COLLEGE OUTLINE SERIES

LATIN AMERICAN
HISTORY

A. Curtis Wilgus
University of Florida

Raul d'Eça
*Formerly at University of
Minas Gerais, Brazil*

 BARNES & NOBLE, INC. · NEW YORK
PUBLISHERS · BOOKSELLERS · SINCE 1873

This book is an original work written by distinguished educators, carefully edited, and produced in accordance with the highest standards of publishing. The text was set on the Linotype in Granjon by the Plimpton Press (Norwood, Mass.). The paper was manufactured by P. H. Glatfelter Company (Spring Grove, Pa.) and supplied by Perkins & Squier Company (New York, N.Y.). This edition was printed by General Offset Company (New York, N.Y.) and bound by Sendor Bindery (New York, N.Y.). The cover was designed by Rod Lopez-Fabrega.

TABLE OF CONTENTS

LIST OF MAPS AND CHARTS

NOTE TO THE READER

In this volume the authors have attempted to provide a brief, well-balanced summary of the essential facts about the political, economic, and cultural history of Latin America from its beginnings to the present. The book is comprehensive enough to be used either as an adopted text for college and university courses or as a companion book providing a condensed view of the subject. In either case the maps and charts will be found most useful for quick-reference purposes. The selected bibliography will facilitate independent study of the most significant literature in the Latin American field.

The authors have divided the labor of writing as follows: Dr. Wilgus prepared Chapters I through XIII and assumed responsibility for the maps (with his wife's assistance) and for the brief selected bibliographies. Dr. d'Eça supplied the remaining chapters. However, each author has benefited from mutual consultation at all stages and from numerous suggestions of the other. Both wish to thank Dr. Laurence F. Hawkins, of the publisher's editorial staff, for his invaluable assistance in the preparation of the final manuscript.

A. CURTIS WILGUS
RAUL D'EÇA

TABULATED BIBLIOGRAPHY OF STANDARD TEXTBOOKS

The following are the books referred to in the column headings of the Quick Reference Table:

Bailey, Helen M., and Nasatir, Abraham P., *Latin America: The Development of Its Civilization* (Englewood Cliffs, N. J.: Prentice-Hall, Inc., 1960)

Bannon, John F., and Dunne, Peter M., *Latin America: An Historical Survey* (Milwaukee: The Bruce Publishing Company, 1963)

Herring, Hubert, *A History of Latin America from the Beginnings to the Present* (New York: Alfred A. Knopf, 1961)

Munro, Dana G., *The Latin American Republics: A History* (New York: Appleton-Century-Crofts, Inc., 1960)

Rippy, J. Fred, *Latin America: A Modern History* (Ann Arbor: The University of Michigan Press, 1958)

Thomas, Alfred B., *Latin America: A History* (New York: The Macmillan Company, 1956)

Williams, Mary W., Bartlett, Ruhl J., and Miller, Russell E., *The People and Politics of Latin America* (Boston: Ginn and Company, 1958)

Worcester, Donald E., and Schaeffer, Wendell G., *The Growth and Culture of Latin America* (New York: Oxford University Press, 1956)

CHAP–TER	TOPIC	BAILEY & NASATIR	BANNON & DUNNE (1963)	HERRING (1961)
I	The American Background	3, 4, 5	1	1, 2
II	Spain and Portugal in the Age of Discovery	1, 2	2, 3	3, 4
III	Columbus and His Contemporaries	1, 6	3	5, 6
IV	The Great Conquerors	7, 8	4–6	5, 6
V	The Great Explorers	7, 8	4–6, 10	5, 6
VI	Colonial Administration	6, 9, 14–16	7–10	7, 12
VII	The Colonial Economic System	6, 10, 14–16	7–10	9, 10, 12
VIII	Colonial Society	12, 14–16	8–10	11, 12
IX	Colonial Culture	11, 13–16	8–10	8, 11, 12
X	Prelude to Colonial Independence	17	11, 12	13
XI	Independence of Spanish North America	18	15	14
XII	Independence of Spanish South America	18	12, 13	15
XIII	Independence of Brazil	21	14	16
XIV	Latin America at End of Revolutions for Independence	19	16, 17	17
XV	Mexico	20, 28, 29	**28, 32**	18–25
XVI	The Five Republics of Central America	27, 38	**29, 32**	29
XVII	The States of Northern South America	25, 26, 36, 37, 38	25–27, 29, **32**	29–32
XVIII	Peru, Bolivia, and Chile	23, 25, 34, 36	**22–24, 32**	33–36
XIX	The River Plata States	22, 24, 32, 33, 35	**19–21, 32**	37–46
XX	Brazil	21, 30, 31	**18, 32**	47–53
XXI	The Caribbean Insular States	27, 39	**30, 32**	26–28
XXII	Inter-Latin American Relations	40, 41	31	56
XXIII	Latin America and the United States	40, 41	31	54–56
XXIV	The Pan American System	40, 41	31	54–56
XXV	Latin America and Non-American Nations	40, 41	31	

STANDARD TEXTBOOKS

MUNRO (1960)	RIPPY	THOMAS (1956)	WILLIAMS, BARTLETT, & MILLER (1958)	WORCESTER & SCHAEFFER	THIS BOOK
1	1, 2	1	1, 2	2	I
2	3	2	3	1	II
2	4	3, 4	·4	1	III
2	4, 5	3, 4	4	2, 4–7	IV
2	4, 5	3, 4	4	4–7	V
3–5	6–8	5, 7–11	5, 11	2, 3	VI
3–5	6–8	7, 10, 11	6, 8, 11	7, 9–19	VII
3–5	6–8	6, 10, 11	10, 11	7, 9–19	VIII
3–5	6–8	6, 10, 11	7, 9, 11	9–19	IX
5	9	12	12, 13	14–20	X
6	10, 11	14	13	20, 23	XI
6	10, 11	12, 13	13	20–22	XII
6	10, 11	13	13	13, 20, 24	XIII
7	12		14	25	XIV
18, 19	14, 21, 28, 31, 32	28	19, 30, 31	29, 30, 33, 36	XV
20–22	15, 21, 28, 31, 32	27	18, 30, 31	29, 30, 33, 37	XVI
14–16, 20	16, 17, 21, 28, 29, 31, 32	22–24	20–22, 30, 31	28, 30, 32, 33, 37, 40	XVII
11–13	18, 21, 29, 31, 32	19–21	23–25, 30, 31	26, 28, 30–32, 39, 40	XVIII
8–10	19, 21, 30–32	15–17	26–28, 30, 31	26, 27, 30–32, 39, 40	XIX
17	20, 21, 30	18	29–31	24, 26, 30, 34, 38	XX
23–25	13, 21, 27, 31, 32	25, 26	12, 15–17, 30, 31	30, 33, 37	XXI
26, 27	25, 33	29	32, 33		XXII
26, 27	22, 23, 33	29	32, 33		XXIII
26, 27	25, 33	29	32, 33		XXIV
	22–24, 26, 33		32, 33	35	XXV

ABOUT THE AUTHORS

Dr. A. Curtis Wilgus has been Director of the School of Inter-American Studies at the University of Florida since 1951. Previously he was on the faculty of The George Washington University, where he organized and served as first Director of the Center of Inter-American Studies. He is the author of six college textbooks and hundreds of monographs on Latin American subjects, and has edited some forty-five volumes on Latin America. For many years he has served as editor of *World Affairs* and other periodicals in this field.

Dr. Raul d'Eça, who was born in Portugal, has taught at The George Washington University and has served in important posts in the United States government programs for Latin America. He has been Acting Chief, Brazil Desk, in the United States Department of State and an executive officer with the United States Information Agency, both in Brazil and in Washington. He was recently Visiting Professor of American History at the University of Minas Gerais in Belo Horizonte, Brazil.

PART ONE

COLONIAL LATIN AMERICA

PART ONE

COLONIAL LATIN AMERICA

THE BASIC FACT of Latin American history is that for more than three hundred years (some eleven generations) the peoples of Latin America were under the paternalistic and repressive control of the mother countries Spain and Portugal, which discouraged political self-government, stifled individual economic initiative, and suppressed intellectual ambition. Nevertheless, these subject peoples were always ready to sacrifice their lives and resources for king or pope. Throughout these ages the colonists lived in much the same manner as did the people in Europe of their day, but in most instances they were more handicapped by nature and natives and by disease and disaster. Certainly, Europeans at home did not have to cope with enormous stretches of roadless, inhospitable, and partially explored territory as did these sturdy pioneers. We must honor the intrepidity of the founders of the Spanish and Portuguese empires in the strange, remote, and dangerous lands of America.

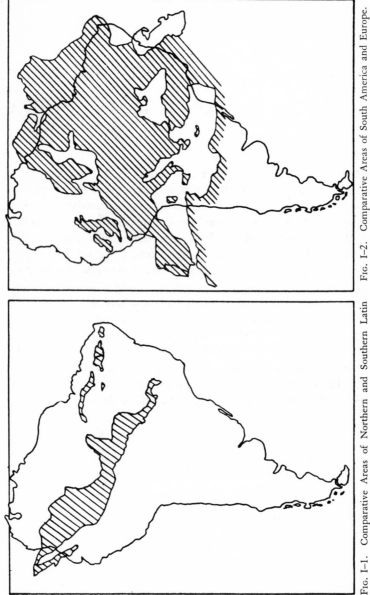

Fig. I-1. Comparative Areas of Northern and Southern Latin America.

Fig. I-2. Comparative Areas of South America and Europe.

CHAPTER I

THE AMERICAN BACKGROUND

GEOGRAPHY TREATS, among other things, of the earth as the home of man. It describes the environment in which man acts out his life, and it gives history a stage upon which human actions take place. An understanding of the stage and the actors is essential to an appreciation of the life and culture of any part of our globe. It is important to view here the environment as a whole and in its component parts and to see how human beings lived and acted in the Americas from the earliest times.

THE GEOGRAPHICAL BACKGROUND

Extent of Latin America. Latin America includes twenty countries: Mexico, the six states of Central America (Guatemala, Honduras, El Salvador, Nicaragua, Costa Rica, and Panama), the West Indian islands of Cuba and Hispaniola (divided into Haiti and the Dominican Republic), and the ten states of South America (Venezuela, Colombia, Ecuador, Peru, Bolivia, Chile, Paraguay, Uruguay, Argentina, and Brazil). This comprises a total area of almost eight million square miles, or over twice the area of Europe. It is a distance of some 7,000 miles from the northern tip of Mexico to the southern extremity of South America, which is greater than the distance from London to Capetown, South Africa. Extending the length of Latin America and forming its geographical backbone is one continuous chain of mountains in which earthquakes are frequent and volcanic eruptions have occurred.

Mexico. Mexico has a total area of about 760,000 square miles, which makes it slightly smaller than Greenland, or about one-fourth the size of the United States (excluding Alaska). The Tropic of Cancer divides it about equally north and south. Much of Mexico is a lofty plateau with mountains on the eastern and western sides of

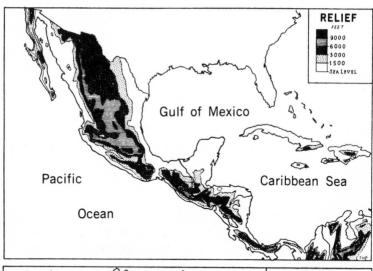

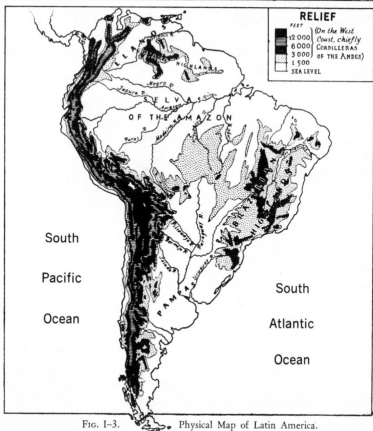

Fig. I–3. Physical Map of Latin America.

the country. A narrow coastal plain on the west and a wide coastal plain on the east border the Pacific Ocean and the Gulf of Mexico, respectively. In the high plateau of south central Mexico lies the "Valley of Mexico," called by the natives *Anáhuac,* or the "Country by the Waters," because of the many lakes in the region. Here, at about 7,800 feet above sea level, is located Mexico City, with a mean annual temperature of about 62 degrees, which is about that of San Francisco, California. The plateau region is generally temperate in climate; the temperature in the mountains is cold and that along the seacoast is hot. Mexico has few rivers, the longest being the Río Grande, which runs along its northern boundary. The harbors are few, and no first-class natural harbors exist. Regions of heaviest rainfall are in the southern and eastern portions of the country. Agricultural products are those which grow in both temperate and tropical climates, and mineral products are varied and abundant, with silver and petroleum ranking high in importance.

Central America. The six Central American states embrace an area of some 200,000 square miles, or about twice the area of the state of Colorado. Guatemala and Honduras are, separately, about the size of Tennessee; Nicaragua is about the size of Wisconsin; El Salvador is about the size of Connecticut and Massachusetts; Costa Rica is almost as large as West Virginia; and Panama is a little smaller than South Carolina. The colony of British Honduras is not included in Latin America. The Central American states consist largely of mountains, plateaus, valleys, and coastal plains. The most important water system in Central America (except the Panama Canal) is that formed by Lake Nicaragua, which is about twice the area of Great Salt Lake in Utah, and the San Juan River. There are no first-class harbors in Central America. As in Mexico, there are temperate, tropical, and cold regions, with the temperate plateaus most densely inhabited. The yearly rainfall is heavy. Agricultural products which flourish in both temperate and tropical areas are produced. Minerals are widely distributed but little exploited.

The West Indies:

Cuba. Cuba is the largest of the Caribbean islands, being about 730 miles long. It contains some 44,000 square miles, which makes it about the size of Pennsylvania. It is a country of mountains, plains, and small lakes with small unimportant rivers and a few harbors. The climate is tempered by the trade winds, and the rainy season extends from May to October. Hurricanes occur frequently. Most tropical and temperate products can be raised in Cuba. There are few minerals.

HAITI. Haiti lies in the western portion of the island of Hispaniola (in Spanish, Española), which contains some 30,000 square miles, about the size of South Carolina. Haiti itself, with an area of about 10,000 square miles, is a little larger than Vermont. It is a mountainous country, which fact somewhat tempers its climate. The rainfall is abundant, with the rainy season occurring in the summer months. The products are largely those of a tropical climate, and minerals are few. There are no first-class harbors.

DOMINICAN REPUBLIC. The Dominican Republic in the eastern two-thirds of the island of Hispaniola has an area of about 19,000 square miles, or about the size of New Hampshire and Vermont combined. Like Haiti, it is mountainous, with a similar climate and similar products. It also has no first-class harbors.

South America. The continent of South America is some 4,600 miles from north to south and, at its widest, some 3,000 miles from east to west. The total area of the continent is almost 7 million square miles, which is about a million square miles smaller than North America. The greatest bulk of South America lies in the Torrid Zone, although the Tropic of Capricorn divides it nearly equally north and south. Besides the ten Latin American republics on the continent, there are three European colonies: the British, Dutch, and French Guianas, roughly equal in area to Kansas, Wisconsin, and Maine, respectively. Argentina is about equal in size to the eleven Pacific and Mountain states of the United States; Bolivia is almost as large as Texas and California; Brazil is almost as large as the United States, including Alaska; Chile is somewhat larger than Texas; Colombia is about the area of Washington, Oregon, California, and Arizona; Ecuador is just as large as Colorado; Paraguay is about the size of California; Peru is larger than Texas, Oklahoma, Kansas, and Nebraska; Uruguay is about the size of North Dakota; and Venezuela is larger than Texas and Oklahoma.

About one-sixteenth of the area of South America lies at an elevation of 10,000 feet or above. The backbone of the continent is the great Andean range, running from Colombia to the southern tip of Tierra del Fuego. It varies in width from 100 to 400 miles, with the highest peak, Aconcagua, in Argentina, at about 23,000 feet, with more than fifty peaks above 20,000 feet, and with a broad, bleak plateau, or *altiplano,* in Bolivia. Glaciers are numerous, and earth-

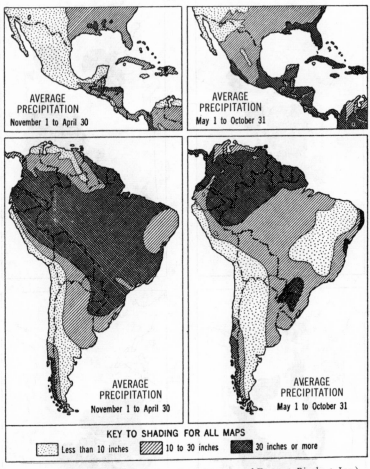

AVERAGE
PRECIPITATION
November 1 to April 30

AVERAGE
PRECIPITATION
May 1 to October 31

AVERAGE
PRECIPITATION
November 1 to April 30

AVERAGE
PRECIPITATION
May 1 to October 31

KEY TO SHADING FOR ALL MAPS

Less than 10 inches   10 to 30 inches   30 inches or more

Fɪɢ. I–4. Rainfall Map of Latin America. (Courtesy of Farrar & Rinehart, Inc.)

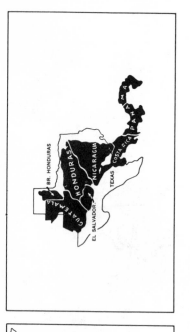

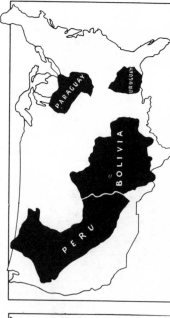

FIG. I–5. Comparative Areas of Latin American Countries and the United States.

quakes shake the whole region. Two older, but lower, mountain regions are found on the continent: the Brazilian Highlands and the Guiana Highlands. About three-fifths of the continent may be classed as plains, with elevations not exceeding 1,000 feet. Coastal plains extend around the edge of the continent except in southern Chile and in a few scattered localities. In Argentina the plain broadens into the *pampas* and surrounding areas; in Brazil the large central plains are called the *selvas;* and in Venezuela the plains are called the *llanos.*

Each of these regions is watered by a great river system: in Argentina it is called the Plata system, composed of the Uruguay, Paraná, Salado, and other rivers; in Brazil it is the Amazon River and its many tributaries; and in Venezuela it is the Orinoco River and its tributaries. All other South American rivers are dwarfed by these three great systems. High in the Bolivian Andes is the greatest lake on the continent, Lake Titicaca. It lies at an elevation of nearly 13,000 feet and is about the size of Lake Nicaragua. The best harbors on the continent are on the Atlantic side, with that of Rio de Janeiro in Brazil ranking foremost.

About two-thirds of South America is in the Torrid Zone, but the great altitude tempers much of this area. In the midsection of the Pacific coast lies a great desert, while other dry regions are found in northwest Argentina and in southern and western Argentina. The heaviest rainfall occurs in the Amazon Basin and in southern Chile. Temperatures in South America vary so widely that any agricultural product found elsewhere may be grown there. Mineral products are varied and numerous.

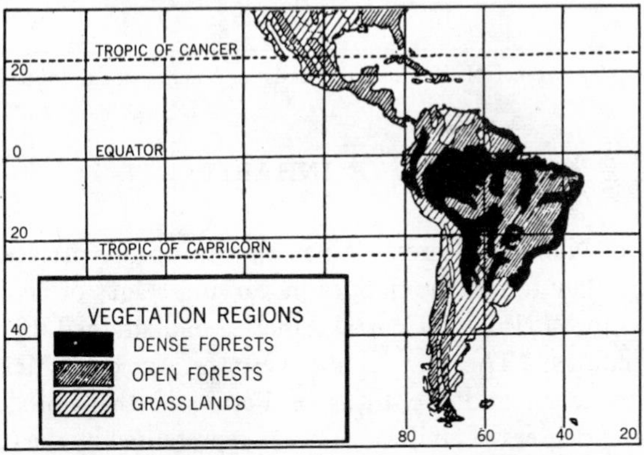

Fig. I–6. Vegetation of Latin America. (Reproduced with permission from *The New World Atlas and Gazeteer* published by P. F. Collier and Sons Company, New York, 1921.)

Fig. I–7.   Chief Native Cultures in Latin America about 1500.

THE NATIVE INHABITANTS

Extent of Native Cultures.   When the Europeans arrived in this
hemisphere they found the natives in varying stages of civilization.
The Mayas in Mexico and Central America had attained the greatest
degree of culture.   The next in line were the Aztecs of Mexico and
their predecessors, and the Incas of Peru and their predecessors.
Diminishing degrees of civilization were represented by the Chibchas
in northern South America and by the Pueblo Indians of southwest-

ern United States. Many other scattered native groups, however, were struggling up the ladder of civilization.

Theories of Native Origin. The question of the origin of the American natives has for centuries furnished a topic for popular and scientific discussion. It is now believed that some of the American Indians originated in Asia and migrated to this hemisphere by way of the Bering Strait and the Aleutian Islands. Theories of native origin which have been suggested are the Indigenous theory, the Lost Ten Tribes of Israel theory, the Malay-Polynesian theory, the Japanese-Chinese theory, the Phoenician theory, the Egyptian theory, the Mormon theory, the Lost Atlantis theory, the Lost Continent of Mu (or Lemuria) theory, the Ayar theory, the African theory, and many others.

The Mayas. In the first millennium B.C. these Indians, or their predecessors, inhabited parts of Mexico and Central America. It seems that a group of these peoples appeared in Guatemala about the beginning of the Christian era, and from there spread into Yucatan, where their civilization reached its greatest height about 500 A.D. Living in large cities, they built great pyramids and temples, worshiped many gods, practiced agriculture and various manufacturing pursuits, and were ruled over by hereditary chiefs. They developed a form of writing which has not been interpreted fully, and they wrote many books, of which only a few exist today. They developed a surprisingly accurate calendar and seem to have understood certain facts concerning astronomy. When the Spanish conquerors arrived in the region, they found only ruined cities, and the natives appeared to know nothing of their ancestors. The mystery of the origin and disappearance of Mayan civilization is still unsolved.

The Aztecs and Their Predecessors. About the sixth century A.D. there came into the Valley of Mexico a group of Indians known as the Toltecs, who may have been related to the Mayas. They built cities, temples, and pyramids, practiced agriculture, worshiped many gods, and practiced human sacrifice. About the tenth or eleventh century the Chichimec peoples conquered the Toltecs in the Valley of Mexico and adopted their civilization. Finally, probably in the twelfth century, the Aztecs, coming from the north, conquered the Valley and began to extend their sway over the other peoples of Mexico. A great centralized confederation headed by an emperor was established; one of the emperors, Montezuma II, ruled from 1503 until he was conquered by the Spaniards. The Aztec capital,

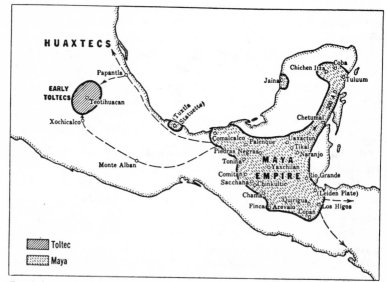

Fig. I–8. First Empire of the Mayas, 100 B.C.–630 A.D. According to Dated Monuments. Indicates Maya influence on the early Toltecs (500 A.D. and later). (Courtesy of the American Museum of Natural History.)

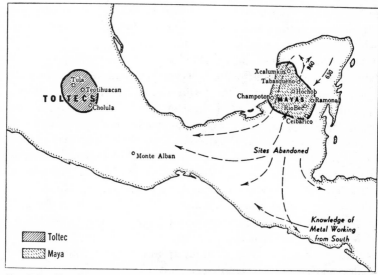

Fig. I–9. Transitional Period of the Mayas. Showing the abandonment of many of the First Empire sites with movements northward and southward. (Courtesy of the American Museum of Natural History.)

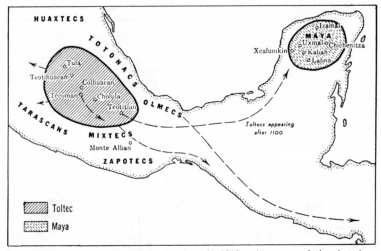

Fig. I–10. Second Empire of the Mayas, 960–1200. (Courtesy of the American Museum of Natural History.)

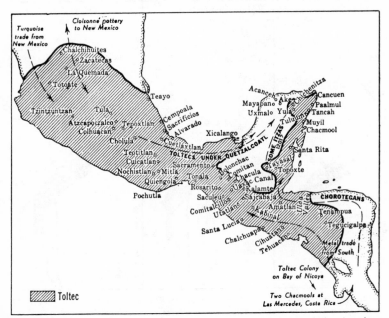

Fig. I–11. Toltec Period of the Mayas, 1200–1450. (Courtesy of the American Museum of Natural History.)

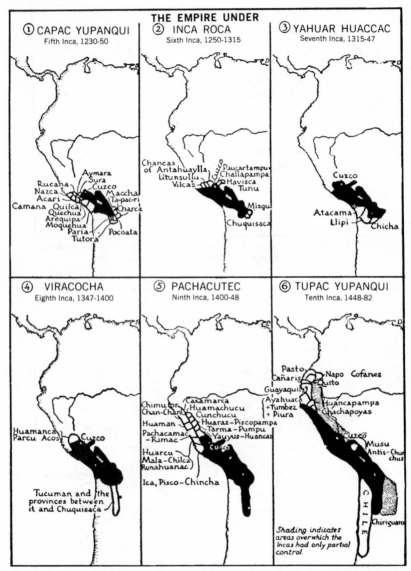

Fig. I–12. Growth of the Inca Empire. (From *Ancient Civilizations of the Andes*, by Phillip Ainsworth Means, courtesy of Charles Scribner's Sons.)

Tenochtitlán, stood on an island in the middle of Lake Texcoco within the area now occupied by Mexico City. The Aztecs worshiped many gods and goddesses and practiced human sacrifice in the temples on the tops of their pyramids. They also practiced slavery. Agriculture and mining were important occupations; weaving and the making of gold and silver objects were developed to a high degree; taxes were collected; and trade was engaged in throughout the confederation. The Aztecs spoke one language, recorded their thoughts in picture writings, developed a highly effective calendar, and enjoyed the dance, drama, and a variety of athletic activities. Their civilization astonished the Spaniards.

The Incas and Their Predecessors. The so-called "pre-Incas" may have developed an empire in the vicinity of Lake Titicaca as early as 400 A.D. By 900 A.D., however, they had declined after having attained a high degree of civilization expressed in great fortifications and other buildings and in pottery and weaving. In the thirteenth century the Incas appeared in the region as conquerors and extended their power north and south of Lake Titicaca, until in the fifteenth century their empire extended from present-day Colombia to Argentina and Chile. In most cases the Incas appear to have adopted the pre-Inca civilization as their own. They were ruled by a *Sapa Inca* (chief). One of their chiefs, Atahualpa, was conquered by the Spaniards. The Incas worshiped a number of deities and seem to have practiced human sacrifice to some extent. They did not construct temples like the Aztecs, but they built palaces. Their society was classified and effectively organized for the service of the state. Agriculture was practiced and the use of irrigation, fertilizers, and terraces enabled a large number of people to be supported by the land. Mining was widely engaged in, as was the manufacturing of textiles, pottery, and gold and silver objects. Rapid communication by highways, footpaths, and bridges was possible. The Incas embalmed their dead. They kept records by means of cords called *quipus,* but they had no means of writing like the Mayas or Aztecs. Nevertheless, we have considerable knowledge of the history of this people.

The Chibchas. In the temperate uplands of present-day Colombia, in the vicinity of Bogotá, lived a group of Indians contemporary with the Incas. These were the Chibchas, who, when conquered by the Spaniards, were emerging into a higher state of civilization than the surrounding natives. They practiced agriculture and mined salt, gold, and emeralds. They had a medium of exchange, manufactured textiles and pottery, and carried on a regulated trade. They worshiped many gods, especially spiders; they sacrificed human beings and animals to their deities, and built temples. At the head of the government were two rulers called the *Zipa* and the *Zaque,* both of whom the Spaniards conquered. About the person of one of these rulers probably grew up the story of El Dorado.

Other Indian Groups. Among other Indian tribes whom the early Spanish or Portuguese conquerors encountered were the Moundbuilders and Pueblo Indians of the United States, the Caribs and Arawaks of the West Indies and northern South America, the Tupí-Guaraní Indians of Brazil and Paraguay, the Patagonian Indians of Argentina, and the warlike Araucanians of Chile. These groups were in varying stages of development, some being cannibals and many being hardy and vigorous fighters. Despite this, however, most of the natives were conquered by force of arms, fear, or faith, for churchmen accompanied most of the conquistadores.

CHAPTER II

SPAIN AND PORTUGAL
IN THE AGE OF DISCOVERY

ONE OF THE MOST amazing facts of European history, and of world history as well, is found in the rise to world powers of Spain and Portugal in a few brief generations. Their claim to and occupancy of the Western Hemisphere thrust them into the front rank of fifteenth- and sixteenth-century history. The Iberian geographical environment was a unique stage on which a number of unique peoples performed unique feats of historical prowess.

IBERIAN GEOGRAPHY

Iberian geography has many of the characteristics of Latin American geography, with high mountains, bleak plateaus, semitropical lowlands, moist and dry areas, a few harbors, and navigable rivers. The area of the Iberian Peninsula is some 230,000 square miles, or almost the size of Texas. Spain proper has an area of about 195,000 square miles, which makes it about the size of Utah and Nevada, or somewhat over half the area of Venezuela. Portugal has an area which is about equal to that of the state of Indiana and smaller than that of Cuba. Yet these two small countries of Iberia together conquered and claimed more territory than any other powers in history prior to the twentieth century.

The peninsula is entirely surrounded by water except where it is connected to France by the rugged Pyrenees. Central Iberia is a high plateau with a bleak winter climate, while parts of the south are semitropical. The rainfall is heavy in the northwest and light in parts of the east and south, where irrigation must be practiced for the production of crops. The scattered mountain areas affect the climate considerably. Valleys are formed by the five largest rivers: the Tagus, the Duero, the Guadiana, and the Guadalquivir flowing into the Atlantic Ocean, and the Ebro flowing into the Mediterra-

19

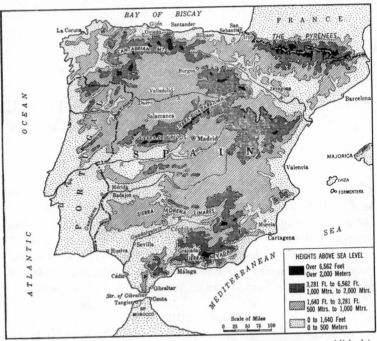

Fig. II–1. Physical Features of the Iberian Peninsula. (Based on a map published in *The New York Times,* August 23, 1936.)

nean Sea. There are harbors along the rivers as well as along the seacoast. For centuries Portugal has faced on the Atlantic, and Spain has faced on the Mediterranean.

The topography of Spain, more mountainous than that of Portugal, has tended to divide the inhabitants into small groups so that Spain has been harder to conquer by outsiders and likewise more difficult to unite from the inside than Portugal. Local patriotism and individualism early developed in Spain as a result of the varied geographical nature of the country, and people in isolated communities acquired distinct characteristics of language, thought, and customs. In consequence, Spain became a region of separately developed principalities or kingdoms, while Portugal was achieving political unity.

IBERIAN HISTORY

The Iberian Peninsula has witnessed the invasion of many peoples, and the resultant racial mixture has produced composite traits which can best be described as the "Spanish character" and the "Portuguese character."

Invaders. Little is known of the original inhabitants of the peninsula. About 1100 B.C. the Phoenicians entered the region and remained in partial control until about 200 B.C., if the Carthaginian period is counted. At this time also, Greek colonies were established in the peninsula, while the Celts had settled in the north.

The next invaders were the Romans, who occupied the territory from about 200 B.C. to the fifth century A.D. The peninsula was called Hispania by the Romans. The country was unified, cities were founded, Roman law and customs were established, and Christianity was introduced.

In the fifth century the Vandals, the Suivians, and finally the Visigoths overran Hispania (except for Asturias in the north) so that by 623 the country was under "barbarian" rule, which modified Roman society and institutions but maintained Roman law.

Into the midst of this Visigothic state came the highly civilized Moslems, first in 710. The next year they began the conquest of the peninsula, which by 718 they had overrun except for Asturias. By the tenth century their culture was well established. They introduced a new social order, founded schools, educated women, encouraged the arts and classical learning, modified architecture, improved agriculture, stimulated industry, and in general modified the customs and habits of the Iberians. The Mohammedan religion became widespread in the country, although some religious toleration was practiced.

Rise of Portugal. Portugal attained its present boundaries some two hundred years before the Spanish portion of the peninsula. The expulsion of the Moslems began in the northwest in the eleventh century and was completed about 1250, chiefly through the activities of Sancho I and II and Afonso II and III. National consolidation was brought about under Dinis, Afonso IV, Pedro I, and Fernando I, so that under João I, "The Great," of the House of Avis, who ruled from 1385 to 1433, national political unity was consummated. In the following years the king's powers were strengthened and the government became more centralized. In 1496 the Jews were expelled.

Rise of Spain. The Spanish reconquest began in 718, when Pelayo in Asturias defeated the Moslems. Gradually the Christian fighters extended their conquests, until by 910 the kingdoms of León and Navarra and the County of Barcelona had been founded. Then

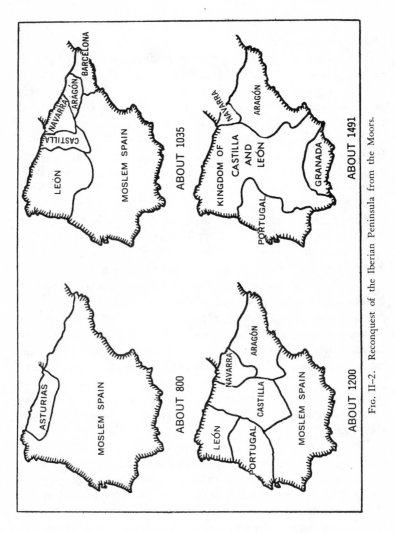

Fig. II–2. Reconquest of the Iberian Peninsula from the Moors.

León and Castilla united and Aragón appeared. By the middle of the twelfth century about half of the peninsula had been reconquered from the Moslems. In 1236 Córdoba was taken from the invaders, and in 1248 Sevilla was captured. By 1252 the reconquered territory included about two-thirds of the peninsula, and by 1491 all of present-day Spain, except the region about the city of Granada, had been recaptured. Finally, in 1492 Ferdinand and Isabella seized this region and the present boundaries of Spain were reached.

As the reconquest proceeded, the numerous Christian states began to consolidate their political and economic life under ruling noble families. This resulted in civil struggles within their boundaries and in warfare with the neighboring kingdoms. Local jealousies thus prevented effective national co-operation, and it became apparent that a strong centralizing force would be necessary to unify the many kingdoms and principalities. This centralizing force appeared in the persons of Ferdinand of Aragón and Isabella of Castilla (the "Catholic Kings"), who, fortunately for the future of Spain, were married in 1469, thus uniting two of the chief kingdoms of the peninsula. Into this union were gradually forced most of the other political units. With political consolidation came social and economic consolidation, and in 1492 the Jews were expelled from Spain. The Inquisition was reorganized as a political and religious instrument; the Catholic Kings thus established internal order.

EARLY PORTUGUESE EXPANSION

Because Portugal was unified before Spain, the government and people were ready at an earlier date than in Spain for exploration and conquest overseas. In the fourteenth century the Canary Islands were discovered, and in 1415 Ceuta, on the north coast of Africa, was captured. The son of John (João) "The Great," known to history as Prince Henry the Navigator, became interested in searching for the golden kingdom of Timbuktu and for the fabled kingdom of Prester John, a Christian ruler supposedly surrounded by pagans somewhere in Africa. In 1419 Prince Henry began to send out ships along the west coast of Africa. By 1431 the Azores were discovered; by 1434 Cape Bojador was reached; and by 1445 the Cape Verde Islands were reached. By 1448 a colony was established at Agadir. By 1460, when Prince Henry died, Portuguese discoveries had extended as far south as 6 to 8 degrees North Latitude.

It was now that a new incentive arose to give impetus to African discoveries, for the Turks at the eastern end of the Mediterranean, with the capture of Constantinople in 1453, had begun the seizure of trade routes to the East. In 1462 the great bend of Africa was rounded, and finally in 1487 Bartolomeu Dias discovered the Cape of Good Hope. In 1497–99 Vasco da Gama went around Africa to India. The Portuguese thus acquired their own private trade route to the East. Pedro Alvares Cabral, driven off course on his way to India in 1500, found himself on the coast of Brazil.

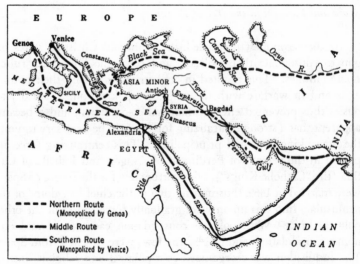

Fig. II–3. Fifteenth-Century Trade Routes between Europe and Asia.
(Courtesy of Farrar & Rinehart, Inc.)

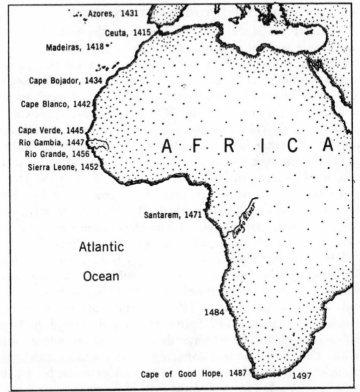

Fig. II–4. Portuguese Exploration along the West Coast of Africa. (Based on
map in *Historia de México,* by Chávez Orozco.)

EARLY SPANISH EXPANSION

Because Spain faced the Mediterranean Sea rather than the Atlantic Ocean like Portugal, her interests were early turned eastward. In the fourteenth century a company of Catalán adventurers established the Duchy of Athens, maintained from 1326 to 1388. In 1349 Pedro IV of Aragón took over the island of Majorca, and shortly afterward he took Minorca. Enrique III of Castilla sent embassies to the Sultan of Babylon and to Tamerlane (1402). He sought the kingdom of Prester John in the East, where it was often rumored to be located. Thus Spanish interest in the East was early manifest. In 1402 the Spaniards began the move to take the Canary Islands from the Portuguese, and in 1480 Ferdinand and Isabella took possession of Grand Canary Island, which they soon colonized. The experience gained in occupying and governing this latter territory served as a training school for the later occupation and administration of the Spanish American colonies.

EUROPEAN CONDITIONS AFFECTING SPAIN
AND PORTUGAL

Trade with the East. Spain and Portugal attained unity in the Age of the Renaissance, which had been ushered in partly as the result of the Christian Crusades against the Mohammedans who expanded out of Arabia. As a result of the Crusades many Eastern products and ideas were introduced into Europe, and a desire arose to travel in the Orient in emulation of the Polos and others and to trade with the East. Italy, in the path of the Crusaders, was prepared to take advantage of this demand for Eastern products, and she sent her merchants to the cities at the eastern end of the Mediterranean to purchase Oriental goods brought there by the merchants of Asia, and to sell European goods. The western termini of the three chief routes were Constantinople, Antioch, and Alexandria. But in 1453 the Turks seized Constantinople, and thereafter by various restrictions gradually discouraged the use of these routes by European merchants. Therefore, Italy and Portugal became interested in finding a new route to the East. In this aim Portugal was successful by going around Africa, but Italy failed, and many of her adventurous citizens went to England, France, Spain, and Portugal, where they aided these countries in their exploring activities.

Geographical Knowledge. When the "Dark Ages" in Europe came to an end with the Renaissance, not all of the superstitious be-

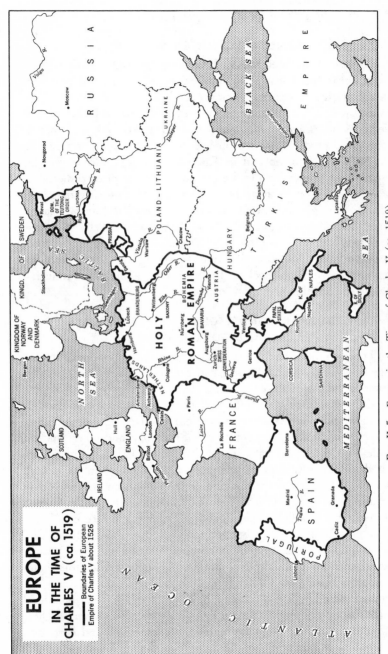

Fig. II-5. Europe in the Time of Charles V (ca. 1519).

liefs regarding the earth and its inhabitants vanished. Many people still believed that the earth was flat, that it was surrounded by water or by fire, and that the seas were full of great, horrible monsters. Although Greek, Roman, and Arabic thinkers had believed that the earth was a sphere, they did not conceive of the earth as being as large as it actually is. Hence some geographers theorized that by sailing westward one could reach the East. The idea that a continent intervened was almost unthought of, though reports concerning such land occasionally circulated in Europe.

As men speculated about the earth's surface they began to draw maps on which they placed islands and names conceived largely from their own imaginings. These places shifted from time to time as the whims of the map-makers changed. But some of these names may have represented actual discoveries in the fourteenth and fifteenth centuries, and some authorities are of the opinion that Cuba, Jamaica, Florida, and the Atlantic seaboard of the United States and Canada had been visited by Europeans. However, if this knowledge existed, no one had made use of it. Even the fact that the Scandinavians had discovered and colonized certain sections of the North Atlantic coast of America from the tenth to the fourteenth centuries was unknown to the rest of Europe.

Inventions. Further knowledge regarding other parts of the world, it was soon realized, would not be forthcoming until better ships were built and more satisfactory methods of reckoning distance, location, and direction could be devised. In the fifteenth century these problems were partly solved by the use of the compass and the astrolabe and by improvements in ship construction. In these matters the Italians and Portuguese took the lead. It was not possible to estimate longitude until the Portuguese, in 1514, developed a method. In the fifteenth century the use of gunpowder spread widely, and guns and cannon were improved. The development of printing by the use of movable type made possible wider dissemination of knowledge about scientific and geographical discoveries, stimulating a wider interest in contemporary events. Finally, in the sixteenth century, by means of Mercator's projection, charts could be made with compass sailings drawn in a straight line. Late in the fifteenth century, therefore, the time was ripe for the nations best prepared to take advantage of their opportunities for overseas expansion. In this activity Spain and Portugal played a prominent role.

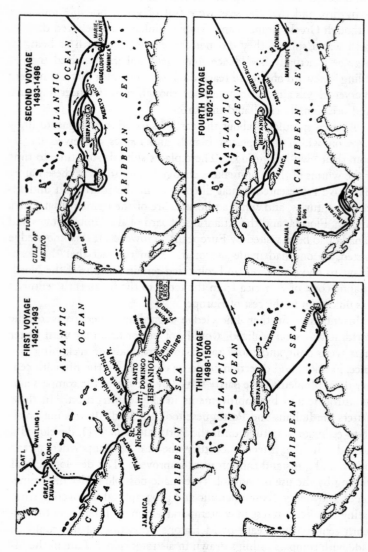

Fig. III–1. Routes of Columbus in the New World. (Courtesy of Farrar & Rinehart, Inc.)

CHAPTER III

COLUMBUS AND
HIS CONTEMPORARIES

By 1492 CONDITIONS in Spain and Portugal were ripe for overseas expansion, and Columbus and his contemporaries appeared on the scene at a most propitious time not only for themselves but for Western Europe. With the discovery of America several European nations began to think of acquiring overseas colonies, and the rising state systems, as they became consolidated, began to participate in the important movement in world history known as "the Expansion of Europe."

CHRISTOPHER COLUMBUS

The Enigma of Columbus. The story of Columbus has suffered from too much telling, for gaps in our knowledge concerning him have been filled with speculation. We do not know with certainty when or where he was born, what his early life was, what he looked like, whether or not he could read and write, where he first landed in America, or where he is buried.

Columbus was probably born in Genoa between 1446 and 1451. He may have received a fair education as a youth. He may have traveled by land and sea before he went to Portugal, probably in 1470, where he was attracted by the exploits of the Portuguese. There he married the daughter of one of Prince Henry's navigators, and he probably acquired the idea of sailing westward about this time. He may have then visited France and England in search of aid. Certainly he received no help from the Portuguese king, and in 1485 he went to Spain. But there he obtained no official encouragement from Ferdinand and Isabella until they had defeated the Moslems at Granada in January, 1492.

The First Voyage. With assistance from persons at the Spanish court Columbus was able to sign a contract with the Catholic Kings on April 17, 1492, which made possible his first voyage. He was to be admiral, viceroy, and governor of all mainlands and islands which he might find and to have 10 per cent of all net proceeds of the trade with these lands. The cost of the expedition, however, was not to be borne by the sovereigns.

On August 3, 1492, in the hurricane season, Columbus set sail for the West with a cosmopolitan crew of adventurers. The three ships, after leaving the Canary Islands, sailed steadily westward through severe storms. Finally, on October 12, they sighted what to-day is called Watling Island. From there they sailed to Cuba, which they called "Juana," and then to Haiti, which they named "Española," or "Little Spain." On December 25, they founded the town of La Navidad and built a fort from the timbers of the wrecked *Santa María*.

Leaving twenty-nine men there, Columbus sailed away on January 2, 1493, and after a stormy passage, finally was forced to land on the coast of Portugal. When he told King John II of his discoveries, the ruler believed that the Admiral had reached India, which Portugal claimed. On March 15, Columbus returned to Palos, Spain, and reported to the Catholic Kings, who, like Columbus, seem to have believed that he had reached Asia.

The World Divided. Certain problems concerning rights to newly discovered land confronted Spain and Portugal as a result of Columbus' voyage. If Columbus had reached Asia, Portuguese prior claims had to be considered. If he had reached new lands, then claims by Spain had to be made legal. The Spanish Pope, Alexander VI, was asked by the sovereigns of both countries to help settle the problem, and as a result the New World was divided between Spain and Portugal by three Bulls of Demarcation (May 3 and 4, 1493). These provided for a north-south line in the Atlantic running 100 leagues west of the Azores, with the territory east of the line belonging to Portugal and the territory west of the line belonging to Spain. When this arrangement caused Portugal to complain that she did not have sufficient sea space to go around Africa, the two countries signed the Treaty of Tordesillas (June 7, 1494) moving the line westward to 370 leagues west of the Cape Verde Islands. Though it was not known at the time, this arrangement gave to Portugal a toe hold on the eastern bulge of South America, from which Brazil later developed. The Demarcation Line was extended to the Pacific Ocean by the Treaty of Zaragoza (April 22, 1529), and this gave to Portugal the Philippine Islands, which were later exchanged with Spain for Brazilian territory west of the Demarcation Line in South America.

The Second Voyage. On September 25, 1493, Columbus sailed from Spain with seventeen ships carrying 1,500 colonists, soldiers, laborers, and missionaries (but with no women and with about one hundred stowaways). Cattle, seeds, and agricultural implements were taken for the purpose of founding a permanent colony. Columbus was captain general of the fleet and was to be the civil head of the government in the colony. On November 27, the colonists reached La Navidad but found it deserted. The next month they founded the town of Isabella some thirty miles away, where disease, mutiny, and troubles with the Indians beset the colonists during the winter. In the spring of 1494 Columbus discovered the island of Jamaica and explored the coast of Cuba. Meanwhile, his brother Bartolomé came to Isabella as provincial governor, but he proved a harsh ruler. Finding fierce Indians and little gold, the colonists spent their time in quarreling. Finally, in March, 1496, Columbus began his return voyage to Spain with many sick colonists and some thirty Indian slaves. At the court of Ferdinand and Isabella, Columbus attempted to explain away the complaints which had been raised against him.

The Third Voyage. The fortunes of Columbus now began to decline. On May 30, 1498, the Admiral left Spain with six vessels containing crews of men freed from prison on condition that they be exiled in the colony. At the Canary Islands the fleet divided, three vessels going direct to Española, and three sailing along the Equator under the command of Columbus. On August 1, Columbus reached South America in the vicinity of the Orinoco River, and then sailing northward he discovered Trinidad and several islands of the Lesser Antilles. Finally, he reached Santo Domingo, recently founded by his brother in a better location than that of the town of Isabella. The colony, however, was more troubled with dissension than before. Columbus endeavored to establish peace, and at the same time he sent to Spain for assistance. But instead of the desired aid, there came from Spain in August, 1500, Francisco de Bobadilla, appointed by the king to inquire into the complaints against the Admiral. After a brief hearing before this official, Columbus, his brother Bartolomé, and his son Diego were sent to Spain under arrest. There, however, the sovereigns released all of them and

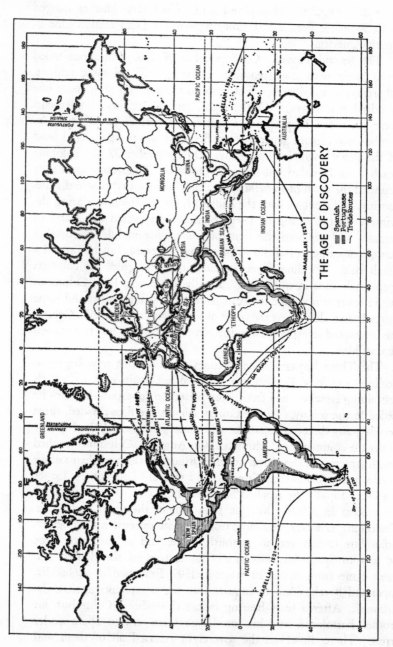

Fig. III-2. The Age of Discovery.

assured Columbus that their agent had overstepped his instructions.

The Fourth Voyage. It was some months before Columbus could assemble another expedition. Finally on May 9, 1502, the Admiral left Spain with four small ships with orders not to touch at Santo Domingo. In spite of these commands, however, Columbus put into that port for repairs on June 2. Forced to leave by the officials, he sailed westward and coasted the shore of Central America, finally landing in Panama, which he called "Veragua," and founding the town of Santa María de Belén. He was attacked by savage Indians and left Panama on Easter, 1503. After encountering severe storms, he was finally wrecked on the island of Jamaica in May, from which predicament he was rescued by the new Governor of Española, Nicolás Ovando. It was not until November, 1504, that the Admiral reached Spain.

The Death of Columbus. Shortly after his arrival in Spain, Queen Isabella, his chief supporter, died. Columbus himself was ill, probably from syphilis, which caused a brain disorder. His enemies continued to hound him, and his poverty increased. He died on May 20, 1506. To this day the exact location of his remains is unknown.

OTHER LEADING EXPLORERS

While Columbus was engaged in the work of discovery, others were planning or making similar expeditions. For England, John Cabot sailed westward in 1497 and reached North America; his second expedition (1498) was lost. For Portugal, the Cortereal brothers were exploring toward the northwest (1500–1502), and Pedro Alvares Cabral was sailing along the coast of Brazil while driven far off course on the way to India (1500). Two other names deserve mention: Vespucci and Magellan.

Amerigo Vespucci. This boastful adventurer, who was born in Florence, Italy, in 1454, served in Spain as the agent of the Medici commercial house. Becoming interested in overseas voyages, he sailed to America, so he claimed, on four expeditions—two under the Spanish flag (in 1497 and 1499) and two under the Portuguese flag (in 1501 and 1503). On these trips he alleged that he explored the coasts of the continent from about 52 degrees South Latitude to about 16 degrees North Latitude. Finding a wood similar to the brazilwood of Asia along the South American coast, he gave the name of Brazil to the region. Upon his return to Europe in 1504,

Vespucci seems to have visited Columbus, and shortly afterwards he wrote a series of accounts of his own experiences, giving himself a more prominent place on each voyage than was actually the case. In 1507, in the College of St. Dié, a professor of geography named Martin Waldseemüller, learning of Vespucci's accounts, published a map of the New World using the name "America" in connection with it as an honor to Amerigo Vespucci. Later, learning of his mistake, the professor published a new map with the old term replaced by the words "Terra Incognita." The term used by the Spaniards and the Portuguese, however, was more convenient, for they spoke of their possessions as the "Indias."

Ferdinand Magellan. Fernando de Magalhães, as his name is spelled in Portuguese, was born about 1480 into a family of the fourth order of Portuguese nobility. He served his king in India, in the Moluccas (the Spice Islands of the East Indies), and in Africa, where he was wounded and crippled. Being accused unjustly of trading with the enemy in Morocco, he fell into disfavor with King Manuel of Portugal, and decided to offer his services to Charles V of Spain. To that monarch Magellan suggested the possibility of sailing around the newly found continent in the west and reaching the East Indies and Asia. With the financial backing of a friend, Magellan set sail with five Spanish ships for South America in September, 1519. On December 13, the expedition arrived at what is now Rio de Janeiro. From there Magellan sailed to the Río de la Plata and then (in March, 1520) on to about 49 degrees South Latitude, where he wintered, crushed a mutiny, and made contacts with the natives, whom the Spaniards called Patagonians ("Big Feet"). Leaving there in August, 1520, the fleet went southward and on October 21 entered the strait which now bears Magellan's name. In 38 days of trial and error they traversed the 360 miles of the strait, and then for 98 days they sailed northwestward, reaching the Ladrones (now Marianas) Islands on March 6, 1521. On this voyage food and water were exhausted, but at Guam these were replenished.

On April 7, 1521, they reached the Philippines, where on the island of Mactán, Magellan allied himself with a native chief and was killed in the ensuing struggle. Having been in the East Indies before, he was the first man to circumnavigate the globe. His ships continued on, but only one returned to Europe in September, 1522. It was now definitely proved that Columbus had discovered a new continent.

MAPPING THE ATLANTIC COAST OF AMERICA

A swarm of Spanish and a few Portuguese adventurers, with a small mixture of other nationalities, followed closely on the heels of Columbus' second voyage. These men were chiefly inspired by the desire to gain personal riches and glory, but whatever land they discovered they claimed in the name of their king. Within about three decades after the first voyage of Columbus most of the Atlantic coast line of America was known and mapped.

The South American Coast. On the northern coast of South America, Columbus had discovered pearls, and thereafter that region was known as the "Pearl Coast," although it also came to be called the "Spanish Main." To this region, after Columbus, came Alonso de Ojeda, Vespucci, Juan de la Cosa (the map-maker), Pedro Alonso Niño, and Diego de Lepe (1499–1500).

Along the Brazilian coast before the coming of Cabral from Portugal, were the Spaniards Diego de Lepe and Vicente Yáñez Pinzón (1499–1500).

Vespucci claimed that from 1501 to 1503 he was twice along the South Atlantic coast of America. In 1509 Juan Díaz de Solís and Vicente Yáñez Pinzón were in the same region. In 1515 the former, while exploring the Río de la Plata, was killed and eaten by Indians in that territory.

The Coast of Mexico and Central America. In 1500 Rodrigo Bastidas and Vasco Núñez de Balboa preceded Columbus in exploring the Caribbean coast of Central America. In 1506 Juan Díaz de Solís and Pinzón explored the region. In 1517 Francisco Hernández de Córdoba explored Yucatan, and the next year Juan Grijalva sailed along the Mexican coast. In 1519 Alonso de Pineda explored the Gulf coast of Mexico, while in the same year Hernando Cortés began his famous conquest of Mexico from his base at Veracruz.

The Coast of the United States. In 1513 Juan Ponce de León sailed along the Atlantic coast of Florida, and in 1519 Alonso de Pineda explored the Gulf coast of the United States. Finally, in 1521 the eastern seaboard of the country was explored by Francisco Gordillo and Pedro de Quexos.

SETTLEMENTS IN THE CARIBBEAN AREA

In the Islands. In 1508 Sebastián Ocampo circumnavigated the island of Cuba, and in 1511 the conquest of Cuba began under Diego Velásquez de León, who founded Santiago in 1514 and

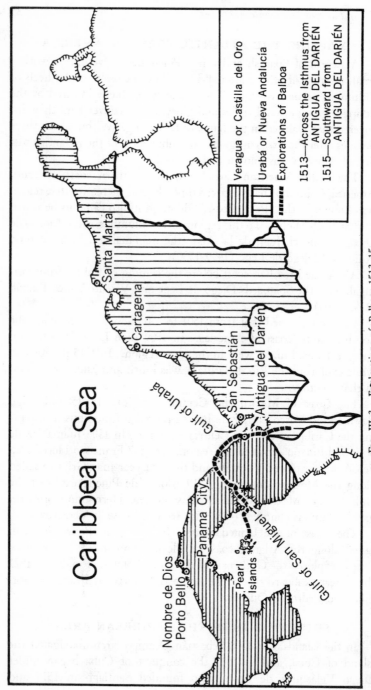

Fig. III-3. Explorations of Balboa, 1513-15.

Havana about 1515. Meanwhile, Puerto Rico was conquered by Juan Ponce de León in 1509, and the city of San Juan was established in 1511. Also in 1509, Juan de Esquivel settled the island of Jamaica, calling it "Santiago."

On the Mainland. In 1503 Columbus had founded the short-lived town of Santa María de Belén on the Isthmus of Panama. Five years later, in 1508, Alonso de Ojeda received a grant of land on the Pearl Coast east of Panama, while at the same time Diego de Nicuesa obtained a grant of land from Panama northward. In 1509 Ojeda founded the town of San Sebastián, which was later moved to a new site called Antigua del Darién. In 1510 Nicuesa founded a colony at Nombre de Dios.

In 1513 the governor in the colony of Darién was the red-headed, blue-eyed, energetic Vasco Núñez de Balboa. In September of that year, after one of the most difficult marches in recorded history, he discovered the Pacific Ocean, which he called the "South Sea," and took possession of it and all the lands bordering it in the name of the king of Spain. But the next year, with the arrival of a new governor, Pedro Arias d'Avila (called Pedrarias), the fortunes of Balboa declined, and he was finally executed by Pedrarias in 1519. The same year, Pedrarias moved across the Isthmus and founded the town of Panamá on the Pacific side, the first Spanish settlement on the Pacific Ocean.

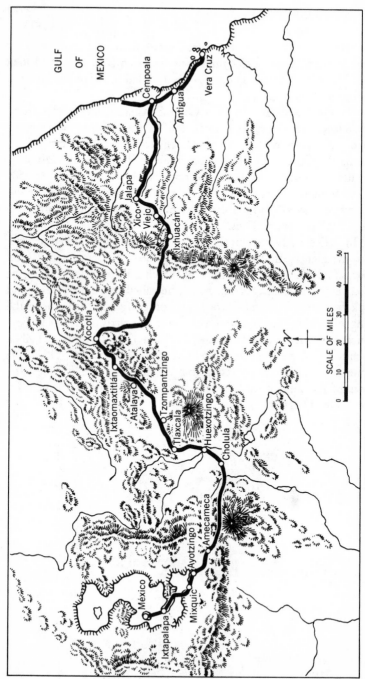

Fig. IV-1. Route of Cortés from Vera Cruz to Mexico City.

CHAPTER IV

THE GREAT CONQUERORS

THE CONQUEST OF America by the Spaniards and the Portuguese was carried out by private individuals at their own expense; the rulers gave only their permission and their good wishes. Thousands of adventurous souls from the Iberian Peninsula sold their worldly goods and went to the Indies. Three motives for conquest developed: gold, glory, and gospel. The first and second aggrandized the state and the individual, while the third contributed to the glory of the Roman Catholic Church, whose interests the Iberian sovereigns had at heart.

Among the leaders of the conquest in America were four individuals, who, because they fought and overcame the greatest native opposition, prepared the way for the exploration of many adjacent regions and made possible the establishment of permanent colonial governments and the consolidation of vast territories.

HERNANDO CORTES

His Early Life. Born in Medellín, Spain, in 1485, Cortés came of a noble family. He attended the University of Salamanca for two years, but was more interested in dissipation than in studies. In 1504 he went to Santo Domingo, where he became a planter. In 1511 he went to Cuba with Governor Diego de Velásquez, whose sister-in-law he married. But a quiet, domestic life was not to the liking of Cortés, and in October, 1518, he obtained a commission from Velásquez to find and to conquer the kingdom of the Aztecs on the mainland to the west.

Cortés Conquers Mexico. On November 18, 1518, at the age of thirty-three, Cortés sailed from Cuba with a dozen ships, more than five hundred soldiers, one hundred sailors, many servants and slaves, sixteen horses, and a number of cannon. At the island of Cozumel,

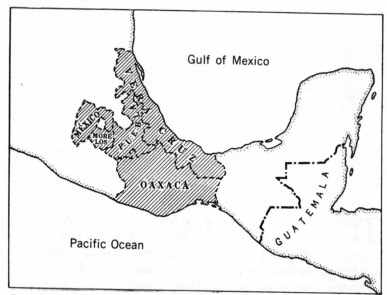

Fig. IV-2. Territory in Which Towns Were Granted to Cortés. (Courtesy of Farrar & Rinehart, Inc.)

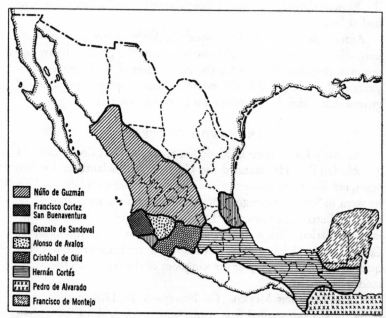

Fig. IV-3. Early Mexican Conquerors and the Regions Conquered. (Based on data from *La Conquista de la Nueva Galicia*, by José López-Portillo y Weber, Mexico, 1935.)

off the coast of Yucatan, Cortés found a shipwrecked Spaniard named Aguilar, who understood the Mayan language. In March, 1519, the expedition left this island and soon afterward landed on the Tabasco coast, where they found a girl, Malinche (called Doña Marina by the Spaniards), who understood the Aztec language. With these two interpreters, the Spaniards were enabled later to converse with the Aztecs.

On April 21, Cortés landed his forces at the present site of Veracruz, which he named. After burning his ships in order to prevent his dissatisfied men from returning to Cuba and in order to use the sailors on land, Cortés began in August to fight his way inland to the Aztec capital high in the great Valley of Mexico. With the aid of Indian allies and with the judicious use of his cannon, firearms, and horses, Cortés overcame all opposition, and on November 8, he arrived at the edge of the lake on which was the great Aztec island capital ruled over by Montezuma II. The emperor greeted the Spaniards and gave them quarters in the city. But the handful of conquerors, fearing treachery, forced Montezuma to live with them, to declare his allegiance to the Spanish king, and to make payment of gold to the Spaniards.

In the meantime, Velásquez had sent a fleet from Cuba under Pánfilo de Narváez to limit the authority of Cortés. When this force reached Veracruz, Cortés hastened there and persuaded his enemies to join him in winning riches from the Aztecs. With this assistance Cortés returned to the capital, where he found Pedro de Alvarado, whom he had left in command, besieged by the Indians under a leader elected to succeed Montezuma. Failing to quiet Aztec enmity, Cortés led his forces, on the night of June 30, 1519, out of the city and along the causeway to the border of the lake. By the time they reached the edge of the lake, they had lost more than half of their men in this bloody retreat of *"La Noche Triste."* Thereupon Cortés resolved to build a fleet on the lake and to capture the city from the water. In May, 1521, these ships attacked the capital, and after a siege the city fell on August 13.

Cortés Establishes a Government. Immediately the rebuilding of the city on a Spanish pattern was begun, and Cortés established a Spanish municipal government, with Pedro de Alvarado as mayor. Lands and Indians were assigned to the followers of Cortés, and plans were made for seizing the surrounding territory. New officials were sent from Spain to take over the new government and to supervise mining and all other economic matters. In October, 1522, the king named Cortés governor and captain general of New Spain, as Mexico was then called.

Cortés after the Conquest. Despite his achievements, the enemies of Cortés in New Spain and in Old Spain caused him to suffer many indignities, and in 1528 he went to Spain to present his defense to the Crown. Charles V was much impressed; he granted Cortés twenty-two towns and 23,000 vassals in Mexico and gave him the title "Marquis of the Valley of Oaxaca." In 1530 Cortés returned to New Spain, where he found life unpleasant, and he returned to his native land. Later he fought in Algiers. He died in 1547.

FRANCISCO PIZARRO

Preliminaries of the Conquest of Peru. The conqueror of Peru was born in Spain between 1470 and 1478. An illegitimate son of a Spanish army officer, he was deserted by his parents and was in early life a swineherd. In 1509 he went to the Indies, and the next year he went to the Isthmus of Panama with Ojeda. In 1513 he crossed Panama with Balboa, the discoverer of the Pacific. Hearing of rich native kingdoms lying to the south, he resolved to search for them. At the time, however, he was too poor to equip an expedition. Therefore, he settled down to farming near Panama City in partnership with a friend, Diego de Almagro, who was also an illiterate adventurer of unknown parentage.

In 1524 these men sold their farm and fitted out two ships to search for the kingdoms to the south. On November 14, they sailed from Panama but were soon back with both ships damaged. They had, however, reached about 4 degrees North Latitude.

Nothing daunted, they planned a second expedition. With the financial aid of a renegade priest, Hernando de Luque, and the Mayor of Panama, Gaspar de Espinosa, they equipped two vessels with 160 men and five horses and sailed from the Isthmus on March 10, 1526. Proceeding against adverse currents, they ran out of supplies, for which they had to send back to Panama, but they finally reached a point about 9 degrees South Latitude in 1527. Then they returned to the Isthmus with stories of the rich nations of Peru.

Pizarro now resolved to go to Spain to obtain from the king an official patent to the country. As a result Charles V granted land to Pizarro and to Almagro and appointed de Luque as Bishop of Tumbes. Pizarro was also given a coat of arms and made a noble.

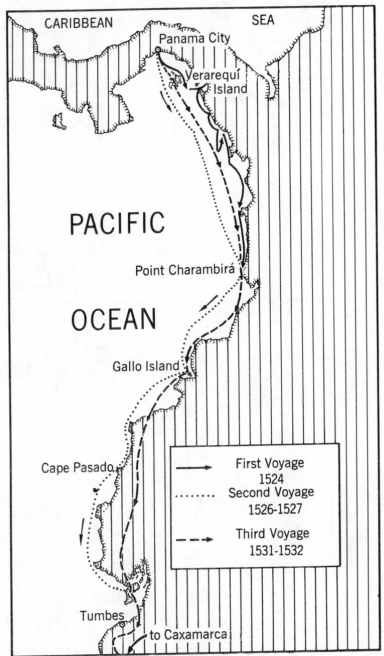

CARIBBEAN SEA

Panama City

Verarequí
Island

PACIFIC

Point Charambirá

OCEAN

Gallo Island

Cape Pasado

	First Voyage 1524
....	Second Voyage 1526-1527
	Third Voyage 1531-1532

Tumbes

to Caxamarca

FIG. IV-4. Voyages of Pizarro, 1524-32.

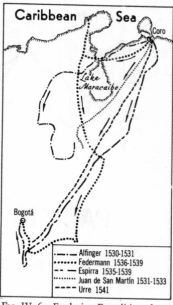

Fig. IV-5. Route of Jiménez de Quesada, 1536–38.

Fig. IV-6. Exploring Expeditions from Coro, 1530–41.

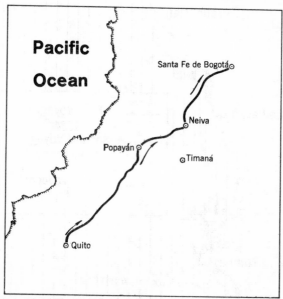

Fig. IV-7. Route of Sebastián de Belalcázar, 1536–38.

When Pizarro returned to America in January, 1530, he took with him his four half-brothers.

The Conquest of Peru. In January, 1531, Pizarro led a third expedition, consisting of three ships, 183 men, and thirty-seven horses, southward from Panama. In November, 1532, the adventurers reached Caxamarca, where they met the Inca ruler, Atahualpa, then at war with his half-brother Huascar. By treachery the Spaniards seized the native monarch and held him a prisoner. However, it was agreed that if he would fill a room 22 feet by 17 feet to a height of 9 feet with gold, he would be allowed to go free. But when this task was accomplished, the conquerors decided not to free Atahualpa, and shortly afterwards an excuse was found to execute him on August 29, 1533.

From Caxamarca the conquest of the Incas was extended in all directions. In November, 1533, Hernando de Soto took Cuzco, and the next year Quito was founded. In January, 1535, Pizarro founded Lima, "The City of the Kings," as his capital, and Trujillo, Guayaquil, and other towns were established. As in New Spain, the surrounding territory was rapidly explored and subjugated. But it was not long before quarrels among the conquerors caused civil wars in Peru, which for a decade prevented the establishment of an orderly government and the exploitation of the riches of the country.

JIMENEZ DE QUESADA

Preliminaries of the Conquest. Gonzalo Jiménez de Quesada was born about 1499 in Córdoba, Spain. He came from a noble family and was educated for the law. But although he was a scholar, he was interested in horsemanship and in the use of arms. In 1535 he went to America and became a magistrate at Santa Marta on the Pearl Coast, where the governor of the region, Fernando de Lugo, was interested in finding gold among the neighboring Indians. Early in 1536 he commissioned Quesada to lead an expedition southward to look for riches.

The Conquest of the Chibchas. On April 6, 1536, Quesada set out with six hundred infantrymen, one hundred horses, and six ships with two hundred men on board. The fleet was to go up the Magdalena River while Quesada was to lead his men overland into the high plateau of central Colombia. Clothed in heavy cotton armor as protection against the poisoned arrows of the Indians, the men cut their way foot by foot through the steaming jungles, making contacts occasionally with the ships ascending the treacherous river. Finally, after going four hundred miles in eight months and having lost two-thirds of his men, Quesada founded the town of La Tora on the Magdalena River. After resting there, the Spaniards moved into the mountainous region to the east. By now their clothes, which had been torn to shreds, offered slight protection against the cold. They dragged their cannon up precipices and toiled through deep drifts of snow. At last, 166 men reached the great plain near the present city of Bogotá where the Chibchas lived.

Because the Chibcha kingdom was divided into two parts, each with a ruler, the Spaniards were able eventually to overcome native resistance and to seize several native leaders. On August 6, 1538, Quesada founded the town of Santa Fe de Bogotá, which he planned to be the capital of the country. There he left his brother in charge and returned to the coast. Expansion from this city began in all directions, and some gold and emeralds were found.

Quesada after the Conquest. From the Pearl Coast, Quesada went to Spain, where he obtained a grant to the land he had conquered. But his enemies complained against him and he was tried for the torture of a Chibcha chief, fined, and banished from the country. In 1549 his rights were restored and he became an official at Bogotá. Twenty years later he led an expedition eastward from the city in search of "El Dorado," and in the following years he engaged in Indian warfare. On February 16, 1579, Quesada died at the age of eighty, probably from leprosy.

PEDRO DE VALDIVIA

Valdivia before the Conquest. One of the conquerors of Peru was Pedro de Valdivia, born in Spain of noble parents about 1500. He served in the army of Charles V in Italy, and in 1530 went to America. Two years later he was in Peru, where he won the confidence of Pizarro and became rich from a mine he had discovered. Interest in the country south of Peru was keen, and in 1535 Almagro set out to conquer Chile. But after terrible hardships he was forced to return to Peru, having reached as far south as the present city of Santiago. This disaster only stimulated Pizarro with a greater desire to occupy Chile, and in 1539 he commissioned Valdivia to undertake the task.

The Conquest of Chile. In 1540 Valdivia with two hundred Spaniards and a thousand native servants started southward over a route different from that taken by Almagro. From the very beginning his men were mutinous. Fighting the fierce Araucanian Indians as they advanced, Valdivia and his men finally founded the city of Santiago on February 12, 1541. When the natives burned this town, Valdivia founded La Serena. With the help of sorely needed reinforcements which arrived from Peru, the Spaniards built the town of Valparaíso in September, 1544. By 1546 Valdivia had extended his influence as far south as the Bío-Bío River, near the mouth of which he founded Concepción in January, 1550. The next year he built Imperial, and in 1552 he founded the town of Valdivia. With further aid from Peru, Valdivia sent an expedition across the Andes to found towns in present-day Argentina.

Meanwhile, Valdivia wrote Charles V asking for a confirmation to the land which he was conquering. At the same time, Indian fighting began anew, and on December 31, 1553, Valdivia was killed in a battle. The Spaniards were seized with panic and fled northward, hotly pursued by the Araucanians under two leaders, Caupolicán and Lautaro. For a time the Indians swept all before them. But at last, after nearly half a century of warfare, the Spaniards fortified the Bío-Bío River as their southern boundary and attempted with partial success to keep the natives south of that line.

PINZÓN & SOLÍS — 1506
OJEDA & NICUESA — 1509
PONCE DE LEÓN — 1513
ESPINOSA — 1516-19
CÓRDOBA — 1517
GRIJALVA — 1518
PINEDA — 1519
GORDILLO & QUEXOS — 1520-21
NIÑO & GONZÁLEZ — 1522
GOMES — 1525
ULLOA — 1539
CABRILLO — 1542-43
VIZCAÍNO — 1602-03

FIG. V-1. Water Explorations in Northern Latin America in the Colonial Period.

CHAPTER V

THE GREAT EXPLORERS

MOST OF THE TERRITORY conquered by Spain and Portugal was not obtained in so spectacular a fashion as was that described in the previous chapter. Indeed, land was explored and conquered chiefly by small bands of men with the assistance of firearms, horses, and fierce dogs trained to fight. Conquest involved at times a conscious attempt to spread disease, especially measles, among the Indians. Thousands of small expeditions, often consisting of a handful of soldiers and a priest, helped to give Spain and Portugal their claims to America. Often the natives were not completely subdued for centuries.

The motives for exploration and conquest remained constant throughout nearly three centuries: gold, glory, and gospel. Everywhere the Europeans went they heard tales from the natives of strange lands and peoples, of rich cities and kingdoms. In North America the explorers searched for the Fountain of Youth, the Seven Cities of Cíbola, the Island of the Amazons, Chicora, Quivira, and other fabulous places of great riches, while in South America they sought El Dorado (the Gilded Man), the Kingdom of the Amazons, the Land of Cinnamon, Omagua, Meta, and similar places of supposed wealth. Needless to say, these "mysteries" were never found, but the search for them led the explorers into many far corners of America.

EXPLORATIONS IN NORTH AMERICA

Southeastern United States. Many expeditions went to Florida from the West Indies. Juan Ponce de León, in 1521, went to the Gulf coast of Florida with some two hundred men hoping to found a colony, but in a battle with the fierce natives the Spaniards were defeated and the leader was killed.

× o × o	SANDOVAL — 1520-21
× × × ×	ALVARADO — 1522-24
o o o o	GONZÁLEZ — 1524
-o-o-	CORTÉS — 1524-26
o o o	CABEZA DE VACA — 1528-36
- - - -	GUZMÁN — 1529-31
- - -	DE SOTO — 1539-42
————	CORONADO — 1540-42
-×o×-	IBARRA — 1564-67
-o o-	ESPEJO — 1582
-×-×-	OÑATE — 1598-1609

Fig. V-2. Land Explorations in Northern Latin America in the Colonial Period.

Lucas Vásquez de Ayllón, in 1526, sailed from Española with three ships and five hundred colonists hoping to land in what are now the Carolinas, but the leader died and the colonists returned home late in 1528.

Pánfilo de Narváez, on April 15, 1528, en route from Spain with six hundred persons and eighty horses, landed near the present Tampa Bay. Marching inland, his company fought the Indians but failed to find riches. At the end of July, they reached St. Mark's Bay, hoping to find ships which would take them to the West Indies. But no aid came, and they killed and ate their horses, using the skins to make five small boats in which they set sail on September 22. A hurricane blew them along the Gulf coast, sinking all but one ship, which was wrecked on the coast of Texas. In this craft was the treasurer of the expedition, Alvar Núñez Cabeza de Vaca, with several companions. These survivors set out to walk to Mexico City, but along the way they were detained by numerous Indian tribes, and found themselves at Culiacán on the Pacific coast of Mexico April 1, 1536, after having walked several thousands of miles. The stories they told of the things they had seen and heard led other adventurers to explore the southwestern part of the United States.

Hernando de Soto, on May 25, 1539, landed at Tampa Bay with about 600 men and 223 horses to look for riches and several of the northern mysteries. For about four years this band wandered through present Georgia, the Carolinas, Alabama, Mississippi, Arkansas, and Louisiana. But they found no wealth of any consequence, and when on May 21, 1542, the leader died, the explorers, under Luis de Moscoso, turned back, floated down the Mississippi River, and finally reached Mexico in 1543.

In June, 1559, Tristán de Luna landed at Pensacola Bay with 1,500 men in thirteen ships, prepared to establish a colony. But hardships and mutiny ensued, and de Luna was replaced by Angel de Villafañe, who had come from Mexico with supplies and who now moved the colony to Santa Elena on Port Royal Sound. However, all attempts to found a permanent colony failed, and in 1561 Philip II of Spain declared that no more attempts should be made to colonize Florida.

But because the French Huguenots took an interest in Florida, the Spanish king changed his mind and sent Pedro Menéndez de Avilés with 1,500 colonists in nineteen ships to Florida, where on September 6, 1565, the town of St. Augustine was founded. From

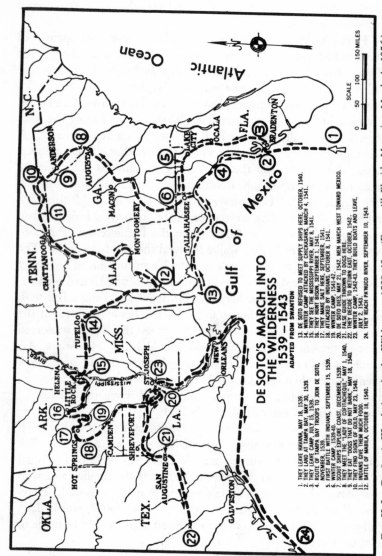

DE SOTO'S MARCH INTO THE WILDERNESS
1539 – 1543
ADAPTED FROM SWANTON

1. THEY LEAVE HAVANA, MAY 18, 1539.
2. THEY LAND AT TAMPA BAY, MAY 30, 1539.
3. THEY LEAVE CAMP, JULY 15, 1539.
4. ROUTE OF TAMPA BAY TROOPS TO JOIN DE SOTO, NOVEMBER, 1539.
5. FIRST BATTLE WITH INDIANS, SEPTEMBER 15, 1539.
6. WINTER CAMP 1539-40.
7. SCOUT SHIPS EXPLORE COAST, DECEMBER, 1539.
8. THEY MEET THE "LADY OF COFITACHIQUI," MAY 1, 1540.
9. THEY EAT DOGS THAN DO NOT MARCH," MAY 18, 1540.
10. THEY FIND SIGNS OF GOLD, MAY 23, 1540.
11. INDIANS GIVE THEM MUCH FOOD.
12. BATTLE OF MABILA, OCTOBER 18, 1540.
13. DE SOTO REFUSED TO MEET SUPPLY SHIPS HERE, OCTOBER, 1540.
14. WINTER CAMP ATTACKED BY CHICKASAWS, MARCH 4, 1541.
15. THEY SEE THE MISSISSIPPI RIVER, MAY 8, 1541.
16. THEY HUNT BISON, SEPTEMBER 1, 1541.
17. THEY MAKE SALT HERE, OCTOBER 1, 1541.
18. ATTACKED BY INDIANS, OCTOBER 8, 1541.
19. WINTER CAMP, 1541-42.
20. DE SOTO DIES, MAY 21, 1542. MEN MARCH WEST TOWARD MEXICO.
21. FALSE GUIDE THROWN TO DOGS HERE.
22. THEY DECIDE TO RETURN EAST, OCTOBER, 1542.
23. WINTER CAMP, 1542-43. THEY BUILD BOATS AND LEAVE, JULY 2, 1543.
24. THEY REACH PÁNUCO RIVER, SEPTEMBER 10, 1543.

FIG. V–3. De Soto's Wanderings in the Wilderness, 1539–43. (From *All Florida Magazine*, March 4, 1956.)

that time on, this city was used as a base for further expansion in Florida. Menéndez, however, died in 1574, and the colony was never prosperous.

Southwestern United States. Alvar Núñez Cabeza de Vaca had returned to Mexico with tales of the famous Seven Cities of Cíbola, and the viceroy commissioned a Franciscan, Marcos de Niza, and a Negro named Estevanico to find these cities and to bring back a full report. In March, 1539, they set out northward, with Estevanico going ahead and promising to send back a token if he found the cities. When this was received Marcos hastened on, but he learned that the Negro had been killed by the Indians and that the supposed Seven Cities was only a Zuñi pueblo. Returning to Mexico, Father Marcos, however, reported that he had found the Seven Cities of Cíbola and that they were richer than Mexico City itself.

As a result of this report, the viceroy decided to send a great expedition to the region, and he commissioned Francisco Vásquez de Coronado to seize it. In February, 1540, Coronado took two hundred horsemen, seventy infantrymen, and nine hundred Indian servants with cattle and horses overland toward the north. For nearly two years the explorers searched for a land of riches and passed through the present states of New Mexico, Arizona, Texas, Oklahoma, and Kansas. In 1542 they finally returned to Mexico.

In the years that followed, only small exploring parties were sent out toward the north, chiefly with the aims of finding and opening mines or of establishing missions and towns. One of the most important of these was led by Juan de Oñate, who, in 1595, received the right to colonize New Mexico. In 1598 he set out with one hundred soldiers, some missionaries, slaves, and cattle. By 1601 he may have gone as far as Wichita, Kansas, returning to Mexico in 1609, the year in which Santa Fe was founded by Pedro de Peralta. From this region and from northern Mexico expeditions were sent into Upper California, where many missions were founded by the regular clergy in the two following centuries.

Water Explorations from New Spain. Cortés showed an early interest in mapping the Pacific coast of New Spain and in making discoveries in the ocean. In 1527 he sent an abortive expedition under Alvar de Saavedra Cerón across the sea to the Moluccas, and in 1532 his agents explored the Gulf of Lower California, which came to be called the "Gulf of Cortés." In 1533 Lower California was discovered; it was believed to be an island. In 1535 Cortés founded a

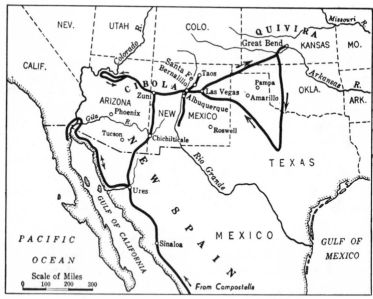

Fig. V–4.   Route of Coronado's Expedition, 1540–42.   (Reproduced with permission from *The New York Times*, January 7, 1940.)

colony on the peninsula of Lower California at La Paz.   Finally, in 1539 an expedition under Francisco de Ulloa proved that Lower California was a peninsula; but the belief that it was an island persisted for many years.

Juan Rodríguez Cabrillo, in 1542, sailed along the coast of California to perhaps 40 degrees North Latitude, but he died before returning to Mexico.

Ruy López de Villalobos led an expedition across the Pacific in 1542 and took possession of the Philippines for the Spanish king, but he was captured by the Portuguese there and died in the Moluccas.

Miguel López de Legazpi, with four hundred men and four ships, left Mexico in November, 1564, for the Philippines.   There they had trouble with the Portuguese, but in the end founded Manila in 1571, as a Spanish city.   The next year the leader died.

Sebastián Rodríguez Cermeño, in 1595, tried to map the California coast but was wrecked in Drake's Bay.

Sebastián Vizcaíno, in 1602, explored the California coast as far north as Oregon and mapped Monterey Bay as a port of call for ships returning from the Philippines.

Central America. Central America was explored both from Mexico and from Panama. Cortés was especially interested in exploring and conquering the territory. In 1523 and 1524 Alvarado extended his influence as far south as present-day El Salvador. In 1524 Cristóbal de Olid, under the direction of Cortés, went to Honduras, and Cortés himself went to Honduras shortly thereafter. In 1526 the conquest of Yucatan was undertaken. Frequently in Central America the forces of different Spanish leaders clashed, and especially was there rivalry between the forces coming from Mexico and those sent by Pedrarias from Panama.

In 1522 and 1523 Andrés Niño and Gil González Dávila explored northward from Panama along the coast of Nicaragua. In 1524 the latter went from Española to Honduras, where he engaged in warfare with other Spanish forces. In all of this exploring many towns were founded, including Trujillo, San Gil de Buenavista, Bruselas, León, Granada, and others.

In 1532 Bartolomé de las Casas, "The Apostle of the Indies," went to Nicaragua as a Dominican missionary to convert the natives, and in 1536 he was in Guatemala in a region of warlike Indians whom he pacified without the use of firearms.

EXPLORATIONS IN SOUTH AMERICA

Northern South America. Several towns were founded along the Pearl Coast: Cumaná in 1520; Santa Marta in 1525; Coro in 1527; Cartagena in 1533; and others, all of which were used as bases from which to send exploring parties into the interior of what are now Colombia and Venezuela. All of the explorers were looking for the southern mysteries and especially for El Dorado.

In 1527 the Augsburg banking house of the Welsers obtained, as security for money which they loaned Charles V, the right to conquer and settle in Venezuela. In February, 1529, the colonists sent by the Welsers reached Coro. But the Indians were warlike, the leaders were incompetent, and the colony did not prosper. Finally, after eighteen years, the grant was given up, but not until Federmann, von Speier, and Alfinger, three of the leaders, had explored several hundred miles inland.

Among early explorers in this territory were Diego Ordaz (1531–35), Pedro de Heredia (1534), Gerónimo Ortal (1535), and others. Later a number of towns were founded in the interior: Pamplona

FIG. V–5. Water Explorations in Southern Latin America in the Colonial Period.

1 LIMA
2 QUITO
3 BOGOTÁ
4 ASUNCIÓN
5 BUENOS AIRES
6 CÓRDOBA

–•–• ALEIXO GARCIA — 1524-25
–•×•– SEBASTIAN CABOT — 1526
–•–•– DIOGO GARCIA — 1526
–×××– HERRERA — 1534
××××× MENDOZA & AYOLAS —1534
–×•– ALMAGRO — 1535
••••• BELALCÁZAR — 1536
–×–×– JIMÉNEZ DE QUESADA — 1536-38
–•–• FEDERMANN — 1539
——— ORELLANA — 1539-41
–×•×– CABEZA DE VACA — 1540
×•×• ROJAS — 1542
–•–•– IRALA — ABOUT 1548
– – – AGUIRRE — 1560
–•–•– GARAY — AFTER 1576

Fig. V–6. Land Explorations in Southern Latin America in the Colonial Period.

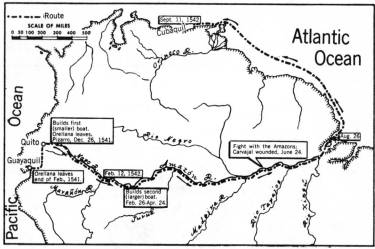

FIG. V–7. Orellana's Voyage of Discovery down the Amazon, 1541–42.

FIG. V–8. Route of Lope de Aguirre from Peru to Venezuela, 1560–61.

(1549), Ibagué (1551), Barquisimeto (1552), Valencia (1555), Trujillo (1556), Mérida (1558), Caracas (1568), La Guaira (1588), and others.

Peru and Bolivia. Civil war between the Pizarro brothers and the Almagros (father and son) prevented for a decade the effective organization of exploring expeditions in and from Peru. In 1538, Almagro, Pizarro's partner in the conquest, was executed, and in 1541 the conqueror himself was murdered. The younger Almagro was finally executed in 1542 and the control of Peru fell to Gonzalo Pizarro, a half-brother of the conqueror. In 1539 he set out to look for the Land of Cinnamon eastward across the Andes in the Amazon Valley. From 1539 to 1542 Francisco de Orellana explored the Amazon, which for a time was known as the "Río Orellana."

In 1560 Viceroy Mendoza of Peru sent Pedro de Ursúa to further explore the Amazon. With him went Lope de Aguirre, who murdered the leader and most of the party and then escaped northward to the Orinoco River. He was finally caught and executed for his crimes.

Expeditions into Bolivia, or Upper Peru as it was called, were sent from Peru. In 1538 the town of La Plata (later called Chuquisaca, Charcas, and Sucre) was founded, and other settlements were made.

Water Explorations from Peru. The people of Peru, like the people of New Spain, were interested in exploring the Pacific. About 1564 Alvaro Mendeña de Neyra sailed from Callao, the seaport of Lima, and discovered the Solomon Islands. In 1595 Mendeña, on another expedition, discovered the Marquesas Islands.

In 1579 the viceroy of Peru sent Pedro Sarmiento de Gamboa to the Strait of Magellan to intercept Francis Drake and to consider fortifying the region, but it was not until 1583 that the first settlement was made there at San Felipe.

La Plata. From 1516 to 1525 several of the survivors of the expedition of Solís, who was killed in this region in 1515, explored part of present-day Bolivia and Paraguay.

In 1527, Sebastián Cabot, then pilot major of Spain, stopped in La Plata on his way to the Moluccas and the East and explored the region until 1530, building a fort at San Espíritu and finding some gold.

In September, 1534, Pedro de Mendoza led an expedition of eleven ships carrying 2,500 colonists, cattle, seed, and agricultural implements to La Plata. In 1535 they built a fort at Santa María

Atlantic
Ocean

Gurupá 1623
Manaus 1674
Tabatinga 1780
Pará (Belém) 1619
Santa Maria 1614
Ceará (Fortaleza) 1612
Natal 1597
Paraíba (João Pessoa) 1583
Olinda 1535
Pernambuco (Recife) 1536
São Cristóvão 1589
Penedo 1620
Santa Ana 1736
Bahia (Salvador) 1549
Vila Bela 1752
Cuiabá 1722
Minas Novas 1727
Paracatú 1744
Pôrto Seguro
Diamantina 1730
Corumbá 1788
Ouro Prêto 1698
Nova Coimbra 1775
Espírito Santo 1535
São Paulo 1532
São Vicente 1532
Rio de Janeiro 1555
Santos 1545
Laguna 1654
Atlantic
Ocean
Pôrto Alegre 1743
Rio Grande 1737

Pacific Ocean

FIG. V–9. Colonial Settlements in Brazil.

de Buenos Aires, which was soon attacked by the Indians. In consequence, the colony was moved up the river to Corpus Christi. In 1536 the town of Asunción was founded. With this city as a center other towns were established in the interior of Argentina, including Santa Fe and Córdoba in 1573. Finally, in 1580 a town was built at Buenos Aires, and in the following years towns were laid out at Tucumán (1585), Corrientes (1588), Rioja (1591), and San Luis (1596). Four leaders in this region were Domingo Martínez de Irala, Juan de Ayolas, Alvar Núñez Cabeza de Vaca, and Juan de Garay.

Brazil. Although Cabral had discovered Brazil in 1500, the Portuguese government seemed to take little interest in Brazil until about 1530. In the next few years several Portuguese adventurers settled or explored the coast, including Diogo Alvares Correa and João Ramalho. In 1526 Diogo Garcia landed in the present state of

Santa Catarina and with a band of natives marched overland toward the Inca kingdom, but his party perished. In the same year Cristovão Jacques landed north of present-day Pernambuco.

Finally, in 1530 the Portuguese government sent Martim Afonso de Sousa with settlers, cattle, seeds, and agricultural implements to colonize the country. They built a fort at Rio de Janeiro, but it was destroyed early the next year, and in 1532 they founded São Vicente. Sousa was to be governor and to lay out a dozen *capitanias,* or feudal estates, each to be in charge of a noble, called a *donatário,* who was to build towns and forts, explore, and carry on trade with the mother country. These estates were laid out facing the coast and extending inland to the Demarcation Line. But the Portuguese sent over so many criminals as colonists, and the climate proved so enervating, that the colony got a poor start.

However, several towns were founded during this period. About 1535 Duarte Coelho Pereira founded Olinda, in 1536 Pero Lopes de Sousa established the towns of Santo Amaro and Itamaracá, and in the same year Pernambuco was settled.

In April, 1549, Tomé de Sousa brought more colonists to the country in six ships and founded the town of Bahia. From this period interest in explorations of the interior increased. In 1560 Brás Cubas at São Vicente led an expedition north and west in search of the headwaters of the São Francisco River and to look for gold. Also in 1560 Vasco de Caldas led an exploring party westward from Bahia. Sebastião Tourinho explored the present state of Minas Gerais for minerals in 1572 and 1573.

In 1580 the colony of Brazil became a Spanish possession, when Philip II of Spain inherited the throne of Portugal. Spanish rule lasted until 1640, and during the period renewed exploring activities occurred. But it was not until the eighteenth century that many towns were opened in the interior, and especially in the southern part of Brazil, where gold and diamonds were found by the roaming Paulistas from southeastern Brazil. For much of her colonial life Brazil remained a coastal colony.

Fig. VI–1. Government Divisions and Grants in South America by 1534.

CHAPTER VI

COLONIAL ADMINISTRATION

THE PROBLEM OF THE political administration of vast areas had to be solved by Spain and Portugal with practically no political precedent available and with only a minimum of applicable political experience. It is amazing that a trial and error procedure produced political theory that at first proved so sound in practice. At the same time political, religious, and military leaders from all classes appeared from all parts of the peninsula to implement the royal orders, rules, and regulations. It is regrettable and tragic that colonial administration in the sixteenth century set standards which were not followed in the seventeenth and eighteenth centuries.

COLONIAL GOVERNMENTS IN THE MOTHER COUNTRIES

Theory of Colonial Government. From the standpoint of theory the methods devised for controlling the Iberian colonies in America were carefully planned, but in actual practice the colonial governments of Spain and Portugal in America were burdensome, slow, expensive, and at times almost unmanageable. The supervision of the colonies was paternalistic and the colonists were in relation to the mother countries as children to parents—they were to do as they were told without asking why. In a modified form the two countries applied the mercantile system to their colonies and held them in bondage as the best way in which to exploit them profitably.

Power of the Kings. By virtue of the papal grants of demarcation the Spanish and Portuguese kings owned in person all land and water in their respective colonies. Thus, the rulers could grant or refuse to grant territory in America, and they could claim all or part of the products from the land and water there. The kings could allow or refuse to allow any person to go to the colonies, they could super-

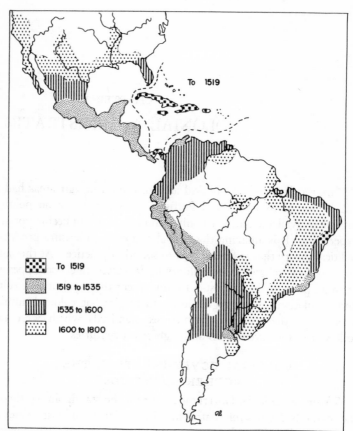

To 1519

To 1519
1519 to 1535
1535 to 1600
1600 to 1800

Fig. VI–2. Spanish and Portuguese Occupation of America to 1800.

vise all trade to and from the colonies, and they could force the
colonists to produce certain products and could prevent their production of other products. The kings collected all revenue and spent
it as they pleased. As the heads of the Catholic Church in their separate kingdoms, the sovereigns could collect and spend church
revenues, could approve or disapprove the appointment of church
officers, and could veto or sanction any papal decree which might be
directed at their colonies by the pope. Through the Church the monarchs controlled all colonial education, printing, and literature. As
the source of justice, the kings could make and execute all colonial
laws. All amusements, public activities, and even private affairs
were subject to the control and regulation of the Iberian rulers. In-

dians, likewise, were subject to the authority of the kings and could be enslaved or protected as the sovereigns saw fit. Thus, nothing (and no one) was free from the absolute power of the monarchs.

Colonial Government in Spain. Because the Spanish king could not personally perform all the functions described above, he had to delegate some of his authority to officials both in Spain and in the colonies.

THE CASA DE CONTRATACIÓN. In 1503 the Crown established at Sevilla the *Casa de Contratación,* which was a combination immigration office, trade clearing-house, mercantile tribunal, and nautical college for the general control of colonial economic affairs. As the years passed and the functions of this body became modified, the number of officers in the body increased. In 1717 the *Casa* was moved to Cádiz, and in 1790 it was abolished. During its lifetime it served to systematize and unify the economic life of the colonies.

THE CONSEJO DE INDIAS. It was soon apparent that the *Casa* could not handle all colonial affairs, and in 1524 the king created the *Consejo de Indias* to supervise and control all noneconomic matters pertaining to the colonies. Like the *Casa,* this body grew in membership and developed many special functions which were dealt with in a systematic fashion at regular stated times. Its members were to be noble Spanish Catholics with administrative, legal, or other specialized training and ability. The *Consejo,* which reflected the general policies of the kingdom and usually exhibited little initiative, lasted throughout the colonial period.

Colonial Government in Portugal. In the early part of the sixteenth century, primarily because its interest in Brazil was eclipsed by interest in its possessions in the Far East, the Portuguese government paid slight attention to its American colony. The king was assisted by an inspector of finance who was to supervise the exploitation of Brazil. But in 1580, when Philip II of Spain inherited the crown of Portugal, he established a Finance Council (*Conselho da Fazenda*) which had about the same relation to Brazil as the *Casa* and *Consejo* had to the Spanish colonies. With the aid of this body the king legislated for the colony. In 1604 Philip III of Spain created the *Conselho da India* copied after the Spanish *Consejo de Indias,* but in 1640, when Portugal regained its independence, the name was changed to *Conselho do Ultramar* and it was given supervision of colonial civil, religious, and military affairs. Colonial officers were nominated by the king's Council of State.

THE FIRST COLONIAL GOVERNMENTS
IN AMERICA

In the West Indies. Columbus established the first colonial government in the West Indies. He had the title of governor, and he appointed all officers, distributed land and natives to his fellow countrymen, and supervised further exploration. In 1502 Nicolás de Ovando became governor with almost absolute authority from the king, and the capital of the colony was moved to the city of Santo Domingo. Ovando was assisted by royal treasury officials who had charge of economic matters and who set aside one-third of the mining revenues for the Crown. In 1509 Diego Columbus (a son of the Admiral) succeeded Ovando as governor, remaining in office until 1522.

In Mexico (New Spain). Cortés had founded Mexico City as the capital of Mexico, or New Spain as it came to be called, and in 1524 the king sent royal officials to take over the government. In 1527 the Crown established the first *audiencia,* or supreme court, which was also to act as an advisory body in matters of government. Finally, in 1535 Charles V founded the Viceroyalty of New Spain and appointed Antonio de Mendoza to be the first viceroy.

In Peru. The wars in Peru between the Pizarros and the Almagros hampered the exploitation of the riches of that country, and the king appointed Blasco Núñez Vela as a special official with the title of viceroy to establish order, to develop the region, and to take away from the Pizarro family the function of governor, the title which had been given to Francisco Pizarro, the conqueror of Peru. The viceroy arrived in 1544 and was forced to fight Gonzalo Pizarro, who had assumed the title of governor. But in 1546 the viceroy was killed, and two years later the king replaced him by Pedro de la Gasca, who succeeded in capturing Gonzalo Pizarro and executing him. Finally, in 1551 the first viceroy of New Spain, Antonio de Mendoza, was promoted to the viceroyalty of Peru, thus setting a precedent which was often followed later. The greatest viceroy in Peru in the sixteenth century was Francisco de Toledo, who held office from 1569 to 1581.

In Brazil. The first form of government in Brazil was the *capitania,* or feudal principality, ruled over by a Portuguese noble called a *donatário* appointed by the Crown to colonize, exploit, and fortify his grant. Thirteen *capitanias* were laid out along the coast in 1534, extending westward to the Demarcation Line. It was not long before the king regretted having made these extensive grants, and in 1549 he revoked the powers of the *donatários* and sent royal governors to take over their authority. Over all of the colony was placed a governor general, with his capital at Bahia. The first governor general was Tomé de Sousa, who served from 1549 to 1553.

THE VICEREGAL SYSTEM IN AMERICA

The Viceroyalty in the Spanish Colonies. The predecessors of the viceroys were the governors and *adelantados,* each holding temporary power from the king and usually serving as leaders of exploring or conquering expeditions. As more territory was seized in America, it became necessary to consolidate vast areas, and a higher official called a *viceroy* was sent by the Crown to represent the kingly power and authority.

The viceroy was the personal representative in America of the Spanish Crown. He lived in a palace in the capital city, maintained a court and all forms of royal pomp and prestige, appointed all officials with the king's authority, and supervised the economic, religious, intellectual, and social affairs of the colony. The early viceroys were chosen with great care by the king, and they served at the king's pleasure. The later viceroys were not so carefully selected, and they served usually from three to five years. The great majority of the viceroys were born in Spain and lived in the colonies only during their terms of office. The salary varied with the viceroyalty, the viceroy of Peru receiving the highest compensation. In his political control of the colony the viceroy headed the government, was supreme judge (although advised by the *audiencia*), and made and enforced the laws. To see that he functioned honestly and efficiently, the viceroy was often spied upon by a visitor-general sent by the Crown to report on colonial matters. At the end of his term of office the viceroy had to remain in his viceroyalty for six months and had to undergo a *residencia,* which amounted to a trial before the *audiencia,* to whom anyone could complain concerning the acts of the viceroy while he had been in office.

In the sixteenth century there were two viceroyalties in Spanish America: New Spain, created in 1535, and Peru, created in 1544. In the eighteenth century two more were added: New Granada, created in 1718, and La Plata, or Buenos Aires, created in 1776. These were established to better govern and defend large territories in South

Fig. VI–3. Viceroyalties in Latin America about 1800. (Courtesy of Farrar & Rinehart, Inc.)

America remote from the seat of government at Lima. The bound-aries of the viceroyalty were fixed by the Crown. In each viceroyalty was a capital city, where the viceroy resided. The viceroyalty was divided into a number of judicial districts called *audiencias* (and in a few cases *presidencias*) in charge of each of which was a court also called an *audiencia*. A military subdivision was generally called a captaincy general, but the captain general was not always subordi-nate to the viceroy. The smallest political division of a viceroyalty was a municipality.

The *Audiencia* in the Spanish Colonies. There were no *audien-cias* in Brazil, but in the Spanish colonies they constituted both a territorial subdivision of a viceroyalty and a judicial, administrative, and advisory body. In the capital city of the viceroyalty the *audi-encia* was presided over by the viceroy, while in some other places it was presided over by either a captain general or a president, in which case it was often called a captaincy general or a *presidencia*. The members usually had legal training and were men of good char-acter. They were paid high salaries so that they would not be tempted by bribery. As the conquest progressed, the number of *audiencias* increased until there were thirteen in the eighteenth cen-tury. Serving within the *audiencia* structure were several officials whose titles and functions varied but who were in intimate contact with the natives and the colonists. Among the officials were *gober-nadores* in charge of *gobiernos* and *provincias, corregidores* in charge of *corregimientos,* and *alcaldes mayores* in charge of *alcaldías*. Their functions were chiefly judicial, financial, and administrative in their respective districts.

The Municipalities in the Spanish Colonies. Colonial towns or municipalities were classified according to their size and impor-tance; they were all similar in structure, being based on the old Spanish municipality, and they included the territory surrounding the town proper. Some of the towns held charters from the Crown and had coats of arms, and many of them were named after saints. In the sixteenth century the colonial towns were theoretically and practically autonomous in their political affairs, but they gradually lost this character in the next two centuries, and near the end of the colonial period their governments were mere hollow political shells whose officials had some social prestige but little political im-portance. The landholding white citizens of the towns chose *regi-dores,* or aldermen, who were known collectively as the *regimiento*.

Fig. VI-4. *Audiencias* in Spanish America in the First Half of the Sixteenth
Century. (Map based on Chapter 3, Volume III, of *The Rise of the Spanish Em-
pire*, by R. B. Merriman, published by The Macmillan Company,
New York, 1925.)

From their number these men selected *alcaldes,* or justices, over
whom presided an *alcalde mayor,* or mayor. Together with other
minor officials these men sat in a *cabildo,* or *ayuntamiento,* which
was a town council with power to legislate for the municipality.
All towns were eventually laid out in uniform fashion according to
a royal ordinance dated July 3, 1573.

The Viceroyalty in Brazil. The Portuguese government did not
use the title of "viceroy" during the early history of Brazil, but the
governor general was for all practical purposes a viceroy and had
functions similar to those of the Spanish viceroy. In the eighteenth
century the term was generally employed in the same sense as it
was in the neighboring Spanish colonies.

Between 1572 and 1577 the experiment was tried of dividing the
colony into North and South Brazil, with capitals at Bahia and at

Rio de Janeiro. Thereafter the capital was fixed at the latter city. In 1645 the colony was temporarily made a *principado,* with the heir to the Portuguese throne as Prince of Brazil. But eventually the whole colony was placed under the authority of a viceroy, and its boundaries became fixed, although they remained throughout the colonial period a matter of dispute with the neighboring Spanish colonies. The interior divisions consisted of provinces, several of which were founded on the bases of the original *capitanias.* In charge of each was a captain or governor subordinate to the governor general and later to the viceroy. The municipalities were the smallest political divisions.

The Municipalities in Brazil. The Brazilian municipalities were somewhat similar to those in the Spanish colonies. Most of the towns had charters with a governing council called a *senado da câmara* or a *câmara municipal,* the members of which were chosen by the citizens of the town from among those on an eligible list.

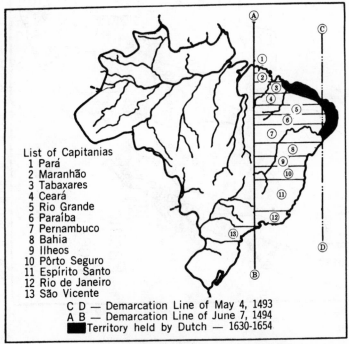

List of Capitanias
1 Pará
2 Maranhão
3 Tabaxares
4 Ceará
5 Rio Grande
6 Paraíba
7 Pernambuco
8 Bahia
9 Ilheos
10 Pôrto Seguro
11 Espírito Santo
12 Rio de Janeiro
13 São Vicente

C D — Demarcation Line of May 4, 1493
A B — Demarcation Line of June 7, 1494
■ Territory held by Dutch — 1630-1654

Fig. VI–5. Territorial Divisions in Colonial Brazil.

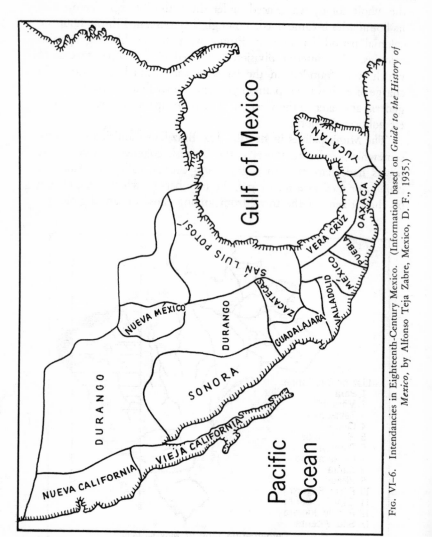

Fig. VI-6. Intendancies in Eighteenth-Century Mexico. (Information based on *Guide to the History of Mexico*, by Alfonso Teja Zabre, Mexico, D. F., 1935.)

The members of this council selected other town officers, including a judge, justices, police, and various civil officials. The powers of the *senado da câmara* rapidly declined during the colonial period until it ceased to have local legislative authority and became an advisory body for local affairs to the governor of each province.

ADMINISTRATION OF JUSTICE

In the Spanish Colonies. Justice was usually administered locally in the name of the Crown. There were courts of first instance in the municipalities, and some appeals might be carried to the *audiencia* and then to the viceroy. Important cases might eventually reach the *Consejo de Indias,* and finally the Crown. Cases concerning commercial and maritime matters might be decided by the seaboard tribunals known as *consulados.* Cases concerning questions of religion were usually settled by church officials, although civil officers might take cognizance of certain religious matters which were submitted to them by the courts of the Inquisition.

In Brazil. The judicial system was not so well regulated or so effective in Brazil as it was in the Spanish colonies. At times the judiciary practically ceased to function. The town courts were tribunals of first instance, and appeals might be taken to the governor, to the governor general or the viceroy, and eventually to the king.

LAWS AND CORRUPTION

In the Spanish Colonies. The Spanish government was always concerned with laws for the regulation of its colonies. When America was first settled, the laws of Spain were applied there. Thus, *Las Siete Partidas* and other codes of law became the bases for Spanish American law. As time passed, new laws were made and old ones were dropped. In the sixteenth century Philip II prepared a code called the *Nueva Recopilación* (1567). This was followed by other codifications of law, the most important of which was the *Recopilación de Leyes de los Reinos de las Indias* (1680). Near the end of the colonial period *La Novísima Recopilación* was compiled under Charles IV. In the colonies themselves many laws originated, and these likewise had to be considered.

In spite of all laws, political corruption occurred, especially when the Spanish Crown, after the sixteenth century, decreed that public offices could be sold at auction to the highest bidder. In this way many incompetent and corrupt individuals got into colonial offices.

In Brazil. The Portuguese government never attempted such a systematic compilation of laws for Brazil as did Spain for her colonies, but during the years from 1580 to 1640 the Spanish legal influence in Brazil was marked. Thereafter, except for a brief period in the eighteenth century when Prime Minister Pombal in Portugal attempted a political house cleaning in the colony (1750–77), peculation and corruption among government officials were almost universal. As in the Spanish colonies, the sale of offices was permitted.

THE INTENDANCY IN THE SPANISH COLONIES

After the War of the Spanish Succession, which ended in 1713 with the Treaty of Utrecht, the French House of Bourbon came into control of the Spanish throne, which had been held for nearly two hundred years by the Hapsburgs. One of the French political institutions introduced into Spain was the intendancy. This was taken to the Spanish American colonies when the first intendancy was set up at Havana, Cuba, in February, 1765. In 1786 the system was extended to New Spain when eleven (later twelve) intendancies were created there. By 1790 the system had been extended to all of the Spanish American colonies.

As a result of this innovation the viceroyalty was divided into districts called *intendencias*. Over each, an *intendente* was appointed by the Crown. His functions were divided into four classes: justice, finance, war, and industry (*policía*). Each *intendente* was immediately responsible to an intendant general, who in turn was subject to the Council of the Indies. The intendant eventually took over most of the functions of the viceroy except his social duties, and that official became largely a figurehead. It was expected that this simplification of colonial government would raise the general efficiency and honesty of officers, but in reality the intendants had too many duties to perform to carry them all out efficiently and effectively.

CHAPTER VII

THE COLONIAL ECONOMIC SYSTEM

S PAIN, AND TO SOME extent Portugal, developed the mercantile system in the sixteenth century. Since then "colonialism" has been
adopted (and modified) by many large and small powers until at
last the word *colonialism* has become a term of reproach. At the
heart of the mercantile system was the theory that colonies were
acquired as markets where the products of the mother country could
be sold. To a lesser extent, the colonies were to produce the materials needed by the mother country. Thus a family relationship
developed of parent and children united in one economic family
which should be self-sufficient, with an economic surplus. Various
countries, with their colonies, became international economic rivals
in which each national system attempted to keep ahead of all others.
This rivalry inaugurated a struggle for power among European
nations.

GENERAL ECONOMIC ORGANIZATION

The Spanish and Portuguese colonial empires in America, at their
greatest extent, included all of South America, Central America,
Mexico, the West Indies (except certain small islands), and large
parts of present-day United States. In this vast territory there existed
such a great variety of climate, soil, and topography that every
product known to man could be grown there.

Both the Spanish and the Portuguese kings owned the land and
water in their respective domains as well as everything in the air,
water, and land. Whatever they wished for themselves they could
keep, and whatever they did not want they could give away. In any
case, however, the rulers of both countries recognized a difference
between the products of the surface soil (agricultural products) and
those of the subsoil (mineral products).

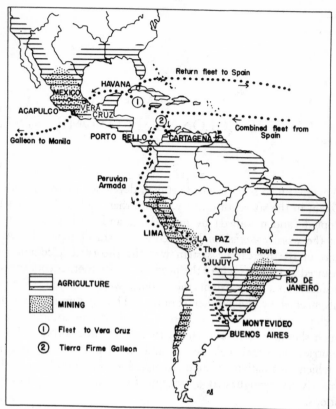

FIG. VII–1. Colonial Trade and Commerce of Latin America.

At first, the kings retained one-half of all the products from their colonies, but later they reserved for themselves only one-fifth (called the Royal Fifth, or *Quinto*) of certain products, usually minerals.

To supervise these vast possessions (the *real hacienda*), the monarchs appointed royal treasury officials with wide powers. They were responsible to the kings through the Spanish *Casa de Contratación* or the Portuguese Finance Council (*Conselho da Fazenda*).

Under the mercantile system, as practiced by Spain and Portugal, the colonists (like dutiful children) had to produce what the mother countries desired and were restrained from producing what the mother countries did not want. The colonies existed only for the economic good of the parent country.

TAXATION

The Spanish and Portuguese crowns expected both a personal and state revenue from the colonies. To the latter end the colonists were taxed for the support of the colonial establishment in America and for the mother government in Europe. As the years passed, both the kings and their governments required more and more funds, and revenues from the colonies had to be increased. Thus, taxes in America not only grew larger but their number multiplied until there were more than forty kinds of taxes in the Spanish colonies and nearly as many in Brazil. Among these were taxes on trade, sales taxes, stamp taxes, excise taxes, land taxes, property taxes, import and export taxes, church taxes (tithes, Bulls of the Crusades, etc.), income taxes, and taxes on special commodities, such as salt, snow and ice for refrigeration, manufactured articles, etc.

The methods of collecting taxes were often vicious and cruel, and property was frequently seized by force. The collectors, too, were dishonest, and peculation was almost the rule. Often when a tax collector arrived in a community, people fled in fear of their lives.

LANDHOLDING

Since all land in the colonies belonged to the kings personally, they could dispose of it according to their own wishes. Both the Spanish and Portuguese crowns made regulations for occupying, holding, and inheriting land.

In the Spanish Colonies. The founders of towns were called *empresarios,* and they had the right to grant to the citizens lots in the towns and lands outside of the towns. In the towns there were also common lands administered by the town councils. Rural lands were granted by the government to individual families on the condition that they occupy and improve such grants. Small grants of land to small farmers were called *peonías,* while larger grants to important families were termed *caballerías.* Agricultural lands with Indians living on them were called *encomiendas.* The natives here were enslaved or reduced to the status of feudal serfs. An *encomienda* was usually granted for the lifetime of the grantee, but at times it could be passed on to heirs. The Church might obtain land by bequest and could hold it in perpetuity.

In Brazil. On the great feudal *capitanias* in the sixteenth century, the *donatários* were empowered to make grants of land to Christians who applied, while other colonial officers had similar

powers. Such grants were called *sesmarias* and were made for perpetuity with the provision that the owner pay one-tenth of the produce of the soil to the Crown. Later this tax was paid in the form of
a quit rent (*fôro*). The Church could acquire land only by bequest.
In the north, where great plantations were the rule, the feudal system gradually reduced the small landholder to the position of a
feudal serf, if not to that of a slave. In the south, however, this
condition was not so common.

PRODUCTS AND INDUSTRIES

America had been colonized with the hope that great mineral
wealth would be discovered. In the case of the Spaniards this desire
was fulfilled almost from the beginning. But for almost a century
the colonists in Brazil looked in vain for minerals.

Mineral Products in the Spanish Colonies. Great quantities of
gold and silver were immediately found in Mexico and Peru, and
as the conquest progressed new mines were opened. Throughout
the whole colonial period, new mineral deposits were discovered in
sufficient numbers to justify a continuous search for riches. Other
important minerals present in the Spanish colonies were quick-
silver (Mexico), tin and copper (Bolivia), nitrates (Chile), and semiprecious stones such as emeralds (Colombia).

In the Spanish colonies, in 1525, mining regulations were issued
by the Crown. Frequently thereafter, and from time to time, these
were carefully revised in the light of needs and experiences. Often
these laws contained ordinances for the control of life in mining
towns where vice and corruption were rampant and where the cost
of living was high. In most mining communities, smelting houses
were established in which royal officials supervised the smelting,
weighing, and stamping of the metal.

Mineral Products in Brazil. In the sixteenth century the Portuguese government, in order to encourage the search for minerals,
promised a title of nobility to any person who opened a mine. In
1618, in anticipation of the finding of minerals, the government
issued a detailed code of mining regulations for Brazil. This law
provided for the granting of land titles in mining areas and for the
smelting of ore in properly supervised furnaces. In 1702 new mining
regulations were issued by the Crown.

About the middle of the seventeenth century gold was finally
found in south central Brazil, and shortly thereafter many gold mines

were opened. About 1727 diamonds were discovered in the interior of southern Brazil, and emeralds were found in northwest Brazil. As a result of these discoveries many agricultural regions along the coast were nearly depopulated when their inhabitants joined the gold and diamond rush into the hinterland. These periodic "rushes" brought immigrants from various parts of the world to the colony, and considerably disturbed not only the economic life of the colony but that of the mother country as well.

Agricultural Products in the Spanish Colonies. As early as 1532 the Spanish government decreed that all ships taking colonists to America should carry plants and animals there. Thus, cattle, sheep, swine, etc., and bananas, sugar cane, grapes, olives, coffee, rice, citrous fruits, and many cereals and vegetables were taken to America. It was not long before several native products, such as the potato, certain beans, and corn, were adopted by the colonists.

Several regions were found to be excellently suited for agricultural production, especially in Argentina, Uruguay, Paraguay, Chile, Colombia, Venezuela, and the West Indies. Even in the mining regions, agriculture became well established, and before the end of the colonial period Mexico, for example, produced agricultural products of greater value than her minerals.

From time to time the Crown compelled the colonists to raise certain products for which there was a demand in Spain, while at other times the production of certain things was forbidden because of the competition they afforded to the disposal of similar products in the mother country. In the case of tobacco, the government sometimes established a royal monopoly for its production. Another product of the soil which the king often considered his own was timber, of which there was a great variety.

Agricultural Products in Brazil. The chief agricultural products of colonial Brazil were sugar cane, brazilwood (from which dyes were made), cacao, coffee, tea, vanilla, cloves, manioc (or cassava, an edible root), tobacco, indigo, rice, cotton, various citrous fruits, tropical woods, cattle, sheep, swine, etc. As in the Spanish colonies, a variety of products was introduced into the colony from Europe.

The most prosperous agricultural regions in Brazil were situated in the northern part of the country along the coast, where the establishment of large plantations was the rule. Cattle and sheep raising were carried on chiefly in the uplands and interior of southern Brazil, until mining became more profitable there.

Industries in the Spanish Colonies. Besides mining and agriculture, pearl fishing was an important industry, especially along the Pearl Coast (Colombia and Venezuela), off the Pacific coast of Panama, and in the Gulf of Lower California. Because of the demand for fish as food, offshore and deep-sea fishing were important. In some localities the dairy industry grew in importance during the colonial period. The manufacture of textiles, pottery, jewelry, and furniture, especially by the natives, constituted important industries. The manufacture of wines and liquors was almost a personalized industry, as was the making of cigars and cigarettes.

Industries in Brazil. Pearl fishing in Brazil never reached the importance which it did in the Spanish colonies, but offshore and deep-sea fishing were important industries. Wine and liquor making were likewise important occupations, while textile, pottery, and jewelry manufacturing were encouraged and carefully regulated by the government.

LABOR

Indian Labor in the Spanish Colonies. Much to the horror of Queen Isabella, who attempted ineffectively to prevent it, Columbus began the enslavement of the Indians in America. But it was not long before the Spanish government halfheartedly sanctioned native slavery provided the Indians were cannibals or exceptionally warlike. And since the Spaniards did not always wish to test the nature of the natives, they found it convenient to consider all as fit subjects for slavery. Hence the conquerors, by the *repartimiento* system, divided the Indians among themselves as spoils of war, despite the fact that the Spanish government by the New Laws of 1542 decreed that the Indians should be paid for their labor and Christianized. But the colonists ignored these laws, and the natives succumbed by the thousands to the hard labor required of them, while many more were driven to suicide.

Indian labor under the *repartimiento* system was of two types: the *encomienda,* in which Indians were employed on farms and in household work; and the *mita,* in which they worked in the mines, in pearl fishing, in transport service, etc. Of the two types the latter was more hated by the Indians, for thousands died in the mines. Finally, in 1720 the Spanish government tried to abolish the harsh system, but in practice it continued throughout the colonial period, and remained for a century more as the peonage system.

Indian Labor in Brazil. The first colonists from Portugal inter-married with the Indians in Brazil and also reduced many to slavery. But in 1570 the Portuguese government decreed that unless the Indians were cannibals or had been captured in war, they must not be enslaved. Many other decrees dealing with native slavery were issued from time to time, but practically no attention was paid to such legislation, since it ran counter to the interest of the colonists. As the result of harsh treatment, the Indians often escaped into the interior or committed suicide. In several instances Indian rebellions occurred with all of the attending horrors of racial warfare.

Negro Labor in the Spanish Colonies. The first Negro slaves were probably imported into the West Indies from Africa in 1502, in order to replace the native laborers as Queen Isabella wished. From this date on, the Spanish government regularly granted contracts (*asientos*) to individuals or companies to import Negroes into the colonies at an average rate of about 3,000 yearly during the colonial period.

The Negro slaves were generally considered animals and treated as such. The owners had the power of life and death over their slaves and many cruelties were perpetrated. Occasionally Negro uprisings took place, but generally the slaves were thoroughly cowed.

During the transportation of the Negroes from Africa to America, often as many as one-half of the Negroes died on shipboard. Once in America, they spread diseases, especially leprosy, and they mingled everywhere with the white and red races in marriage or in clandestine union. It was not until 1789 that the Spanish government made any serious attempt to improve the lot of the Negroes, and then it simply decreed better treatment for them and some educational and religious training.

Negro Labor in Brazil. Because of the high mortality among the Indian slaves of Brazil, the Portuguese government, about 1532, allowed the importation of Negroes from its African possessions, and by the end of the eighteenth century the Negroes in the colony outnumbered the whites by about 50 per cent.

Negro slavery in Brazil was probably not as cruel as in the Spanish colonies, but attempts at civilizing and Christianizing Negro slaves were of little avail. Numerous slave rebellions took place, the greatest occurring in the middle of the seventeenth century, when some 30,000 slaves fled into the forests west of Pernambuco and established the Palmares Republic. From 1650 to 1695 these Negroes raided white settlements and carried off white women and other plunder. Finally, in the latter year they were overcome and killed or forced into slavery by the whites.

Skilled Labor in the Spanish Colonies and Brazil. Both Indians and Negroes furnished skilled laborers in the colonies, and many were freed from bondage because of their exceptional abilities. The two mother countries encouraged their own skilled white laborers to go to the colonies to practice their professions and to teach their trades to the colonists. Though the colonies were generally closed to foreigners, some German laborers went to America in the sixteenth century, and some French laborers entered the colonies in the eighteenth century. Skilled craftsmen were generally members of guilds, which regulated the quality and quantity of their products.

TRADE

Control of Trade in the Spanish Colonies. Under the mercantile system the Spanish government developed a method of monopolistic trade control. All trade with the American colonies was confined to the Spanish ports of Sevilla and Cádiz, while all trade with Spain was confined to the American ports of Havana, Veracruz, and Portobelo (in Panama) on the eastern side of the colonies. From 1561 to 1748 the Spanish government allowed two merchant fleets to be equipped in Spain annually (in March and April) for trade with the Indies. These ships were convoyed to America by war vessels. On entering the Caribbean, the fleet divided, one part going to the Isthmus and the other part to Mexico. After unloading and reloading at Portobelo and Veracruz, the fleets met at Havana and began the return voyage to Spain, thus completing a round trip within the year.

Goods destined for southern South America were shipped across the Isthmus, put on board the Peruvian galleons at Panama City, and taken to Callao (the port of Lima). Then they were carried overland to La Plata and intermediate points. Products from these regions were sent back to Spain over the same route.

Goods destined for the Philippines were landed at Veracruz, carried overland to Mexico City, and thence to Acapulco on the Pacific, where they were placed on the Manila galleons for the East. Oriental products returned by way of the California coast to Mexico and thence to Spain via Havana.

Trade between colonies was generally discouraged and often forbidden by law. At the chief colonial ports there were finally established *consulados,* or consulates, for the supervision of trade, while the coasts were guarded from smugglers by *guardas costas* (coast guards) and by fortifications.

All transportation by sea and by land was slow. It often took two years for a round trip on land and sea between Buenos Aires and Spain.

In the middle of the eighteenth century, under Charles III and his successor, the Spanish government, realizing that its trade control was ineffective and that the French, English, and Dutch merchants enjoyed as large a commerce (although illegal) with its colonies, gradually relaxed its commercial regulations by first abolishing the fleet convoy system (1748) and allowing individual ships to sail for the colonies, and finally (1778) by opening more colonial and Spanish ports to direct trade with each other.

Trade within individual colonies was handicapped throughout the colonial era by poor roads, lack of bridges, difficult terrain, bandits, and natural catastrophes. However, the government gradually did what it could to improve river and land transportation, so that by the end of the eighteenth century communication was more rapid and safe.

Control of Trade in Brazil. Portugal, like Spain, attempted to monopolize the trade of its colony, but it never attempted such absolute control. At first, trade was carried on with the colony by individuals or companies acting independently at their own risk, but before the end of the sixteenth century a "caravan system," like the Spanish fleet system, was devised whereby merchant ships were convoyed to Brazil by war vessels. This arrangement lasted until 1765, when the Portuguese Crown again allowed individual ship sailings to America.

Foreign merchants, especially Jews, were allowed to settle in Brazil and to carry on trade. Since the colony chiefly bordered the seacoast and since there were many harbors, it was possible and expedient to carry on a considerable coastwise commerce. Many Portuguese vessels found it profitable to trade illegally in La Plata. Because of the poor roads in the interior of Brazil, overland trade was handicapped and at times impossible.

Fairs in the Spanish Colonies. A method employed by the Spanish government to facilitate trade and to supervise the exchange of products was the holding of fairs in centrally located communities, such as Jalapa, Mexico City, Acapulco, Santa Fe, Saltillo, Portobelo, Cartagena, Lima, etc. To these centers merchants came once a year to buy and sell goods and to exchange products brought from Spain and elsewhere. Usually a fair lasted several weeks, but an outbreak of disease often terminated it after a few days. The greatest and most picturesque of the fairs was held after 1597 at Portobelo on the Isthmus. When the fleet came in, merchants from all of the colonies gathered in a tent town built especially for the purpose. Thousands of people attended and the crowds were gay and boisterous. Sometimes exchange was effected by barter, while gold, silver, and other mediums were often accepted as payment. Prices of commodities were generally regulated, but the cost of living at the fairs was exorbitant and profits on necessities of life were often increased by 1,000 per cent.

Trading Companies in the Spanish Colonies. As a means of regulating colonial trade in the seventeenth century, and especially in the next century after the failure of the fleet system, the Spanish government created trading companies with monopolistic trading rights in certain regions and with the express purpose of underselling merchandise brought to the colonies illegally by English, French, and Dutch traders.

However, it was not until the eighteenth century that these trading companies were seriously promoted. In 1728 the Quipúzcoa Company was founded at Caracas on the Pearl Coast to compete with the Dutch smugglers in the region. In 1734 the company expanded its trade northward to the Mexican coast. The company existed until 1784, but it failed to carry out the aims projected. In 1755 the Barcelona Company was created to control the Spanish trade with the West Indies, but this too proved a failure, as did a number of other similar attempts.

Trading Companies in Brazil. After the middle of the eighteenth century, the Marquis of Pombal, chief minister of King José I of Portugal, began to reform colonial commerce by creating two exclusive companies to monopolize the trade of certain parts of Brazil. In 1755 he founded a company to trade with Maranhão and Pará, and in 1759 he created a company to trade with Pernambuco and Paraíba. Both companies existed only until 1777 and were not financially successful. However, a third company was later established to trade in regions not covered by the first two companies and to have exclusive monopolies of fishing in Brazilian waters and of supplying the colonists with salt.

The *Asiento* in the Spanish Colonies. For the double purpose of creating revenues for the Crown and of regulating the importation of Negro slaves into the colonies, the Spanish government in the sixteenth century instituted the practice of granting *asientos* (contracts) to individuals or companies in Spain or elsewhere. Such a contract allowed an individual or a group of individuals, for a fixed sum to be paid in advance to the king, to sell into the Spanish colonies a fixed number of Negro slaves for a certain period of years at a fixed price per slave. The first *asiento* was granted to a Genoese company in 1517. Other contracts were granted to Spanish, Portuguese, French, Dutch, German, and English companies. In 1713, as a result of the Treaty of Utrecht, the English South Sea Company received the right to import into the Spanish colonies 144,000 Negro slaves at the rate of 4,800 yearly for thirty years, and it paid $200,000 to the Spanish government for the privilege. Included in this agreement was the right of the English to send, annually, one ship of five hundred tons to the fair at Portobelo, where English goods could be sold. The English were also allowed to establish trading posts at Cartagena, Veracruz, and Buenos Aires. Needless to say, the English exploited these rights to their fullest extent, and charges of violating the terms of the *asiento* were frequent and were doubtless justified.

FOREIGN ATTACKS ON THE COLONIES

Because Spain and Portugal attempted to monopolize the trade of their rich American colonies, England, Holland, and France, trade rivals of the Iberian countries, early tried to break this monopoly by illegal trade in the regions. By the eighteenth century, the illegal foreign trade of these three nations in the colonies was greater than the legal trade of the colonies with the mother countries. Moreover, the great wealth of the Spanish and Portuguese colonies led the European nations to covet their territory, and often colonial towns were seized or destroyed by citizens of foreign states, especially during periods of general European warfare.

Early in the sixteenth century a group of "buccaneers," or "freebooters," established themselves on small West Indian islands and began a systematic plunder of neighboring Spanish territory. In these pirate bands were men of all nationalities, and they often plun-

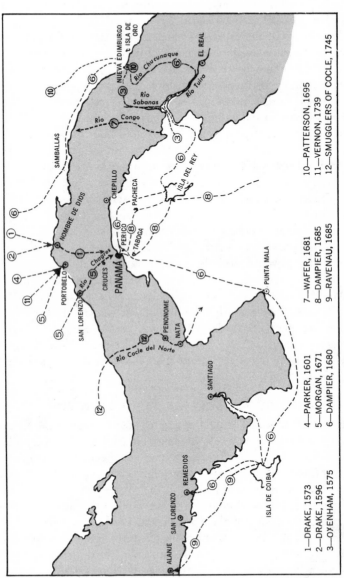

Fig. VII-2. Piracy in Panama in the Sixteenth to Eighteenth Centuries. (From *Panamá—Eslabón entre Dos Mundos*, U. S. Information Service, 1953.)

1—PARKER, 1601
2—DRAKE, 1596
3—OYENHAM, 1575

4—PARKER, 1601
5—MORGAN, 1671
6—DAMPIER, 1680

7—WAFER, 1681
8—DAMPIER, 1685
9—RAVENAU, 1685

10—PATTERSON, 1695
11—VERNON, 1739
12—SMUGGLERS OF COCLE, 1745

dered and murdered merely for the thrill of it. Generally their activities were not sanctioned by the governments of England, Holland, and France; yet they often co-operated with these powers in their attacks upon the colonies and they quite often succeeded in demoralizing colonial trade with the mother countries, which was one of the aims of the European enemies of Spain and Portugal.

Attacks on the Spanish Colonies:

By the English. In 1588 the Spanish Armada was defeated by England, and Spain lost control of the seas. Even before this disaster, English seamen, including Drake, Raleigh, Hawkins, and others, had begun to "singe the beard of the Spanish king" by attacking his colonial possessions in America. Francis Drake, in 1565, began a career of plunder and illegal trade in the Spanish colonies. In 1578 he entered the Pacific and spread terror among the peoples of the coastal towns. In 1585 he was again burning and plundering in the Caribbean area.

In this and the following century Englishmen seized many small Caribbean islands and gained footholds in Central America and in northern South America. From 1698 to 1700 William Paterson attempted without success to establish a Scotch colony on the Isthmus of Panama. Sir Henry Morgan, Bartholomew Sharpe, William Dampier, Edward Davis, and other English subjects spread terror in the Caribbean in the last half of the seventeenth century.

In the eighteenth century the English pirate, Thomas Colb, and such men as Woodes Rogers, Edward Vernon, George Anson, and others made their names feared in both the Atlantic and Pacific colonies by their plundering and seizure of treasure fleets.

By the Dutch. The people of the Netherlands were stirred to make attacks upon the Spanish colonies by the bloody activities of the agents of Philip II in their country. Accordingly, they came with fleets and armies to seize lands for their West Indian Company organized in 1621. They not only occupied small islands in the Caribbean but plundered colonial coast towns, seized treasure fleets bound for Spain, and spread terror in the Pacific as well as in the Atlantic. Among the Dutch leaders of the seventeenth century were Piet Heyn, Henrik Brouwer, Van Horn, and other picturesque characters.

By the French. Before 1700, when the French House of Bourbon gained the throne of Spain, French Huguenots, as well as agents of the Catholic French government, became interested in Spanish territory in America. Attempts to settle Florida were made in the sixteenth century by such leaders as Jean Ribaut, René Goulaine de Laudonnière, Jacques le Moyne, the artist, and others. However, the French did not appear in the Spanish colonies in such large numbers as did the English and the Dutch. Besides taking possession of several small islands in the West Indies, the French often collaborated with the English, Dutch, and buccaneers in raiding the Spanish coast towns. Between 1698 and 1703 the French Compagnie Royale de la Mer du Sur financed expeditions against the Viceroyalty of Peru.

Attacks on Brazil:

BY THE ENGLISH. The government of England was generally friendly with the Portuguese government, but from 1580 to 1640, while Spain controlled Portugal and her colonies, the English considered Brazil as a fair field for attack. In consequence, in this period raids were made upon the colony by Edward Fenton (1582), Robert Worthington (1586), Thomas Cavendish (1591), James Lancaster (1595), Robert Harcourt (1608), and others.

BY THE DUTCH. One of the chief purposes for creating the Dutch West Indian Company in 1621 was the conquest of Brazil. In 1623 a Dutch fleet under Jacob Willekens and Piet Heyn sailed for Brazil and seized São Salvador da Bahia in 1624. In 1630 Hendrick Loncq captured Pernambuco, and from then until 1661, the Dutch maintained as a possession several of the best provinces of Brazil, with Maurice of Nassau as the first governor. The region was called "New Holland" and the capital was at Recife, which the Dutch called "Mauritiopolis." The colony proved profitable to the Dutch, but they were finally forced to abandon it and to leave the country.

BY THE FRENCH. France took an interest in Brazil before Portugal, and Frenchmen had explored the coast and had founded a trading post at Pernambuco before 1530. In 1556 a band of Huguenots under Nicolas Durand built a fort at Rio de Janeiro and named the colony "Antarctic France." The French colonists were finally expelled from the region in 1567. In 1583 the French seized the port of Paraíba, which they held only for a short time. In 1612 the Huguenot, Daniel de la Touche, founded a colony on the island of Maranhão which lasted for three years. The next century, in 1710, a French force captured Rio de Janeiro but was unable to hold it very long. In 1763, when France lost all her territory on the North American mainland, she turned covetous eyes upon Brazil, and in

1777 she founded a military post at Mayacau. However, this and subsequent French attempts were generally failures, and France had to be content with her Guiana territory, which she had acquired in 1626.

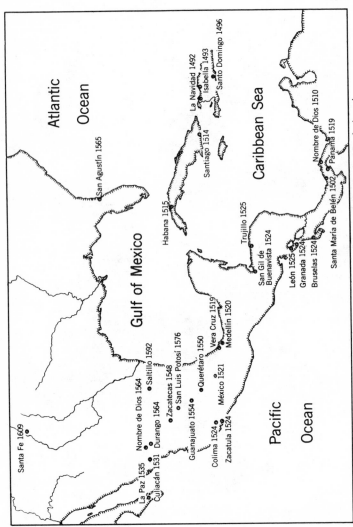

Fig. VIII–1. Some Early Settlements in the Spanish Colonies in North America.

CHAPTER VIII

COLONIAL SOCIETY

THE SPANISH AND Portuguese colonies contained castes and classes, and slavery was the fundamental basis for all relations between the colonials. But the present-day meaning of these words cannot be carried back to the colonial centuries. In the Iberian Peninsula, from Roman times at least, slavery, classes, and castes had existed. The American natives, also, had castes and classes when they first came into contact with the Europeans. This fact made it comparatively easy for the Indians to fit into the social system brought from Europe. To a lesser extent, the Negroes too had their social castes in Africa, and even under the conditions of slavery these were perpetuated and accentuated in America. In other aspects of society the colonies more or less reflected the mother countries, with important exceptions due chiefly to environment.

SOCIAL CLASSES

The classes of society were essentially the same in both the Spanish colonies and Brazil, although the names applied to the several groups sometimes varied.

The Peninsulars. At the top of the social scale were the whites born in the Iberian Peninsula, who were generally known as "peninsulars," but who were often called *chapetones* (wearers of spurs) or *godos* (Goths) in the Spanish colonies. These persons were frequently of noble birth and were inordinately proud of their heritage. They came to the colonies to hold the highest offices, received large salaries and perquisites, lived well, and attempted to maintain a social superiority above the other social groups. They were the upper crust of the social structure, and they helped the viceroy to maintain a sumptuous court in the viceregal capital. One of the chief ambitions of this small caste appears to have been to get rich as quickly as possible and then return to Spain and live in luxury for the remainder of their lives. Because of their arrogance they were hated by the other social groups.

The Creoles. Just below the peninsulars in the social scale were the Creoles (called *criollos* in the Spanish colonies and *mazombos* in Brazil), who were pure-blooded whites born in the colonies. This growing group held many of the lesser offices of small honor and smaller pay. The law allowed them equal political privileges with the peninsulars, but their rights were often denied them by the ruling peninsulars. Being educated, intelligent, and dissatisfied, the Creoles constituted, especially in the eighteenth century, a growing threat to the mother countries' continued paternalistic control of colonial affairs. The Creoles and the peninsulars hated each other, and rivalry was general and friction frequent. The Creoles sought assistance from the mixed elements in colonial society, which may here be designated as "half-breeds."

The Half-breeds. From the first days of the conquest the whites had intermarried with the natives, and this mingling of blood continued and increased during the colonial period. In the Spanish colonies persons resulting from such unions were called *mestizos,* and in Brazil they were known as *mestiços* or *mamelucos.* They were most numerous in the regions where the Indian population was greatest, especially in the viceroyalties of New Spain and Peru and in Brazil. Often this class displayed the worst characteristics of both the white and red races, but there were many prominent colonial leaders from this group.

Another half-breed element in society was the mulatto (called *mulato* in the Spanish colonies and in Brazil). Being part Negro and part white, this group was most numerous in the regions where Negro slavery was practiced, especially in the West Indies, in Brazil, and in northern South America. The mulattoes likewise often showed the worst traits of both the whites and the blacks, but there were also some prominent colonials among them.

A third half-breed element in colonial society resulted from the mixture of the Indians and the Negroes. In the Spanish colonies these people were called *zambos* and in Brazil *cafusos.* Members of this group were most numerous in Brazil and in northern South America.

The Indians. As already noted, the natives of Ibero-America varied widely in civilization. Some tribes were easily conquered by the whites, while others resisted white control for centuries. In the latter class were the Araucanians of Chile and the Patagonian Indians of southern Argentina, as well as certain fierce tribes on the northern border of New Spain. In Brazil and in other parts of tropical South America, the natives were of a primitive type, and even to this day some remain out of contact with civilization. During the early period of the conquest of America, the Indians were destroyed in large numbers by warfare, oppression, and disease, but it was not until the natives were completely cowed that they were enslaved and that attempts were made to hispanicize them. As the colonial period progressed, the Indians regained some of their lost rights, and in many localities they were free to come and go as they pleased. However, the life of this social group was a hard one, for they were generally exploited by the whites throughout the colonies.

The Negroes. The Negroes were brought to the colonies as slaves, and most of their race remained slaves until the era of independence. Occasionally Negroes were freed by humane masters, but generally their lot was a hard one. Their presence in the colonies enabled many colonists to maintain the conviction that it was undignified and degrading to do manual labor. Later in the colonial period, when attempts were made by the governments to improve the lot of the Negroes, the masters were made responsible for the actions of their slaves and could be punished for their misdeeds. But even then the masters had the right to maim or kill an unruly slave.

POPULATION

In both the Spanish colonies and Brazil the population was scattered over wide areas, and towns were often separated by great distances. The birth rate was high, but the death rate was generally higher. The increase in population figures was partly due to immigration and partly due to the conversion and counting of an increasing number of Indians. Population figures for the colonial period are untrustworthy, but some estimates can be made.

In the Spanish Colonies. About 1600 the total white population of the Spanish colonies was probably about 200,000, divided about equally between the Viceroyalty of New Spain and the Viceroyalty of Peru. In this period there were probably some 500,000 Indians classed as civilized.

By 1800 the population numbered some 15 million, of whom 30,000 were peninsulars, 3 million were Creoles, 6 million were

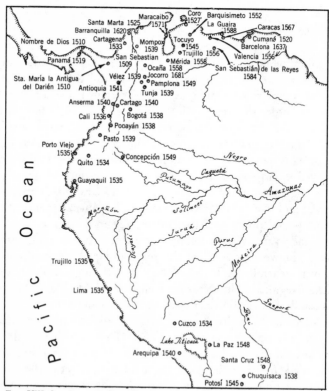

FIG. VIII–2. Some Early Settlements in the Spanish Colonies in Northern
South America.

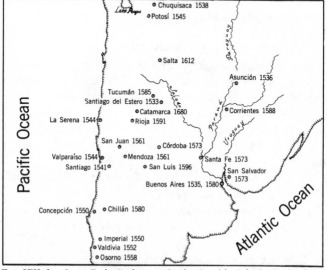

FIG. VIII–3. Some Early Settlements in the Spanish Colonies in Southern
South America.

mestizos, and the remainder were Indians and Negroes. The population of the viceroyalties in 1800 is estimated as follows: New Spain, 7 million; New Granada, 2.5 million; Peru, 4 million; and La Plata, 1.5 million. The largest municipalities were Mexico City with about 140,000 inhabitants, Lima with 80,000, Quito with 70,000, Buenos Aires with 60,000, and Santiago, Chile, with 30,000.

In Brazil. At the beginning of the period of Spanish domination of Brazil (1580–1640), the population of the colony numbered about 50,000. By 1600 there were about 70,000 inhabitants, of whom one-third were white. At this time the region of greatest population was in the north about Pernambuco and Bahia. By 1700 there were perhaps 750,000 people in Brazil classified as civilized. By 1800 the number of inhabitants had grown to about 2.5 million, of whom 400,000 were classed as white, 1.5 million were Negroes, and 600,000 were Indians. The largest city in the year 1800 was Rio de Janeiro, with a population of about 30,000. By this period the centers of population had shifted to the southern section of Brazil.

RURAL LIFE

In both the Spanish colonies and in Brazil there were great plantations (called *estancias* or *haciendas* or *fincas* by the Spaniards and *fazendas* by the Portuguese), comprising thousands of acres of land, on each of which were the palatial home of the owner, the more modest home of the overseer, and the huts of the freemen and slaves. Often, especially in Brazil, there was a close resemblance to plantation life in the southern English colonies on the mainland of North America. Each estate was self-sufficient. Frequently the owner lived on his plantation only a part of the time, spending most of his life in a neighboring town or in the capital city, where comforts were greater. Thus, the estates were often left to the supervision of an overseer who was sometimes brutal and incompetent. The practice of absentee landlordism, especially in Chile, Mexico, La Plata, and Venezuela, had a pernicious influence upon the social and economic life of the plantation.

In all of the colonies there were small rural landholders, but their wealth was not great and they were frequently reduced to a position of vassalage by the encroachment of the great landowners. Rural life was generally dreary and discouraging, and whenever possible the countrymen went to the nearest town to take part in the church festivities and other amusements.

URBAN LIFE

In all of the colonies there were many small villages and a few larger towns, and all were social and amusement centers for the people in the surrounding territory. Especially in the Spanish colonies, great care was taken to locate the towns on healthful sites and to lay them out in a uniform manner, each with one or more public squares for the exercise of horses, for military drill, and for the promenade of the citizens. About the principal square were situated the church and other religious buildings, government structures, and other important edifices.

Colonial homes, like public buildings, were built with thick walls for protection against the climate and earthquakes. Windows were protected by bars and sometimes by shutters. Balconies extended from the upper stories, some being of beautiful iron or stone work, and others of carved wood. The homes contained an interior patio, where there might be a fountain or a well and where, in the case of poorer families, the pigs, chickens, and other animals were kept. Sanitary conditions in the towns were generally poor, and epidemics of disease were frequent and serious. The wealthy class imported rich furnishings for their homes, but the other classes made use of whatever could be manufactured locally in the form of furniture and household goods.

AMUSEMENTS

In the Spanish colonies as well as in Brazil, amusements were controlled by both the State and the Church in accordance with the paternalistic theories of government practiced by the mother countries. Therefore, it was chiefly in the towns, where the supervising influence of the government and church officials could be best exercised, that amusements and entertainment were provided.

One of the leading colonial amusements was gambling, which became such a vice that the mother governments attempted to control it, but without success, by prohibiting the importation of playing cards into the colonies. Other amusements were bullfights, cockfights, animal torture, jousting, horsemanship, dancing, singing, etc. Vice and crime were rampant, and promiscuity was extremely common among all classes so that illegitimacy was high. Drinking of alcoholic beverages was universal, as was smoking. Even children engaged in both pastimes from early childhood.

Church holidays and civil holidays were all too frequent, and in some cases it took the populace several days to recover from an unusually strenuous *fiesta*. On the occasion of these celebrations there were fireworks, processions, and the display of physical skill. Night was turned into day, and people roamed the streets in gay crowds, often being showered from the balconies with confetti and paper bags filled with water or colored liquids.

Love-making on the part of young people was carefully regulated. Marriages were arranged by their families, and the wedding ceremonies were regulated and controlled by the Church. After marriage, family life was usually one-sided. The husband had few family obligations, and he could form outside attachments with other women. Men seldom were at home except to sleep, and they spent much of their leisure at their club or at places of amusement. Wives seldom went anywhere with their husbands.

Especially in mining towns, where great wealth accumulated, the leading families tried to outdo each other in brilliance of weddings, balls, etc. The women, particularly, attempted to dazzle others by the splendor of their costumes, often going so far as to embroider their overshoes with pearls and diamonds.

One of the more innocent amusements was the composing of verses and setting them to the improvised music of a guitar or of other stringed instruments. Frequently poetry contests of this nature were staged for the edification of a newly appointed royal official, whose praise was sung by the contestants.

Reading by the literate Creoles made them conversant with a variety of serious literature. They often engaged in both public and private debates. Especially popular were the salacious European comedies and romances of chivalry, which the mother countries tried in vain to suppress.

Another amusement was resting or sleeping, or simply killing time. In all parts of the colonies the midday *siesta* was the rule, and places of business were closed and the streets were deserted.

Eating and drinking became a ritual among the Creoles and peninsulars. A whole morning might be consumed in sipping a gourd of yerba mate (Paraguayan tea), a cup of coffee, or a glass of wine. Several hours might be spent in eating a many-course dinner. Much time was also devoted to conversation and horseplay. Great quantities of meat, fowl, fish, and fruits were consumed by the wealthy classes, while the poorer elements of society lived largely on beans, corn, rice, fruits, etc.

FIG. IX–1. Jesuit Missions in Spanish North America, 1566–1767.

FIG. IX–2. Sixteenth-Century Spanish Missions and Settlements in Florida.

CHAPTER IX

COLONIAL CULTURE

C OLONIAL CULTURE was both imitative of the mother countries and original because of environment and the individual and racial characteristics of the morose Indian and the buoyant Negro and their hybrid combinations. Religion never had the leveling influence it was intended to have; colonial morality was probably no better and no worse than it was in Europe; and to be educated was to be superior to almost everyone else.

THE CHURCH

Both the Spanish and Portuguese kings were nominal heads of the colonial church, and only Roman Catholicism was recognized in the colonies. The popes could not issue papal bulls or other decrees for the colonies without the consent of the Iberian rulers. Moreover, the monarchs had control over the collecting of church revenues and the spending of the church income. In some cases the kings appointed and controlled the church officials. The royal control over the Church in America is usually referred to as the *real patronato*.

The Secular Clergy in the Spanish Colonies. For the purposes of religious control the Spanish Crown first divided the colonies into Northern and Southern Hemisphere sections, in each of which were two archbishoprics (Mexico City, Santo Domingo, Bogotá, and Lima) subdivided into bishoprics. Later, three more archbishoprics were created at Guatemala, Caracas, and Charcas. In all there were thirty-five bishoprics, which in turn were divided into parishes. The secular clergy was continually engaged in preaching and teaching and in the administration of the sacraments.

The Secular Clergy in Brazil. The first bishopric, including the whole of Brazil, was established with the seat at Bahia in 1552. In 1676 Brazil was made an archbishopric with its seat at Bahia, and

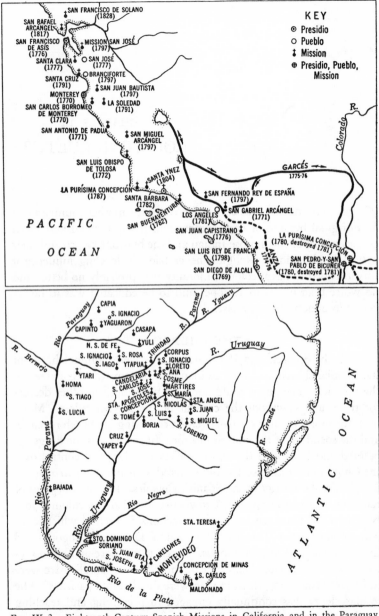

Fig. IX–3. Eighteenth-Century Spanish Missions in California and in the Paraguay Region. (Upper map reproduced with permission from *History of the Americas,* by H. E. Bolton, published by Ginn and Company, Boston, 1928; lower map reproduced with permission from *Breve historia de América,* by Carlos Pereyra, published by M. Aguilar, Madrid, 1930.)

the colony was subdivided into three bishoprics at Maranhão, Pernambuco, and Rio de Janeiro. Later, three more bishoprics were created. As in the Spanish colonies, the smallest division was the parish in charge of a priest.

The Regular Clergy. The regular clergy—those who lived by the rule of a religious order—included the Jesuits, Franciscans, Dominicans, Augustinians, Carmelites, and several others. These orders were generally in charge of missionary activity and were often the shock troops of the conquest. They were organized under rigorous discipline and were subject to commanding officers in the mother countries. Everywhere the regular clergy converted the natives to Christianity and helped to carry civilization to the most remote parts of the colonies.

When the Iberians first reached the Western Hemisphere, the missionaries immediately began to master the Indian dialects and languages, which probably numbered over a thousand, and they set about preparing grammars of some of these languages. The difficulties of communication with the natives were often ingeniously overcome by these intrepid men, sometimes at the cost of having the Indians consider them crazy because of the many manual gyrations they practiced in attempting to explain Holy Writ without words.

Wherever the missionaries went, they founded missions, monasteries, convents, churches, and schools, and they taught the natives useful arts as well as the Christian doctrine. Many of the regular clergy deliberately sought martyrdom.

In the Spanish Colonies. Everywhere in the Spanish colonies the regular clergy aided in advancing the frontiers, their efforts being greatest in Florida, New Spain, Paraguay, and on the borders of Peru.

Among the regular clergy the Jesuits were perhaps the most energetic in their promotion of Indian missions. In Paraguay they segregated the natives in towns (*reducciones*), where they could be more easily Christianized and hispanicized, and where they could be taught useful trades and the practice of agriculture. But eventually this order became rich and worldly from the fruits of Indian labor; it engaged in trade, organized the Indians into military forces, and became a threat to the colonial government. Hence, in 1767 the Spanish king Charles III expelled the members of this order from Spain and the colonies.

The Franciscans and Dominicans, like the Jesuits, had many representatives in the Spanish colonies, but they did not antagonize the government as the Jesuits did, and therefore they prospered, taking over many of the Jesuit activities.

IN BRAZIL. Besides the Jesuits, the other religious orders in Brazil were the Benedictines, Carmelites, and Capuchins, who were under the direct control of the Portuguese Crown. As in the Spanish colonies, the Jesuits took the lead in introducing the natives to civilization, and as in the Spanish colonies, settled them in towns, especially in southern Brazil, from which whites were excluded. The same complaints, however, were made against the Jesuits in Brazil as in the neighboring colonies, and in 1760 they were expelled from the colony and the mother country by King José I and his minister Pombal.

The Inquisition and the Index. In the Spanish colonies and Brazil the Church established the Inquisition in much the same form as it existed in the mother countries.

IN THE SPANISH COLONIES. By a royal decree of January 25, 1569, the Inquisition was extended to America, where the first tribunals were set up at Lima, Peru (January 29, 1570), at Mexico City (November 4, 1591), and at Cartagena (1610). Although not so active in the colonies as in Spain, the officials of the Inquisition sought out Jews, heretics, bigamists, witches, and others for persecution. No one, except Indians, was safe from its jurisdiction. Among the functions of the Inquisition was that of maintaining a list of books (the Index) which no one might read; nevertheless, it was possible for certain privileged persons to secure permission not only to read such books but to own them. In its 277 years of activity in the Spanish colonies the Inquisition probably executed no more than one hundred people.

IN BRAZIL. During the period of Spanish control in Brazil, the first visitor for the Inquisition came to the colony in 1591. In 1618 an Inquisitor arrived at Rio de Janeiro and made a number of arrests and seizures of property. From 1640 to about 1707 the power of the Inquisition declined, but from the latter year to 1711 some 160 persons were persecuted, of whom most were sent to Lisbon for trial. However, the Inquisition was never so active in Brazil as it was in the neighboring colonies, and the use of the Index was never so effective as it was in the Spanish colonies. Generally the Portuguese government was disinclined to exclude from Brazil colonists of non-Catholic faiths, and in consequence, many Jews and Protestants settled peacefully in the country.

Religious Life. The practice of religion in the Spanish colonies and in Brazil was often superficial, and women more than men were affected by the teachings of the Church. The clergy were frequently illiterate, especially in Brazil, and often immoral as well. Hence they frequently set a bad example for the people, who in some cases lost all respect for the clergy.

In even the smallest towns in the colonies there was at least one church, and in some of the cities there were more churches than the people needed or could support. In every community the populace was appealed to by the Church through the use of religious festivals, processions, and celebrations of all descriptions. Especially in Indian towns, the ceremonies of the Church appeared inseparable from the old pagan forms of idol worship. It may be safely said that in many communities in the colonies the Roman Catholic religion had broken down and had become devoid of much of its European significance by the grafting upon it of many non-Christian practices.

Throughout the colonies saints were venerated. In Mexico, the Virgin of Guadalupe, and in Peru, St. Rose of Lima (the first American saint) were deeply revered by the people.

EDUCATION

Education in the Spanish colonies and Brazil was carried on by the Church with the backing of the government, and it was generally more cultural than practical. Many plans for educational changes were made for the colonies, but these usually remained on paper and were never carried out.

From the beginning of the conquest the Spanish and Portuguese governments planned to educate the Indians—at least to teach them the Spanish or Portuguese languages—but even though schools for this purpose were early established, only a small minority of natives succeeded in becoming literate. The Indians converted to Christianity and hispanicized were taught by missionaries only to repeat phrases in Spanish, Portuguese, or Latin, none of which was understood.

Girls were given no formal education except in convents, and this was of a superficial nature. Coeducation was unheard of and unthought of, and there were no schools which both sexes could attend.

Lower Education in the Spanish Colonies. In 1536 the first school for Indian boys was founded at Mexico City. Subsequently, attempts were made in the other colonies to found similar schools of an elementary nature for Indian children, and usually these were attached to some mission. Some schools for white boys existed, but often parents chose to educate their sons by tutors or to send them abroad in later life. Secondary schools, as known today, were nonexistent, and as a result the system of higher education was at a much lower level than it would have been otherwise.

Lower Education in Brazil. The regular clergy, chiefly the Jesuits, were active in Brazil in founding elementary schools, especially after the sixteenth century. In 1718, in the province of Bahia, there were forty-six elementary schools, and in the same century six "academies" were founded for the education of children in the colony.

Higher Education. There were no universities in colonial Brazil, but from the beginning the Spanish government took an active interest in higher education in its colonies. In 1538 the University of Santo Tomás de Aquino was founded at Santo Domingo. In 1551 Charles V decreed the establishment of the Royal University at Mexico City and the University of San Marcos at Lima, Peru, to offer courses in theology, sciences, languages, history, and anthropology. Other leading universities founded by the Spanish government in the colonies were at Córdoba (1613), Sucre (1623), Cuzco (1692), Caracas (1721), Havana (1728), Santiago, Chile (1743), and Quito (1787). In most institutions of higher learning students were taught law and medicine, as well as theology and other subjects, and in the latter part of the eighteenth century they were allowed to study philosophy.

University enrollment was generally large, in some instances numbering several thousand students. The faculties were composed of churchmen, and the chancellors, or presidents, were likewise religious officials. All university officers were subject to appointment by the viceroy, who often taught or served as chancellor. The degrees of bachelor, master, and doctor were granted by the universities, and the ceremonies used in the conferring of degrees were similar to those employed today.

Many colonials were dissatisfied with the type of education available in the colonies, and some of them went to European universities, especially to the University of Paris, the University of Salamanca in Spain, and the University of Coimbra in Portugal.

LITERATURE

Throughout the colonial period, in the Spanish colonies and Brazil, literary production was not only discouraged but practically prevented at times by the activity of the Inquisition, the Index, government regulations, and the lack of printing presses. Moreover, the cost of printing everywhere was high, and the necessity of publishing a book at private expense tended to limit the number of printed works to persons who could afford the original outlay of funds. However, many works were written during the colonial period, even if they did not at the time see the light of day in print.

Printing. Only two printing presses were established in Brazil during the colonial period: at Pernambuco from 1701 to 1706 and at Rio de Janeiro, beginning in 1747.

The first printing press in the Spanish colonies was set up at Mexico City in 1532. The second press was located at Juli, Peru, in 1579. The first book printed in America appeared at Mexico City in 1539, while the first volume to be published in Peru appeared in 1584. In the next two centuries, printing presses were established in Mexico in 1640, 1720, 1764, 1793, and 1794; in Guatemala in 1660; in Cuba in 1707 and 1796; in Colombia in 1738; in Ecuador in 1754 and 1760; in Peru in 1610; in Paraguay in 1705; in Chile in 1747 and 1776; and in Argentina in 1765 and 1780.

All of the early presses were under the control of the Church, especially of the regular clergy. Only works of a religious nature or works approved by the Church could be printed on these presses. Hence colonials were often forced to send their manuscripts abroad and risk the hazard of loss in transit in order to have them printed in Spain or Portugal or in France, England, Italy, or Holland.

Poetry. The improvising of poetry in the colonies was a favorite pastime, but only a comparatively few individuals could be classed as important poets or could get their poetry into print. The subjects dealt with by the colonial poets were the same in America as elsewhere. However, the spectacular nature of the conquest of the continent inspired many poets to write epic and heroic compositions in poetry, prose, and drama, some of which have considerable significance.

In the Spanish Colonies. Among the epic or heroic poems written in the Spanish colonies were: *La Araucana,* by Alonso de Ercilla y Zúñiga (1533–94), about the conquest of Chile, and a continuation of the poem by Diego de Santisteban Osorio; *Arauco domado,* by Pedro de Oña (b. c. 1570), on a similar topic; *Purén indómito* by Hernando Alvarez de Toledo, recounting his adventures in South America at the end of the sixteenth century; *Compendio historial de Chile,* by Melchor Xufra del Aguila (1568–1637), telling of his experiences in Chile and elsewhere; *Conquista del nuevo mundo,* by Gaspar Pérez de Villagrá (1555–1620), telling of the conquest of northern New Spain: *Elegías de varones ilustres de Indias,* by Juan de Castellanos (1523–1605), giving the lives of the early conquerors of America; *La Argentina y conquista del Río de la Plata,* by Martín del Barco Centenera (b. 1535), telling of the conquest of the Plata region; *Peregrino indiano* by Antonio Saavedra de Guzmán, describing the conquest of New Spain; and *Lima fundada* by Pedro de Peralta Barnuevo (1663–1743), recounting the story of Peru following its conquest.

Some poets dealt with religious subjects, especially the lives of the saints, while still other poets turned to lyric verse. In the seventeenth century much of the Spanish colonial poetry was dominated by Gongorism (named after the Spanish poet Luis de Góngora y Argote), which was characterized by an elegant, artificial, and metaphysical style.

Perhaps the greatest poet of the colonial period was Juana Inés de Asbaje y Ramírez de Santillana (1651–95) of Mexico, who, as a nun, was known as Sor Juana Inés de la Cruz and who published three volumes of poetry.

In Brazil. Poetry in Brazil was dominated by European influences, especially Gongorism, as well as by native and environmental factors. The chief literary center was first at Bahia in the north, but in the eighteenth century Rio de Janeiro became a rival.

As in the Spanish colonies, several heroic poems were written. The two outstanding were *O Uruguai* by José Basílio da Gama, who dealt with Brazil's neighbor and its natives, and *O Caramuru* by José de Santa Rita Durão, who told of the adventures of one of the earliest Portuguese to arrive in Brazil. Both were published in the eighteenth century.

The earliest Brazilian poet to publish a book of verse was Manuel Botelho de Oliveira (1636–1711), who wrote *Música do Parnaso.* Other outstanding Brazilian poets of the colonial period were Gregório de Mattos Guerra (1633–96), and Antônio José da Silva (1705–39), who was a dramatist as well as a poet.

Prose. The chief prose produced in the colonies was of a serious nature, and many works were scientific and historical treatises. Numerous grammars, dictionaries, and religious works were also written. Comedies, romances, and similar types of prose were generally poor in quality and of little permanent value.

IN THE SPANISH COLONIES. Among the innumerable historical writers native to the Spanish colonies were two of Indian descent who should be mentioned: Garcilaso de la Vega (1540–1616), a descendant of the Incas of Peru, who wrote the *Comentarios reales de los Incas,* dealing with Inca civilization, and *La Florida del Inca,* treating of the activities of Hernando de Soto in Florida; and Fernando de Alva Ixtlilxochitl (c. 1568–1648), a descendant of the Aztec rulers of Mexico, who wrote, among other things, the *Historia chichimeca.*

Other sixteenth-century historians born in the colonies were: Juan Suárez de Peralta (b. 1536), who wrote on New Spain; Diego Durán (d. c. 1588), who wrote about the Indians of New Spain; and Agustín Dávila Padilla (1562–1604), who dealt with the missions of New Spain.

One of the leading scientists born in the colonies was Carlos Sigüenza y Góngora (1645–1700), who lived in Mexico and distinguished himself as a poet, philosopher, mathematician, engineer, cartographer, geographer, astronomer, philologist, ethnologist, archaeologist, and historian.

IN BRAZIL. The earliest writer in colonial Brazil was probably José de Anchieta (1530–97), a Jesuit who compiled grammars, lexicons, hymns, etc. Among the other Jesuit writers were Fernando Cardim (1540–1625) and Eusébio de Mattos (1629–92). Another historical writer of some consequence was Sebastião da Rocha Pitta (1660–1738), who wrote the *História da América portuguêsa.*

Literary Societies and Periodicals:

IN THE SPANISH COLONIES. Many colonial leaders organized and belonged to literary "circles" or clubs in which philosophical, scientific, and literary topics were discussed. The members of these groups often wrote articles and books, and some of the clubs issued learned periodicals.

During the colonial period newspapers and magazines appeared, although neither were quite of the same nature as modern newspapers and magazines. The leading periodicals were: *El Mercurio Peruano,* of which the first number appeared at Lima on January 1, 1791; *La Gaceta de Lima,* printed from 1791 to 1821; *El Telégrafo*

Mercantil, first issued at Buenos Aires on April 1, 1801; *El Semanario de Agricultura, Industria, y Comercio,* printed at Buenos Aires from 1801 to 1807; *El Semanario de la Nueva Granada,* published in the late eighteenth century; *La Gaceta de México,* printed at Mexico City from 1722 to 1739; *El Diario de México,* begun in 1805; and numerous others.

IN BRAZIL. In the eighteenth century many educated Brazilians joined literary and scientific societies located at Bahia, Rio de Janeiro, and elsewhere for the purpose of discussing new philosophies and learning from Europe. Among such groups were the *Acadêmia Brasílica dos Esquecidos,* founded in 1724; the *Sociedade dos Felizes,* founded in 1736; the *Sociedade dos Selectos,* established in 1752; the *Sociedade dos Renascidos,* established in 1759; the *Sociedade Literária de Rio de Janeiro,* created in 1786; and others. Little interest seems to have been shown in the publication of literary periodicals, owing in part at least to the scarcity of means of publication.

THE ARTS

Architecture. In both the Spanish colonies and Brazil, architectural development was influenced chiefly by Iberian and European trends modified somewhat in America by the demands of the environment and the skill of native labor.

The first Europeans brought to the Indies the plateresque style, in which skilled ornamentation was concentrated about doors and windows, and the Gothic style. From about 1550 to about 1650, however, a new trend appeared under the influence of the Herreran style, which caused buildings to be constructed after austere and massive Greco-Roman patterns. During the next hundred years to about 1750, the baroque, or churrigueresque, style was in vogue, characterized by intense and universal ornamentation. This period also saw the spread of the French neo-classical type of architecture to the colonies. But despite all such European influences, everywhere in the colonies the Moslem tradition of architecture, with its characteristic arches and balconies, was in evidence.

Carving, Sculpture, and Painting. Metal work and the carving of wood and stone provided important artistic occupations in the colonies. The Indians of certain regions showed remarkable skill in these activities and were given considerable encouragement in the practice of them by the Church, which utilized art as an inspiration to worshipers. The Church laid down definite specifications for carvers, sculptors, and painters of religious subjects, requiring them to use certain stereotyped patterns for the production of religious figures. In the making of saints and other religious images, for example, the Church decreed the use of real hair, nails, eyelashes, etc., in order to render them as lifelike as possible.

Other artistic pursuits in which the Indians were especially skilled included the making of jewelry, furniture, textiles, and pottery.

Most of the colonial arts were supervised by guilds, which were often closed corporations controlling the membership and regulating the quality and quantity of the artistic output through traveling inspectors. Thus there was as little opportunity for the development of individualism in art as in economic and political affairs. But such supervision was in accord with the paternalistic policies of the mother countries.

Music. Colonial music was generally more profoundly affected by American influences than by European, although the peninsulars and Creoles chiefly enjoyed European types. Everywhere in the Indies, the Indians had their own peculiar musical instruments and their own characteristic music. With the coming of the Negro, new musical characteristics were introduced. Hence nearly every colony developed its own type of music.

In the Viceroyalty of Peru, for example, the Inca influence showed itself in music based on a minor diatonic scale in which songs of sorrow (*yaravíes*) and songs of joy and happiness (*marineras* and *pampeñas*) were found. The Negro influence there was shown in the *tendero*. The Incas used instruments, such as drums, whistling jars, pipes (*quenas*), rattles, whistles, etc., while in Mexico the natives used the drum (*huehuetl*), horns, seashells, and the flute (*teponaztli*).

Everywhere in the colonies folk songs were enjoyed, and the colonials with the aid of a guitar readily improvised both words and music of this nature. Everywhere also, church music played an important part in developing musical patterns and characteristics.

PART TWO

THE REVOLUTIONS
FOR INDEPENDENCE

FIG. X–1. The Americas about 1800. (Reproduced with permission from *History of the Americas,* by H. E. Bolton, published by Ginn and Company, Boston, 1935.)

PART TWO

THE REVOLUTIONS
FOR INDEPENDENCE

THREE HUNDRED YEARS of colonial life under the paternal tutelage of Spain and Portugal had poorly prepared the American colonies of the Iberian states to assume an existence independent of the mother countries. Yet because of world forces beyond their control, which were then manifesting themselves in Europe, chiefly owing to the machinations of Napoleon, the colonists, between the years 1808 and 1825, found themselves faced with making a decision as to whether they wished to remain attached to their parent countries or to sever their connections and strike out for themselves as independent political entities.

The Creoles, who constituted the educated and thinking elements in colonial society, finally resolved, after varying lengths of time in the different colonies, to follow the examples of the English colonists in North America and of the French people in Europe, and to take advantage of the opportunity providentially sent them to strike off the fetters which bound them to royalty, and to declare their independence. But with this decision reached, it became evident that fighting for their ideals was necessary.

The winning of colonial independence, especially by the Spanish American colonists, was made easier owing to the fact that from 1808 to 1824 the Spanish people were occupied first in fighting the French invaders (1808–14) and then with civil disorders incident to the restoration of Ferdinand VII, who wished to rule as an absolute monarch.

When Joseph Bonaparte was placed on the Spanish throne by his brother Napoleon in 1808, the cities of Spain organized themselves into a league for defense, and in 1812 they established a constitution for a limited monarchy with a regency to rule until Ferdinand should return. In March, 1814, Ferdinand was freed by the abdication of Napoleon and he assumed his kingly powers, established an absolute monarchy, and repudiated the Constitution of 1812. This alienated many of his people, and considerable unrest developed in Spain. Finally, on January 1, 1820, the Spanish army rose in rebellion and declared itself for the Constitution of 1812 (thereafter called the Constitution of 1820), which Ferdinand, fearing for his crown, agreed to uphold. But it was not long before the king returned to his reactionary methods. Again he was faced with a rebellion, which he was eventually able to put down with the aid of French troops in 1823. Thus his illiberal and absolute regime was restored by 1824.

During the years 1808 to 1814 the people of Spain made several unsuccessful attempts to persuade the colonists in America to help them in the cause which they had in common: that of establishing political equality in the government. But after Ferdinand's restoration, the Spanish Crown appeared anxious only to suppress the colonial rebellion, and it opposed any negotiations which looked toward the recognition of independence. But because of peninsular unrest the Spanish government was not able to spare the necessary troops to suppress the American rebels. The colonists were therefore considerably aided in their rebellion, and the winning of independence was undoubtedly hastened because of Spain's preoccupation with her serious problems at home.

Thus in the critical years of the first quarter of the nineteenth century the colonists followed their Creole military and political leaders toward the goal of freedom, fighting and negotiating, as the situation demanded, with the mother country. But with separation once achieved, the colonists found it necessary to justify their fitness for independence by organizing stable and workable governments and by showing the world of nations that without either political training or experience they could build national states and maintain their national political equilibrium in the realm of practical politics. Such a task was to prove extremely difficult.

CHAPTER X

PRELUDE TO
COLONIAL INDEPENDENCE

THE INEVITABLE OUTCOME of three centuries of colonial exploitation and repression by the Spanish and Portuguese governments was revolution, which stirred the colonies to their foundations and which resulted in the severing of the ties which bound them to the mother countries. The causes for the revolts of the colonists may be classed as (1) internal and fundamental, and (2) external and immediate. The first class of causes was inherent within the colonial system as practiced by the mother countries, while the second class of causes came from outside the colonial system—it was the breath of liberalism fanning the smoldering embers of internal dissatisfaction into the flames of revolution.

INTERNAL CAUSES

The paternalistic and blighting control of the mother countries over the colonies described in previous chapters constituted the fundamental internal causes for revolt. Under the mercantile system economic exploitation was consistent and continuous, with greed rather than intelligence acting as the guiding principle. Taxes were numerous and high. The whole oppressive colonial economic system was maintained by the combined and co-ordinated activities of the State and the Church, aided and abetted by the maintenance of a social-caste system which held the people of the colonies at various levels of social inequality and by a system of education which made possible a superficial literacy among a few but perpetuated illiteracy and ignorance among the masses.

In the more sophisticated and enterprising English colonies in North America, a state of oppression much less grievous caused those colonies to revolt and seek independence. But in the Spanish and Portuguese colonies there was an appalling degree of apathy among the masses owing to ignorance of any better conditions elsewhere. Not until foreign ideas (which constitute the external causes) came in, did the colonists realize that their own condition was relatively bad. Thereupon, colonial leaders turned to revolutionary action.

Furthermore, in the Iberian colonies there was an almost universal patriotic fervor for king and pope, and since State and Church were combined, a criticism of one was a criticism of the other. Daring, indeed, was the colonist who would criticize the acts of his sovereign or of his God. It was only when the Creoles learned that this had happened elsewhere with impunity that they took courage to make such a break with tradition.

EXTERNAL CAUSES

In the latter half of the eighteenth century the minds of the Creoles in the Iberian colonies were gradually being influenced by events in the outside world. Many of the Creoles were well educated, some having studied abroad in the great universities of Europe. A few had studied in the United States. Once outside of the narrow colonial intellectual atmosphere and in the more exhilarating atmosphere of European thought, these Creoles eagerly accepted the opinions of great leaders elsewhere, and, being philosophical by nature, they began to regard their homelands as ready to profit from the new ideas which they had discovered. Hence, the Creoles began to spread their philosophies and doctrines through university students, through secretly printed and circulated pamphlets and books usually in Spanish translation, and through the medium of secret societies organized for the ostensible purpose of debate, study, and scientific experimentation. As a result of this activity, the years from about 1750 to about 1808 marked the growth of colonial self-analysis, with all of the accompanying mental and physical dissatisfaction with existing political, economic, social, and intellectual conditions and with the hope that an excuse for seeking freedom from the mother countries might be found.

Influence of the American Revolution. Admiration for the United States was expressed in the Spanish and Portuguese colonies from the beginning of our national life. When Spain joined in the war against England, at the time of the American Revolution, she could not convince her own colonies that she was not attempting thereby to aid England's colonies to obtain independence. Some Creoles had traveled in British North America before its independence, and more visited that region shortly after the Revolution. All returned imbued with a new spirit, and all praised the military, political, economic, social, and intellectual achievements of the young republic. Such revolutionary Americans as George Washington, Thomas Jefferson, and Thomas Paine were fervidly admired and were looked to for inspiration. Translations of United States books, pamphlets, and public documents began to circulate in the Iberian colonies. Everywhere there was keen interest in the working of our political machinery and in our success as a state, and everywhere, a desire to emulate us. What the English colonists had been able to do, the Spanish and Portuguese colonists believed they could do also.

Influence of the French Revolution. The French Revolution, following close on the heels of the American Revolution, gave a concrete example of what an oppressed people could do through concerted effort. Creole travelers from the Iberian colonies had observed in France before the Revolution the wide interest in political and social philosophy. Some Creoles had even participated in the Revolution and had learned at first hand the methods of revolution. The works of Montesquieu, Voltaire, Rousseau, Raynal, and many others, read by the colonists in the original language or in translation, had sown fruitful seed in the colonial intellectual soil, and the French Revolution stimulated its growth.

Influence of England. From England came the philosophies of Hobbes, Locke, Bentham, Hume, Malthus, and others and the example of a long national struggle for popular political rights. English trade, both illegal and legal, had brought to the Iberian colonies not only welcome products but ideas expressed in printed works. Some Creoles studied and traveled in the British Isles.

English influence was particularly effective at two points in the Spanish colonies.

At Trinidad. In 1797 the English occupied the island of Trinidad off the coast of Venezuela. There, Governor Thomas Picton not only was interested in promoting trade with the nearby Spanish colonies, but he believed that by offering them assistance in munitions and men he could encourage them to rise in revolt, become independent, and perhaps ultimately, for the greater glory of England, attach themselves to the British Empire. The colonists were, however, lethargic and they lacked the proper leaders. In consequence, nothing was accomplished immediately.

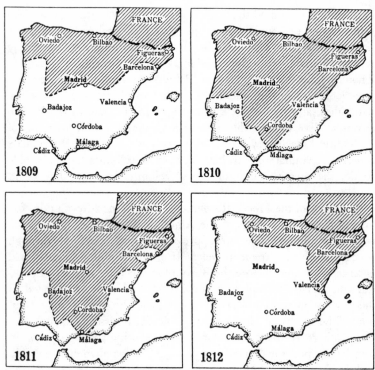

Fig. X–2. The French in Spain, 1809–12. (Courtesy of Farrar & Rinehart, Inc.)

At Buenos Aires. Because of enmity for Spain and because of
the desire to tap the riches of the Plata region, the British attempted,
from June to August, 1806, to take possession of the city of Buenos
Aires. But the colonists under the Creole Jacques Liniers of Montevideo drove the British out. The next year, in June and July, a
second English expedition was prevented from seizing the city.

These English attacks influenced the colonists of the Plata region
in several ways: (1) they revealed the weakness of their colonial
government because the viceroy deserted them in their time of need;
(2) they learned their own strength in defeating the forces of a great
nation; (3) they learned the use of firearms in self-defense and in
aggression; and (4) their experience with the English invaders
proved to be a training school for later activities.

Influence of Napoleon. The most immediate external cause of
the movements for independence, and the one which fanned the

flame of colonial unrest into colonial revolt, occurred in 1807 and 1808 in the Iberian Peninsula.

In Portugal. Napoleon, to enforce his Continental System, which aimed to close European ports to English trade and thus starve his greatest enemy, ordered Portugal to cease her trade with England, to renounce her alliance with that country, and to declare war upon Great Britain. The Regent John, who was acting for his demented mother, Queen Maria, attempted to put off Napoleon by protracted negotiations. This the Frenchman would not allow, and in the fall of 1807 he sent French troops into Portugal. They reached Lisbon late in November, but not in time to prevent John, his mother, his wife Carlota, some 15,000 of the Portuguese nobility, and 50 million dollars of state funds from being put on board British and Portuguese ships and taken to Brazil. On January 25, 1808, the Portuguese refugees reached Bahia.

In Spain. While Napoleon negotiated with Portugal on the one hand, he attacked Spain on the other. In the latter country an unhappy situation existed in the royal family. King Charles IV was a weak, vacillating monarch, little interested in the affairs of government, which he left largely in the ambitious hands of Queen María Luisa and Prime Minister Manuel Godoy, her lover. The heir to the throne was Prince Ferdinand, a young man of weak character. His sister was Carlota, the wife of John of Portugal.

When Napoleon, in trying to punish Portugal, demanded certain concessions from Spain, the Spanish king, queen, and minister decided to flee to the American colonies. But at this point, Ferdinand had Godoy seized as a traitor. In the confusion, Charles resigned in favor of his son, Prince Ferdinand, who became King Ferdinand VII. Thereupon, Napoleon caused Charles to retract his abdication, and he offered to settle the royal family's problems if the members would come to Bayonne in France. There, on May 6, 1808, the principals met Napoleon, who forced both Charles and Ferdinand to abdicate the throne of Spain, which Napoleon gave to his brother Joseph a month later.

News of these events was carried to the Spanish colonies by the agents of Napoleon and Joseph. When these emissaries arrived with the intention of declaring the colonists subjects of Joseph, many of them were seized and imprisoned or sent back to Europe. There was general indignation in the colonies at such high-handed French procedure, and the first reactions were anti-French and pro-Spanish.

At first, a patriotic movement to maintain Spanish control, called the "Volunteers of Ferdinand VII," began in many of the colonies. But soon the Creoles realized that this was the opportunity they had been longing for, and taking advantage of the difficulties and confusion in the mother country, they began anti-Spanish movements which ultimately resulted in colonial declarations of independence and in fighting to maintain it.

EARLY UNREST IN THE SPANISH COLONIES

Minor Revolts. The last half of the eighteenth century in the Spanish colonies was marked by growing unrest among the Creoles, assisted by *mestizos* and Indians.

Some unrest was due to trade restrictions, as in the case of the revolt at Caracas, Venezuela, in 1749, when the Creole Juan Francisco de León led a protest against the trade monopoly of the Quipúzcoa Company. But for their efforts the revolutionists were executed.

In Chile, in 1776, the Creoles protested against high taxes and the oppressive activities of the Church, but they, too, were suppressed.

From 1780 to 1783 the Indians of Peru and neighboring regions rose in revolt under the Indian Tupac Amarú II, later assisted by the Creoles and *mestizos*. After his death, his cousin continued the revolt in a fruitless effort to win reforms from the Spanish authorities. In all, probably 80,000 Indians lost their lives in the bloody uprising.

In 1781, while the struggle in Peru was in progress, the Creoles in New Granada rose against unjust taxes, and some of them were treacherously captured and executed. At the same time, another revolt, in which independence was to be declared and a republic established, was planned in Chile by several Creoles and two Frenchmen, but came to nothing.

In 1797, at Caracas, a revolt, led by Creoles and stimulated in part by the influence of Governor Picton of Trinidad, failed to win independence.

Miranda's Attempt to Revolutionize Venezuela. One of the most important single attempts, before 1808, to revolutionize a region in the Spanish colonies occurred in 1806, when the great Creole Francisco de Miranda, a native of Caracas, Venezuela, attempted with outside assistance to land forces on his native soil and to free his country from Spain.

Miranda had served in the Spanish army assisting the American colonists during their War of Independence and traveled in the United States during 1783 and 1784. From there he went to Europe, traveled widely, served as an officer in the French Revolution, and finally settled in England, where he devoted himself to securing assistance in his attempt to create a revolution in Venezuela.

Failing to obtain English aid, Miranda returned to the United States to seek help. In February, 1806, he sailed from New York City with a ship containing munitions and about two hundred men, chiefly Americans. In the West Indies he added two small ships to his expedition and sailed for the Venezuelan coast. Near Puerto Cabello he attempted to put his plans into effect, but his two small vessels were seized by a Spanish fleet, and Miranda fled to the Barbados, where he met the English Admiral, Alexander Cochrane. After discussing plans with Miranda, this British commander agreed to assist him in return for British commercial privileges in Venezuela. Accordingly, from June to August, 1806, Miranda again attempted to land his forces and to obtain local assistance from his compatriots in freeing his native soil from Spain. But with no local co-operation, Miranda was forced to leave the country. Returning to England, he again began to make plans for freeing his homeland.

EARLY UNREST IN BRAZIL

In Brazil, Creoles interested in reform found it practicable to organize themselves into discussion groups, often disguised as literary societies. Among the leaders the most outstanding was Joaquim José da Silva Xavier, called "Tiradentes," or tooth-puller, since he was a dentist.

This first martyr of Brazilian independence was a self-made man, who practiced dentistry, medicine, mineralogy, and engineering. He also served in the army for a time. Tiradentes traveled widely in Brazil and had occasion to meet many persons and to make many influential friends. He also read widely and became acquainted with European philosophies, so that at last he decided to win the freedom of his native land from the mother country. Associated with Tiradentes were many Creoles, literary and professional men, poets, merchants, miners, and army officers. These conspirators laid detailed plans for an independent state. But the plot was discovered by the government, and Tiradentes was arrested at Rio de Janeiro on April 10, 1789. After a long trial, in which Tiradentes took all of the blame, he was executed by hanging on April 21, 1792.

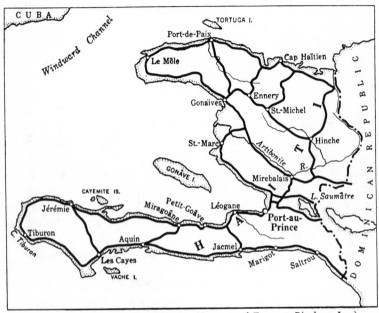

Fig. XI–1. The Republic of Haiti. (Courtesy of Farrar & Rinehart, Inc.)

CHAPTER XI

INDEPENDENCE OF SPANISH NORTH AMERICA

In 1808 the Spanish possessions in North America comprised the Viceroyalty of New Spain and included Mexico proper, present-day Central America (except Panama), portions of the West Indies, the Philippine Islands, and the Spanish territory within the present limits of the United States. This vast region did not gain independence all at once, and the movements for independence within it were scattered and frequently unrelated.

INDEPENDENCE OF THE ISLAND OF HISPANIOLA

Even before 1808 a part of this region had declared its independence of European control. This was the island then called Haiti, originally called "Española" by Columbus, who set up its first government.

In 1795, by the Treaty of Basel, France gained possession of the whole island, which at that time was virtually under the control of the Negro Toussaint L'Ouverture. On July 1, 1801, Toussaint promulgated a constitution for the country and declared the island independent of all foreign connections.

But Napoleon had plans for using the country as a base for his occupation of the recently acquired territory of Louisiana. In consequence, he sent troops to occupy the island, but the Negroes and yellow fever defeated him. He did, however, seize Toussaint in May, 1802. Toussaint's place was taken by Henri Christophe and Jacques Dessalines. On January 1, 1804, the country was again declared independent under the name of the Republic of Haiti, and General Dessalines became governor for life, and later became Emperor Jacques I. It was, however, not until 1825 that the French acknowledged the independence of the western part of the island as the Republic of Haiti.

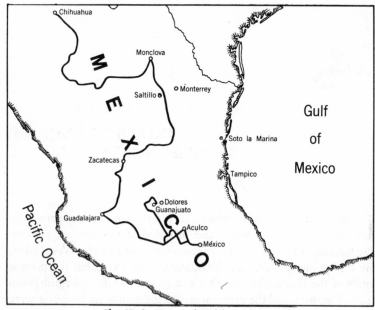

Fig. XI–2. Route of Hidalgo, 1810–11.

Fig. XI–3. Mexican Territory in Control of the Revolutionists, 1811–13.

Meanwhile, in 1806, the Spaniards regained the eastern portion of the country, or Santo Domingo, which, in 1821, came under the influence of Bolívar's Colombian government, declaring its independence from Spain on November 30 of that year. But in January, 1822, President Boyer of Haiti forcibly attached Santo Domingo to the Haitian Republic, of which it remained a part until 1844.

INDEPENDENCE OF MEXICO

Beginnings. In 1808 the Viceroy of New Spain, José de Iturrigaray, took over the government in the name of Ferdinand VII and refused to take orders from the representatives of Joseph or Napoleon. Later, he refused to accept orders from the Spanish people's government, and in consequence of this, on the night of September 15, 1808, a group of Mexicans, called the "Volunteers of Ferdinand VII," made the viceroy a prisoner. He was succeeded in office by Pedro de Garibay, nearly eighty years of age and feeble. Dissatisfaction among the Creoles increased and the agents of the French secretly encouraged the unrest. Again the "Volunteers of Ferdinand VII" intervened and asked the Spanish government to send a more suitable representative. In July, 1809, therefore, Garibay was followed by Archbishop Francisco Xavier de Lizana, also aged and infirm. Again the Creoles plotted revolt, but their plot was discovered. The viceroy was then replaced in August, 1810, by General Francisco Xavier Venegas, sent from Spain. As dissatisfaction steadily increased, the Creoles began to plot ways and means of winning independence, or at least reforms.

Miguel Hidalgo. One of the Creole leaders who seems to have been content with seeking reforms rather than independence was the priest of Dolores, Miguel Hidalgo. Longing for political, economic, and social betterment, he plotted with friends to seize the colonial government officers and to institute the desired changes. The uprising was planned for October, 1810, but the plot was discovered and on September 16, Hidalgo assembled his parishioners and other followers, took as his slogan, "Long live our Lady of Guadalupe! Perish the government! Perish the Spaniards!" and began to seize the neighboring towns. Marching from place to place, freeing prisoners from jails, and promising reforms, Hidalgo and his followers won over several of the central provinces of Mexico. At Guadalajara, Hidalgo organized a government, abolished slavery, and restored the lands to the Indians. But on January 17,

1811, Hidalgo was defeated by the viceroy's forces and forced to flee. Shortly afterward, in attempting to go to the United States for aid, Hidalgo was captured (March 21), condemned by the Inquisition, tried by the government, and shot on July 26, 1811. Hidalgo had not proclaimed the independence of Mexico.

José Morelos. A follower and student of Hidalgo was the Creole priest, José María Morelos, who gave up his profession to head the patriots' cause after the death of their leader. From 1811 to 1815 he revolutionized the central provinces of Mexico from the Pacific to the Caribbean. In November, 1813, he convened a congress at Chilpancingo which declared Morelos head of the government and commander in chief of the army. At the same time, a declaration of independence was issued on November 2, 1813, and a constitution was promulgated on October 22, 1814. The patriots abolished slavery and class distinctions, corrected tax abuses, and made plans to raise a state militia. But in December, 1813, Morelos was defeated trying to take Valladolid. Pursued by the royalists under Agustín de Iturbide, Morelos gave up his executive authority although he retained command of the army. Like Hidalgo, Morelos was condemned by the Inquisition. When he was captured late in 1815, he was tried by the government and shot at Mexico City on December 22, 1815. He had, however, declared Mexican independence.

Francisco Xavier Mina. With the death of Morelos the patriots only halfheartedly continued to fight in guerrilla bands which were never able to co-operate. Finally, however, there landed on Mexican soil a Spaniard who had ambitions to free Mexico from the tyranny of Spain. This man was Xavier Mina, who had fought for Spain against the French invaders, and had been captured and imprisoned in France in 1811. Freed in 1814, he returned to Spain to fight against the illiberal King Ferdinand. Forced to flee, he went to England, and in 1816 he sailed for America with men, money, and munitions, hoping to aid the patriots of Mexico. At Baltimore he recruited more men and sailed for the West Indies and then to the Texas coast, again adding men and supplies. From Texas he went to Soto la Marina, on the Gulf, arriving on April 15, 1817, with the title "General of the Relief Army of the Republic of Mexico." Marching inland with three hundred men, he was at first victorious, but soon he was defeated by the viceroy's forces, captured, and shot on November 11, 1817. Again patriot opposition degenerated into guerrilla warfare, lasting until 1820.

Agustín de Iturbide. Fighting on the royalist side, because he thought it would win, was the Creole Agustín de Iturbide, who was responsible for several royalist victories over the patriots. A soldier by profession, Iturbide was interested only in his own personal aggrandizement. Therefore, in 1820, when he saw an opportunity to promote his ambitions, he deserted to the patriot cause. On February 24, 1821, at the town of Iguala, Iturbide issued his scheme for an independent Mexican state with a constitution outlined in his "Plan of Iguala." To put his new government into effect, he corresponded with the viceroy, but that official declared Iturbide an outlaw and took steps to crush the patriots.

In July, 1821, a new viceroy, Juan O'Donojú, came from Spain. Without authority he reversed the policies of his predecessor and agreed, in the Treaty of Córdoba (August 24, 1821), to recognize the independence of Mexico. On September 27, Iturbide entered Mexico City in triumph. When the Spanish government learned of these developments, it refused (February, 1822) to recognize the treaty. But by then it was too late, for on February 24, 1822, Iturbide assembled a national congress at Mexico City, and on May 19, this body declared him Emperor Agustín I of an independent Mexican Empire. Thereafter, his family was ennobled, and his image was stamped on the coin of the realm.

Hardly had these steps been taken when revolt broke out under Santa Anna and others, and on March 19, 1823, Iturbide was forced to abdicate and leave the country. In July, 1824, he secretly returned to Mexico, was captured by the government and was shot on July 19.

INDEPENDENCE OF CENTRAL AMERICA

José Matías Delgado. The colonial population of Central America was widely scattered, and the strong arm of the Spanish government was felt less there than in many parts of the Spanish colonies. Hence there was comparatively little unrest in this region at a time when the other colonies were fighting for their independence.

Between 1811 and 1814 the chief disturbances were instigated largely by the Creole José Matías Delgado, a native of San Salvador, who was not only a lawyer but a priest. Joining with other priests and with Manuel José Arce, he organized a revolt for independence which commenced on November 5, 1811. Removing the Spanish officials from office, the patriots proclaimed the national independence of San Salvador. But the Spanish authorities in Guatemala quickly suppressed the uprising and transferred Delgado to Guatemala as a prisoner, where he continued unsuccessfully to agitate for independence.

When news came from Spain of the promulgation of the Constitution of 1812, many Creoles in Central America wished to adopt its principles and to remain within the Spanish Empire. But when news of the restoration of Ferdinand VII reached them in 1814, their hopes collapsed. It was not until the Creoles learned of the Revolution of 1820 in Spain that they again successfully planned revolt.

José Cecilio del Valle. In 1820 the Creoles were divided into two groups. Delgado's party wished an immediate declaration of independence and to promote its ideas began to publish a periodical called *El Editor Constitucional,* founded by Pedro Molina. The other party believed that the time was not yet ripe for independence; it published a periodical called *El Amigo de la Patria* under the leadership of José Cecilio del Valle.

But when Iturbide in Mexico, in February, 1821, announced his Plan of Iguala for an independent Mexican government, the Central American Creoles decided to follow his example, and on September 15, 1821, a declaration of independence, drafted by del Valle, was issued at Guatemala City. The revolutionists temporarily adopted the Spanish Constitution of 1820.

Union with Mexico (1822–23). An independent Central America was destined at this time to be short-lived, for hardly had a government been organized when Iturbide invited the people of Central America to join his empire. Most of the Creoles accepted his offer, but under Delgado's influence San Salvador refused, on the ground that such a step would nullify Central American independence. Thereupon, Iturbide attempted unsuccessfully to establish unity by force.

Central America Wins Complete Independence. The union with Mexico proved generally unsatisfactory for all concerned, and because of the continual agitation of Delgado and the abdication of Iturbide there was finally convened at Guatemala City on June 24, 1823, a constitutional assembly, with Delgado as president, which, on July 1, issued a declaration of independence and created "The United Provinces of Central America," composed of five provinces. After the formulation of a constitution, adopted on November 22, 1824, a national Central American congress was finally assembled on

February 25, 1825, which elected Manuel José Arce the first president of the new state. But union did not bring political peace, and within a year Arce quarreled with other rival leaders of local forces which fought among themselves.

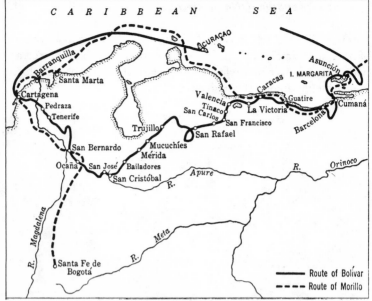

Fig. XII–1. Campaigns of Bolívar and Morillo, 1812–16. (Courtesy of Farrar & Rinehart, Inc.)

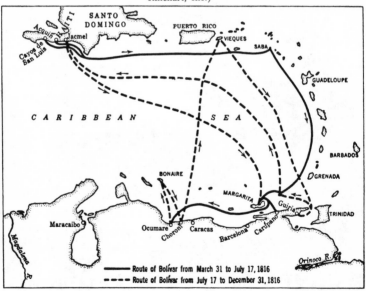

Fig. XII–2. Expeditions of Bolívar in 1816. (Courtesy of Farrar & Rinehart, Inc.)

INDEPENDENCE OF
SPANISH SOUTH AMERICA

T HE INDEPENDENCE OF Spanish South America was achieved not as a concerted unified movement but by scattered groups of patriots attempting to win freedom from the mother country by force of arms, and in some cases by force of words. Since the greatest stronghold of Spain in South America was in Peru, it was to be expected that that region would be the last to win independence. And it was not until patriot invaders from the north and from the south entered Peru that the country was finally freed from Spanish domination and Spanish South America became free forever.

INDEPENDENCE OF NORTHERN SOUTH AMERICA

Miranda Returns. Miranda had returned to England after his failure to revolutionize Venezuela in 1806. But he had not given up hope of aiding his people; he was only waiting for them to begin the movement for independence.

When news reached Venezuela that Napoleon had replaced Ferdinand by Joseph, the Creoles began to make plans to seize the opportunity to separate from Spain. Accordingly, the patriots of several provinces, with those of Caracas leading, convened in March, 1811, a congress which on July 5 of that year declared the independence of Venezuela from Spain. On December 21, 1811, they promulgated a constitution.

Meanwhile, in 1810, Miranda had heard the patriots' call and had returned to take part in their activities. When the new government appointed him commander-in-chief of the patriot forces, he set out to compel the remaining provinces in Venezuela to join the patriot cause. But reverses followed. Suddenly on March 28, 1812, an earthquake rocked the patriot provinces, killing twenty thousand people and demoralizing the patriot forces. Since the royalist provinces had not been affected by this disaster, the Spanish government sent priests to tell the revolutionists that this was an act of God to show his displeasure at their rebellion.

In consequence, Miranda's army dissolved, and although he was made head of the patriot Venezuelan government on April 4, 1812, he was finally forced to capitulate to the Spanish commander at San Mateo on July 25. All subsequent attempts to reassemble his army failed, and Miranda decided to seek aid abroad. But on July 31, just before embarking, Miranda was seized by a group of men headed by Simón Bolívar, as a deserter of the patriot cause, and shortly thereafter he was turned over to the Spaniards. In 1813 Miranda was confined in a dungeon in Puerto Rico, but the next year he was removed to Spain, where he died on July 14, 1816, in a dungeon at Cádiz. Thus did fate misuse the great precursor of South American independence.

Simón Bolívar Frees Venezuela and Colombia. The Creole Simón Bolívar, like Miranda, was a native of Caracas. With the wealth left by the early death of his parents he was educated in Spain and traveled widely in Europe and the United States. In 1807 Bolívar returned to his estates in Venezuela to live the life of a rancher. But in 1810, heeding the patriots' call, he was sent to England as one of three commissioners to endeavor to obtain aid. Failing in this, he returned to his native land and with several others seized Miranda. This unjustified act left Bolívar the leading Creole patriot.

But finding that the patriot cause in Venezuela was hopeless for the present, Bolívar, in December, 1812, went to Colombia (or New Granada), where he offered his services, and early in 1813 he defeated several royalist forces. Then marching overland across the Andes into Venezuela, the patriots fought their way to Caracas, which Bolívar entered on August 4, 1813. Meanwhile, Bolívar had declared "War to the Death" (June 8), thus giving no quarter and expecting none.

In January, 1814, the second Venezuelan Republic was created, and Bolívar became its head with the title of "Liberator." But the royalists under the brutal José Tomás Boves and others attacked the revolutionists under Bolívar, Santiago Marino, Campo Elias, and others, and on July 10, 1814, the Spaniards captured Caracas. Forced to flee, Bolívar went again to Colombia, arriving at Cartagena on September 25. Once more in command of the patriot forces, he occupied Bogotá and established a government with himself as head.

However, royalist successes caused Bolívar to leave Colombia a second time; he resigned the command of the army and in May, 1815, went to Jamaica to obtain aid.

Meanwhile, in April, 1815, Venezuelan royalists under Tomás Morales were reinforced by fresh troops from Spain under Pablo Morillo, and the patriot forces under José Antonio Páez were hard pressed. When Bolívar learned of these facts, he obtained assistance from Haiti and sailed for the island of Margarita, which he planned to use as a base of attack on the Spaniards. But this expedition was not permanently successful, and in March, 1816, Bolívar again returned to Haiti for aid.

At last, in January, 1817, the Liberator returned to Venezuela, captured several towns, and with the aid of Páez overran much of the Orinoco River valley by the end of 1818. On November 20, 1818, at Angostura, the independence of Venezuela was again proclaimed. However, the patriots were prevented from taking Caracas by the Spanish General Morillo.

Fortunately for the patriot cause, there now began to arrive in Venezuela the first of some six thousand soldiers of fortune from

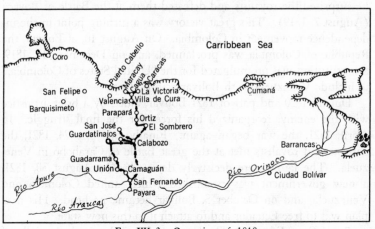

Fig. XII–3. Campaign of 1818.

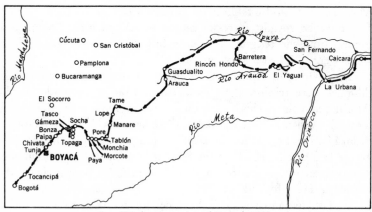

Fig. XII–4.   Campaign of Boyacá, 1819.

Great Britain, recruited by the Venezuelan agents in England headed
by the Creole López Méndez. With a mixture of these and patriot
troops Bolívar, late in June and early in July, 1819, marched across
the Andes into Colombia in a most spectacular maneuver. There
he surprised the royalists and defeated them at the Battle of Boyacá
(August 7, 1819). This great victory was a turning point in the independence movement in Colombia. On August 10, at Bogotá, the
Republic of Colombia was proclaimed, and on December 17, 1819,
a constitution was promulgated for the "United States of Colombia,"
to include Venezuela, with Bolívar as president.

During 1820 and part of 1821 Bolívar, aided by a brief armistice
with the enemy, reorganized his forces for the final struggle. In
April, 1821, the war began again. Finally, on June 24, 1821, the
patriots and royalists met at the great Battle of Carabobo in Venezuela. The latter were decisively defeated. On August 30, 1821,
a new government was established which united Colombia and
Venezuela, and on October 3, Bolívar became its head. His next
plan was to free Ecuador and to attach it to this new state.

Sucre Frees Ecuador. The Creoles of Ecuador, and especially of
Quito, attempted an uprising in the middle of 1809, but by October
they were put down by the government. Again in 1810 they rose
in rebellion, but were crushed. Nevertheless, in December, 1811,
the patriots succeeded in issuing a declaration of independence, al-

though by the end of the next year they were again subdued. Thereafter, the country remained generally quiet until 1821.

In May, 1821, Bolívar's right-hand assistant, the able Creole, General Antonio José de Sucre, reached Guayaquil to carry out the Liberator's plans to revolutionize Ecuador. Sucre brought with him Colombian and Venezuelan troops, but they were not successful until after they were joined by some 1,200 men sent by San Martín from Peru. After considerable maneuvering, the Spaniards and patriots faced each other on May 24, 1822, at the decisive Battle of Pichincha. In this conflict Sucre won a great victory, and the independence of Ecuador was assured. A few days later (June 16, 1822), Bolívar reached Quito and soon persuaded the patriots to join with Colombia and Venezuela in his Republic of Gran Colombia. From Quito, Bolívar went to Guayaquil to meet San Martín and to decide the future fate of the independence movement in South America.

INDEPENDENCE OF SOUTHERN SOUTH AMERICA

Independence of Argentina. The repulse of British attacks on Buenos Aires in 1806 and 1807 had inspired Argentine patriots with considerable self-confidence. Hence, when news reached them of the accession of Joseph to the Spanish throne, many Creole leaders became interested in winning early independence from the mother country. On May 20, 1810, under the leadership of Manuel Belgrano and other Creoles, a demand was made that the viceroy resign. The Spaniards attempted to compromise, but on May 25, 1810, the Creoles overthrew the viceregal government and set up a supreme governing council to rule in the name of Ferdinand VII. At the same time, they sent to England for aid.

With Buenos Aires in Creole hands, the next step was to revolutionize the outlying parts of the viceroyalty. Accordingly, troops were sent into Bolivia, Paraguay, and Uruguay, but in all three regions the Buenos Aires forces were eventually unsuccessful: Bolivia was defended by Spanish troops sent from Peru; the people of Paraguay wished to remain free from all outside influences; Uruguay became a bone of contention between local factions stirred by José Artigas and the covetous influences of Brazil and Buenos Aires, and it did not become independent until 1828.

Meanwhile, in Buenos Aires several Creole leaders, including Cornelio de Saavedra, Mariano Belgrano, Bernardino Rivadavia, and others, attempted to decide whether the monarchical or republican

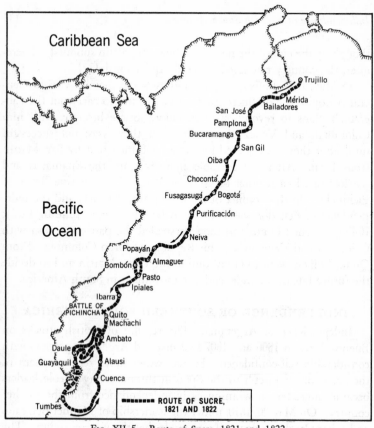

Fig. XII–5. Route of Sucre, 1821 and 1822.

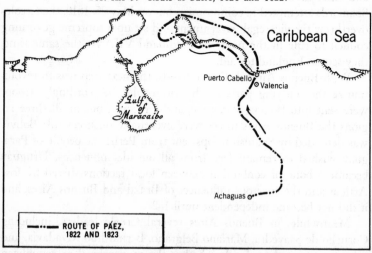

Fig. XII–6. Route of Páez, 1822 and 1823.

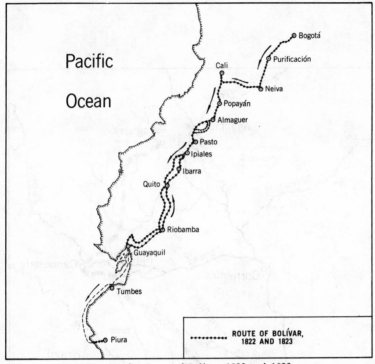

Fig. XII-7. Route of Bolívar, 1822 and 1823.

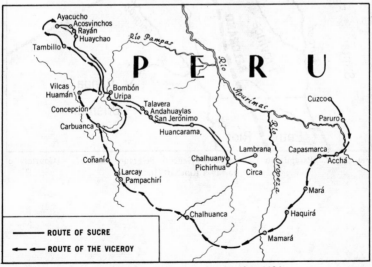

Fig. XII-8. Campaign of Ayacucho, 1824.

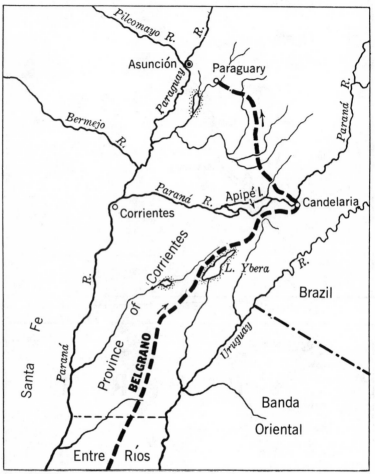

FIG. XII–9. Paraguayan Campaign of General Belgrano, 1810–11. (Courtesy of Farrar & Rinehart, Inc.)

form of government would best meet their needs and whether or not complete independence from Spain should be proclaimed.

While leaders of the metropolis were thus engaged, the Creoles of the provinces were gradually coming to desire complete independence from the mother country. Accordingly, a congress of representatives of the provinces was assembled at Tucumán on March 24, 1816, and on July 9, the delegates declared absolute independence from the mother country and organized themselves into the United Provinces. However, the immediate future of the new state was to be marred by the growing rivalry between the province of Buenos Aires on the one hand and the thirteen interior provinces on the other.

San Martín and O'Higgins Free Chile. While the Argentines were trying to settle some of their perplexing problems there appeared in their midst at Buenos Aires in 1812, the Creole José de San Martín, who had served in the Spanish army and navy since 1789 and had won fame for his military ability. Avoiding politics, San Martín saw that he might best serve the Creole cause by attempting to drive the Spaniards out of their greatest stronghold in South America—Peru. Accordingly, he asked to be appointed governor of the Argentine province of Cuyo at the eastern border of the Andes, where he proposed to prepare a well-drilled and well-equipped army which he might lead into Chile and, using that country as a base, strike at Peru by sea. Thus, from 1814 to the end of 1816, San Martín molded a cosmopolitan body of men into a military machine. In this he was aided somewhat by Chilean patriots, especially by the Creole Bernardo O'Higgins.

This Chilean revolutionary, whose father Ambrosio had gone to Spain from Ireland and had later become viceroy of Peru, had been a friend and student of Miranda in England, where he had been sent for an education and from which he had returned imbued with ideas of freedom. But the Creoles in Chile, led by Juan Martínez de Rozas, José Miguel Carrera and his two brothers, Bernardo O'Higgins, and others, had been unable to agree on methods of revolution and had in consequence not only quarreled among themselves but, because of their mutual dissension, had been defeated by the royalists and forced to flee from the country in 1814. Many of these patriots joined San Martín in Cuyo.

At last, San Martín was ready to cross the Andes with his army, and on January 17, 1817, he began his advance, dividing his forces

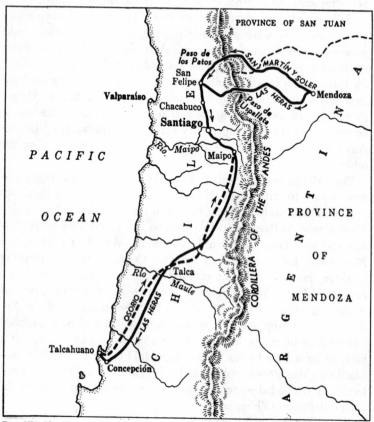

FIG. XII–10. Route of San Martín's Passage over the Andes and His Liberating Campaign in Chile, 1817 and 1818. (Courtesy of Farrar & Rinehart, Inc.)

into two parts, each going by a different pass across the great mountain barrier. After overcoming tremendous difficulties, his men assembled on Chilean soil, surprised the royalists, and defeated them at the important Battle of Chacabuco near Santiago on February 12, 1817. The next day the victorious patriots entered Santiago, and San Martín was offered the headship of the Chilean government. But he declined this honor in favor of O'Higgins, preferring to remain in command of the army.

Until the end of 1818 the Chilean patriots were engaged in fighting the remaining Spanish forces in the country. During this campaign O'Higgins declared the absolute independence of Chile at Talca on January 2, 1818. The second and last great battle in the Chilean revolution occurred at Maipó on April 5, 1818. Thereafter eventual victory was certain.

San Martín Invades Peru. Meanwhile, San Martín had returned to Argentina to obtain men, money, and munitions for his attack upon Peru. While he was thus engaged, O'Higgins had begun to assemble a fleet which could be used both as a patriot navy and as transports to carry San Martín's troops to Peru. Fortunately for the patriot cause, Miranda's friend, the Englishman Thomas Cochrane, in disgrace with the British government, was now employed to organize and command this fleet.

By the end of 1819 San Martín had an efficient navy and a well-trained army of six thousand men, and he began his plans for the attack on Peru. Finally, on August 20, 1820, the expedition got under way with the army on board Cochrane's fleet. On September 7, troops were landed south of Lima on the coast of Peru, but failing to revolutionize that region, San Martín re-embarked his men and took them several miles north of Lima, where they were again landed. Now began a period of troop maneuvering and diplomatic correspondence which was generally more favorable to the royalists.

Such results were due to the fact that the Spaniards in Peru had complete control over the country. The early Creole uprisings (1808 to 1813), in part under the inspiration of José de la Riva Agüero, had been thoroughly crushed. An Indian uprising in 1814 and 1815 was ruthlessly suppressed. Thereafter, there was little opportunity for the Creoles to agitate even for reform, let alone for independence.

Because of the conditions which he found in Peru, San Martín sought to negotiate with the viceroy early in 1821. Failing to accomplish his aims in this manner, he decided to fight, and on July 9, 1821,

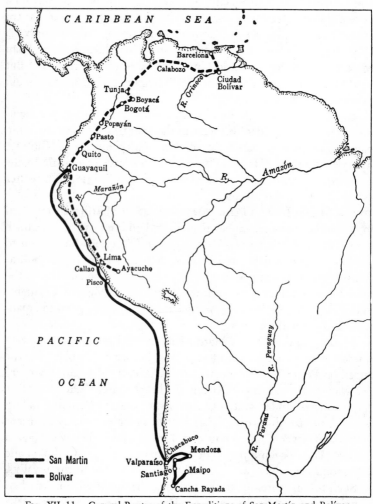

Fig. XII–11.   General Routes of the Expeditions of San Martín and Bolívar.
(Courtesy of Farrar & Rinehart, Inc.)

his forces entered Lima, where on July 28, he issued a declaration of independence from Spain. On August 23, San Martín was named "Protector" of the new Peruvian government. But since only a small portion of the country was in patriot hands, three more years were to pass before Peruvian independence could be made good.

INDEPENDENCE OF PERU AND BOLIVIA

San Martín and Bolívar Meet. After Sucre had defeated the royalists at the Battle of Pichincha (May 24, 1822) with the aid of troops sent by San Martín, he and Bolívar planned to move into Peru and to assist the Argentine general. Both Bolívar and San Martín had corresponded, and the former invited the latter to meet him at Guayaquil, Ecuador, in July, 1822. Accordingly, on July 26 and 27, the two great South American military leaders came together for the first time. What happened at this conference is not completely known. But shortly after it terminated, San Martín returned to Lima, said farewell to the Peruvians on September 20, and returned to Chile. Unfortunately, conditions there prevented his staying, and he went to Buenos Aires. But conditions there, likewise, were not to his liking, and with his daughter he sailed for France, where he died in 1850 at Boulogne. He had fulfilled his role in helping to win the independence of South America.

Bolívar and Sucre Free Peru. In Peru, Bolívar and Sucre began immediately to make final plans to win the complete independence of the country. After months of maneuvering, the patriots and royalists faced each other at the Battle of Junín on August 6, 1824. This patriot victory was followed on December 9 by a more decisive victory at the Battle of Ayacucho, which was won by Sucre while Bolívar was away seeking reinforcements. This was the last great battle for South American independence, although the last of the Spanish troops were not driven from the country until January, 1826.

Bolivia Becomes Independent. Upper Peru, or Bolivia, like coastal Peru, was freed by revolutionists from the outside. Scattered Creole uprisings from 1808 to 1814 were unsuccessful, although on July 16, 1809, the Creoles at La Paz declared for separation from Spain and for war if necessary. In 1810, and again in 1815, forces from Argentina failed to revolutionize the country. Finally, in 1822 Bolívar took an active interest in Upper Peru, and in that year and the next, two successful expeditions were sent into the region. It was, however, not until after the patriot victories at Junín and

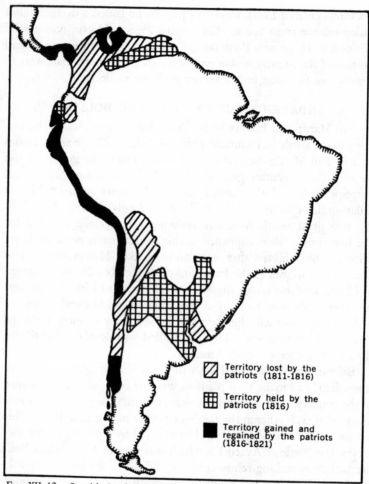

Fig. XII–12. Spanish South America: Areas of Revolutionary Activity, 1811–21.

Ayacucho in Peru that the royalists could be defeated in Upper Peru.

Finally, on January 5, 1825, the Bolivians proclaimed their independence at La Paz, and on April 1, the royalists were at last defeated. Meanwhile, Bolívar had been declared the "Father of Upper Peru," and on August 25, the country took the name of Bolivia in honor of the Liberator. The next year a constitution which Bolívar planned was adopted and the country was launched on its career of national existence.

CHAPTER XIII

INDEPENDENCE OF BRAZIL

T̲HE INDEPENDENCE OF Brazil was achieved in an offhand and almost accidental manner. Yet this was the logical outcome of events which took place in the Iberian Peninsula as one small phase of the life-and-death struggle between France and England on a world-wide scale.

THE ROYAL PORTUGUESE FAMILY IN BRAZIL

When Napoleon's troops caused the Portuguese royal family to leave Lisbon in November, 1807, they sailed with British ships to Brazil, arriving at Bahia on January 25, 1808. But finding that region too tropical in climate, they moved on to Rio de Janeiro, which they reached on March 8.

The regent John was surprised to find his colony so backward and took immediate steps to modernize it and to repeal colonial restrictions. Soon he had founded schools, a printing press, a bank and a mint, factories, hospitals, a national library, etc. Health conditions were improved; vaccination for smallpox was introduced. Rio de Janeiro was made the capital, and the city was beautified with broad streets and numerous parks. Foreign immigration was encouraged. Artistic and scientific projects were planned.

On December 16, 1815, the colony was given the title of "realm" and made a part of the "Kingdom of Portugal, Brazil, and Algarves." When the demented Queen Maria died on March 20, 1816, the regent became John VI. He surrounded himself with a royal court and, to the disgust of the Creole Brazilians, he placed many of the Portuguese nobles in local offices. Commerce was increased, but the financial situation remained unsatisfactory, in part because of a costly conflict with Argentina over Uruguay, which was finally attached to Brazil as the "Província Cisplatina."

Some Brazilians looked with growing disfavor upon the continuation of their ruler in their midst, and the Creoles especially wished that he would return to Portugal. In March, 1817, a revolt broke out in Pernambuco which turned into a secession movement, but it was finally suppressed by royalist troops.

In 1820, after the revolution in Spain, the Portuguese people decided to overthrow the regency ruling in the name of John and to demand his return to the mother country. In Brazil the people eagerly welcomed the idea, and the Creoles took steps to persuade the king to go to Portugal. Accordingly, on April 26, 1821, John and his family and many Portuguese nobles sailed for Europe.

INDEPENDENCE WON UNDER PEDRO I

King John left his son, Pedro, then twenty-one years of age, in charge of the government of Brazil. Pedro was handsome and popular, but had little education except that of a soldier.

Such a political arrangement for Brazil, however, did not satisfy the people of Portugal, and the Côrtes (parliament) demanded that Pedro also return to Europe. When the Creoles in Brazil learned of this order, they requested, under the leadership of José Bonifácio de Andrada e Silva, "The Father of Modern Brazil," that Pedro remain as their ruler. As a result, on January 9, 1822, Pedro announced that he would remain in the country. Ever since, this day has been celebrated as the "I Remain Day." This was the first step in Brazilian independence.

The second step in Brazilian independence occurred on May 13, 1822, when Dom Pedro assumed the title, "Perpetual Defender and Protector of Brazil." The following month he issued a call for a constitutional assembly.

The third step was taken on September 7, 1822, when Dom Pedro declared on the bank of the Ypiranga River that his motto henceforth would be "Independence or Death." This is known as the *"Grito do Ypiranga."*

The fourth and final step in consummating Brazilian independence occurred on October 12, 1822, when Dom Pedro was proclaimed constitutional emperor of Brazil at Rio de Janeiro. On December 1, 1822, he was crowned amid inspiring ceremonies. A constitution for the new state was finally adopted in 1824.

CHAPTER XIV

LATIN AMERICA AT THE END OF THE REVOLUTIONS FOR INDEPENDENCE

THE WARS OF EMANCIPATION in Latin America ended with the surrender, on January 23, 1826, of the last Spanish garrison occupying the *Castilla* of Callao, in Peru. However, Spain withheld recognition of the new nations for many years and in several instances endeavored to recover parts of her lost empire. Portugal recognized the independence of Brazil in 1825, and France that of Haiti in the same year.

TERRITORY

Although bound together by a common political, religious, and cultural heritage, the Spanish colonies in America did not constitute themselves into a single nation after emancipation as did the English colonies of North America. At the end of the wars there were the following states: Mexico and the United Provinces of Central America, comprising the territory of the Viceroyalty of New Spain; Great Colombia, including the territory of New Granada (Colombia, Venezuela, and Ecuador); Peru, Chile, and Bolivia, carved out of the territory of the Viceroyalty of Peru; and the United Provinces of the River Plata and Paraguay, formed out of the Viceroyalty of La Plata.

Brazil retained the whole territory of the former Portuguese colony of that name, with Uruguay (Banda Oriental) added to it under the name of "Cisplatine Province" from 1822 to 1828; and Haiti included the present territory of the Dominican Republic from 1822 to 1844. Cuba remained a Spanish colony until 1898.

Later on, new political subdivisions took place until the total number of the Latin American nations became twenty, as it is today. The boundaries of these nations were for many years, and still are in a few cases, a matter of dispute, causing intermittent irritation and international friction.

FIG. XIV–1. Latin America after the Wars of Independence, 1825. (Based on text and map from *The Cambridge Modern History Atlas*. Used by permission of the publishers, Cambridge University Press, England, and The Macmillan Company, New York.)

POPULATION

No reliable statistics exist in regard to Latin America during the period here studied. About 1825 the total population of Spanish America was roughly estimated at 15 millions: about 7 millions lived in Mexico and Central America; 2.5 millions in Great Colombia; three-quarters of a million in Chile; over 3 millions in Peru; and the rest in Argentina, Bolivia, and Paraguay.

Brazil's population was approximately 2.5 millions, and the island of Hispaniola (Española or Santo Domingo) had a total of about one million inhabitants.

SOCIAL CONDITIONS

Measured by contemporary European standards, society in the new nations was in general primitive and crude. Except for the inhabitants of a few larger cities, such as Mexico City (140,000), Lima (80,000), Quito (70,000), Buenos Aires (60,000), Santiago de Chile (30,000), and Rio de Janeiro (30,000), the population lived scattered in small villages and on isolated farms. The hinterland of South America and portions of Mexico and Central America were inhabited by primitive Indians who were at war with the civilized population most of the time.

Many of the rural people lived on immense estates owned by a few wealthy families. Life on these estates was patriarchal if not feudal, the owners exercising all the rights of feudal lords even though no such rights were given them by the laws.

In the cities—which usually were seats of government, provincial or national—there was always a small group of old families, wealthy and bound together by ties of blood relationship and friendship, constituting an aristocracy. Below this group, and imitating it as much as their background and wealth permitted, was a large group consisting of traders and owners of small shops and industries. The rest of the urban population were artisans, servants, slaves, peddlers, beggars, etc.

Despite the fact that in all these nations (except Brazil, Mexico, and Haiti) the form of government adopted was republican and democratic, society was to remain essentially aristocratic for many years to come.

In some sections the wars of emancipation were bloody and lasted for several years, depopulating the rural districts as well as the towns. Some of the most prominent families were completely wiped out;

others lost their wealth and social prestige. On the other hand, the wars brought into prominence men who until then had occupied a humble place in society. Among these latter were some who had distinguished themselves for military ability—rude, unprincipled, and ambitious persons who struggled, often successfully, to gain control of the government. These were the *caudillos* and dictators of the next half century of general political disorder.

Even in countries where independence was secured with little or no shedding of blood, such as Brazil and Central America, hatred toward those who had remained loyal to the mother country throughout the wars persisted after peace was re-established. In many cases these persons formed the nuclei around which were organized the conservative parties or factions.

POLITICAL CONDITIONS

At the end of the wars of emancipation the new nations found themselves freed from the restraints imposed by the mother countries; but they were not prepared for self-government and, least of all, for republican and democratic government as provided in their constitutions. Politically, the Spanish colonies, as well as Portuguese Brazil and French Haiti, had been accustomed to the monarchic form of government, as represented by the king, the viceroy, the captain general, and the *cacique*. Colonial government was always autocratic, and the Creoles were seldom given the opportunity to gain political experience. Even the municipal governments, which allowed a certain amount of self-government, had gradually lost many of their democratic features, because of the custom of selling offices to the highest bidder.

Nevertheless, it must be kept in mind that whatever political experience the leaders of the new nations possessed had been acquired in municipal governments (*ayuntamientos, cabildos,* or *senados das câmaras*). In many cases these city governments formed the nuclei of the national governments.

The large mass of people were illiterate, ignorant, and inexperienced in all matters of government except unconditional obedience to the constituted authorities. That they were not prepared for republican government was realized by some of the patriot leaders, such as San Martín, Belgrano, Rivadavia, Pueyrredón, Bolívar, Sucre, Lucas Alamán, and many others, who at one time or another favored a monarchic form of government. But the majority of the patriots, with the examples of the American and French revolutions before them, could not be persuaded to accept a monarch as their ruler, except in Brazil and, for shorter periods, in Mexico and Haiti.

The constitutions adopted were drafted, for the most part, by lawyers, theorists, and some literary men—most of them idealists who had no experience in democratic government. When it came to the election of executive officers, men of power and prestige, usually prominent veterans of the emancipation wars, were chosen. Most of these men knew little or nothing about political theory. Confronted with the problems of creating an effective government, they acted in accordance with their own military experience. Accustomed to being obeyed, they expected prompt and blind obedience from legislatures and the people. When this did not happen, they resorted to force. The result was a perpetual struggle between idealistic theories of government and the reality of immediate practical needs. Soon constitutions and laws were set aside, and despotism, tempered by revolution and assassination, became the prevailing form of government in most of the new nations.

The situation was further aggravated by rivalry between leaders; by racial antagonism between the ever-increasing *mestizos* and mulattoes on one hand and the pure-white Creoles on the other; and by regional patriotism, which further tended to break up the national units.

ECONOMIC CONDITIONS

In colonial days manufacturing had been discouraged by the authorities to prevent competition with the mother country, and agriculture had often been sacrificed to the exploitation of mineral wealth. During the wars of independence, and thereafter for many years, owing to general disorder, mineral and agricultural production decreased and in some regions almost disappeared. A great deal of property was destroyed because of hatred toward the owners or for tactical reasons. Much of the property and trade had been in the hands of peninsulars who were either killed or compelled to leave the country. Even when they sided with the patriots, as some did to save their lives and property, they remained under the cloud of public suspicion, jealousy, and hatred, and their economic activities were hindered. In some of the new nations these economic and financial ailments were further aggravated by the abolition of slavery and the extravagance of government expenditures.

Means of communication were unsatisfactory for the most part, or even nonexistent. Restrictions on foreign commerce were abolished everywhere at the outset of independence, and trade pacts were signed, especially with Great Britain and the United States. This resulted in the flooding of local markets with foreign goods, which further discouraged local industries.

CULTURAL CONDITIONS

During colonial days, with little or no public instruction in the modern sense, the masses were illiterate. Provisions for general public education were included in the constitutions and legislation adopted at the outset of independence. Efforts were made to establish elementary schools, but lack of funds and general disorder impaired to a great extent the success of these efforts. In some countries private associations under the auspices of the government were organized to introduce the Lancasterian system of instruction; in others the Scottish educator James Thomson was invited to establish schools based upon that system. The well-to-do continued to be educated by private tutors or in small private schools or abroad, as during colonial days. Higher and professional education was centered in convents, seminaries, and a few government-supported universities, such as Chuquisaca in Bolivia, San Marcos in Peru, Santa Fe de Bogotá in Great Colombia, Córdoba in Argentina, and Santiago in Chile. There was no university in Brazil until the twentieth century, although separate faculties of law, medicine, and theology were established earlier.

Education was classical and humanistic. Despite the low general level of education, there existed in the various countries men of great culture, such as José Bonifácio de Andrada e Silva (1765–1838), a Brazilian scientist of European renown; Andrés Bello (1781–1865), a Venezuelan jurist, educator, and writer, who spent the greatest part of his life in the service of Chile; Lucas Alamán (1792–1853), a historian and statesman of Mexico; Antonio José Irisarri (1786–1868), a brilliant philologist, poet, and writer on political science born in Central America; and José Joaquín Olmedo (1780–1847), an illustrious poet of Ecuador.

RELIGIOUS CONDITIONS

The predominant religion of the Latin American peoples was, as it is still today, Roman Catholicism. The constitutions of all the new nations adopted it as the official religion of the state, the latter assuming all the prerogatives in religious matters that the Spanish Crown had previously held. The *real patronato* became in most cases the *patronato nacional*.

Although most of the upper hierarchy of the Church had sided with the mother countries at the outbreak of the wars of independence—as was to be expected since most of them were Spaniards—the lower clergy, mostly native, sided in general with the patriot cause and in some instances became leaders of the revolutionary movement. At the end of the wars the prestige of the Church remained undimmed. There is no doubt that during the wars and the following period of disorder the Church contributed in no small degree to stability and national unity, although in many cases it sided with the military and the landed aristocracy in opposition to progressive legislation and democratic government.

In general, the religion of the lower classes, particularly of the Indians, Negroes, mulattoes, and *mestizos,* was a crude mixture of Catholicism, idolatry, and superstition.

In a few countries Protestants, mostly foreigners, were allowed the exercise of their faith, with restrictions.

PART THREE

RISE OF NATIONALISM,
1825 TO THE PRESENT

PART THREE

RISE OF NATIONALISM, 1825 TO THE PRESENT

THE HISTORY OF MANY of the Latin American nations since their independence is an almost continuous succession of revolutions, dictators, and constitutions. Superficial students are prone to look at this perpetual turmoil with a smile of amusement, if not with a sneer of disgust. They are apt to think that this disorderliness indicates a congenital incapacity for self-government. The facts, however, are much more tragic than that and demand a less shallow interpretation.

The revolutions, the dictators, and the constitutions are only symptoms of maladjustment. They reveal the struggle of those peoples to overcome the handicaps of adverse physical environment and racial heterogeneity as well as the curses, inherited from their mother countries, of an aristocratic attitude toward physical labor and an autocratic concept of government.

It is with these points in mind that the history of the Latin American nations since independence must be studied. And whatever progress these peoples have made must be measured, not by the yardstick of other more fortunate peoples' advancement, but by the magnitude of the obstacles overcome.

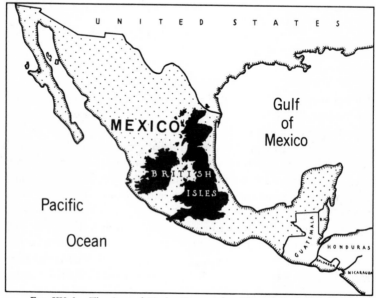

Fig. XV–1. The Area of Mexico Compared to That of the British Isles.

CHAPTER XV

MEXICO

IN BRIEF, THE HISTORY of Mexico since independence is the story of the struggle of the despoiled native races to shake off the dominance—political, social, and economic—of the descendants of the Spanish conquerors. Three distinct stages may be pointed out in this struggle. The first period is from 1821 to 1855, during which time the white aristocratic element was in control and the country was ruled by military *caudillos*. This period is characterized by anarchy, rivalry among political leaders, and corruption and incompetence in matters of government. In the second period, from 1855 to 1910, liberalism gained control of the government, struck at the most scandalous privileges of the conservative classes, and attempted to redistribute the land and property accumulated by the Church during three centuries. The third period, from 1910 to the present time, is properly called the Mexican Revolution. The most distinctive features of this period are: the breaking up of the large estates; the distribution of land among the peasants; the enactment of social legislation favoring the laboring classes; the struggle against the Church and, later, foreign capitalism; and a general rise of the standard of living.

MILITARY ANARCHY AND *CAUDILLISMO* (1821–55)

It has already been shown how Agustín de Iturbide, a royalist army officer who had fought against the revolutionary forces of Hidalgo, endeavored to reconcile the royalists with the patriots by issuing the Plan of Iguala, which proposed the maintenance of the Roman Catholic religion and the establishment of an independent limited monarchy with equal rights for both Spaniards and Mexicans.

When, on February 24, 1822, a national congress assembled at

159

Mexico City, three parties emerged. One favored the placing of a Bourbon prince upon the Mexican throne; the second stood for the occupation of the throne by Iturbide himself under the Plan of Iguala; and the third advocated the establishment of a federal republic. The Spanish government, by refusing to recognize the Treaty of Córdoba and to consider the independence of Mexico, offered Iturbide and his followers the opportunity for which they had been waiting. Quarreling with the congress over financial matters and the maintenance of an army, Iturbide gained the support of the conservative classes. On May 18, 1822, he was acclaimed emperor by a group of soldiers in the streets of the capital. The next day the congress was overawed by the same rowdy element into formally electing Iturbide emperor under the title of Agustín I. On July 21, he was crowned in the cathedral. The congress declared the monarchy hereditary and gave the title of prince to Iturbide's sons.

Iturbide's Empire. The first Mexican Empire was short-lived. On October 31, the emperor dissolved the congress because of the opposition to his rule on the part of the republican element. A legislative junta composed of persons favorable to him was created. Pressed for money, he had this junta approve forced loans. The wealthy began to lose their enthusiasm for the emperor, and the liberals took advantage of the situation to incite the people to revolt. On December 2, Antonio López de Santa Anna began his career as a professional revolutionist by leading the garrison of Veracruz in revolt against the government. Although defeated at Jalapa, he and some of his followers were able to take refuge in Veracruz.

On February 1, 1823, the revolutionists proclaimed in Veracruz the Plan of Casa Mata, favoring the re-establishment of the sovereignty of the national congress and the calling of a new congress. Then they marched against the capital. Iturbide, seeing that all was lost for him, convened the old congress and abdicated (March 19). Upon meeting, the new congress refused to accept Iturbide's abdication, since that would have amounted to recognition of his right to the Crown, declared his government null and void, and exiled him to Italy with a generous annual pension.

Iturbide left the country. But returning secretly to Mexico in 1824 in the hope of regaining favor with the people, he was recognized, arrested, tried, and executed in Padilla, state of Tamaulipas— the first of a long list of Mexican executives who have been removed by the bullets of a firing squad. He was vain, egotistical, and incompetent, representing that aristocratic Creole element to which so many of the political leaders of this period belonged.

The First Federalist Constitution. After deporting Iturbide, the national congress declared itself in favor of the establishment of a republic, appointed a governing junta, called a constituent assembly to draft a constitution, and adjourned.

The constituent assembly met late in 1823, and after protracted discussion between the centralists, who favored the concentration of political power, and the federalists, who advocated the division of powers between the states and a central government, it adopted a constitution embodying the main ideas of the latter. This constitution, promulgated on October 4, 1824, divided the country into nineteen autonomous states and established a federal government composed of the executive body (president and vice-president elected for four years by the state legislatures), a bicameral congress, and a judiciary. The Catholic faith was declared the official religion of the state, and other religions were prohibited. Guadalupe Victoria (assumed name of Juan Manuel Félix Fernández) was elected president, with Nicolás Bravo as vice-president. They were inaugurated on October 10, 1824.

The Masonic Parties. During the following year many Masonic lodges of the York Rite were organized throughout the country by the liberals, federalists, and republicans, whereas the monarchists, centralists, and conservatives in general organized themselves into lodges of the Scottish Rite. Thus appeared the two main parties or factions of this period, the *yorkinos* and the *escoceses*. When the former won the congressional elections of 1826, the latter rose in revolt, calling for the suppression of all secret societies, for the overthrow of the government, and for the dismissal of Joel Roberts Poinsett, then United States Minister to Mexico. Poinsett was often consulted by the *yorkinos* and by his freely expressed opinions had won the antagonism of the conservatives.

As a result of the *yorkinos'* propaganda, a decree expelling all Spaniards from the country was adopted by the congress on December 20, 1827. This resulted in the emigration of a considerable number of people and in the consequent loss of much capital for Mexico at a time when the country needed it badly.

The elections of 1828 were won by the *escoceses,* whose candidate, General Manuel Gómez Pedraza, was elected president, with Anastasio Bustamante as vice-president. The *yorkinos* at once revolted under the leadership of General Santa Anna. President-elect Pedraza was forced to leave the country, and thereupon the congress (on January 12, 1829) declared the previous election null and void and elected General Vicente Guerrero president, with Anastasio Bustamante as vice-president.

Guerrero, Bustamante, and Santa Anna. Under Guerrero the abolition of slavery was decreed (September 16, 1828) and other reforms were undertaken. But the conservatives, who were in control in most of the states, revolted against the federal government. The government forces were defeated, and the congress deposed Guerrero, who was assassinated the following year.

During Guerrero's administration a Spanish expedition under the command of General Isidro Barradas landed in Mexico to attempt the reconquest of the country, but this was defeated by General Santa Anna, who thereby gained great prestige with the Mexican people.

Bustamante was declared president and assumed the government on January 1, 1830. He belonged to the conservative faction and was helped by one of the ablest leaders Mexico has ever had, Lucas Alamán, a wealthy aristocrat who, despite his great culture and ability, possessed the prejudices of his class.

The assassination of General Guerrero by a group of soldiers caused general indignation throughout the country. In 1832 General Santa Anna, always ready to take advantage of any opportunity to promote his own selfish purposes, denounced the government in Veracruz. Bustamante was compelled to resign in favor of General Pedraza, who had been elected president in 1828, but who had never assumed the government. He was now allowed to finish the presidential term for which he had been elected; at the end of this term, Santa Anna was declared president, with Dr. Valentín Gómez Farías as vice-president. Directly or indirectly, Santa Anna was to remain in control of Mexican politics until 1855. He was an incompetent and corrupt individual, indifferent to the best interests of his country or the common people, but not without personal charm and a political talent which enabled him to retain the loyalty of the Mexican populace and keep the support of the conservative classes despite his many and costly failures.

On April 1, 1832, Gómez Farías assumed the presidency while Santa Anna absented himself from the capital. A staunch liberal, he soon antagonized the upper classes by proposing measures against the Church. Returning to the capital, Santa Anna attempted to make himself dictator with the support of the conservatives. But seeing that the country would not stand for that at the time, he gave up the attempt to unseat Gómez Farías. New laws were adopted against the Church; the California missions were secularized; a board of public instruction was appointed; and the compulsory payment of the tithes was abolished.

The Centralist Constitution of 1836. The antagonism against the Federalist Constitution of 1824 culminated in a revolt of the Conservatives under the cry of *"Religión y Fueros"* (religion and privileges). General Santa Anna, seeing his opportunity, sided with the conservatives and in 1834 proclaimed the Plan of Cuernavaca, which replaced the liberal laws and called for the replacement of the federal form of government by one which was centralized. At his suggestion a constituent convention met in 1835, and a new government embodied in seven laws called *Las Siete Leyes Constitucionales* (December 29, 1836) was adopted. The presidential term was increased to eight years; the states were abolished, and for administrative purposes the country was divided into departments ruled by governors appointed by the central government; the legislature was made unicameral; and the executive was to be advised by a council of state. A Supreme Conservative Power was also created, consisting of a commission of citizens to supervise the actions of the various branches of government.

The Loss of Texas. The abolition of the federal system resulted in the immediate secession of Texas and indirectly, ten years later, in war with the United States.

Texas formed part of the state of Coahuila and was inhabited by many American citizens who had settled there because of the liberal Mexican immigration laws. Dissatisfied with political conditions after the Revolution of 1834, the Americans rose against the central government and established a provisional government on November 7, 1835, at San Felipe de Austín, declaring themselves in favor of the Constitution of 1824. On March 2, 1836, at a convention held at Washington, on the Río Brazos, they issued their first declaration of independence. General Santa Anna marched against them and at the Alamo (a fortified building in San Antonio) defeated the revolutionists despite the heroic resistance of the defenders. The massacre of the inhabitants of the town that followed aroused intense indignation among the Texans and in the United States. On April 21, 1836, General Santa Anna was attacked on the banks of the San Jacinto River and completely routed. The Mexican general himself was captured by the Texans and sent to the United States. The situation remained more or less stationary for the next ten years, while the Texans negotiated for admission into the United States.

Bustamante's Second Administration. General Anastasio Bustamante was elected president under the new constitution and took office on April 21, 1837. His second administration was full of turmoil and complications with foreign nations. Between January, 1838, and March, 1839, the so-called "Pastry War" took place with France, because of unpaid claims (especially the claim of a French baker) arising from political disturbances. The incident resulted in an attack on Veracruz by a French fleet. During this affair Santa Anna, who had returned from the United States, was shot in the knee; the wound, which made necessary the amputation of his leg, added to his prestige. The war ended by the recognition of the French claims.

Antagonism to the Centralist Constitution of 1836 resulted in several uprisings. One of these was led by Mariano Paredes y Arrillaga, who had the support of Santa Anna and the conservatives. On September 28, 1841, the Plan of Tacubaya was proclaimed, advocating the overthrow of the government and the calling of a congress to formulate a new constitution. Bustamante was compelled to resign. On October 7, General Santa Anna entered the capital and two days later he was declared provisional president.

The *Bases Orgánicas* of 1843. A congress controlled by the liberals met on June 10, 1842. But the constitution drafted was rejected by Santa Anna, who also dissolved the congress and called together a Council of Notables. This council met in January, 1843, and a few months later adopted a new charter known as the *Bases Orgánicas*, granting broad powers to the executive.

Under this constitution Santa Anna ruled as dictator amidst regal luxury. But the liberals revolted. While he was away from the capital attempting to put down the revolution, the congress declared Santa Anna a rebel (December, 1844), and General José Joaquín de Herrera was chosen to replace him. Attacked by the forces of the new government, Santa Anna was defeated and captured near Jico, impeached and banished. He sailed to Havana on June 3, 1845.

Yucatan Attempts to Secede. Since about 1838 Yucatan had shown a tendency to separate from Mexico. On May 29, 1839, a revolution against the central government broke out in that province. The following February a federal form of government was adopted. The war continued until December of the following year, when a treaty which recognized the autonomy of Yucatan was negotiated between the central government and the Yucatan revolutionists. The treaty was rejected by Santa Anna, and war continued until 1843, when Yucatan's autonomy was recognized. Five years later the territory of Yucatan was finally incorporated into the Mexican nation.

War with the United States. At this time relations with the United States became strained because of unpaid claims arising from damages suffered by American citizens living in Mexico and by the introduction of a bill in the American Congress for the annexation of Texas. Taking advantage of this situation, General Mariano Paredes y Arrillaga, commander of the Mexican troops at San Luis Potosí, declared himself against the government, deposed Herrera, and assumed the government (January, 1846). He was backed by the conservatives and the clergy.

Meanwhile, Texas had become a state in the American Union (December, 1845), and President Polk had sent an army to the region of the Río Grande del Norte under the command of General Taylor. There, on April 26, 1846, the American and Mexican forces clashed. The incident gave President Polk the opportunity, for which he had been waiting, to declare to Congress that a state of war existed between the United States and Mexico.

In the war that ensued, Mexico had little chance of victory. The country was divided by political strife, her financial and economic forces were disrupted, and her army was poorly equipped. The American forces, despite the valiant resistance of the Mexicans at certain points, were able quickly to occupy northern Mexico and later to invade the central region by way of Veracruz. Santa Anna, who had been returned to Mexico on an American man-of-war under the persuasion that he would put an end to the war, revived Mexican hopes of victory and was elected provisional president (December, 1846). As commander-in-chief, he blundered and was defeated by General Winfield Scott. The latter entered the Mexican capital at the head of the American forces on September 14, 1847.

Meanwhile, an American army had also seized Alta (Upper) California. Helpless, Mexico accepted the peace terms dictated by the United States. The treaty of peace was signed at Guadalupe-Hidalgo, on February 2, 1848, Mexico ceding Texas, New Mexico, and Alta California to the United States in exchange for payment by the United States of an indemnity of 15 million dollars. The United States also agreed to pay any claims against Mexico by American citizens up to a total of $3,250,000. As a result of this war Mexico lost more than half of its national territory.

Herrera, Arista, and Santa Anna. After the war General José Joaquín de Herrera was again elected president. He was faced by problems of reconstruction and an uprising of the Yucatan Indians. This uprising, which started in the middle of 1847, is called the "War of Castes." It was a bloody affair, in which both whites and Indians showed the utmost cruelty and vengefulness. The Indians were at last subdued by the federal forces, and Yucatan, which during the war with the United States had declared itself neutral, was unconditionally incorporated into the Mexican nation on August 17, 1848.

Three years later (January 15, 1851), after one of the few peaceful elections the nation had seen until then, General Mariano Arista was inaugurated president. But on July 26, 1852, a revolution favoring the recall of Santa Anna to the presidency broke out in Guadalajara and spread to other sections. Powerless to resist, Arista resigned on January 4, 1853. On April 20, General Santa Anna was once more selected by a combination of militarists, clericals, and conservatives.

Once in power, Santa Anna strengthened the army, imposed heavy taxes, and sold a strip of land along the Río Grande called La Mesilla to the United States (Gadsden Purchase, 1853) for 10 million dollars. Dissatisfaction was rife throughout the country. Santa Anna flouted public opinion by assuming the title of "His Most Serene Highness" and declaring himself permanent dictator.

In 1854 a French nobleman, Count Auguste de Raousset de Boulbon, with a motley army of adventurers, invaded the provinces of Sonora and Baja (Lower) California with the intention of establishing an independent nation there. He was defeated by Mexican troops, taken prisoner, and shot.

Revolutions broke out in various regions, and Santa Anna, unable to crush them, resigned, leaving the country on August 9, 1855. Thus ended the political career of a man who by his selfishness and incompetence brought more losses to his country than anyone else.

LIBERALISM AND DESPOTISM (1855–1910)

With the disappearance from the scene of General Santa Anna and the coming into power of a new group of people, mostly belonging to the middle class, Mexico was about to experience a radical change in her politics.

On October 4, 1855, one of Santa Anna's opponents, General Juan Alvarez, a full-blooded Indian, was elected president. Alvarez had signed the Plan of Ayutla, which voiced the opinions of all persons opposed to the political dominance of the privileged classes. Once in power, the liberals carried into effect some of the tenets of this Plan, striking at the privileges of the Church and the military.

President Alvarez's cabinet soon divided itself into two factions: the *puros,* who had radical ideas, and the *moderados,* who wished to adopt a conciliatory attitude toward the Church and the landowning class. The *moderados* were led by Ignacio Comonfort, Minister of War. Among the *puros* was another full-blooded Indian, Benito Juárez, who had won a reputation for integrity and liberalism as governor of Oaxaca and as a member of the national congress. Born in Oaxaca of Zapotec stock, he was raised by an Italian trader and studied first for the Church; later he became a successful barrister.

As Minister of Justice and Ecclesiastical Affairs, Juárez drafted a bill which was adopted by the congress and became known as the "Juárez Law" (November 23, 1855). This act, which limited the jurisdiction of military and ecclesiastical courts, increased the enemies of the administration. On December 1, 1855, President Alvarez was forced to resign in favor of Ignacio Comonfort. Despite continual unrest, the new president endeavored to carry into effect some of the liberal reforms of the Plan of Ayutla. The Society of Jesus was abolished, and on June 25, 1856, another important piece of legislation, the "Lerdo Law"—named after Miguel Lerdo de Tejada, its proponent and a member of the cabinet—was passed in an effort to release from the dead weight of mortmain the enormous ecclesiastical holdings. From one-third to one-half of all valuable land in the republic belonged to the Church at this time. The new law provided for the sale of that land under favorable terms, the proceeds to revert to the Church.

The Constitution of 1857 and the "War of Reform." Despite the opposition, conspiracies, and even revolts inspired by the Church and by the conservative classes, a constituent assembly was summoned by President Comonfort, and a new constitution was adopted. This constitution, promulgated on February 5, 1857, represents the first effective step toward liberating the common people of Mexico from the dominance of the privileged classes. It granted freedom of speech and of the press; it abolished hereditary titles and forbade monopolies and the confiscation of property; a federal form of government was again established, the country being divided into twenty-three states and one territory; the supremacy of the State over the Church was recognized; and religious freedom was granted to all. This constitution remained in effect until 1917. It was, however, too far in advance of the political experience of the Mexican people as a whole.

The new constitution was strenuously opposed by the conservatives, and Comonfort was forced to resign. Juárez, who was president of the Supreme Court of Justice at the time, assumed the executive power in accordance with the constitution, on December 1, 1857. The conservatives arose in rebellion against the government, under the leadership of General Félix Zuloaga, who was proclaimed by them president of the republic on January 11, 1858. The war between the two governments lasted three years and is known as the "Three Years' War" or "War of Reform." During the struggle, Juárez and his cabinet had to leave the capital and take refuge, first in Guadalajara, where he was nearly assassinated, and later on in Veracruz. Fortunately for the liberals, the Juárez government was recognized by the United States on April 6, 1859, and thus was enabled to negotiate foreign loans and to buy armaments. In July, Juárez issued the famous "Laws of Reform," disestablishing the Church and providing for the suppression of all religious orders and the confiscation of all ecclesiastical property not yet sold under the Lerdo Law. Civil registration of marriages, births, and deaths became compulsory.

By December, 1860, the conservative forces, divided among themselves, had been decisively defeated, and the following month Juárez returned to the capital. In June he was re-elected.

Foreign Invasion and Maximilian's Empire. For years foreign creditors had endeavored without success to secure the repayment of loans made to Mexico. Ill-advised, the Mexican Congress, on July 17, 1861, declared the suspension for two years of the payment of all debts of the nation. England, France, and Spain decided to take action and at London (October 31, 1861) signed an agreement to intervene jointly in Mexico to protect the interests of their nationals.

An expedition was sent to Veracruz, and that port was occupied in January, 1862. Negotiations with the Mexican government failed to bring about satisfactory results. Nevertheless, when it became apparent that France wished to conquer the country, instead of merely to collect the claims of her nationals, the British and Spanish forces withdrew.

Napoleon III, then Emperor of France, under the influence of his wife, Empress Eugénie, and some Mexican conservatives, had conceived the dream of establishing a great Catholic empire in Mexico to serve as a bulwark against further expansion of the United States, and to provide France with raw materials.

The Mexican clericals and conservatives saw an opportunity of permanently overthrowing the liberals. In April, 1862, General Juan Nepomuceno Almonte declared himself against Juárez and in favor of a government under French control. French troops began the conquest of the country. Although defeated near Puebla (May 5, 1862), they eventually captured the capital, which had been abandoned by President Juárez a short while before. On July 8, an assembly of notables convened under the auspices of the French and adopted a limited hereditary monarchy as the form of government, inviting the Archduke Ferdinand Maximilian Joseph, a brother of Franz Joseph, Emperor of Austria, and a Hapsburg descendant of Charles I, to rule over the Mexican Empire.

On May 28, 1864, Maximilian and his wife Carlotta landed in Mexico. The French, under the command of General Bazaine, were in control of the central part of the country, while Juárez and his partisans were in the north, near the United States border, keeping up a desultory war against the French.

Maximilian was well-meaning but he had little practical sense or experience in government. He antagonized the Church by refusing to return its recently nationalized property. He also indulged in reckless spending. On the other hand, the United States government, after the Civil War, not only refused to deal with Maximilian, but continued to recognize the Juárez government and demanded the withdrawal of the French from Mexico. Left without the necessary support, Maximilian was surrounded in Querétaro by Juárez's forces and surrendered. He was tried, condemned, and, despite foreign pressure, shot by a firing squad on June 19, 1867.

Opposition to Juárez. On July 15, 1867, President Juárez reentered the capital. The following December he was re-elected.

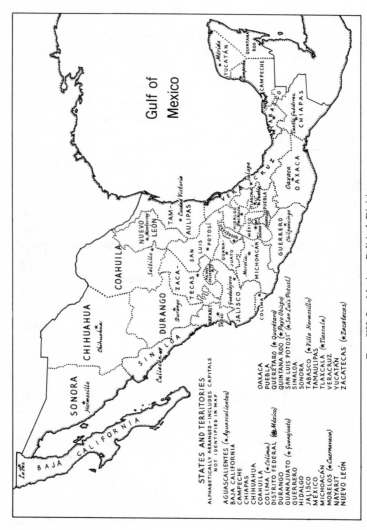

Fig. XV-2. Mexico: Political Divisions.

However, there were those who, out of personal ambition or fear that Juárez might make himself dictator, opposed the president. Among these was a young *mestizo* born in Oaxaca, who had distinguished himself in the war against the French. This man, Porfirio Díaz, was soon to become the supreme ruler of Mexico.

Juárez set himself to reorganize the nation, but revolutions in various parts of the country broke out as a protest against his re-election. Suddenly, on July 18, 1872, he died of heart failure. The president of the Supreme Court, Sebastián Lerdo de Tejada, assumed the executive power.

The new president continued Juárez's policies. In 1875 he was re-elected. Porfirio Díaz led the opposition in revolt against the government. On March 22, he proclaimed a new scheme of government (Plan of La Noria) favoring the fulfillment of the Constitution of 1857 and prohibition of the re-election of a president. Defeated at first, and forced to leave the country for a while, Díaz returned to Mexico and on November 16, 1876, at Tecoac, he in turn defeated the government forces. On May 2, 1877, he was recognized as the president by the Mexican Congress.

Díaz as Dictator. Thus began what is generally known as the "Age of Díaz." Porfirio Díaz was a man of great power and shrewdness. Under his strong administration, internal peace was established and Mexico recovered from the effects of its many revolutions and wars. To maintain order, Díaz created a mounted police force, the *Rurales,* recruited in many cases from among ex-bandits. He rid the army of turbulent officers, and by murder or imprisonment he did away with his most dangerous enemies. Careful to render lip service to the Constitution of 1857, he built up a strong, centralized, and effective government machinery through which he controlled all branches of public administration both in the federal government and in the states. Elections continued to be held as prescribed by the constitution, but no one was ever elected without his consent. The congress passed all the bills he wanted passed, and no others. Local politics were managed by Díaz through local political leaders.

In the beginning of his rule, Díaz reorganized the civil service on sound foundations, remodeled the consular service, and improved the finances of the nation. He also gradually gave back to the Church the property recently confiscated and allowed the rich landowners to despoil the peasant communes of their lands. He particularly fostered the economic progress of the nation by granting generous concessions to foreign capitalists. The latter, at the end of the Díaz regime, became the real masters of Mexico. On the other hand, social legislation was lacking. Popular education was deficient. The agricultural workers continued to live in virtual servitude.

With the exception of the period of 1880 to 1884, when General Manuel González was allowed to fill out the term for which he was elected—under congressional provision that no president might succeed himself—Díaz, who was again elected in 1884, remained in power until 1911.

THE MEXICAN REVOLUTION (1911–40)

President Díaz allowed the conservative classes to regain most of their lost privileges at the expense of the lower classes. The latter, especially the peasants, were now worse off than at any time since independence. All liberal-minded persons chafed under the Díaz dictatorship, and when, in 1908, the dictator insincerely declared to an American journalist that he would allow the Mexican people to choose their next president freely at the elections of that year, they sprang to action.

Francisco I. Madero, a wealthy liberal of high ideals, became the candidate of the opposition. When he charged Díaz with numerous irregularities, he was arrested and tried for sedition. While in jail, Madero drafted a proclamation (Plan of San Luis) favoring the overthrowing of the dictator and the redistribution of the land among the peasants, as well as other reforms.

By November, 1910, the whole country was in a turmoil. Government troops proved unable decisively to defeat the revolutionists, who were united under the battle cry of "Effectual Suffrage, Non-re-election, and Redistribution of Land." On May 25, 1911, Díaz, now eighty-five, gave up the struggle, resigned, and left the country with his family a few days later. Madero entered the capital, was recognized president, and assumed the executive power on December 11, 1911.

Thus begins the period known as the "Mexican Revolution," during which the common people succeeded in freeing themselves from the control of the conservative classes.

Madero, Huerta, and Carranza. For the next few years the country was in constant turmoil. Madero showed himself weak and impractical. He forgot his promised reforms and became more and more dependent on the army for support. The latter was commanded by General Victoriano Huerta. A number of uprisings occurred. Between February 9 and 18, 1913, during the so-called "Tragic Ten Days" (*La Decena Trágica*), there was continuous fighting in the capital. Huerta betrayed the president and joined the rebels, whom he in turn also betrayed. He next caused the president to be arrested. While Madero was being moved from one prison to another, he was assassinated.

Thereupon, Huerta made himself dictator. He attempted to pacify the country, but without success. Several revolutions broke out under the leadership of Venustiano Carranza, Francisco "Pancho" Villa, Emiliano Zapata, and others. Huerta's difficulties were increased by the refusal of recognition on the part of the United States government. The tension between the two countries increased when, in March, 1914, a party of American Marines was arrested in Tampico. Huerta apologized but refused to salute the American flag, as demanded by President Wilson. This resulted in the seizure of Veracruz by American forces on April 1. War was averted only by the threatening European situation and by mediation on the part of Argentina, Brazil, and Chile (the so-called ABC countries). Huerta resigned (July 15, 1914) and left the country, as did many wealthy aristocrats and clergymen.

On August 20, 1914, General Carranza became the executive and was recognized as *de facto* president of Mexico by the United States government. The following year he summoned a constituent assembly to draft a new constitution embodying the principles of the Revolution.

Meanwhile, a council of revolutionary generals assembled in Aguascalientes. Dominated by Villa, this group selected General Eulalio Gutiérrez to rule the country, replacing Carranza. The latter abandoned the capital and took refuge in Veracruz. Gutiérrez occupied Mexico City, but another convention of revolutionary leaders gathered, refused to recognize his authority, and proceeded to govern the country in its own name. At this time Alvaro Obregón, in command of Carranza's forces, defeated and annihilated Villa's army, entered the capital, and dismissed the convention. A few months later Carranza returned to the capital and was installed as president.

Relations with the United States continued to be strained because of the murder of several American citizens and the destruction of American property by soldiers of Villa in an attack on Columbus, New Mexico (March 9, 1916). This resulted in an American punitive military expedition against Villa, led by General Pershing in the latter part of that year. This expedition accomplished little and returned to the United States after some fruitless maneuvering in northern Mexico.

The Constitution of 1917. On December 1, 1916, the constituent assembly called by President Carranza met at Querétaro, and on February 5, 1917, a new constitution was promulgated, similar in some respects to the one of 1857, but containing several new provisions of radical character. Among these, Article 27 provided that the Church could not acquire, hold, or administer real property and stated that the ownership of the land and water within the republic was originally vested in the Mexican people; Article 33 conferred upon the president the power to expel without judicial process any foreigner whose presence in Mexico might be deemed inexpedient; and Article 123 provided that workers in industrial or commercial enterprises should have the right to share in the profits of those undertakings and be allowed the right to strike. The new constitution also provided for the distribution of land among the landless agricultural peons.

During the remainder of his administration Carranza showed himself unwilling to carry out in full the program of the Revolution and attempted to dictate the election of his successor. This resulted in revolutions, during which he was assassinated, and General Obregón assumed the executive power. On April 10, 1919, Emiliano Zapata, a representative of the common people fighting for land distribution, was captured and killed in an ambuscade prepared under the orders of President Carranza.

Reforms under the New Constitution. President Obregón, inaugurated on December 1, 1920, endeavored to enforce the new constitution. A number of laws on financial, educational, and land questions were promulgated. The large estates were broken up and the land distributed among the peasants. Industrial workers were organized into labor unions. The army was reorganized. The president endeavored to settle the remaining difficulties with the United States; his efforts resulted in the recognition of his government (August 31, 1923).

Obregón was succeeded by General Plutarco Elías Calles in 1924.

The new president enforced the religious provisions of the constitution and carried out an extensive program of educational reforms and land distribution. In 1928 the constitution was amended, extending the presidential term to six years and allowing the president to appoint supreme court judges.

The Church opposed the Calles government in every possible way. In July, 1928, General Obregón, who had succeeded Calles as president, was assassinated by a religious fanatic. Emilio Portes Gil was then chosen chief executive for a term ending in 1930. In the elections of 1929 Pascual Ortiz Rubio, candidate of the National Revolutionary Party, was elected. Despite attempts from the conservative elements to prevent his inauguration, Ortiz Rubio became president on February 5, 1930. Three years later he resigned because of a quarrel with General Calles, leader of the Revolutionary Party. General Abelardo L. Rodríguez then became provisional president, and on November 30, 1934, he was succeeded by General Lázaro Cárdenas, elected for a term ending in 1940.

During this period conditions in Mexico improved considerably. A labor code was promulgated on August 28, 1931, and a civil code, adopted in 1928, became effective on October 1, 1932. In 1933 a Six-Year Plan was adopted to hasten the socialization of Mexico, aiming at improving the standard of living of workers, promoting public education, completing agrarian and public works programs, and improving foreign relations.

President Cárdenas, a descendant of Tarascan Indians, was able to consolidate his power with the aid of the labor unions and the Agrarian Party, even to the point of forcing General Calles to relinquish the leadership of the Revolutionary Party and to leave the country (1935).

Cárdenas endeavored to carry out all the principles of the Revolution. He greatly increased the number of public schools; redistributed to the peons some 24 million acres of land; improved means of communication by building automobile roads and railroads; fostered betterment of the conditions of industrial workers by sponsoring the organization of the Confederation of Mexican Workers and aiding them to secure higher wages; and carried out a program of nationalization of the great industries by securing the adoption of a stringent expropriation law in 1936 and two years later by taking over the oil wells from the foreign corporations when the latter refused to increase the wages of their laborers and adopt other welfare measures as provided in a decision of the Federal Labor Board (December 18, 1937), later sustained by a decision of the Supreme Court (March 1, 1938). In May, 1940, President Cárdenas signed an agreement with one of the oil companies which set a pattern in subsequent years for the Mexican government to follow in settling with other foreign oil companies.

The presidential election held on July 7, 1940, was a contest between General Manuel Avila Camacho, the government's candidate, and General Juan Andreu Almazán, an independent candidate who was endeavoring to unify all opposition parties. General Avila Camacho was backed by the Mexican Revolution Party and by the Confederation of Mexican Workers. Both candidates supported the redistribution of land, some rehabilitation of the Church, protection for foreign capital, friendship with the United States, and opposition to Nazism and Communism. Despite unrest and threats of revolt, the government's candidate, General Avila Camacho, was declared elected and was inaugurated on December 1, 1940. The inaugural ceremonies were attended by Henry Wallace, the Vice-President-elect of the United States, who represented the American government as special ambassador of President Roosevelt.

Soon after his inauguration President Avila Camacho distributed among about 1.5 million peasants over 63 million acres of land formerly held in communal ownership; restored to the Church a good deal of its lost influence; reformed the judiciary; and took other measures of a conservative nature.

POLITICAL DEVELOPMENTS SINCE WORLD WAR II

Problems of War and Peace. As early as 1941 the United States and Mexico agreed on united defensive action in the event of foreign aggression. This agreement provided for reciprocal use of airfields, trade concessions, credits, and the regulation of certain exports. The claims of United States citizens arising from expropriated land property and oil concessions in Mexico were settled.

The following year an agreement was signed between the two countries providing for the purchase of Mexican silver by the United States to help to stabilize the Mexican currency.

Mexico broke off diplomatic relations with Japan on December 8, 1941; with Germany and Italy on December 11; with Bulgaria, Hungary, and Rumania on December 23; and with Vichy France on November 9 of the following year. On June 1, 1942, Mexico declared war on Germany, Italy, and Japan. President Roosevelt arrived in Mexico City on April 20, 1943, for negotiations with President Avila Camacho on questions of mutual interest. A few days later an agreement was announced to set up a joint commission on military and economic co-operation.

The United States supplied "lend-lease" aid and helped to train the Mexican naval and air forces which participated in the Pacific campaigns of World War II. In 1945 Mexico became a charter member of the United Nations.

A semireligious, fascistic group known as the *Unión Nacional de Sinarquistas,* organized in 1930, became very active after the war and was accused of plotting against the government. With Falangist affiliations, it was opposed to close relations with the United States and in favor of co-operation with Spain. This group, which at one time claimed a million members, was outlawed early in 1948.

In the election of July 7, 1946, Miguel Alemán Valdés, the candidate of the Party of Revolutionary Institutions, was elected president, easily defeating Dr. Ezequiel Padilla, of the Mexican Democratic Party, and two other candidates.

President Alemán visited the United States as an official guest April 29–May 13, 1947, returning the March 3–4 visit of President Truman to Mexico. It was announced at that time that the United States would purchase 50 million dollars' worth of Mexican pesos, over a period of four years, to help stabilize the peso-dollar exchange rate. A loan of an equal amount was to be granted to the Mexican government to finance economic projects.

In September, 1947, President Alemán announced that an agreement had been reached with another of the foreign oil companies settling the latter's claim in regard to properties expropriated in 1938.

By the middle of 1948 the financial situation of the country had become quite critical. On July 22, all foreign-exchange operations were suspended following negotiations with the International Monetary Fund, to establish a new peso-dollar exchange rate. To offset the unfavorable trade balance, the government imposed an embargo on the import of luxuries and increased the import duties on semi-luxury articles.

Three years later (July 27, 1951) a new agreement with the U. S. Stabilizing Fund was announced under which the Fund would purchase up to 50 million pesos, if necessary, to help to stabilize the peso-dollar rate of exchange. A period of considerable prosperity followed, due to increased commerce, great industrial development, and enlarged tourist travel.

Recent Progress. Adolfo Ruiz Cortines, the candidate of the Party of Revolutionary Institutions, won the election of July 6, 1952, defeating Vicente Lombardo Toledano, the candidate of the left-wing Popular Party and prominent labor leader.

The right to vote was granted to Mexican women by constitutional amendment approved by the Senate on March 11, 1953.

Since 1951 the Communist Party has not been legally sanctioned in Mexico, as it did not comply with the electoral law which requires that a political party should have at least 30,000 members in order to be officially recognized.

The election of 1958 was won by Adolfo López Mateos. President Eisenhower visited Mexico in February, 1959. Although no important discussions took place at that time, the pending questions between the two countries, mostly of an economic and financial nature, were discussed informally in August of that year by Dr. Milton Eisenhower and the Mexican authorities. President López Mateos returned President Eisenhower's visit in October, 1959.

Mexico broke off relations with Guatemala on January 23, 1959, following an incident in which Guatemalan planes machine-gunned three Mexican shrimp boats off the Pacific coast of Guatemala. Relations were resumed in September.

Mexico participated in the Punta del Este Conference (August, 1961) for implementation of the Alliance for Progress and in the January, 1962, meeting of the American ministers of foreign affairs at the same place to consider the Cuban question. Mexico was one of seven countries which opposed sanctions against Cuba.

Late in 1963 the dispute with the United States over the Chamizal tract of about 600 acres north of the Rio Grande in El Paso, Texas, was settled with recognition of Mexican rights to the land.

On July 5, 1964, Gustavo Díaz Ordaz was elected president to succeed López Mateos.

ECONOMIC, SOCIAL, AND CULTURAL DEVELOPMENT

Economic Development. Mexico today is a prosperous and fast-developing country. Its greatest source of wealth is found in its mineral and petroleum deposits, although agriculture is the basic occupation of the people. Variations of climate and soil permit a great diversification of crops ranging from henequen fiber, cotton, and sugar in the lowlands to wheat, corn, and coffee in the higher lands. The government has helped the rural population by the extension of agricultural credit, the promotion of irrigation projects, the division of farm lands, and mass education. Corn is the most important crop, and most of it is consumed domestically, as are cotton, beans, chick peas, and a variety of vegetables and fruits. A large percentage of the henequen fiber produced in Yucatan and Campeche is exported, as are bananas, chicle, and coffee. Cattle raising is increasingly important, although twice in recent decades foot and mouth disease has necessitated, with the co-operation of the United States, the killing of large herds in order to prevent a serious national disaster.

Mexico is one of the richest mineral countries in the world, and about half of the total exports consists of these products. Mexico produces about 40 per cent of the world's silver. Other important minerals are gold, lead, zinc, copper, iron, coal, and sulfur. About 2.6 billion barrels of petroleum reserves are known to exist. Since the expropriation of the foreign-owned oil properties in 1938, petroleum production has been controlled largely by Petróleos Mexicanos (PEMEX), a government corporation. About 30 per cent of the output of refineries is exported.

Manufacturing is devoted mainly to supplying finished goods to the nation's people and is concentrated chiefly in and near Mexico City. The greatest increase in manufacturing (43 per cent) occurred in the decade 1937–47. The construction industries have increased rapidly, leading to an expansion of the iron and steel industries. Highway building, constantly increasing, has promoted a cement industry of considerable proportions. Railroads are being improved and in some cases extended, while air traffic, with new and improved airfields, has expanded rapidly in recent years.

Social Development. The population of Mexico is estimated at more than 33 million, with most of the people living in rural districts and small towns. The capital, Mexico City, has more than 4 million inhabitants. Standards of living vary, but compared to those of some other Latin American countries they are relatively high. Mexico should not be classed as an "underdeveloped country." Living conditions among the industrial and agricultural laboring classes have steadily improved in recent years because of labor and social legislation, and there is a growing middle class with considerable political and economic influence. Since the Revolution the

Mexican people have become very conscious of their Indian origins, and a cultural re-evaluation of Western civilization in terms of the Indian is in progress.

Education. The responsibility for public education is shared jointly by the federal and state governments. Primary education is free and compulsory. Special emphasis has been placed on rural education, and cultural missions composed of educators, health workers, teachers of arts, crafts, and music, moving picture operators, and authorities on community leadership are regularly sent to the rural districts. In 1944 a nation-wide anti-illiteracy campaign was inaugurated aiming to teach, in two years, some 10 million people to read Spanish. The National University in the capital is one of the leading institutions in the Hemisphere. Many other schools of higher learning and for special technical training are located in the capital and in other cities of the country.

Literary and Artistic Development. Mexico has a varied and rich literature. Among the most important writers of the nineteenth and twentieth centuries are the following: Ignacio Rodríguez Galván (1816–42), author of *Muñoz, visitador de México, La Hija del oidor, La Visión de Moctezuma,* and many other romantic dramas; Fernando Calderón y Beltrán (1809–45), dramatist and lyric poet, author of the plays *Reynaldo y Elina* and *El Torneo;* José María Roa Bárcena (1827–1908), poet and author of the *Ensayo de una historia anecdótica de México* and *Leyendas mexicanas;* Juan Díaz Covarrubias (1837–59), poet and novelist, author of *Gil Gómez, el insurgente;* Ignacio Manuel Altamirano (1833–93), poet, essayist, novelist; José Joaquín Fernández de Lizardi (1774–1827), author of the novel *Periquillo sarniento,* still read today; Justo Sierra (1814–61), novelist, author of *Un Año en el hospital de San Lázaro* and *La Hija del judío;* Pantaleón Tovar (1828–76), novelist inspired by social conditions in Mexico; Vicente Riva Palacio (1832–91), author of *Calvario y tabor,* an historical novel; Manuel Sánchez Mármol (1839–1912), a prolific novelist, author of *El Misionero de la Cruz, Pocahontas,* and *Juanita Sousa;* Alfonso M. Maldonado (b. 1849), author of *Nobles y plebeos* and other novels; Manuel José Othón (1858–1906), one of the best Mexican poets; Manuel Gutiérrez Nájera (1859–95), a poet of gentle melancholy; Federico Gamboa (b. 1864), realistic novelist of merit; Amado Nervo (1870–1919), the greatest modernist poet of Latin America after Rubén Darío; Mariano Azuela (b. 1873), one of the greatest Latin American novelists, author of *Los de abajo, La*

Malhora, and *La Luciérnaga;* Martín Luis Guzmán, author of *El Aguila y la serpiente* and *La Sombra del caudillo*, powerful novels of the Mexican Revolution; Gregorio López y Fuentes (b. 1895), author of *Campamento, Mi General*, and *El Indio;* Xavier Icaza, Jr., author of *Panchito chapopote*, a very humorous novel in the modern manner; Rafael F. Múñoz, author of *Vámonos con Pancho Villa, Si me han de matar mañana, El Hombre malo*, and many other popular novels; Nellie Campobello, author of *Cartucho;* Cipriano Campos Alatorre, author of *Los Fusilados;* José Manuel Puig Cassauranc, author of *Los Juan López Sánchez y López Sánchez de López*, a novel; José Mancisidor, Francisco Sarquis, and Lorenzo Turrent, recent revolutionary writers; José Vasconcelos (1882–1959), a distinguished educator and writer, author of the important sociological study *La Raza cósmica;* Alfonso Reyes (b. 1889), poet, essayist, and literary critic.

In recent years the plastic arts have been intensively cultivated in Mexico. Among the most important painters, the following may be mentioned: Diego Rivera, the best-known Mexican painter; Roberto Montenegro, Adolfo Best Maugard, Rodríguez Lozano, José del Pozo, Francisco Gómez Rul, Alfonso Cardone, Saturnino Herrán, José Clemente Orozco, Agustín Velázquez Chávez, David Alfaro Siqueiros, Rufino Tamayo, and Julio Castellanos. Among the well-known sculptors are Gabriel Guerra, Manuel de Arzave, and Luis Hidalgo.

In music, Mexico has long been famous for its folk songs of great beauty and captivating rhythm. In recent years two great composers have appeared—Manuel Ponce and Carlos Chávez, the latter being one of the outstanding musical composers of the whole Hemisphere at the present time. Daniel Ayala and Luis Sandi should also be named.

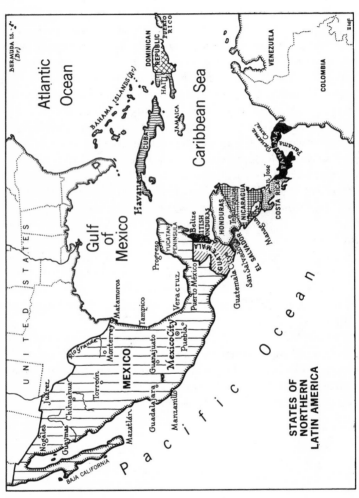

Fig. XVI-1. States of Northern Latin America.

CHAPTER XVI

THE FIVE REPUBLICS OF
CENTRAL AMERICA

THE DISASTROUS CONSEQUENCES to the body politic resulting from the lack of a self-conscious middle class are more noticeable in Central America than perhaps in any other Latin American group of countries. Here, too, the privileged classes have struggled to remain in control of government, opposed by a few well-intentioned but inexperienced liberals, while the common people in general have looked upon the struggle with indifference. The consequences have been revolutions, despotism, and general chaos.

UNITED CENTRAL AMERICA (1821–38)

Before independence, the territory of Central America formed the Captaincy General of Guatemala, including the province of Guatemala, the intendancies of Chiapas, San Salvador, Nicaragua, and Honduras, and Costa Rica. A section of Nicaragua and Honduras, on the Caribbean (Mosquito Land or Mosquitia), was inhabited by primitive Indians who maintained their independence from Spain during colonial days. Buccaneers established posts along the coast, and gradually British settlements grew there. In 1786 Spain recognized British sovereignty over a portion of Yucatan and present Guatemala in exchange for the withdrawal of the British from the rest of Central America. Today this territory forms the British colony of Belize (British Honduras).

Of the other Central American provinces, Chiapas declared its independence at about the same time as the rest (1821), but separated from Guatemala and adhered to the Mexican Empire independently, remaining as part of that country to the present day; and Soconusco, also a part of Guatemala, was annexed to Mexico in 1842. The other five provinces formed the present nations Guatemala, Honduras, El

Salvador, Nicaragua, and Costa Rica. Panama, occupying the rest of the Isthmus, was part of Colombia until 1903; it will be studied in a subsequent chapter.*

Central America as Part of Mexico. In 1821 Agustín de Iturbide, Emperor of Mexico, wrote to the patriot junta of Guatemala urging that Guatemala join to Mexico. Despite opposition from many patriots, the local aristocracy was able to bring about a favorable decision. On January 5, 1822, Central America was declared annexed to Mexico. Deputies were then sent to the Mexican capital, where the imperial congress declared the people of Central America to be Mexican citizens.

Nevertheless, sections of El Salvador, Honduras, and Nicaragua held aloof, and Iturbide sent an army under the command of Brigadier Vicente Filísola to enforce his authority there. Filísola had just finished establishing order when he received the news of Iturbide's abdication. He immediately called a general congress of the Central American provinces. This congress met on June 24, 1823, and declared the former provinces of the Captaincy of Guatemala free and independent as a confederation under the name of *"Provincias Unidas del Centro de América."* Their independence was soon after (August 1, 1824) acknowledged by the Mexican Republic. Filísola and his soldiers had left Central America in August, 1823.

The United Provinces of Central America. The same congress then proceeded to discuss and adopt a constitution and to legislate in regard to various matters. This assembly was presided over by the distinguished patriot, José Matías Delgado, known as the "Father of the Central American Fatherland." Two major parties or factions appeared: the *Serviles,* who wished to have a centralized and strong government; and the *Radicales,* who favored a federal republic and the abolition of the abuses and privileges of the conservative classes. A provisional governing junta was appointed. The constitution adopted (promulgated on November 22, 1824) was modeled after that of the United States. It provided for a federal government of the five states (Chiapas was not included, although given an opportunity to join later on), with the traditional division of powers. The executive power was to be exercised by a federal president and a chief of state for each of the confederated states. No provision was made for the establishment of a federal capital. Guatemala City, the stronghold of the conservatives, became the seat of the federal gov-

* For Panama, see pages 221–227.

ernment. Slavery was abolished by the assembly (April 17–23, 1824), and the Catholic faith was declared to be that of the State.

When the first congress met under the new constitution, it elected Manuel José Arce, a liberal, president of the Confederation, and José Cecilio del Valle, a conservative, as vice-president. The latter refused to accept the position and was replaced by Mariano Beltranena.

Although well-intentioned, Arce soon quarreled with his own party and with the state authorities of Guatemala. When he summoned an extraordinary congress to deal with the political situation in that state, a military uprising took place in El Salvador under the pretext that the president had exceeded his powers (December 6, 1826). Other states (Honduras, Nicaragua, and Costa Rica) joined El Salvador, and in 1828 General Francisco Morazán at the head of a Honduran army defeated the federal forces and compelled them to evacuate El Salvador, which they had invaded in an effort to quell the rebellion. Morazán then entered El Salvador's capital in triumph and, collecting new forces, marched against Guatemala City. Although repulsed at first, he later defeated the federal forces again, captured the city (April 13, 1829), and established a military dictatorship. The congress was recalled and a new president, Pedro Molina, was elected. Many conservative leaders, including several churchmen, were expelled. The monasteries were abolished, except the Bethlehem Order, to which was entrusted the conduct of religious services. Church and monastical property was confiscated.

Morazán's Regime. In 1830 General Morazán was elected president of the Confederation. He was a man of strong character, cultured, capable, and liberal-minded. During his ten-year administration he promoted public education, fostered industry and commerce, and reorganized the administrative machinery. He also encouraged immigration. The crime code drafted by Edward Livingston for Louisiana and rejected by that state was adopted in Central America in 1832. Marriage became a civil contract, and the civil registration of births and deaths was made compulsory. In 1835 Morazán moved the capital to San Salvador.

These reforms stirred the antagonism of the conservative classes. Several uprisings took place. An epidemic of cholera was attributed to the government, which, so the country people were told, had caused the waters to be poisoned in order to destroy all the Indian population. The Indians rose in rebellion, led by a half-caste named Rafael Carrera, born in Guatemala of the humblest parents. Although illiterate, he possessed great native powers of leadership and inspired his Indian soldiers with absolute devotion to him. Under the battle cry of "Long Live Religion and Death to Foreigners," Carrera and his followers murdered several judges appointed under the Livingston code and committed all sorts of depredations. Defeated in his first encounters with the government forces and compelled to take refuge in the mountains, Carrera rallied his forces and in 1838 marched against Guatemala City. The authorities of that city warded him off by paying a large ransom. Carrera then marched against the city of Mita, which he occupied. There followed a series of battles in which Carrera was sometimes defeated and sometimes victorious over government troops.

The Collapse of the Confederation. In the midst of this turmoil the Confederation collapsed. Authorized by the federal congress— which on May 18, 1838, passed an act permitting the various states to assume the form of government they wished—Nicaragua declared herself independent, and her example was followed by Honduras and Costa Rica.

General Morazán was elected head of the government of El Salvador on July 8, 1839. Suspicious of his intentions, the other states made war against him. In this struggle Carrera, then in control of Guatemala, joined against Morazán, who was defeated and in 1840 compelled to leave the country. There followed a general massacre of liberals throughout Central America.

In 1842 Morazán returned to Central America, overthrew Braulio Carrillo, the dictator of Costa Rica, was himself elected president of that country and at once endeavored again to bring about the union of the several states. Defeated once more by the united forces of the other states, he was captured, condemned to death, and shot on September 15, 1842.

The same year delegates from El Salvador, Honduras, and Nicaragua met at Chinandega to draft a new constitution creating a league of states to be called "The Central American Confederation." This league ended two years later when Honduras and El Salvador attacked Nicaragua. Since then, from time to time other attempts have been made to bring about the political union of all or some of the Central American states. These attempts have all failed, in great measure because of regional jealousies.

GUATEMALA

Among the Central American states, Guatemala has suffered perhaps the most from despotism. From the dissolution of the Confederation to 1944 her politics were under the control of four strong men: Rafael Carrera (1838–65), Justo Rufino Barrios (1873–85), Manuel Estrada Cabrera (1896–1920), and Jorge Ubico (1931–44). Since then the political life of the country has been confused and disorderly.

The Rule of Carrera. From 1838 to his death in 1865, the actual ruler of Guatemala was Rafael Carrera. In 1839 he deposed the president, General Carlos Salazar, and put Mariano Rivera Paz in his place. One of the first acts of Rivera Paz was to declare the independence of Guatemala. In 1843 Carrera himself became president. He made war against the neighboring nations whenever their governments did not suit him. He hated all liberals and took great pleasure in helping to overthrow liberal presidents in El Salvador and Honduras. Compelled to retire from power in 1847, he came back two years later as commander of the army. In 1851 he was elected president once more, and three years later he was declared president for life.

The Rule of Barrios. After Carrera's death in 1865, another conservative, Vicente Cerna, became president. But in 1871 the liberals regained control of the government, under the leadership of Justo Rufino Barrios, who ruled despotically for twelve years (1873–85). He was a man of progressive ideas and brought about many reforms: railroads were built, public education was fostered, and the country experienced a certain amount of economic prosperity. During his regime many large landowners were deprived of their property, several conservative leaders were exiled, and the religious orders were expelled. On December 11, 1879, a new liberal constitution was promulgated.

In 1885 President Barrios was killed while engaged in war against El Salvador in an endeavor to bring about once more the union of the Central American states. Manuel Lisandro Barillas thereupon became president and ruled until 1892. In November, 1887, the constitution was amended in order to allow the election of the president by direct popular vote and to extend the presidential term to six years.

After Barillas, José María Reyna Barrios, a nephew of the great liberal leader, became president, being elected in a comparatively free election. In 1897 he made himself dictator and was assassinated the following year. The vice-president, Manuel Estrada Cabrera, became acting executive and later was regularly elected to the presidency of the republic.

The Rule of Estrada Cabrera. Estrada Cabrera was a cultured, suave, but ruthless man who ruled for twenty-two consecutive years. He suppressed his enemies and intimidated the legislature into complete obedience to his wishes. There were many rebellions during his regime. In 1906 a revolt led by General Barillas spread to the other Central American states. The United States and Mexico intervened, offering their mediation, with the result that a Central American Peace Conference assembled in Washington (1907) and a Central American Court of Justice was created to settle disputes between any of the Central American states. The representatives of the five states signed a treaty of peace and friendship, another of extradition, a convention on the Court of Justice, and another establishing an International Bureau and a Pedagogic Institute. The Court of Justice was inaugurated in Cartago, Costa Rica, on May 25, 1908, and the International Bureau was opened on September 15 of the same year in Guatemala.

Several cases were submitted to the Court, but it ceased to function after Nicaragua, in 1918, refused to recognize the Court's jurisdiction in a decision regarding the Bryan-Chamorro Treaty with the United States.

In 1920 Estrada Cabrera was finally overthrown, being succeeded first by Carlos Herrera y Luna and a few months later by General José María Orellana, who governed until his death on September 26, 1926.

General Lázaro Chacón was the next president. In 1928 the constitution was again amended to provide for universal suffrage. General Chacón's administration was a progressive one; but in 1930, because of a serious illness, he retired, and a conservative, Baudilio Palma, was elected provisional president. Palma was forced to resign, being replaced by General Manuel Orellana. The United States did not recognize the latter's government, and on January 3, 1931, the national assembly elected José M. Reyna Andrade to rule during President Chacón's illness. The latter, however, died on April 10, 1931, while abroad in search of medical assistance for his ailments, and General Jorge Ubico was regularly elected for a term of six years, until February 14, 1937.

The Rule of Ubico. General Ubico gradually assumed the dictatorship of the country. He carried out certain reforms: wages were improved under government legislation; the Alien Law was amended to afford a certain measure of protection to native workers and business men against foreign competition; and means of communication were improved. In 1936 a reciprocal trade agreement was signed with the United States, and treaties of limits were agreed upon with El Salvador and Honduras settling the boundary questions with those two nations. Attempts at revolution were severely suppressed. In 1935 a "plebiscite" called by a constituent convention provided for General Ubico's continuation in office without re-election. The following year the president announced that he would remain in power for another period of six years at the expiration of his term in 1937.

When General Ubico assumed the presidency in 1931 the public debt of Guatemala was $22,237,315, of which $6,426,977 represented internal indebtedness. By refunding the bonds held by United States citizens and other measures, President Ubico was able to reduce the public debt to $10,246,507 (April, 1940). The Financial Committee of the Guatemalan Congress voted, on that account, to make a gift of $80,000 to President Ubico.

There were, however, some people in Guatemala who criticized the administration and conspired against the president. On December 28, 1940, thirteen would-be rebels were shot by order of General Ubico.

Political Developments since World War II. Guatemala declared war on Japan, December 8, 1941, and on the other Axis powers, December 12. The United States established an air base in the country to aid in the protection of the Panama Canal and Central America. In 1945 Guatemala became a charter member of the United Nations.

On July 1, 1944, President Ubico resigned as a result of widespread public disturbances following the suspension of constitutional guarantees. A junta of four army officers took over the government. Three days later the congress selected General Federico Ponce to be provisional president. However, on October 22, rioting in the capital led to the overthrow of General Ponce's government and its replacement by a junta of two army officers and one civilian.

Presidential elections were held on December 21, Dr. Juan José Arévalo, a liberal, being elected by a large majority. He took office on March 15, 1945, for a four-year term, which he finished despite political unrest and plots against his government.

The presidential election of November 10, 1950, was won by Lieutenant Colonel Jacobo Arbenz Guzmán, the candidate of the Revolutionary Action and the National Regeneration parties. Inaugurated on March 15, 1951, he soon showed extreme leftist tendencies. Extensive land-reform legislation was adopted by the congress with the president's backing, giving the state the power to expropriate land not in cultivation and to lease it in small holdings to peasants. Other measures of a socialist character were adopted. As the administration became more and more infiltrated by Communists, violence and persecution against the conservative classes and the Church were undertaken. When arms were shipped to Guatemala from Communist countries, the United States decided to supply Honduras and Nicaragua with arms, at the same time prohibiting the sale of war weapons by American citizens to Guatemala.

President Arbenz appealed to the United Nations Security Council and suspended constitutional guarantees throughout the national territory.

On June 18, a group of armed Guatemalan exiles led by Colonel Carlos Castillo Armas crossed the frontier from Honduras. After defeating the government troops, the revolutionists marched against the capital. President Arbenz resigned on June 27 in favor of Colonel Carlos Díaz, head of the national armed forces. Before entering the capital, Castillo Armas demanded the arrest of all Communists in the country. On June 29, Colonel Díaz was replaced by Colonel Monzón, who promptly ordered the arrest of some two thousand persons known to be Communists or Communist sympathizers and who had been officeholders under Arbenz.

The armed struggle ended on July 2, with the appointment of a five-man military junta headed by Colonel Monzón as interim president. A few days later Colonel Castillo Armas was made president. An officer in the Guatemalan army, and a devout Roman Catholic, he had been arrested in 1950 after an abortive revolution against the government but had escaped and taken refuge abroad.

On March 1, 1956, a new constitution went into effect. A Communist plot to spread panic and disorder in the country was discovered and a state of emergency was decreed by President Castillo Armas.

The president was shot dead in the presidential palace on July 26,

1957, by one of the palace guards who apparently had Communist affiliations. Vice-President Luis Arturo González López assumed the presidency in a provisional character.

Presidential elections were then announced to be held on October 21. Rioting and violence led to the replacement (October 24) of González López with a three-man military junta, headed by Colonel Oscar Mendonza Azurdía. The election of October 21 was then annulled by the congress and Second Vice-President Guillermo Flores Avendano assumed the government as provisional president.

On January 19, 1958, new presidential elections were held, and on February 14 General Miguel Ydígoras Fuentes was declared elected by the congress. General Ydígoras took office on March 2, 1958.

In November, 1960, an uprising broke out in Puerto Barrios and other places, apparently inspired by Communist and left-wing agitators. President Ydígoras accused Cuban Premier Castro of complicity and requested United States planes and warships to protect the country's shores from further attempts at invasion.

Diplomatic relations with Mexico, broken off early in 1959, when Guatemalan planes had attacked three Mexican shrimp boats off the Pacific coast of Guatemala, were resumed in September.

Early in 1960 Guatemala protested against inclusion of British Honduras (Belize) in the British Commonwealth, claiming that Belize was part of its territory. Britain rejected the claim.

Guatemala is a signatory of the Central American Economic Integration Treaties of 1960.

On March 30, 1963, Ydígoras was overthrown by an army coup led by Colonel Enrique Peralta Azurdía, who temporarily suspended the constitution and dissolved the congress.

Economic, Social, and Cultural Development. Guatemala has the largest population of the Central American republics, with about 3.5 million people, or about 40 per cent of the total population of the five republics. The great majority of the people are Indians who have retained the languages and customs of their Maya ancestors.

Significant economic progress has been made in the past few years, and in 1956 a five-year economic development plan and an agrarian reform law were adopted. The latter gave the government power to expropriate agricultural lands to be distributed under certain conditions in small holdings to peasant farmers. Special loans for special purposes have been frequently made by the United States and by international agencies.

Coffee is the leading export product, with about 80 per cent being sent abroad. Bananas are exported in large amounts. Sugar is a fast-growing industry. Cotton is produced widely, since the boll weevil is not found in the country. The cattle industry has developed steadily and herds are being improved gradually. In 1934 a new mining and petroleum law was enacted with highly favorable provisions for operating companies which have engaged in prospecting in various parts of the country. Manufacturing is limited largely to textiles and other products for local consumption. Railroad mileage has remained static, but highway mileage is slowly increasing and air transportation is now important.

At the head of the educational system is the National University of San Carlos in the capital, which, especially in its summer sessions, attracts students from the United States. Several technical schools and public and private primary and high schools provide an inadequate education for the increasing population.

Many native Guatemalan writers have achieved fame outside of their country. One of these was Antonio José de Irisarri (1786–1868), a wealthy man who went to live in Peru and Chile, where he played an important part in the independence movement. He founded periodicals which greatly influenced cultural development in South America. He also wrote poetry. Another distinguished writer born in Guatemala was José de Batres y Montúfar (1809–44), a poet of note and a writer of prose. Other writers were: Juan Diéguez (1813–66), a popular poet; José Milla (1822–82), a prolific writer, author of a *Historia de Guatemala* and several historical novels; Máximo Soto Hall, historian and journalist; José Cecilio del Valle (1780–1834), a sociologist and a thinker far ahead of his time; Monteforte Toledo, novelist; and Miguel Angel Asturias, author of historical fiction.

HONDURAS

Political Affairs to 1940. Honduras was ruled by the liberals from the dissolution of the Confederation to 1840, when President Carrera of Guatemala aided the conservatives to overthrow the party in power. From that year to 1852 the country was ruled directly or indirectly by Francisco Ferrera. Honduras participated in the Chinandega Congress to organize a confederation of El Salvador, Nicaragua, and Honduras. But this confederation lasted only until 1845, ending in war between the three states.

In 1855 the liberal president, Trinidad Cabañas, was overthrown by Carrera of Guatemala, being replaced by a conservative named Santos Guardiola. Seven years later, however, Guardiola was assassinated. His successor, Victoriano Castellanos, who was defeated in war against Guatemala and Nicaragua, was forced to resign and was followed by José María Medina. From 1872, when President Medina was overthrown, to 1911, Honduras had the following principal presidents: Ponciano Leiva, who was forced to resign by President Barrios of Guatemala; Marco Aurelio Soto; Luis Bográn, who ruled for eight years; again Leiva, who was once more forced to leave the presidency; his successor, Domingo Vázquez, who was forced to resign as a result of war with Nicaragua; Policarpo Bonilla, during whose administration the country was united with Nicaragua and El Salvador; General Terencio Sierra; and once more Bonilla, who quarreled with President Zelaya of Nicaragua and involved his country in a dispute with that country and El Salvador. When war seemed imminent, the United States and Mexico offered their mediation and prevented bloodshed. At the Central American Conference held in Washington in 1907, it was agreed that Honduras would henceforth always remain neutral in all Central American conflicts.

Miguel R. Dávila became president and ruled until 1911, when he was overthrown by Manuel Bonilla. The United States again intervened, and a conference between Dávila and Bonilla took place on board the U. S. S. *Tacoma*. As a result, Bonilla was allowed to become president. When he died, in 1913, the Vice-President, Dr. Francisco Bertrand, took his place. He was regularly elected for a term ending in 1920. The next executive was Rafael López Gutiérrez, who governed as a dictator after his term was over. Civil war having broken out as a consequence, the United States offered its mediation, and a new election was held. In 1924 Vicente Tosta was elected president. But the following year he was replaced by Miguel Paz Barahona, who was regularly elected for the term of 1925–29. In that year Dr. Vicente Mejía Colindres was elected to serve until 1933. During his administration several uprisings took place, particularly in 1931, when a revolution of Communist origin occurred.

In 1933 Tiburcio Carías Andino became president for a term to end in 1937. But in 1936 he pushed through the assembly a bill calling for the revision of the Constitution of 1924, nullifying the ban against re-election and extending the presidential term to six years. A constituent assembly adopted a new constitution, which went into effect on April 15, 1936, and extended the incumbent president's term of office until January 1, 1943.

Despite several uprisings, some economic progress was made, but a new agrarian law passed on April 20, 1936, prohibiting the sale of land on the eastern coast, curtailed the activities of the great banana companies and caused unemployment in that region.

President Carías Andino reorganized the country's administration by centralizing power in the hands of the executive. In 1939 the congress extended the president's term until 1949.

Political Developments since World War II. Honduras declared war on Japan, December 8, 1941, and on Germany and Italy, December 12. The Carías regime broke off diplomatic relations with Vichy France on November 13, 1942. In 1945 Honduras became a charter member of the United Nations.

Beginning in 1941 President Carías Andino instituted a national political reorganization which increased the powers of the executive. Most of the municipal governments were replaced by district commissions. On June 4, 1944, widespread discontent caused the administration to declare a state of siege and to ban public demonstrations. The president issued a manifesto pleading for law and order, but resentment over the repressive measures of the government resulted in constant unrest throughout the country. In the election of October 10, 1948, Juan Manuel Gálvez was elected president for a six-year term. The opposition candidates had withdrawn, claiming that the government had not adequately safeguarded the right to vote.

The election of 1954 was won by the liberals, who did not, however, secure an absolute majority, as required by the constitution in the election of a president and vice-president; Julio Lozano Díaz assumed the presidency in a provisional character.

On October 21, 1956, Lozano Díaz was overthrown by a bloodless military coup, and a three-man military junta assumed control of the government. The revolution was caused by alleged irregularities during the election of delegates to a constituent assembly scheduled to meet on October 7.

New elections were held on September 21, 1957, under the sponsorship of the governing junta. The assembly met on the appointed day to elect José Ramón Villeda Morales president of the republic for a six-year term. A new constitution replaced that of 1936.

On October 3, 1963, Villeda Morales was overthrown in a bloody coup headed by Colonel Osvaldo López Arellano.

In 1957 hostilities broke out between Honduras and Nicaragua over an unsettled boundary in the Mosquito Coast region. The Council of the Organization of American States sent an investigating committee to the region and both sides withdrew their troops.

On November 18, 1960, the International Court of Justice stated that it regarded the arbitration award of 1906 by King Alfonso XIII of Spain as valid. Nicaragua accepted the decision, and Honduras took possession of the disputed territory.

Economic, Social, and Cultural Development. Honduras, although it has about the same area as Guatemala, has much poorer soil and a less favorable climate. The population is about two million people, mostly of mixed race: white, Negro, and Indian. Agricultural possibilities have not been fully utilized, but cacao, cotton, corn, sugar cane, coffee, tobacco, henequen, and many other tropical and subtropical products can be produced. Lack of good transportation has hindered economic development of all types. Corn is the most important product but it is consumed locally, while bananas are important chiefly for export. The cattle industry is increasing, and beef and hides are exported to some extent. Mahogany is the leading lumber industry and most of it is exported. Gold and silver are the chief mining products, one mine having produced continuously since 1888.

Honduras has suffered the effects of severe economic depression during the last few years. In 1959, total trade had declined 7 per cent as compared with that for 1958. It was expected that the Economic Integration Treaties of 1960 with other Central American countries would contribute to alleviate the situation.

Schools, both public and private, do not adequately provide education for the national needs. At the head of the educational system is the Central University; there are special schools of music, law, medicine, pharmacy, and engineering.

The following are among the most important writers of Honduras: José Trinidad Reyes, founder of the University of Honduras and author of the famous *Pastorelas;* Juan Ramón Molina, a poet; Rómulo E. Durón, a historian; Arturo Mejía Nieto (b. 1900), novelist and critic; Alberto Membreño (b. 1859), historian and philologist; Luis Andrés Zúñiga, a poet, author of *Aguilas conquistadoras;* Froilán Turcios (b. 1877), poet and novelist; and Rafael Heliodoro

Valle (1891–1959), poet, historian, and bibliographer of note, who lived for a number of years in Mexico.

NICARAGUA

Early Political Developments. From 1821 to 1825 Nicaragua was immersed in civil war, which ended only with the intervention of the government of the Confederation. A constituent assembly met at León on April 10, 1825, electing a chief of the state and other officials. It also adopted a constitution (promulgated the following year) which gave the legislative branch of government predominance over the executive branch. Immediately thereafter, the two main factions (the conservatives, in control of the city of Granada on Lake Nicaragua, and the liberals, centering around León, to the northeast, near the Pacific coast) renewed the war for control of the government. Peace was restored three years later by an army sent from Guatemala by Morazán, then dictator of that country. Dionisio Herrera became chief of state in Nicaragua in 1829.

On April 30, 1838, Nicaragua declared her independence from the Confederation under the presidency of José Núñez. A new constitution was adopted. Four years later the country took part, with other Central American states, in the war against Morazán, who had assumed the government of Costa Rica. The war ended with the defeat of Morazán.

In 1841 Pablo Benigno became supreme ruler of the country. His government was comparatively peaceful. At this time a dispute arose with Great Britain over the sovereignty of the San Juan River. In 1842 Nicaragua participated in the Chinandega convention and became part of the Confederation, which lasted until 1845. In that year new complications with Great Britain ended in the recognition on the part of Nicaragua of the British protectorate over Mosquitia.

In 1845 José León Sandoval took over the government and endeavored to restore peace. The constitution was amended two years later, and the union of El Salvador, Honduras, and Nicaragua was decided upon. This union was dissolved in 1853.

In 1849 Norberto Ramírez was elected president. The following year a contract with United States citizens who had organized a transit company was signed by the Nicaraguan government granting the company the right of way across the Isthmus via the San Juan River and Lake Nicaragua. A treaty of commerce and navigation was also signed with the United States. Rivalry between the United States and Great Britain for control of the Isthmus resulted in the signing of the Clayton-Bulwer Treaty of 1850, under which neither nation was to seek exclusive control over any part of Central America. This treaty was later superseded by the Hay-Pauncefote Treaty of 1901 giving to the United States the right to build a canal across the Isthmus.

In 1853 Frutos Chamorro became the executive. The following year the liberals under the leadership of Máximo Jérez and Francisco Castellón took up arms against Chamorro. They secured the aid of one Byron Cole, an American, with whom they had entered into some sort of immigration contract. This contract was then transferred by Cole to William Walker, who led an expedition of American adventurers to Nicaragua. In 1855 President Chamorro died, and José M. Estrada became president.

Walker in Central America. Born in Nashville, Tennessee, in 1824, Walker was a man with some education and broad experience of the world. He had led an expedition to the northwestern part of Mexico with the intention of declaring that region independent, but had been defeated. When, in 1855, he turned up in Nicaragua, he immediately attacked the town of Rivas, but was compelled to withdraw. Later he returned to battle, defeated the so-called "legitimist" forces, and then marched against their stronghold, the city of Granada. Entering into negotiations with the Granada leaders, he set up Patricio Rivas as president, and was himself appointed commander of the army.

Walker re-enforced his army with more American adventurers, and when General Corral, then Secretary of War, plotted against him, he had Corral arrested and shot. Gradually he antagonized all the Central American states. Walker also made the mistake of quarreling with the managers of the Transit Company, the American corporation enjoying the concession of transit across the Isthmus. As a result, he was deprived of their help in the transportation of soldiers and supplies. Hard-pressed by the united Central American forces, Walker was defeated and eventually surrendered to the commander of an American man-of-war (1857). Three years later he returned to Honduras, but there he was wounded, captured, tried, and shot.

The Rule of Martínez. For a while the two political factions worked together under the leadership of Generals Máximo Jérez (liberal) and Tomás Martínez (conservative). But after 1860 this co-operation ceased. In 1863 General Martínez gained the upper hand, and during nearly thirty years the government remained under the control of the Granada faction, the presidency being passed from one conservative leader to another. Elections were held, but they merely registered the will of the party in power.

Some economic progress was made during this period. Railroads were built, coffee-growing was introduced, and commerce prospered. It was also during this period that the religious orders were abolished.

In 1889 Dr. Roberto Sacasa became president, being the first liberal in many years to be chosen for the position. His administration was bitterly opposed by conservatives, and in 1893 José Santos Zelaya, a young liberal from Managua, became president after a successful revolution. He ruled the country from 1894 to 1909.

Zelaya and His Successors. President Zelaya promoted commerce, agriculture, and transportation. Gradually his methods became dictatorial because of the constant revolts started by the conservatives. In the latter years of his administration he granted monopolies, issued large amounts of unconvertible paper money, and interfered constantly in the affairs of the neighboring states. On June 20, 1895, the Treaty of Amapala was signed between Nicaragua, El Salvador, and Honduras, providing for the restoration of a Central American Union (*República Mayor de Centro América*). This union was dissolved three years later by a revolution that started in El Salvador.

In 1909 a successful revolution placed in power the conservative leader Juan J. Estrada. Zelaya had disregarded the rights of foreigners and had had difficulties with the United States. When he was unable to maintain himself in power any longer, he resigned in favor of José Madriz. The latter was overthrown by Estrada, who assumed the presidency. On November 5, 1910, an agreement was signed with the United States whereby Estrada was recognized as chief executive of Nicaragua. Early the following year he was legally elected by a constituent convention.

In 1911, a new agreement was signed with the United States whereby the latter pledged help in securing a loan for improvements, to be guaranteed through the control of Nicaraguan customs by an American board. The national constituent assembly then elected General Luis Mena president for four years, but the United States demanded that the people of Nicaragua be afforded the opportunity freely to choose their president. Adolfo Díaz was then elected. On May 11, 1911, he was inaugurated and maintained himself in power with the help of a force of United States Marines stationed in the country. During the Díaz administration, the Bryan-Chamorro Treaty between Nicaragua and the United States was signed (1914). The latter nation was granted the right in perpetuity to construct a canal via the San Juan River and Lake Nicaragua, and it also acquired by a ninety-nine years' lease a naval base on the Gulf of Fonseca, as well as two coaling stations. The three million dollars paid by the United States for this lease were to be used mainly for the funding of the public debt of Nicaragua.

In the next election (1916) General Emiliano Chamorro was chosen president with the support of the United States. The same year, the Bryan-Chamorro Treaty was ratified by the United States Senate and went into effect.

In 1921 Diego Manuel Chamorro was inaugurated president. He died before the end of his term and was replaced by Carlos Solórzano. In 1925 a new revolution broke out under the leadership of former President Emiliano Chamorro, and when on January 17, 1926, President Solórzano resigned, Chamorro took his place as executive. The United States refused recognition to his government. As a consequence, a revolution broke out, and American forces were landed to supervise the new elections. Adolfo Díaz was again elected and inaugurated. Thereupon, Juan Bautista Sacasa, who had been chosen vice-president in 1925, with Chamorro as president—but who had been compelled to leave the country—returned to Nicaragua and established an independent government at Puerto Cabezas.

Thanks to the intervention of the United States, a new election was held under the supervision of American officials (1928), and José Moncada, a liberal, was chosen president. He was duly inaugurated, but in 1931 guerrilla warfare broke out under the leadership of Augusto Sandino. In 1932 Dr. Sacasa was elected to the presidency. He governed the country until 1936, when General Anastasio Somoza, commander of the national guard, became candidate for the presidency. Aided by the liberals, headed by former President Moncada, Dr. Sacasa attempted to prevent Somoza from being elected; but the latter started a revolution and Dr. Sacasa had to resign (June 6, 1936). A special congress was convened and Dr. Carlos Brenes Jarquín was elected president. However, a convention at León nominated Somoza, who assumed the executive power. The American Marines were withdrawn from Nicaragua in 1933. On March 11, 1936, a treaty of commerce with the United States was signed.

On March 22, 1939, a new constitution was adopted by a constituent assembly and President Somoza was elected for an eight-year term expiring on May 1, 1947.

Political Developments since World War II. Nicaragua declared war on Japan, December 9, 1941, on Germany and Italy, December 11, and on Hungary, Rumania, and Bulgaria, December 19. During World War II, agreements with the United States provided credits and investments to aid the economic development of Nicaragua in such fields as highway construction and rubber production. Nicaragua was one of the first nations to sign the United Nations Charter (July 6, 1945). In 1947 a serious dispute with Costa Rica was investigated by the Organization of American States (OAS), under the Rio de Janeiro Pact; this dispute was settled amicably in 1949.

Despite a constitutional amendment (April 27, 1944) permitting the president to succeed himself if elected, President Somoza stated that he would not be a candidate in the 1946 election. Dr. Leonardo Argüello, supported by the Liberal and Conservative parties, won the election but served less than a month, for on May 25, 1947, he was ousted and the congress elected Benjamín Lacayo Sacasa as provisional president. He set a general election for August 14, 1947, in which Dr. Víctor Román y Reyes was elected. During his administration the constitution was amended (January 23, 1948) to outlaw the Communist Party. In May, 1950, President Román y Reyes died, and the congress unanimously elected General Anastasio Somoza as president. A national election was held in May, resulting in a substantial majority for General Somoza.

President Somoza died on September 29, 1956, in consequence of gunshot wounds inflicted by a Nicaraguan exile who had been living in El Salvador. The national assembly promptly elected Colonel Luis Somoza Debayle, son of the deceased president, to govern the country until the expiration of his father's term. New elections, held on February 2, 1957, resulted in the election of Colonel Somoza, who was to continue in the presidency until 1965.

In 1948, Nicaragua was accused by Costa Rica of aiding political exiles in an armed invasion of Costa Rican territory. Costa Rica invoked the Inter-American Defense Pact of 1947, and also notified the United Nations Security Council. A commission of the OAS visited both countries, reporting that an invasion had taken place, absolving Nicaragua from complicity, but criticizing it for not having taken steps to stop the invasion. On the other hand, Costa Rica was criticized for permitting formation within its territory of the so-called "Caribbean Legion," which was opposed to General Somoza's control of Nicaraguan politics and to all other dictatorships in the Hemisphere.

In 1955, Costa Rica again invoked the Rio Treaty of 1947 and demanded collective aid against an alleged invasion of its territory by Nicaragua. This conflict was peacefully settled by the Council of the OAS.

In 1957, hostilities broke out between Nicaragua and Honduras over an unsettled boundary in the Mosquito Coast region. As recommended by the OAS Council, both sides withdrew their troops from the disputed territory. On November 18, 1960, the International Court of Justice ruled that the arbitration award of 1906 by King Alfonso XIII of Spain was valid. Nicaragua bowed to the court's decision, and after direct negotiation between the two countries, Honduras took possession of the disputed area.

Attempts in June, 1959, and in November, 1960, to overthrow the government of President Luis Somoza were promptly suppressed by the national guard.

Dr. René Schick Gutiérrez, of the Liberal Party, was elected president on February 3, 1963.

Economic, Social, and Cultural Development. The population of Nicaragua is about a million and a half. As a result of racial intermixture there is more racial homogeneity and less inequality between classes than in most other Latin American countries. The chief agricultural products are corn, beans, and rice, all raised for local consumption. Some sugar, indigo, and fruit—especially bananas—are exported. Coffee is the great export crop. Lumbering is confined chiefly to cabinet woods. Silver is mined in a small quantity, but gold is exported. Railroads and highways are poorly developed, as are airlines.

The educational system is headed by a National University with professional schools. Several normal schools are available to teachers, but primary and secondary schools are inadequate.

In Nicaragua was born one of the greatest poets of all Latin America, Rubén Darío (1867–1916), who spent part of his life in

Europe and Argentina. Other important writers are: Carmen Díaz, Cesario Salinas, Santiago Argüello, and Manuel Maldonado—all poets; Luis H. Debayle, a distinguished scientist and writer on scientific matters; and Jenaro Luga, a historian.

EL SALVADOR

Political Affairs to 1940. From early days El Salvador has been the hotbed of liberalism in Central America. In 1829 this nation united with Honduras in a war against the conservatives of Guatemala. In 1835 General Morazán, president of the Confederation, transferred the seat of government to San Salvador, capital of El Salvador, and from then until the extinction of the Union, El Salvador was involved in every war and revolution that took place in Central America.

A conservative government under the protection of President Carrera of Guatemala was set up in 1840, after Morazán was overthrown. Francisco Malespín, commander of the Salvadorian army, was, however, the real ruler of the country. In 1841 a declaration of independence was issued and a constitution was adopted. In 1843 Malespín became president of El Salvador. The following year, Carrera of Guatemala intervened in El Salvador in favor of the conservative leader, Manuel José Arce, but Eugenio Aguilar, a liberal, was elected (1846). His administration was progressive; he was opposed by the clergy, however, and had to resign. Six years later the conservatives, aided by Carrera, returned to power, and Francisco Dueñas became president. He endeavored to improve the financial condition of the country, promoted public education, and undertook the construction of roads. In 1858 Gerardo Barrios, a liberal, gained control of the government, first as a substitute for President Santín del Castillo, who was ill, and later as a regularly elected president for a term of six years to start in 1860. But three years later he was overthrown by Carrera, and Dueñas became president again. In 1865, after the death of the Guatemalan dictator, a revolution broke out in El Salvador in favor of Barrios; it failed, and Barrios was arrested and shot (August 29). In 1871 Santiago González assumed the executive power and two years later made himself dictator. He promoted public education, commerce, and transportation. In 1875 Andrés Valle was elected president, but war with Guatemala resulted in his overthrow, and Rafael Zaldívar, backed by Guatemalan President Justo Rufino Barrios, assumed the presidency.

In 1880 a new constitution was adopted and President Zaldívar was re-elected for a four-year term. Four years later he was again re-elected. In 1885, when Barrios of Guatemala endeavored once more to unite the states of Central America, El Salvador opposed the idea. War broke out, Barrios was killed in action, and the unionists were defeated. In the same year Zaldívar was overthrown and the government was seized by Francisco Menéndez, who ruled until 1890. In that year General Carlos Erzeta was made army commander to suppress a revolution headed by General Rivas, and the revolutionists were defeated. On June 22, 1890, Erzeta treacherously arrested President Menéndez and members of the cabinet during a ball given in honor of the president. The latter was killed, and Erzeta assumed the government as dictator. War now broke out with Guatemala, which refused to recognize Erzeta. The Guatemalan troops were defeated by the president's brother, General Antonio Erzeta. Despite revolutions, the Erzeta brothers ruled El Salvador until 1894, when a revolution brought Rafael A. Gutiérrez to the executive office. The following year Gutiérrez succeeded in uniting El Salvador with Honduras and Nicaragua again; this union lasted until 1898. In 1899 General Tomás Regalado became president. He made war against Honduras because of help given by the authorities of that country to his enemies. Regalado governed well when sober, but drink, to which he was addicted, made him cruel. In 1903 he was replaced by Pedro José Escalón, who had the backing of Regalado.

In 1906 El Salvador joined Nicaragua in war against Carrera of Guatemala. The Guatemalan forces proved too strong for the allies. Peace was restored by mediation of the United States and Mexico. The treaty of peace, which was signed on the U. S. S. *Marblehead* on July 20, 1906, was followed by a Central American congress at San José, Costa Rica, and later by the Washington Central American Congress of 1907.

From 1911 to 1931 El Salvador had five presidents: Manuel Enrique Araújo, who was assassinated in 1913; Carlos Meléndez, Jorge Meléndez, Alfonso Quiñónez Molina, and Pío Romero Bosque. In the election of 1931 no candidate received a majority, and the congress chose Arturo Araújo to be president. In December a revolution broke out, and the Vice-President, General Maximiliano Hernández Martínez, became the executive. Confirmed by the congress (February 7, 1932), he was regularly elected for a four-year term on

January 13–16, 1935. Although the United States had, at first, refused to recognize his government, recognition was extended on January 26, 1934. President Hernández Martínez promoted the redistribution of land among the peasants in a manner similar to that adopted in Mexico, and favored a new labor law which was passed in 1935 with provisions protecting the laboring classes.

Political Developments since World War II. El Salvador declared war on Japan, December 8, 1941, and on Germany and Italy, December 12. In 1945, like all the other American republics, El Salvador became a charter member of the United Nations. In June, 1950, it ratified the Charter of the Organization of American States and the Bogotá Peace Pact.

President Hernández Martínez was re-elected in 1939, for a six-year term. To keep him in office after the expiration of his term, the congress passed a law in February, 1944, extending his term an additional five years. As a result, a revolution broke out in the capital, and in the following May the president resigned. General Andrés Ignacio Menéndez served as chief executive until October 21, at which time Colonel Osmín Aguirre y Salinas took over the government. Industrial strikes and new revolts induced the administration to declare a state of siege on November 19, 1944. In the election held the following January, General Castañeda Castro was elected president. He held office until December 14, 1948, when he was ousted by a military junta which named Major Oscar Osorio as provisional president. Major Osorio, who resigned from the junta in October, 1949, won the presidency in the 1950 election.

Despite unrest and alleged Communist plots against his government, President Osorio served his full term of office. The elections of 1956 were won by Lieutenant Colonel José María Lemus.

Backed by the Democratic Unification Party, President Lemus showed moderate tendencies, granting a general amnesty to political exiles, selecting able men for his cabinet, and voiding repressive laws. However, political unrest, aggravated by a decline in the prices for coffee and cotton, the main export products of the country, resulted in a new uprising which overthrew the administration on October 26, 1960. A six-man junta headed by Colonel César Yañes Urias seized the government. Other members of the junta were: Lieutenant Colonel Miguel Angel Castillo, Captain Major Rubén Alonso Rosales, Dr. René Fortín Magana, Dr. Ricardo Falla Cáceres, and Dr. Fabio Castillo. The junta alleged that President Lemus had been overthrown because he had governed "outside the law," disregarding the constitutional rights of citizens. The junta promised to hold presidential elections in 1962. The University of El Salvador, closed since August 25 because of a strike of the students, was allowed to reopen. The new regime was recognized by the United States at the end of the year.

El Salvador is a party to the Central American Economic Integration Treaties of 1960.

On January 5, 1962, a new constitution was promulgated to replace that of 1950. On January 8, a provisional president, Eusebio Rodolfo Cordón, was chosen by the constitutional assembly, taking over the government from the Civil-Military Directorate, which had assumed power on January 25, 1961. The sole candidate in the presidential election of April 29, 1962, was Lieut. Col. Julio Adalberto Rivera, of the National Coalition Party, chosen for a five-year term.

Economic, Social, and Cultural Development. The population of El Salvador is about 2.5 million people, with a mixed racial composition somewhat similar to that of Honduras and Nicaragua. Because of its small size, the country is the most densely populated in Latin America. The principal agricultural products are corn, rice, beans, millet, wheat, coffee, indigo, henequen, and sugar. Cattle raising is limited, but hides are important. There is some natural rubber produced. "Balsam of Peru," a valuable drug, is produced for export. About 80 per cent of the valuable coffee crop is annually exported. Among minerals, gold and silver are produced in small quantities, while deposits of copper, lead, and some other minerals are known to exist. The government has built many miles of good roads recently, largely neglecting the railroads, of which there are possibly 100 miles. Some rivers are navigable. Airlines service the country fairly well.

In San Salvador there is a National University, and there are some professional schools. In recent years the government has stimulated educational advancement, but the number of schools is still inadequate to meet the needs of the people.

Among the leading writers born in El Salvador are: Juan Ramón Uriarte, essayist; Claudia Lars, poetess; Juan José Bernal, noted for his mysticism; Juan José Cañas (1826–1900), poet; Isaac Ruiz Araújo (1850–81), a poet of nature, love, and patriotism; Francisco E. Galindo (1850–1900), a poet and dramatist; Joaquín Aragón (b. 1863), a poet of great popularity because of his interpretation of national legends; and Alberto Masferrer, an educator, journalist, and accomplished poet.

COSTA RICA

Political Affairs to 1940. After the extinction of the Confederation, Juan Rafael Mora became president of Costa Rica. He proved to be a good administrator and established an efficient administrative machine, which also promoted the economic development of the country. Independence was declared on November 14, 1838. The same year Braulio Carrillo assumed the presidency. He became very unpopular on account of his dictatorial tendencies, and in 1842 he was overthrown by Francisco Morazán, former president of the Confederation. But Morazán's government was short-lived. Opposed by the other Central American states, he was defeated, arrested, and shot. There followed a period of anarchy which lasted until 1849, when Juan Rafael Mora once more assumed the government. He was re-elected in 1853 and took part in the war against Walker in Nicaragua.

In 1859 Mora was overthrown by a conservative revolution. Two military leaders, Generals Blanco and Salazar, set up José María Montealegre as president. From 1863 to 1882 there were four presidents—Jesús Jiménez, José María Castro, Jiménez again, and Tomás Guardia.

The next president was Próspero Fernández. Upon his death, he was succeeded by Bernardo Soto, who proved to be an enlightened president, introduced compulsory education, and promoted the economic development of the country. He was opposed by the Church. As a result, in 1889, José Joaquín Rodríguez, backed by the conservatives, was elected president.

From 1894 to 1932 there were the following presidents: Rafael Iglesias y Castro (1894–1902), who fostered agriculture and commerce; Ascensión Esquivel (1902–6), whose administration was exceptionally peaceful and prosperous; Cleto González Víquez (1906–10); Ricardo Jiménez Oreamundo (1910–14); Alfredo González Flores (1914–17), whose reforms aroused the antagonism of the conservatives and led to his overthrow in 1917; Federico Tinoco Granados (1917–19), who was not recognized by the United States; Federico Aguilar Barquero (1917–20); Julio Acosta García (1920–24); Ricardo Jiménez Oreamundo (1924–28) again; and in 1928 Cleto González Víquez once more. In 1932 no candidate had a majority vote, and before a new election could take place a revolution broke out. The United States intervened, and Jiménez Oreamundo, one of the candidates, was declared elected by the Costa Rican Congress. On February 9, 1936, León Cortés Castro, Vice-President, became the chief executive, to complete the presidential term of Dr. Jiménez Oreamundo. In the elections of February 11, 1940, Dr. Rafael Angel Calderón Guardia, a physician, was selected as president.

Political Developments since World War II. The Calderón Guardia administration declared war on Japan on December 8, 1941, and on Germany and Italy, December 11. At San Francisco, in 1945, Costa Rica became a charter member of the United Nations.

The presidential election of February 13, 1944, resulted in a decisive majority for Teodoro Picado over his opponent, former President León Cortés Castro. The Picado administration endorsed Calderón Guardia in the 1948 election, which was, however, won by the National Union candidate, Otilio Ulate. The Costa Rican Congress annulled this election as fraudulent. President Picado remained in office during a brief period of civil war which ensued, but was ousted by a junta under the leadership of Colonel José Figueres. A national assembly summoned to draw up a new constitution validated Ulate's election. The Calderón Guardia partisans, who had withdrawn to Nicaragua, then invaded Costa Rica, which accused the Nicaraguan government of aiding the rebels. The invasion came ten days after the Costa Rican Congress had disbanded the national army as unnecessary. Acting under the Rio Treaty of 1947, the Organization of American States sent a commission of representatives of Peru, Brazil, Colombia, Mexico, and the United States to investigate the situation. The dispute was the first settled peacefully (1949) by the Organization of American States under the Rio Pact. Finally, in January, 1949, Ulate was inaugurated as president, the new constitution was put into effect, and the president assumed personal control over the Ministry of Public Security.

The election of 1953, in which women voters participated for the first time in Costa Rica, was won by Colonel José Figueres, the candidate of the National Liberation Party. In January, 1955, a new invasion by Costa Rican exiles from Nicaragua took place with the purpose of overthrowing President Figueres. The Organization of American States once more intervened in the conflict in response to an urgent appeal from the Costa Rican government. Under the Rio

Treaty of 1947, military aid was extended to Costa Rica by the United States. The insurgents were driven out by Costa Rican troops.

The presidential election of February 2, 1958, was won by Mario Echandi Jiménez, backed by the National Union Party. At the invitation of the Costa Rican government, the United Nations Secretary General sent a three-man team to Costa Rica to observe the election, which was declared to have been orderly and truly democratic.

President Echandi expressed dissatisfaction with the Central American Economic Integration Treaties of 1960. He declared that, in his opinion, the treaties represented a setback for the economic integration of Central America. Although Costa Rica participated in the negotiations preceding the signing of the treaties, Costa Rica did not become a party to them on the grounds that they would be detrimental to its economy.

On February 4, 1962, Francisco José Orlich Bolmarcich, supported by ex-President José Figueres, was elected President; he was followed in office by José Joaquín Trejos, elected on February 6, 1966.

President Kennedy and the presidents of the Central American nations met at San José, Costa Rica, March 18-19, 1963, to discuss the Alliance for Progress, the economic integration of Central America, and closer economic and political cooperation between the United States and the Central American nations.

Economic, Social, and Cultural Development. In many respects Costa Rica is quite different from other Central American countries. Her population of slightly over a million people is largely white, the soil is widely cultivated, and much of the population lives on farms and small plantations in relative economic prosperity. Most of the whites are descendants of the Gallegos, one of the most law-abiding and hard-working races in the Iberian Peninsula. Negroes and Indians live chiefly along the coasts and there is little racial mixture, since the whites live for the most part in the cooler plateau regions. Agriculture is the basic industry, with coffee, bananas, and cacao the chief products of export. Because of the large acreage of grasslands the cattle industry has been increasing in importance in recent years. Minerals are of relatively little importance. Transportation has steadily improved within the country until railroads, and especially highways, have reached a degree of adequacy. Air-travel facilities are quite satisfactory.

The country has always prided itself on its well-developed educational system. There are both public and private schools, with the University of Costa Rica in the capital the educational leader for the whole system. Several professional schools help to provide training in special professions and skills. Literacy is at about 80 per cent, being the highest in all Latin America.

The following are among the leading writers of Costa Rica: Juan Diego Braun Bonilla (1759–1855), a poet; Aquileo Echeverria (1866–1909), a very popular poet, author of *Concherías,* a book of poems; Manuel González Zeledón (1864–1936), a prose writer who utilizes the folklore of his country; Manuel Jesús Jiménez (b. 1854), a historian; Joaquín García Monge (b. 1881), a writer of short stories based on national folklore; Ricardo Jiménez (b. 1903), a poet; and Rafael Cardona, Raúl Salazar, and Carlos Luis Sáenz, all modern poets. Ricardo Fernández Guardia (1867–1950), although primarily a historian, is also known for his fine collection of *Cuentos ticos,* short stories based on historical events and personalities.

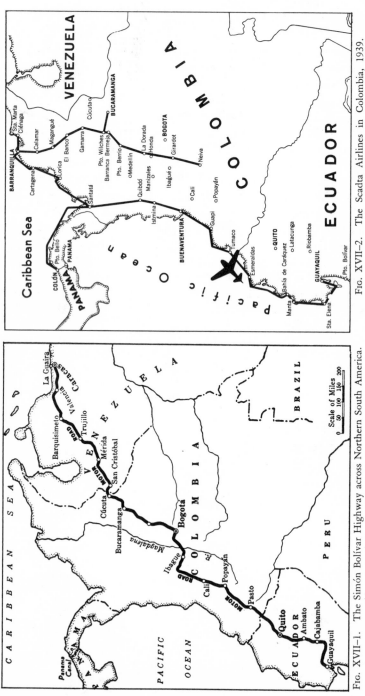

Fig. XVII–1. The Simón Bolívar Highway across Northern South America. (Courtesy of Farrar & Rinehart, Inc.)

Fig. XVII–2. The Scadta Airlines in Colombia, 1939.

CHAPTER XVII

THE STATES OF
NORTHERN SOUTH AMERICA

A T THE OUTSET OF independence, the northern Spanish provinces of South America united, under the genius of Bolívar, to form a single state in the territory of New Granada Viceroyalty, including the Captaincy General of Venezuela, the New Kingdom of Granada, and the Presidency of Quito. However, this union did not last long because of regional jealousies. By 1830, even before the death of the Liberator, the new state had broken up into three independent political units—Venezuela, New Granada (Colombia), and Ecuador. Panama seceded from Colombia in 1903.

GREAT COLOMBIA

The Congress of Angostura created, on December 17, 1819, the Republic of Colombia, comprising Venezuela and New Granada, which was divided into three departments—Venezuela, Quito, and Cundinamarca. Another general congress met at Cúcuta in 1821 and adopted a constitution for the new state, which was then named *Gran Colombia* (Great Colombia). This constitution provided for the usual division of powers in a manner similar to that provided by the United States Constitution. The congress elected Simón Bolívar president of the republic, with Francisco de Paula Santander as vice-president. Quito adhered to the new state in July of the following year.

Santander's Government. From 1822 to 1827, while Bolívar was away continuing the war against the Spanish forces in Ecuador and Peru, Santander acted as president. He was tactless and inclined to rule despotically. At once there were signs of discontent and even rebellion. In May, 1826, General José Antonio Páez, one of the most popular heroes of the wars of independence in Venezuela and commandant general of two Venezuelan departments, rebelled against the central government. He had been accused in the congress of having forced men to enlist in the army and had been suspended from his command.

Bolívar, upon hearing of General Páez's insurrection, returned to Venezuela and on January 21, 1827, at Puerto Cabello, issued decrees of amnesty and restored Páez to his command. Páez was moved by Bolívar's generosity and acknowledged his authority.

But there were other reasons for dissatisfaction, particularly among the conservative classes. Laws adopted by the congress providing for the closing of certain convents and giving the government control over church appointments were vehemently opposed by the clergy.

In 1827 Bolívar returned to Bogotá and assumed the office of chief executive.

Disruption of Great Colombia. Bolívar's return did not restore public peace. An influential group favored the adoption of a monarchic form of government and urged Bolívar to crown himself king. Though favoring a stronger central government for the republic, Bolívar repeatedly denied having royal ambitions.

In April, 1828, a convention assembled at Ocaña to discuss the amendment of the constitution. A bitter controversy began at once over federalism and unitarian government, and the convention adjourned without accomplishing anything. Dissatisfaction increased throughout the republic. On September 25, an unsuccessful attempt was made to assassinate Bolívar, who had assumed dictatorial powers under the constitution to suppress the disorder. A number of conspirators were executed. Santander, suspected of having instigated the plot, was exiled.

Finally, in 1829, General José María Córdoba rebelled against the government in Antioquia. A revolutionary assembly met at Caracas and declared Venezuela separated from Great Colombia. A congress met at Bogotá the following year and tried to prevent the disruption of the republic by adopting a new constitution which granted greater autonomy to the provinces. But it was all in vain. This same congress elected Joaquín Mosquera president of the republic, with Domingo Caicedo as vice-president. On March 1, 1830, Bolívar resigned because of ill health. Intending to go to Europe, he stopped at Cartagena, where he received the news that General José Antonio de Sucre, his best friend and most capable lieutenant, had been assassinated. Broken-hearted, disillusioned, and mortally ill, Bolívar retired to Santa Marta on the northern coast of Colombia, where he died on December 17. "He who dedicates his services to a revolution ploughs the sea," wrote the Liberator to a friend some time before his death. Even before he died, Great Colombia, the creation of his genius, had ceased to exist. In August, Venezuela refused to adopt the constitution drafted at Bogotá and adopted one of its own in September. In August, 1830, a movement for secession also took place in Quito under the leadership of Juan José Flores. Since November of the following year the three component provinces of Bolívar's Great Colombia have remained independent states, known as Colombia, Venezuela, and Ecuador.

COLOMBIA

On account of its proximity to North America, its strategic location—since it borders both the Caribbean Sea and the Pacific Ocean—and its valuable natural resources, Colombia has been one of the most important Latin American countries from the standpoint of United States international strategy.

The history of Colombia as an independent nation may be divided into four periods. During the first one (1832–61), liberalism and conservatism struggled for control of the government. The measures taken by an administration of one of the two parties was, as a rule, annulled and reversed by a succeeding administration of opposite political character. This perennial struggle was complicated by bitter religious controversy and regional jealousies, resulting at the end of the period in the expulsion of the Jesuits and other measures against the Church, as well as in the loss of authority by the central government. During the following period (1861–80), the liberals were in power and carried into effect a broad program of reforms, including the reorganization of the nation as a confederation, and the suppression of all religious orders and other measures limiting the power of the Church and the conservative classes. From 1880 to 1930 the conservatives were in power. Under the leadership of Rafael Núñez a new party was formed by elements from both the conservatives and the liberals; and a new constitution (1886) was adopted providing for an extremely centralized form of government and the restoration of the Catholic Church to its former power and prestige. The fourth period began in 1930, when the liberals returned to power. The constitution was amended in 1936 to allow, among other things, for separation of Church and State.

The continuing struggle between the two parties has led to bitter conflict and revolution.

Liberalism Versus Conservatism (1832–61)

On February 29, 1832, a constitution was adopted for New Granada similar to that of 1830 adopted for Great Colombia. The convention elected General Francisco de Paula Santander first president of the republic. Upon returning from exile, he was inaugurated on October 7. Santander's administration was a progressive one; he was especially interested in fostering public education. At this time a treaty of friendship, commerce, and navigation was signed with Venezuela. Santander was much criticized by his enemies for assuming, in the name of New Granada, half of the debt of the extinguished Great Colombia. Antagonism towards him also resulted from his harsh treatment of his opponents.

In 1837 José Ignacio Márquez, a civilian and eminent jurist, was elected to the presidency. The new executive attempted to reduce the influence of the army in politics, promoted public education, and in general followed an enlightened policy. A new penal code was adopted. For a while the country prospered in peace. But in 1839, after certain monasteries had been suppressed by the congress, a rebellion led by a priest resulted in general disorder throughout the nation. Before the uprising could be put down, Pedro Alcántara Herrán, commander of the government forces, was elected president (1841). Two years later the constitution was amended to give the executive greater power. Herrán continued the liberal reforms of his predecessors. In an attempt to pacify the Church, in 1844 the Society of Jesus was allowed to return to the country and devote itself to educational pursuits.

The next president was Tomás Cipriano de Mosquera, a man of culture and aristocratic family. His administration was very progressive. He initiated negotiations for the construction of a railroad across the Isthmus of Panama. In 1846 he negotiated a treaty with the United States granting American citizens the right of transit across the Isthmus, receiving in return the guarantee of neutrality of Panama and the recognition of Colombian sovereignty over that region. A railroad across Panama built by an American concern was inaugurated in 1855. The monetary system was improved, the slave trade was prohibited, and public education was promoted.

During the latter part of President Mosquera's term, the liberals became stronger as a result of the European revolutions of 1848. In the election of 1849, General José Hilario López, the liberal candidate, was elected. With the victory of the liberals, a period of democratic reforms and of anti-clericalism began. In 1850 the Jesuits were again expelled. Slavery was abolished May 21, 1851, with compensation to slaveholders. The same year the rivers of New Granada were opened to the navigation of foreign vessels.

During General José María Obando's administration (1853–54), laws were passed providing for the separation of Church and State and other measures directed against the Church. The same year a new constitution was drafted guaranteeing complete freedom of thought, liberty of the press, trial by jury, and other individual rights. It also granted universal manhood suffrage and provided for a larger measure of autonomy on the part of the provinces.

These reforms led to a revolution promoted by the conservative classes. President Obando was arrested, and General José María Melo assumed the executive power. But he did not remain in office for a long time. At the end of 1854 Manuel María Mallarino assumed the presidency for the two remaining years of Obando's term. In 1855 the constitution was amended to permit the various provinces to become federal states.

In 1857 Mariano Ospina was inaugurated president. The following year a new constitution was adopted providing for a confederate government under the name of "Granadine Confederation." This constitution gave to the states all the powers not specifically delegated to the confederate government. As a result, General Mosquera, then Governor of Cauca and leader of the Liberal Party, declared in 1860 that his state had decided to assume full sovereign powers. His example was quickly followed by others, and the central government soon lost all of its authority.

War followed, during which Mosquera captured the capital and assumed the title of provisional president (July, 1861).

Predominance of the Liberals (1861–80)

From 1861 to 1867 the country, at first under the name of "United States of New Granada," and later as "United States of Colombia," was ruled by the former president Tomás Cipriano de Mosquera, who upon assuming the government issued a number of decrees against the Church. The Society of Jesus was again expelled, and its property was confiscated. All monasteries were suppressed, and no priest was permitted to perform his religious duties without permission of the civil authorities.

In 1863 a new constitution was adopted decreasing the autonomy of the states. Under this new instrument of government the president was elected for two years by the states. In 1867 Mosquera was accused of malfeasance in office, was arrested, and exiled. The liberals, however, remained in power for almost two more decades.

In 1878, during the government of Aquileo Parra, a concession was granted to a French company to dig a canal across the Isthmus of Panama.

Predominance of the Conservatives (1880–1930)

Rafael Núñez. In 1880 Rafael Núñez became president. A man of advanced political ideas, he had become convinced that the country needed a more centralized form of government. He was also a strong partisan of the Catholic Church. After the interval of one term, Núñez was re-elected in 1884, and helped to form a new political party known as the Nationalist Party, made up of conservatives and independents who had constituted a dissatisfied group within the Liberal Party. In 1885 a national council met at Bogotá and adopted an act providing that the country be called the "Republic of Colombia." Assuming the powers of a constituent convention, the council then proceeded to draft a constitution, which was promulgated the following year (1886). Under this constitution a centralized republic was established; the states were abolished and replaced by administrative departments. The Roman Catholic Church was declared to be the official church. The president was to be elected for six years, directly by the people. This constitution remained in effect until 1936.

The Constitution of 1886 was a great victory for the clericals and conservatives. Núñez, who had assumed the presidency in 1885 and was regularly elected under the new constitution in 1886, and re-elected in 1892, ruled the country until his death in 1894. In 1895 Miguel Antonio Caro was elected. During his administration a concordat with the papacy was signed, restoring to the Church in Colombia most of the powers and privileges it had possessed in colonial days and providing for payment for confiscated ecclesiastical property.

The conservatives continued to rule the country until 1930 in spite of many attempts to overthrow them. In 1899 Vice-President

José Manuel Marroquín broke with President Antonio Sancle-
mente and seized the presidential power; civil war followed until
1903. This is considered one of the most unhappy periods in the
history of Colombia.

The Loss of Panama. The digging of a canal across Panama
started in 1878, but the French company having the concession
stopped work in 1889 for lack of funds. In 1903, after the Spanish-
American War had proved the necessity of a canal across the Isthmus, the United States government signed with Colombia a treaty
(Hay-Herrán) granting to the former a lease for ninety-nine years
of a strip of land across the Isthmus in return for the payment of
10 million dollars at once and an annual rent of a quarter of a million dollars. The treaty was ratified by the United States Senate but
rejected by the Colombian Senate. The inhabitants of Panama were
indignant, and as a result on November 3, 1903, an insurrection
broke out in Panama City and the independence of that province
was declared. The United States intervened under the Treaty of
1846 and prevented Colombian soldiers from using the railroad to
cross from Colón to Panama City. A few days later President Theodore Roosevelt recognized the independence of Panama, despite the
protests of Colombia.

In 1909 an attempt was made to settle the Panama question. But
strong Colombian opposition to the Cortés-Root agreement, which
provided for the payment by Panama to Colombia of the annual
rent received from the United States and recognition of Panama's
independence by Colombia, resulted in the withdrawal of the treaty
by President Reyes of Colombia. In 1914, the Thomson-Urrutia
Treaty was signed, in which the United States expressed regret for
the differences that had arisen between the two nations and agreed
to pay to Colombia 25 million dollars for the loss of Panama. This
treaty, ratified by Colombia, was rejected by the United States Senate.
Eventually, in 1921, the Thomson-Urrutia Treaty was ratified by the
United States Senate without the expression of regret, and this was
accepted by the Colombian Congress. Since then, relations between
Colombia and the United States have been friendly.

In 1922 General Pedro Nel Ospina was elected president of Colombia; he paid a visit to the United States before his inauguration.
The following year a financial mission headed by Professor Edwin W. Kemmerer of Princeton University visited Colombia at the
request of President Nel Ospina and recommended certain changes

in the financial and economic structure of the country. As a result, a national bank was established and the currency reformed.

The Liberals Again in Power (1930–40)

In 1930, owing to a split in the Conservative Party, the liberals won the presidential election for the first time in nearly half a century. Their candidate, Enrique Olaya Herrera, at the time Colombian Minister to the United States, was elected. During the administration of Dr. Herrera national expenditures were reduced and a program of public works was carried into effect to help those without work. The government also tried to help the coffee industry and the planters, then suffering from severe business depression.

In September, 1932, a dispute arose with Peru on account of the seizure by a group of Peruvian citizens of a small settlement called Leticia, which lay in territory ceded by Peru to Colombia under the Treaty of 1927, settling the boundary dispute between the two countries. This new dispute was peacefully settled by the two countries on May 24, 1934.

In February, 1934, Alfonso López Pumarejo, another liberal, was elected president. Two years later the constitution was amended to permit the levying of taxes on income and capital. The Church was disestablished, and its control of public education was ended. Despite the bitter antagonism of the conservatives, in the election of 1937 another liberal, Eduardo Santos, was elected. In 1942 former President Alfonso López was re-elected; he was inaugurated on August 7, 1942.

Political Developments since World War II

Colombia was among the first of the American nations to break off diplomatic relations with Japan (December 8, 1941), with Germany and Italy (December 19, 1941), and with the Vichy French government (November 26, 1942). The López administration declared a state of war against Germany on November 26, 1943. Colombia adhered to the United Nations in 1945, and firmly supported the idea of continental solidarity.

Because of numerous strikes and deep unrest in the nation, President López resigned in July, 1945, and Alberto Lleras Camargo, a distinguished liberal leader, was named by the senate as acting president. Through a division in the majority Liberal Party, the candidate of the Conservative Party, Mariano Ospina Pérez, was elected president in the election of 1946. The democratic tradition and comparative political stability of Colombia were thereby shattered. There followed a succession of uprisings and continuous unrest, including the mob violence of April 9, 1948, during the Ninth Inter-American Conference which was meeting at Bogotá at that time. Because the rioting was attributed, in part, to the activities of Communist agents, Colombia severed diplomatic relations with Soviet Russia on May 3. Serious clashes preceded the 1950 election, at which time the president declared a state òf siege and established rigid censorship over the press and radio.

The 1950 election was won by another conservative, Laureano Gómez. Inaugurated on August 7, he was overthrown by a coup headed by Lieutenant General Gustavo Rojas Pinilla, who immediately thereafter assumed the control of the government. On August 3, 1954, a national constituent assembly elected Rojas Pinilla for a four-year term. Unrest continued throughout the country. On May 8, 1957, the assembly re-elected Rojas Pinilla for another four-year term. The assembly first abolished the constitutional provisions preventing a president from succeeding himself and requiring that a president be chosen by popular election. Two days later a five-man military junta headed by Major General Gabriel París took over the government after rioting in the capital threatened to develop into civil war. Rojas Pinilla and his family left the country. The revolutionary junta released hundreds of political prisoners and took other measures to return the country to normalcy, including abolition of press and radio censorship.

On December 1, 1957, a plebiscite decided—women voted for the first time in Colombia—to amend the 1886 Constitution so as to permit the election of a coalition government including members of the Liberal and Conservative parties. The plebiscite also decided to legalize the rule of the military junta until the 1958 elections.

Congressional elections held on March 16, 1958, gave an overwhelming majority to the right-wing conservatives, headed by former President Laureano Gómez. An agreement between the conservative and liberal leaders resulted in the selection of Alberto Lleras Camargo, a liberal, as a bipartisan presidential candidate.

The presidential election held in May of the same year was preceded and followed by new outbreaks of violence, inspired, for the most part, by partisans of Rojas Pinilla. Despite all this political agitation, Dr. Lleras Camargo was declared elected and assumed the presidency on August 7. Former dictator Rojas Pinilla was then tried by the Senate (March, 1959) and convicted of malfeasance while in office.

During a visit to the United States in April, 1960, President Lleras Camargo urged the United States government to save the underdeveloped countries of Latin America from political extremists by adopting a financial and economic program of assistance. Several loans to Colombia for the development of electric power, railways and highways, and other improvements were granted by the United States and U.S.-supported institutions during his visit.

The May, 1962, presidential election was won by Guillermo León Valencia, who visited the United States before his inauguration.

Economic, Social, and Cultural Development

Coffee is the leading agricultural product of Colombia. Others of importance are sugar, rice, cotton, cacao, tagua (ivory nuts), and fruits. Natural rubber is produced to a limited extent. Mahogany, cedar, and dyewood are exported. Cattle raising has long been important because of the *llanos* (grassy plains) in the east. Mineral resources are significant, the chief being gold, copper, platinum, coal, iron, and petroleum. Salt mines are important, especially in Zipaquirá. Colombia has produced emeralds since pre-Columbian days, and this stone is still of great importance as an export. Manufacturing is steadily increasing, with products used chiefly for local consumption. The railway system (some 1,400 miles) is quite adequate. Highways have been constructed rapidly in recent years, and airlines give satisfactory connections with other countries. The first airline in South America was established in 1920 under the name of Sociedad Colombiana Alemana de Transportes Aéreos (Scadta).

The population of Colombia is estimated at nearly 14 million people, of whom perhaps more than half are part Indian and part white (*mestizos*). Possibly 10 per cent are pure white, living chiefly in the highlands. Negroes and mulattoes are scattered throughout the country.

The educational system has been enlightened and progressive over the years. In the capital are the National University, dating from the sixteenth century, and several new institutions, including the rapidly developing University of the Andes. The Catholic Church has played a leading role in education, with several hundred schools at the primary and secondary levels. Locally and nationally supported schools at these levels are increasing, partly as a result of a good system of teacher training.

Colombia has produced many writers of importance. Among them the following may be mentioned here: José Eusebio Caro (1817–53), a poet, journalist, and politician; José Joaquín Ortiz (1844–92), a romantic poet and journalist; Julio Arboleda (1817–62), a journalist and epic poet; Gregorio Gutiérrez González (1826–72), a romantic poet; José María Vergara y Vergara (1831–72), a poet and historian of Colombian literature; Manuel María Madiedo (1817–88), a philosophical poet and defender of Christianity; Rafael Núñez (1825–94), a statesman and poet; Diego Fallón (1834–1905), a poet of nature; Rafael Pombo (1834–1912), a writer of poetry for children as well as adults; Silvera Espina de Rendón (d. 1886), a poetess of religious inspiration; Mercedes Alvarez de Flórez (b. 1859), a poetess of love; José Asunción Silva (1865–96), a modernistic poet of great merit; Soledad Acosta de Samper (1833–1913), a journalist, historian, and biographer; José Manuel Restrepo (1782–1863), the leading historian of Colombia; Joaquín Acosta (1800–1852), the outstanding historian of the Spanish conquest of New Granada; Eugenio Díaz (1804–65), an idealistic novelist; Jorge Isaacs (1837–95), author of *María,* a novelist and poet and one of the best-known of all Latin American writers; José Joaquín Borda (1835–78), a vigorous promoter of literary periodicals; Rufino José Cuervo (1850–1911), a noted grammarian and philologist; José María Samper (1828–88), a dramatist, poet, and prolific writer; José Eustacio Rivera (1889–1929), one of the outstanding modern writers of all Latin America, author of the novel *La Vorágine;* Víctor M. Londoño (b. 1876), a poet of great inspiration; and Laureano García Ortiz, a historian and writer of *belles-lettres.*

PANAMA

As Part of Colombia. Although Panama did not become a sovereign state until 1903, it had always enjoyed relative autonomy even in colonial days. On November 28, 1821, a *cabildo abierto* declared that territory independent from Spain and annexed to the Republic of Colombia. In 1830 there was an uprising which aimed at making Panama independent from Colombia; but it did not last long. After the dissolution of Great Colombia, Panama joined New Granada (1832). In 1840, however, a revolution led by Tomás

Herrera declared this union at an end. Until December 31, 1841, an independent government ruled the country, which was called "The Free State of the Isthmus."

A railroad across the Isthmus, begun in 1851, and inaugurated four years later, was built by United States engineers under a concession from the government of New Granada. The same year Panama became an autonomous state of the Granadine Confederation, and later (1862) of the United States of Colombia. It was governed by officials elected by a state assembly under a state constitution until 1886, when a centralist constitution was adopted for Colombia. From then until 1903 there were various insurrections against the central government.

After 1878, when a French company received the concession to build a canal across the Isthmus, the desire of the people of Panama for political autonomy increased. And when, in 1903, the Colombian Congress rejected the Hay-Herrán Treaty, antagonism against Colombia led to a new outbreak. On November 3, the people of Panama declared themselves independent, and a provisional governing junta was established, composed of José Agustín Araújo, Federico Boyd, and Tomás Arias. Three days later the independence of the new Republic of Panama was recognized by the United States, and, on November 18, the Hay-Bunau-Varilla Treaty was signed at Washington.

Relations with the United States. By the end of February, 1904, the ratifications of the Hay-Bunau Varilla Treaty were exchanged, and the treaty went into effect. This agreement gave the United States the right to build a canal across the Isthmus on a strip of land leased in perpetuity, in return for the payment of 10 million dollars at once and a quarter of a million dollars as annual rental. Under one of its provisions the United States guaranteed Panama's independence and assumed the maintenance of public order in the country. A similar provision was included in the Constitution of Panama (Article 136). As a result, there has been repeated intervention in that country on the part of the United States.

In 1905 President Manuel Amador Guerrero requested the United States government to supervise the elections in Panama. This the American government refused to do. Three years later, however, troops were landed and American officials undertook to supervise the elections of that year at the request of the Panama government. Troops were landed there again in 1912 and in 1918, on account of political disturbances, despite the suspicion and antagonism that such action evoked throughout Latin America. United States forces have intervened in Panama at various other times to restore and maintain public order.

The Treaty of 1903 has been a source of dissatisfaction for the people of Panama. Controversies have arisen between the United States and Panama on such matters as the right of the United States to open the Canal Zone to commerce and to collect custom duties, and to adopt sanitary measures. Many of these questions have been satisfactorily settled now. In 1926 an agreement was signed doing away with the competition of commercial establishments in the Canal Zone. Other provisions of the treaty granted the United States the right to use airport facilities and radio communications in Panama and to control jointly with Panama all military operations in the country in case of war. This treaty was bitterly opposed in Panama and was refused ratification by the congress of that country. In 1933 President Harmodio Arias visited the United States to discuss the various pending questions. The following year a new dispute arose in regard to the payment of the annual Canal rent. After the devaluation of the American dollar, the government of the United States decided to pay the annual rent in paper dollars instead of in gold, as provided by the treaty, and Panama refused to accept this payment. Two years later (1936) an agreement was signed at Washington providing for the payment, by the United States, of the Canal rent in *balboas* (Panama currency) instead of in dollars, at the rate equivalent to the gold dollar of that date; the United States also gave up the right to intervene in Panama and to guarantee that country's independence. This treaty, negotiated by the very able Panamanian diplomat, Dr. Ricardo J. Alfaro, though criticized for not adequately safeguarding the Canal, was ratified by the United States Senate in 1939. Dissatisfaction on the part of Panama with the treaty provisions led to the revision of this treaty in 1955.

Political Affairs to 1940. The first president was Manuel Amador Guerrero, who was inaugurated on February 20, 1904. One week before, on February 13, a constitution was adopted providing for a highly centralized form of government.

In 1908 José Domingo de Obaldía, a conservative, was elected president. With his death on March 1, 1910, Carlos Antonio Mendoza became temporary executive, followed in September by Pablo

Arosemena, who was chosen by the assembly. On October 1, 1912, Belisario Porras became president; he was succeeded four years later by Ramón M. Valdés. In 1919 Porras again assumed the presidency, but the next year Ernesto Lefevre was elected to the executive office. The next president was Rodolfo Chiari, who was inaugurated on October 1, 1924. Early in March of the following year, a rebellion of the San Blas Indians was crushed. On October 1, 1928, Florencio Harmodio Arosemena, a liberal, was inaugurated. Early in 1931 he was overthrown by a sudden uprising in Panama City on the part of the dissatisfied *Acción Comunal* group backed by independents and conservatives and led by Harmodio Arias on a platform opposed to graft and tyranny. Dr. Ricardo J. Alfaro was chosen chief executive until the end of the term, and on October 1, 1932, Harmodio Arias became the president of the republic. In the election of June, 1936, Juan Demóstenes Arosemena was elected chief executive.

President Arosemena, who is said to have had pro-Fascist sympathies, died in December, 1939, and was succeeded by Dr. Augusto S. Boyd, the Vice-President. The elections of June, 1940, were hotly contested by the candidate of the National Revolutionary Party, Arnulfo Arias, and Dr. Ricardo J. Alfaro, representing a coalition of liberals and socialists, who desired to break the political machinery controlled by the conservatives. Dr. Alfaro, who had been living in Washington, went home and was received enthusiastically by the people of Panama. Before and during the elections there were many disorders, provoked, it was said, by the backers of Arnulfo Arias. Despite the apparent popular support for Dr. Alfaro, the conservative candidate was declared elected.

After his inauguration, on October 1, 1940, President Arias showed decided antagonism towards the United States, declaring publicly that unless properly treated by the American government Panama would seek the protection of other powerful countries.

On December 15, 1940, a new constitution was adopted denying citizenship to non-Spanish-speaking Negroes and to members of the yellow races and races from India and Asia Minor. A clause was included in the new constitution permitting the expropriation of property owned by foreigners or in which foreign capital participates, provided that compensation is made. The president's term was extended from four to six years.

Political Developments since World War II. In 1941 Panama permitted the United States to set up military bases in the country to protect the Panama Canal, but the Arias government was overthrown when it tried to maintain formal neutrality by refusing to allow the arming of American-owned ships under Panamanian registry. Panama declared war on Japan, December 10, 1941, and on Germany and Italy, December 12. Agreements with the United States provided numerous bases for military use during the war. In 1945 Panama became a charter member of the United Nations. All bases in the country were evacuated by the United States in 1947 and 1948.

During the 1940's numerous changes occurred in the government of Panama. President Arias, who had gone over to the Conservative Party in the election of 1940, was ousted by a bloodless coup in October, 1941, and was succeeded by Ricardo Adolfo de la Guardia, formerly Minister of Government and Justice. In 1944, after President de la Guardia's term had been extended by the congress to 1947, the cabinet resigned, the 1941 constitution was suspended, and the assembly was dissolved. Members of the assembly met to proclaim Jephtha B. Duncan president under the 1941 constitution. In June, 1945, however, a constituent assembly elected Enrique A. Jiménez as provisional president. The following year (March, 1946) the assembly adopted a new constitution. After the national election of May, 1948, a National Election Jury adjudged the victor to be the government candidate, Domingo Díaz Arosemena. President Arosemena died in office, August 23, 1949, and was succeeded by First Vice-President Dr. Daniel Chanis, Jr. The latter, in turn, resigned in November, 1949, but later repudiated his resignation and led a march on the Palace, where Vice-President Chiari had been sworn in as president. The Supreme Court then proclaimed Dr. Chanis as constitutional president, but an hour later the police installed ex-President Arias as chief executive and the National Election Jury reversed its previous decision, declaring that ex-President Arias had won the 1948 election. The Arias administration cooperated closely with the United States. In 1950, it outlawed the Communist Party.

On May 9–10, 1951, President Arias was overthrown by a revolution which broke out after he announced that he would suspend the 1946 constitution and restore the 1941 charter. He was arrested by order of the national assembly and later impeached. First Vice-President Alcibíades Arosemena was installed as acting president. Arias was released from prison on February 8, 1952.

The presidential election of May 11, 1952, was won by Colonel José Remón, with the backing of the party in power. He was inaugurated on October 1, for a four-year term. But on January 2, 1955, he was assassinated at the racecourse by a lawyer who later confessed to have acted under the instigations of the president's political enemies. First Vice-President José Ramón Guizado, who had assumed the presidency after President Remón's death and who seems to have been implicated in the plot, was impeached and arrested by order of the assembly. Second Vice-President Ricardo Arias Espinosa was sworn in as president on January 15.

After protracted and often bitter negotiations, a new treaty between the United States and Panama revising the agreement of 1936 on the Panama Canal was signed on January 25, 1955. This new agreement increased the annuity paid by the United States to Panama and, among other things, provided for a revision of the taxing arrangements in regard to certain workers in the Canal Zone.

On May 13, 1956, Ernesto de la Guardia, backed by the National Patriotic Coalition, was elected president; he was inaugurated on October 1.

Dissatisfaction with alleged inequality in the payment of Panamanian workers as compared with American workers in the Canal Zone led to frequent bitter protests and strained relations between Panama and the United States during 1959. Antagonism towards the United States was exploited and fanned by nationalist political leaders and Communist agitators. Especially were relations with the United States strained by rioting in Panama City on November 3, 1959, following an unsuccessful attempt by a mob to enter the Canal Zone to hoist the Panamanian flag. In a note protesting against the depredations that occurred at the time, the Washington government declared itself willing to consider the pending issues provided that the discussions could be carried on under normal conditions. New attempts by a mob to enter the Canal Zone on November 28 were driven back by the Panamanian National Guard. Most of the grievances against the United States derived from contrary interpretations of the 1955 economic treaty, as well as from a dispute over the basic sovereignty over the Canal Zone, the annuity paid by the United States, and the labor policy of the Canal authorities, said to be discriminatory against Panamanian workers. Finally, under orders from Washington, the Panamanian flag was hoisted at one place within the Zone side by side with the United States flag.

In May, 1960, Dr. Roberto Francisco Chiari was elected president (for a four-year term) succeeding de la Guardia. The next constitutional president was Marco Aurelio Robles, elected in 1964.

On January 9, 1963, an alleged insult to the Panamanian flag in the Canal Zone led to bloody riots, and Panama demanded that the Canal Treaty be revised.

Economic, Social, and Cultural Development. The population of Panama is estimated at about one million, with more than half of the people of mixed white and Negro blood.

The soil of the republic is generally fertile and the climate favors the growth of a variety of tropical products, chief of which are bananas, coffee, cacao, abacá, coconuts, sugar cane, and fruits. The forests contain an abundance of cabinet, dye, and building woods. Stock raising has increased over the years. Mining is of little importance, although deposits of manganese and limestone are available. Coral and sponges are found off both coasts, and pearls come from the Pearl Islands in Panama Bay.

The country has less than 300 miles of railroad, but highways are increasing in mileage, especially the roads connected with the Pan American Highway. The country is a center of international airways. The Panama Canal attracts many ships to Panama.

The University of Panama is at the head of the educational system. There are professional schools and many underfinanced elementary and secondary schools.

The following are among the most important writers of Panama: Tomás del Espíritu Santo (1834–62), a classical poet; Mariano Arosemena (1794–1868), a historian; José Dolores Urriola ("El Mulato") (1834–83), a popular poet; Federico Escobar (1861–1912), a poet of great merit; Ricardo Miró (b. 1883), a poet; Rodrigo Miró, poet and essayist; Ricardo J. Alfaro, philologist, historian, and authority on international law; and José Isaac Fábrega, novelist.

VENEZUELA

The history of Venezuela is a succession of dictatorships of more or less benevolent character.

When Bolívar left Great Colombia to continue the wars of independence in Peru, he placed one of his generals, José Antonio Páez, at the head of the government of two provinces in Venezuela. Páez was a typical *llanero,* born and raised on those vast plains of southern Venezuela where cattle raising is the chief occupation of the

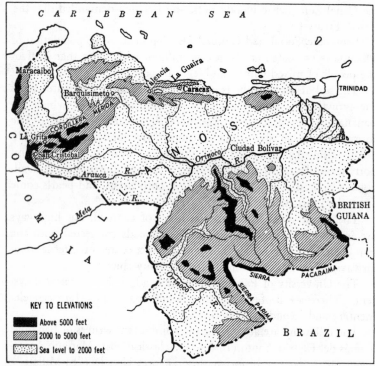

Fig. XVII–3. Physical Map of Venezuela. (Reproduced with permission from *Economic Geography of South America*, by R. H. Whitbeck, F. E. Williams, and W. F. Christians, published by McGraw-Hill Book Company, Inc., 3rd ed., New York, 1940.)

inhabitants. He was bold, a lover of freedom, and sincerely devoted to his country. The Venezuelans were not pleased with the choice of Bogotá as the capital of Great Colombia. When Santander, ruling in the absence of Bolívar, showed despotic tendencies, they decided to secede under the leadership of Páez.

Bolívar's sudden return to Venezuela in 1827 and his diplomatic attitude toward Páez, prevented a breach for the time being. But the secessionist movement continued to grow. At last, on November 19, 1829, an assembly gathered at Caracas declared Venezuela no longer a member of Great Colombia. The following May, at Valencia, independence was reaffirmed by a constituent assembly which drafted a constitution for the new state. This constitution was a compromise between the federalist and centralist tendencies. The executive was elected for four years by an electoral college; the legislature was bicameral; and the country was divided into several autonomous provinces, but their governors were appointed by the national executive. Under this constitution General Páez was elected the first president.

The Age of Páez. Although not all sections of Venezuela accepted the authority of the new government, peace was quickly restored by Páez. A revolution that took place in Caracas, aiming at the extermination of the landed aristocracy, was severely suppressed.

Early in 1835 Páez was succeeded by José María Vargas, a scholarly man who had been rector of the University of Caracas. Disgruntled because of the election of a nonmilitary man, the army rebelled, and President Vargas was compelled to resign. Santiago Mariño then became the chief executive, but not for long. Páez took up arms against him (1836) and forced the legislature to recall Vargas. The legislation suppressing certain monasteries, adopted by the legislature of Great Colombia some time before, was declared in force in Venezuela.

In 1836 Páez was again elected to the presidency. He restored order and ruled until 1843. His administration was progressive: roads were built, the press enjoyed reasonable freedom, immigration was promoted, the army was decreased, and commerce and agriculture were encouraged.

Páez was followed by Carlos Soublette, who continued the liberal reforms of his predecessor. Education was promoted, the national debt was reduced, and a commercial code was adopted. A revolt against the *godos,* or upper classes, was suppressed. As a result of this uprising, the election of 1846 was won by General José Tadeo Monagas, a conservative.

The Monagas Brothers. Despite his early conservative convictions, Monagas showed liberal tendencies after he assumed the presidency. He quarreled with his own party and dissolved the assembly. As a result, General Páez arose in revolt against the government; but he was defeated and exiled (1850). The following year the president's brother, José Gregorio Monagas, was made chief executive. Until 1858 the two Monagas brothers controlled the government.

In 1854 slavery was abolished, with compensation to slaveholders. In 1857 the constitution was amended in order to allow the election of the president for a term of six years, his re-election, and the re-organization of the whole government machinery on a highly centralized basis. This change in the form of government led to a new revolution and the overthrow of the Monagas oligarchy in 1858. A constituent convention was called, and a new constitution was adopted. This new instrument of government granted more autonomy to the municipalities and provided for manhood suffrage. The liberals were not entirely satisfied with these reforms and arose in arms once more. Peace was restored with the return of Páez from exile. He abolished the Constitution of 1858 and ruled as dictator until 1864, when he was once more exiled. War between the centralist and federalist factions continued. Eventually, a new constitution was adopted (1864) which created a confederate government under the name of United States of Venezuela. Juan Crisóstomo Falcón was elected president for four years, and at the end of his term, José Tadeo Monagas, the leader of the conservatives, again assumed the presidency.

The Rule of Guzmán Blanco. Meanwhile, a new leader had arisen. This man, Antonio Guzmán Blanco, was a brilliant, courageous, and energetic liberal with considerable political, diplomatic, and military experience. Taking up arms against President Monagas, he overthrew the government, and by 1872 had restored order, as dictator. In 1873 he was elected constitutional president. From then on until 1888 he ruled Venezuela directly or through his followers. Although despotic, particularly during his latter years, he was wise as an administrator and maintained peace. During his administration many progressive measures were taken: public education was made free and compulsory; the national debt was reduced and public credit restored; means of transportation were improved; import duties were reduced; export taxes were entirely abolished with a view to fostering commerce; and civil marriage was made compulsory.

While Guzmán Blanco was in Europe in 1888 a revolt broke out in Caracas, and his government was overthrown. This brought to the presidency Juan Pablo Rojas Paul, who, two years later, was in turn replaced by Raimundo Andueza Palacio.

The Rule of Crespo and Castro. In 1892 Joaquín Crespo, who had been one of Guzmán Blanco's alternates and was an able man, became chief executive. On July 5, 1893, a new constitution was adopted, providing for a secret ballot, and granting individual guarantees to both foreigners and nationals. Under this constitution Crespo was elected. During his administration a dangerous dispute arose with Great Britain over the boundary in the Guiana region. The two countries severed diplomatic relations with each other in 1887, but eventually decided to submit the question to arbitration, thanks to the intervention of the United States. Although the arbitral award gave Britain most of the disputed territory, the question was settled definitely.

In 1898 José Ignacio Andrade became the chief executive. The following year he was overthrown by Cipriano Castro, who ruled the country as dictator during nine years. He gave considerable attention to material progress, but revealed himself a man of ruthless and extravagant tendencies. The many uprisings that took place against him were brutally suppressed by Castro. During these revolutions considerable property of foreigners was destroyed, and Castro refused to compensate the owners for the damages suffered. As a result, the ports of Venezuela were blockaded in 1902 by warships of Great Britain, Germany, and Italy. Castro was advised by the government of the United States to agree to submit the question of indemnification to arbitration, which he did. Mixed claims commissions, sitting at Caracas, awarded damages proportional to the losses suffered.

The Rule of Gómez. In 1908 Cipriano Castro left for Europe, and while he was there the Venezuelan Congress suspended him from office and allowed the Vice-President, Juan Vicente Gómez, to assume the government. The following year Gómez was proclaimed president.

In 1914 the congress elected General Victoriano Márquez Bustillos provisional chief executive. A few months later a new constitution was promulgated, providing for a federal form of government; an executive to be elected for seven years; no vice-president; and a bicameral legislature. The following year Gómez was again elected president. But he did not take office, preferring to leave the government in charge of the provisional president, Bustillos, and keeping for himself the post of commander in chief of the army.

Gómez ruled Venezuela until his death in 1935. He maintained order. By allowing foreign capitalists to exploit the oil resources of the nation, he increased the national revenues. In 1930, to celebrate the centennial of Bolívar's death, the remainder of the national debt was paid off. During his regime a fine system of automobile roads was built in Venezuela. Other improvements also took place. But the people, in general, remained in poverty and ignorance. Civil liberties did not exist. All opposition to the president was ruthlessly checked, and many citizens were exiled, imprisoned, tortured, and assassinated.

Political Affairs, 1935–41. When Gómez died on December 17, 1935, the whole nation celebrated the event with rejoicing. Riots and attacks on the houses and persons of Gómez's supporters took place. General Eleazar López Contreras was appointed provisional executive by the congress. Later he was regularly elected president for five years. In 1936 a new constitution was adopted. Among other provisions, it contained one authorizing the breaking up of the large landed estates. Social legislation, aiming at the improvement of the conditions of the laboring classes, was also adopted.

President López Contreras followed a moderate policy, promoting harbor improvements and other public works. A Central Bank was established in Caracas early in 1940, with a capital of 3 million dollars. A trade agreement was signed with the United States providing for certain tariff reductions on Venezuelan petroleum imported into the United States. A loan of 10 million dollars was negotiated with the National City Bank for the Central Bank of Venezuela.

As the presidential elections approached (April, 1941), Diógenes Escalante, Venezuelan Ambassador to the United States, had the backing of President López Contreras and a substantial portion of the people. López Contreras himself repeatedly declared that he did not want to be re-elected.

The candidates in the presidential election of 1941 agreed to stop electioneering and allow the national congress to choose between them. Accordingly, General Isaías Medina Angarita, the Minister of War and Navy, was selected as chief executive for the five-year term beginning May 5, 1941.

Political Developments since World War II. Venezuela broke off diplomatic relations with the three principal Axis powers on December 31, 1941, and with Vichy France on November 27, 1942. War was declared on Germany and Japan, February 15, 1945. During World War II, agreements with the United States provided for "lend-lease" aid of more than 10 million dollars, the purchase of large quantities of Venezuelan rubber, and assistance in the campaign against malaria. In 1945 Venezuela became a charter member of the United Nations.

President Medina served until deposed on October 19, 1945, by a revolutionary junta under the leadership of Rómulo Betancourt. A national constituent assembly adopted a new constitution in July, 1947, which granted President Betancourt substantial powers over the economic life of the country. The new constitution guaranteed individual rights relating to property ownership, employment, education, and health. The president's term was changed from five to four years, and he was forbidden to succeed himself for the two following terms. In the presidential election of December 15, 1947, Rómulo Gallegos, the *Acción Democrática* Party's candidate, defeated Rafael Caldera, who represented the Conservative and Independent parties. President Gallegos was deposed in November, 1948, by a military revolution. A junta of three military officers took over the government and Lieutenant Colonel Carlos Delgado Chalbaud became provisional president. His administration outlawed the Communist Party in May, 1950, and promised a new election, a new constitution, and a new congress. These promises had not been kept by November 13, 1950, when President Chalbaud was assassinated.

On November 27, Dr. G. Suárez Flammerich was installed as president of the government junta. He, in turn, was replaced by Colonel Marcos Pérez Jiménez on December 3, 1952.

A revolution in the capital broke out on January 21, 1958, forcing President Pérez Jiménez to flee the country. The revolution was headed by a junta whose leader was Rear Admiral Wolfgang Larrazábal, who restored democratic rights and promised free elections, to be held later in the year, for delegates to a constituent assembly. In the presidential election held on December 7, 1958, Rómulo Betancourt received the majority of votes. He was installed on February 13, 1959.

In July, 1959, President Betancourt submitted to the congress a land-reform bill under which some 350,000 landless peasants would receive small plots of land and credits to purchase equipment, seeds, and fertilizers.

Despite government declarations that no changes would be made in the existing agreements with the foreign oil companies operating in the country, a decree issued on December 19, 1958, increased the income tax to be paid by the oil companies. This broke the 50/50 principle of equal shares in operation until then. Most of the fifty-odd corporations with oil concessions in Venezuela were American companies, representing investments totaling about 28 billion dollars.

In February, 1960, a most outstanding three-year contract was signed by the Oil Workers' Union and the major oil companies operating in Venezuela. This contract gave some 42,000 workers total additional annual benefits of some 100 million dollars, the Venezuelan government assuming responsibility to pay 47 per cent of the increase and the companies the balance. The contract provided for an increase of between 10 and 12 cents an hour in wages, one month's paid vacation, with $60 vacation bonus to each worker. A 40-hour week for salaried employees and a 44-hour week for hourly workers were also provided under the contract.

In November, 1960, there were riots in Caracas, touched off by a strike of the telephone company workers and fanned by leftist agitators. President Betancourt took strong repressive measures, including the suspension of constitutional guarantees. A Communist newspaper which had been inciting the people to revolt was closed by government troops.

Another uprising broke out in Barcelona and other cities in June, 1961, as part of a plot to overthrow President Betancourt. On June 24 an unsuccessful bomb attempt on the President's life was made in Caracas. President Betancourt escaped with burns, but one of his aides and two other persons were killed. Supporters of former dictator Pérez Jiménez were apparently responsible for the attempt, with support from the Dominican Republic. Calling upon the OAS Council to take appropriate action, the Venezuelan government submitted what it called proofs of Dominican complicity. At the meeting of foreign ministers of the American nations held at San José, Costa Rica, August 16–28, a resolution was adopted condemning Dominican acts of aggression and intervention in Venezuela.

A new constitution promulgated January 23, 1961, failed to stop leftist agitation. In June a revolt at the Puerto Cabello naval base was crushed by loyal forces. On June 12, 1963, President Betancourt escaped another attempt against his life, and many Communists were arrested. Amid unrest, elections were held December 1. Raúl Leoni was elected president and was inaugurated March 11, 1964.

Economic, Social, and Cultural Development. The Venezuelan population exceeds 6 million; about 10 per cent are white.

The country is predominantly agricultural, with coffee the leading crop. Other products are cacao, sugar cane, tobacco, cotton, corn, wheat, vegetables, and fruits. The livestock industry is also a source of wealth. Forests cover about half of the area of the country.

The petroleum industry began in 1917 and has now reached tremendous proportions. Other minerals are iron, gold, silver, coal, copper, and salt. Manufacturing, which is expanding rapidly, has been limited chiefly to articles of local consumption.

Transportation is aided by 6,000 miles of navigable rivers, several thousand miles of highways, and a few hundred miles of railroad. National and international airlines serve the country.

There are several universities in Venezuela, including the National University at Caracas, the Universities of the Andes at Mérida, and Catholic and other private universities. There are a number of schools for special instruction in commerce, the arts, and military science. Elementary and secondary schools do not adequately meet the demands of the increasing population.

Venezuela's national literature is extensive and varied. Among the most important writers the following may be mentioned: José Antonio Maitín (1804–74), a romantic poet; Juan Antonio Pérez Bonalde (1846–92), a poet who wrote under the influence of German poets of his generation; José Gil Fortuol (b. 1862), a poet, historian, and novelist of great psychological insight; Manuel Romero García (b. 1865), who portrayed rural life; Gonzalo Picón Febres (1860–1919), one of the greatest novelists of Latin America and author of *El Sargento Felipe;* Manuel Díaz Rodríguez (b. 1868), a novelist, author of *Idolos rotos;* Rufino Blanco Fombona (b. 1874), a modernist poet of great merit, author of *Cantos de la prisión y del destierro* and of the novels *El Hombre de hierro* and *El Hombre de oro;*

Rómulo Gallegos Freire (b. 1884), a novelist whose *Doña Bárbara* is well known everywhere in Latin America; Teresa de la Parra (1895–1936), a novelist of great talent, author of *Ifigenia* and *Las Memorias de Mamá Blanca;* and many others. Andrés Bello (1781–1865) educator, philologist, poet, and one of the greatest literary men of Latin America, was born in Venezuela, although most of his life was spent in Europe and Chile.

Venezuela has produced distinguished artists, such as J. Rojas, a painter of classical inspiration; Martín Tovar y Tovar, a historical painter; Arturo Michelena, a painter of classical subjects; Cabré, López Méndez, Otero, Golding, and Monasterios, modern painters; and Pérez Mujica, a sculptor.

ECUADOR

At the time of independence, the Presidency of Quito veered between adherence to Bolívar's Great Colombia, annexation to Peru, and outright independence. Bolívar was successful in securing the annexation of this territory to Great Colombia. Later (1828) a Peruvian invasion was repulsed by General Sucre. Nevertheless, sentiment in favor of independence did not die out, and in May, 1830, a revolutionary junta met in Quito, declared that province independent from Great Colombia, and elected General Juan José Flores, a hero of the wars of independence as provisional executive. In August of the same year, a congress met at Riobamba, declared the departments of Azuay, Guajas, and Quito as constituting a sovereign state under the name of the "State of Ecuador," and framed a constitution providing for the election of the executive for a term of four years by a unicameral legislature and granting him broad powers of government. The Roman Catholic Church was declared the official church of the republic. A provision of the constitution declared the willingness of the new state to unite with other states of northern South America in some sort of confederation.

From the beginning, Ecuador's political life was disturbed by internal dissension and external disputes: the former caused by rivalry between ambitious *caudillos,* regional antagonism, and resentment against the Church; and the latter by undefined boundaries.

The Rule of Flores. Under the Constitution of 1830 General Flores was elected first president. At once trouble developed in Guayaquil, where General Rafael Urdaneta declared himself in favor of union with Great Colombia. However, the news of Bolívar's death arrived soon after, and opposition to Flores' government gradually subsided. A dispute over the boundary with New Granada in the region of the Cauca and Carchi rivers was settled in 1833 in favor of that country after Ecuadorian forces were worsted in a short armed conflict.

President Flores soon developed dictatorial tendencies. A young liberal named Vicente Rocafuerte who had traveled abroad and had been elected to the congress led the opposition to him. When Rocafuerte was exiled, an uprising took place in his favor in Guayaquil, but it was soon put down and Rocafuerte was imprisoned. However, President Flores feared new outbreaks and decided to enter into an agreement with Rocafuerte whereby the latter would be made governor of an administrative province until Flores ended his term of office; then Rocafuerte would assume the presidency and Flores would be made commander of the national army.

The Rule of Rocafuerte. In accordance with this agreement, Rocafuerte became president in 1835. He at once called a constituent assembly, which met at Ambato and framed a new constitution changing the name of the country to "Republic of Ecuador" and providing for a bicameral legislature. Rocafuerte endeavored to promote public education, commerce, and navigation. In general he was inspired by high ideals.

Flores' Second Regime. In 1839 Flores returned to the presidency. His second administration was at first comparatively free from disturbances. The ports of the nation were opened to commerce with Spain, after that country had recognized Ecuador's independence in 1840. Treaties of commerce were signed with various countries. The failure of Flores to settle satisfactorily the boundary dispute existing with Peru and the general economic depression led to considerable antagonism toward him. Wishing to perpetuate himself in power, he had a new constitution drafted in 1843 extending the president's term of office to eight years. Then he caused himself to be re-elected. Two years later the liberals revolted and Flores was overthrown, agreeing to leave the country in voluntary exile.

The Anarchy of 1845–60. The same year (1845), still another constitution was adopted by an assembly meeting at Cuenca and entirely under the control of the liberals and anti-clericals. According to this new instrument of government, the president's term of office was to be four years. Vicente Ramón Roca was elected president. At once the country was plunged into revolution because of the radical character of the legislation adopted. This condition lasted until 1860. During this period difficulties arose with New Granada on the matter of political refugees from Ecuador, but the dispute was settled peacefully by the agreement of Santa Rosa del Carchi in 1846. In 1850 Diego Noboa took over the government as a result of a military coup. A decree signed by him in 1851 permitted the Society of Jesus to return to Ecuador. A new constitution was adopted the same year, and the capital was moved to Guayaquil; Noboa was declared elected president. In 1852 another constitution was adopted similar to that of 1845 but providing for the election of the president by electoral assemblies. Laws were adopted under this new constitution expelling the Jesuits again and abolishing slavery, with compensation to the owners of slaves. General José María Urbina was elected president in 1852, and four years later Francisco Robles became president.

The country was by now in complete chaos. Taking advantage of this situation, Peru blockaded the port of Guayaquil and forced General Guillermo Franco, in command there, to sign an agreement (1860) whereby Peru acquired sovereignty over the Azuay province. The indignation caused in Ecuador by this humiliating agreement offered General Flores the opportunity of gathering, with the aid of Gabriel García Moreno, a force strong enough to defeat Franco and capture Guayaquil. Flores then retired, and García Moreno was elected president under a new constitution (1861).

The Rule of García Moreno. For the next fourteen years García Moreno ruled the country even when out of the presidency. A well-educated man, energetic, and possessing strong convictions, he had been unfavorably impressed with the results of the European liberal revolutions of the middle nineteenth century and had become convinced that his country could be saved from anarchy only by restoring to the Catholic Church the power and influence it had enjoyed during colonial days.

The 1861 constitution provided for a highly centralized form of government and declared the Catholic Church the official church, to the exclusion of all others.

The following year (1862) Ecuador signed with the papacy a concordat restoring to the Catholic Church all the privileges it had enjoyed before independence, including the complete control of public education and the right to censor all publications.

The president then embarked on a program of the improvement

of roads, harbors, and public buildings, the stimulation of commerce and agriculture, the elimination of corruption in the public administration, and the establishment of a uniform currency.

A war with New Granada, in which the Ecuadorian army was defeated, and García Moreno's severe treatment of his political opponents created unrest. At the end of his term of office (1865), Jerónimo Carrión was elected chief executive. The new president quarreled with the congress, had difficulties with García Moreno, and finally resigned (1867). Two years later García Moreno became president again. Intending to perpetuate himself in power, he caused the constitution to be amended extending the president's term of office to six years and allowing his immediate re-election.

During his second administration García Moreno continued his program of strengthening the Church. His devotion to the Church led him to instruct the Ecuadorian representative at Rome to protest against the confiscation, in 1871, of the papal territory by the Italian government. He also had the Ecuadorian Congress offer gifts of money to the papacy. In October, 1873, a law was adopted by the national congress consecrating the republic to the "Sacred Heart of Jesus."

Despite strong antagonism from the liberals and anti-clericals, García Moreno was re-elected in 1875. But on August 6 of that year he was assassinated. There followed a period of anarchy until 1895, when another strong man, Eloy Alfaro, assumed control of the government.

The Rule of Alfaro. On June 5, 1895, Eloy Alfaro, a liberal of great ability, was declared chief executive by a revolutionary congress in Guayaquil. Alfaro had been exiled by President Luis Cordero. Returning to Ecuador, he organized the opposition against the government, defeated the loyal troops, and the following September entered the capital, where he was soon proclaimed president by the congress.

For the following sixteen years Alfaro was the controlling factor in the political life of Ecuador. In 1897 a new constitution was adopted granting religious freedom and setting aside most of the provisions of the Concordat of 1862. Although the Catholic Church remained the official church, the religious orders were expelled, and only native clergymen were allowed to perform religious functions. Quito again became the capital of the republic. Later, laws were adopted legalizing civil marriage, permitting divorce, and secularizing certain Church properties, the income from which was to be devoted to the maintenance of asylums, hospitals, and other charitable organizations. Complete religious freedom was decreed on October 13, 1904.

From 1901 to 1905 General Leónidas Plaza Gutiérrez ruled in comparative peace. But his successor, Lizardo García, was overthrown by a revolution, and on January 17, 1906, Eloy Alfaro became president again. He at once called a constituent assembly, which met in the capital and drafted a new constitution providing for the election of the president by direct vote of the people for four years, no immediate re-election of the executive, a bicameral legislature, a council of state, public education under the control of laymen, and religious freedom.

Alfaro, inaugurated on January 1, 1907, remained in power for four years. He promoted railroad construction connecting the coast with the plateau where the capital is situated, and other improvements. Opposed by the conservatives and some liberals, he was accused of intending to make himself dictator. In 1911 he resigned and left for Europe. But anarchy followed, and Alfaro was persuaded to return. As he endeavored to regain control of the government, he was murdered on January 28, 1912.

Political Affairs from 1912 to 1940. After Alfaro's assassination another period of anarchy followed. President succeeded president amidst general disorder. In 1914 President Leónidas Plaza Gutiérrez endeavored to bring about a constitutional change to allow the introduction of a parliamentary system, but he failed. In 1918 President Gonzalo Córdoba was deposed, and several government juntas followed at close intervals. In April, 1926, the army proclaimed Dr. Isidro Ayora provisional executive. He initiated serious studies of the economic ailments of Ecuador and engaged for that purpose the services of a group of American economists headed by Professor Edwin W. Kemmerer of Princeton University. As a result, reforms were introduced, a central bank was established (June 1, 1927), and the currency was reformed. In 1929 a new constitution was adopted, not very different from previous ones, and Dr. Ayora was again elected president. In September, 1930, he submitted his resignation to the congress, which did not accept it. The economic depression then felt all over the world resulted in considerable criticism of Dr. Ayora's administration. He decided to resign once more, and this time his resignation was accepted. He was followed in the presidency by Colonel Luis Larrea Alba. Strikes, revolutions, and general disorder made this period a particularly difficult one for Ecuador. In September, 1935, Federico Páez assumed the presidency. His administration became very unpopular in consequence of his measures against so-called "Communist elements." Left-wing activities were suppressed ruthlessly, and a number of the president's political opponents were exiled. Unrest throughout the country finally led the president to resign on October 23, 1937. General Alberto Enríquez, War Minister in the Páez cabinet, assumed the executive power.

A constituent assembly was convened (August 10, 1937) to draft a new constitution. Under this new charter Dr. Aurelio Mosquera Narváez was elected to the presidency in 1939. Dr. Mosquera Narváez died, however, in December of the same year, and the president of the Senate, Dr. Carlos Arroyo del Río, took his place in a provisional character. Despite unrest and rumors of impending revolution, at the elections held on January 10 and 11, 1940, Dr. Arroyo del Río was elected president for the term of 1940–44.

Boundary Disputes. The relations of Ecuador with her neighbors have been rendered difficult on account of boundary disputes. In 1904 a treaty was signed with Brazil accepting as the boundary a line running from the mouth of the San Antonio River to the mouth of the Apaporis River in a region also claimed by Peru and Colombia. In 1916 an agreement with Colombia settled the existing dispute. The remaining claimant to the region, Peru, had agreed to submit the controversy to the arbitration of the Spanish Crown in 1904. But the award was withheld by the arbiter for fear that war might ensue between the two contending parties. Later negotiations led to the decision to submit the dispute to the arbitration of the President of the United States if direct negotiations failed to bring about a settlement. Negotiations dragged on for several years before the question was finally settled in 1942.

Political Developments since World War II. Ecuador maintained very co-operative relations with the United States during and after World War II. Credits and loans from the United States were of considerable assistance to the economy. The United States established a naval base at Salinas in March, 1942, which was returned to Ecuador in February, 1946. The Arroyo del Río government severed diplomatic relations with the Axis powers during the Rio Conference of Foreign Ministers in January, 1942. Shortly there-

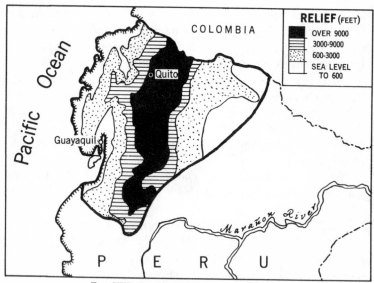

Fig. XVII–4. Physical Features of Ecuador.

after it was revealed that the United States had arranged with Ecuador to take over air bases on the Santa Elena Peninsula and in the
Galápagos Islands. On February 2, 1945, the government stated that
a state of war with Japan had existed since December 7, 1941. Ecuador became a charter member of the United Nations.

In 1941 an uprising in Quito induced the Council of State to con-
fer extraordinary powers on President Arroyo del Río, including
censorship and unlimited economic and military authority. The
objective was to enable the president to cope with an undeclared
war against Peru over a boundary dispute. The dispute was settled
in 1942 through the mediation of the United States, Argentina, and
Brazil. Towards the end of President Arroyo del Río's term, a revolution broke out in Guayaquil (May 29, 1944), and former President José María Velasco Ibarra assumed the presidency as requested
by a revolutionary junta. In August, 1944, a constituent assembly,
meeting at Quito, confirmed Velasco Ibarra's election as president.
A new constitution was proclaimed in 1945. However, Velasco
Ibarra was overthrown by Defense Minister Colonel Carlos Man-

cheno, who instituted a dictatorship. Then a counterrevolution led by Colonel Angel Baquero Dávila split the country into two separate regimes. On September 17, 1947, the congress designated Carlos Julio Arosemena to be temporary president, and in the close election of June 6, 1948, Galo Plaza Lasso was elected president for a four-year term.

Presidential elections held on June 1, 1952, resulted in the victory of Dr. José María Velasco Ibarra, former president and the candidate of the Independent Liberal Party. President Velasco Ibarra was succeeded by Dr. Carmilo Ponce Enríquez, elected on June 3, 1956, and inaugurated on September 1, for a four-year term.

For the last few years, Ecuador has made considerable progress in every realm of activity. It has had an annual trade surplus, its currency is considered solid, and the general economic growth is estimated at about 9 per cent a year. This progress is undoubtedly due to the orderly political life which started with the government of Galo Plaza Lasso. He it was who opened a rich coastal region to agriculture by the construction of some 1,600 miles of roads.

In June, 1960, Dr. Velasco Ibarra again was elected president of the republic. Inaugurated on September 1, he declared in his address to the congress that the agreement for the demarcation of the boundary with Peru under the 1942 treaty was unjust and had been imposed by force. At the request of Peru, the representatives of the four guarantors of the treaty (the United States, Brazil, Argentina, and Chile) met in Rio de Janeiro in October to study the question. They recommended that Ecuador and Peru enter into further direct negotiations with a view to reaching a mutually satisfactory settlement of the dispute.

President Velasco Ibarra has repeatedly expressed his sympathy with Fidel Castro's regime in Cuba. In June, 1961, he sent a mission headed by Vice-President Carlos Julio Arosemena on a goodwill visit to the U.S.S.R. At the end of 1961 Vice-President Carlos Julio Arosemena was proclaimed president by the congress after President Velasco Ibarra resigned under the pressure of rising public and military opposition.

On July 11, 1963, Arosemena was ousted by the military, who set up a governing junta headed by Capt. (later Rear Adm.) Ramón Castro Jijón. On March 29, 1966, the junta was compelled to resign under pressure of public opinion. Clemente Yerovi Indaburo was then set up as provisional President by the armed forces.

Economic, Social, and Cultural Development. The population of Ecuador is estimated at more than 4 million inhabitants, all but perhaps 200,000 of Indian blood.

Ecuador is an agricultural country, producing cacao, bananas, rice, coffee, cotton, palm nuts, and tagua. The forests yield balsa, rubber, kapok, and cinchona. Mining is little developed, although there are gold, mercury, copper, iron, lead, silver, platinum, and sulfur. Petroleum production is on the increase. Manufacturing is varied but not extensive. The "Panama hat" is a well-known product.

There are several universities, including the Central University of Quito and the Universities of Guayaquil and Cuenca. Several professional schools serve the country, and there are a National Conservatory of Music and a National School of Fine Arts. Primary and secondary schools do not meet the country's educational needs.

Ecuador is proud of being the birthplace of José Joaquín Olmedo (1780–1847), one of the greatest poets of Latin America, the author of *La Victoria de Junín,* an ode celebrating Bolívar's victory over the Spanish armies. Other Ecuadorian writers of note are: Juan León Mera (1832–94), a poet and novelist, author of *La Virgen del sol;* Numa Pompilio Llona (1832–1907), who belonged to the romantic school; Juan Montalvo (1833–89), an essayist, philosopher, and imitator of Cervantes; Alejandro Carrio, a modern poet; Jorge Fernández, a novelist; Jorge Icaza, a novelist of great merit and author of the indigenous novels *Huasipungo, En las calles,* and others.

Ecuador has produced many artists of great merit, such as the painters Antonio Salas and his sons Ramón and Rafael. In recent years, Xito Durán, a composer of native inspiration, has become internationally known.

CHAPTER XVIII

PERU, BOLIVIA, AND CHILE

THE POLITICAL LIFE of Peru, Bolivia, and Chile has been closely interwoven since independence, either by temporary union (Peru and Bolivia), armed conflict, or economic interdependence. For many years, because of the difficulty of access to these countries, they were comparatively isolated from the rest of the world. Since the opening of the Panama Canal, however, their influence in the affairs of the Western Hemisphere has grown steadily.

PERU

Until quite recently the history of Peru was a succession of dictatorships made inevitable by the complete lack of political consciousness of the masses (90 per cent of which are Indians and *mestizos*) and the tradition of autocratic government of the ruling minority.

In 1822 the congress convened by San Martín, the Protector of Peru, adopted the basis of a constitution providing for a republican form of government, the division of powers, the election of the executive for four years, and a unicameral legislature. The same congress also elected a governing junta, which was overthrown the following year by dissatisfied army officers. José de la Riva Agüero, a distinguished Creole patriot, was then elected president.

Bolívar, Dictator of Peru. The government shifted from one place to another during the remainder of the war of independence. President Riva Agüero quarreled with the legislature, dissolved it, and created in its place a senate of twelve members. But in the capital the dismissed legislators were reinstalled by José Bernardo Tagle y Portocarrero, Marquis of Torre Tagle, who immediately thereafter was declared by them president, in place of Riva Agüero. Under the circumstances, with two rival governments attempting to rule the country while the war against the royalists was still undecided, the Lima assembly invited Bolívar to come to Peru. Offering him dictatorial powers, the legislature suspended the Constitution of 1823 and adjourned *sine die*.

At the end of the war Bolívar's powers were continued until the meeting of a new congress. The Liberator appointed a governing council headed by José Hipólito Unánue, to rule in his absence. He also issued decrees curtailing the privileges of the Church and providing for other reforms.

In 1826 the situation in the north compelled the Liberator to return to Bogotá, leaving the government of Peru in the hands of a council of which General Andrés Santa Cruz was president. This council proceeded to promulgate for Peru the same constitution drafted by the Liberator for Bolivia, a highly idealistic instrument of government providing for a tricameral legislature and an executive elected for life. Under this constitution the Liberator was elected president of Peru.

All this produced antagonism against Bolívar and his fellow countrymen. This antagonism was intensified by the suspicion that the Liberator wished to join Peru and Bolivia to Great Colombia. The fact that Colombian troops still remained quartered in the country seemed to confirm this suspicion.

The Bolivarian Regime Overthrown. In 1827 several battalions of the Colombian troops mutinied and had to be sent home. Taking advantage of this opportunity, the Peruvians overthrew the governing council left by Bolívar, established a provisional government of their own, adopted once more the Constitution of 1823, and elected General José de La Mar as president.

Meanwhile, resentment against Bolívar's interference in Peru and Bolivia continued to grow. In 1828 some Colombian troops stationed in Bolivia mutinied. Under the pretext of restoring order, Peruvian forces invaded Bolivia, compelled General Sucre, then president of that country, to resign and leave the country, taking with him the remaining Colombian soldiers. The following year relations between Peru and Colombia were strained to the breaking point by a dispute over the division of the debt arising from the war of independence and over the boundary between the two countries. During the short war that ensued, a Peruvian fleet attacked Guayaquil, but the Colombian forces defeated the Peruvian army sent against them. Peace was restored without a definite settlement of some of the pending questions, which later were to bring about new difficulties between the two countries.

In 1828 General Agustín Gamarra was made provisional president of Peru, replacing General La Mar, who was deposed. In 1833 a constituent congress elected General Luis José Orbegoso as president. Gamarra in turn dissolved the congress and proclaimed General Pedro Bermúdez chief executive despite the opposition of the civilian population. Civil war followed, ending with the victory of the civilian party and the return of Orbegoso to the presidency. The same year (1834) a new constitution was adopted. But while the president was away from the capital, a military revolution deposed him and proclaimed in his place General Felipe Santiago de Salaverry as dictator.

Salaverry was an intelligent and courageous young army officer who had distinguished himself in the war of independence. He was well-intentioned but inclined to cruelty.

Intense commercial rivalry developed at this time between the ports of Valparaíso, in Chile, and Callao, in Peru. Realizing the closeness of the commercial interests of the two nations, Salaverry advocated some sort of commercial union between Peru and Chile. In 1835 he signed a treaty with Chile doing away with high tariffs imposed upon Chilean products imported into Peru. This treaty was received with a good deal of antagonism in Peru.

The Peru-Bolivian Confederation. Bolivia was then ruled by General Andrés Santa Cruz, who had favored, to a certain extent, Bolívar's plan of union of Bolivia and Peru to Great Colombia but who had ambitions of his own in regard to the two former states. Invited by the deposed presidents, Gamarra and Orbegoso, to intervene in Peru, Santa Cruz marched at the head of an army into that country, defeated Salaverry, assumed control of the government, and reorganized the nation into two provinces, Northern and Southern Peru, joining them to Bolivia under the name of *"Confederación Perú-Boliviana."* Santa Cruz was appointed Supreme Protector of the Confederation. This union of the two countries did not last long. In 1839 Santa Cruz's troops were defeated by armies sent against them by Chile and Argentina. Santa Cruz himself was compelled to resign and leave the country.

After the disruption of the Confederation, a congress met in Lima, annulled all the acts of Santa Cruz, and adopted a new constitution (November 18, 1839), which provided for a bicameral congress and the election of the executive for a six-year term. Under this constitution General Gamarra was elected president.

Now came the turn of Gamarra to invade Bolivia in order to overthrow General José Ballivián, the successor of Santa Cruz. But the Peruvian forces were defeated, and Gamarra was killed in battle (1841). Thanks to the mediation of Chile, a treaty ending the conflict was signed the following year between the two nations.

Peru made some economic progress during this period. In 1840 the first steamship line was established between Callao and Talcahuano, and in 1841 guano began to be exported to Europe.

The Rule of Castilla. After the death of Gamarra, the country went through a period of anarchy until 1844, when Ramón Castilla was made president. A man of strong character and great ability, although possessing little education, he ruled with a strong hand. His administration was characterized by economic prosperity owing to a great increase in the nitrate and guano exports. The government was enabled through the monopoly of the sale of guano to consolidate the internal debt and to begin payments on the foreign debt. Castilla reorganized the army and the navy, improved means of communication, and built one of the first railroads in South America, connecting the capital with the port of Callao. Immigration was encouraged. Chinese coolies were brought over to work on the farms, but this immigration was stopped in 1874, when the cruel treatment of the coolies led them to rebel against their masters.

Castilla was succeeded in 1851 by José Rufino Echenique, whose administration was characterized by corruption. Four years later Echenique was overthrown, and Castilla returned to power as a dictator. Peru enjoyed a new period of prosperity during Castilla's second administration. Education was promoted, Negro slavery was abolished, and the Indians were freed from the payment of tribute which had been collected since colonial days. In 1856 a new constitution was promulgated. Despite general prosperity, peace was broken by insurrections at various times. Castilla, in 1859, partly to divert the people's attention from internal conflict, provoked a quarrel with Ecuador over the boundary question. The Peruvian fleet blockaded the Ecuadorian coasts, and a treaty was forced upon General Guillermo Franco, then dictator, at Guayaquil (Treaty of Mapasingue, signed in 1860). This treaty was at one time or another repudiated by both nations as not having been signed by a truly national government and therefore not technically legal.

In 1860 a liberal constitution was adopted. Castilla was succeeded in 1862 by General Miguel San Román, who died within a few months of his inauguration and was replaced by the Vice-President, General Juan Antonio Pezet. Another period of corruption and anarchy followed.

War with Spain. In 1864 a war broke out with Spain, Peru being supported by Ecuador, Bolivia, and Chile. Spain had not yet recognized Peru's independence. Attempting to collect damages for injuries suffered by Spanish citizens in Peru during the many revolutions of the period since independence, the Spanish government found it impossible to secure a satisfactory reply. In 1864 a Spanish fleet was sent to the Pacific, and the guano-laden Chincha Islands, belonging to Peru, were occupied. President Pezet endeavored to bring about a peaceful settlement of the dispute. Public indignation at the terms demanded by Spain and accepted by Pezet, resulted in the latter's overthrow. Mariano Ignacio Prado assumed the executive office in 1865 and negotiated an alliance with the neighboring nations against Spain. Military conflict lasted only a few months, and the hostilities were suspended thanks to the mediation of the United States in 1871. But the treaty of peace was not actually signed until 1879.

Prado's Administration. President Prado reformed the administration, curtailed expenses, and promoted industry and agriculture. In 1867 a new constitution not much different from previous ones went into effect. The following year President Prado was overthrown, and José Balta became chief executive. He was honest and well-intentioned. But owing to the financial difficulties of the country, he was compelled to negotiate an unfavorable contract with French bankers whereby, in return for a loan, a monopoly of guano exports up to two million tons was granted to the bankers. Complications developed when the price of guano fell. The foreign debt of Peru rose to enormous proportions.

Balta was overthrown in 1872 and shot during a military revolution headed by Tomás Gutiérrez, who in turn was shot by revolutionists. The congress then elected Manuel Pardo as president. The new executive set himself to reduce the influence of the army in politics and to create a civilian party. He restored the municipalities, which assumed control of local education.

The financial conditions of Peru were rendered worse at this time by the artificial production of fertilizers abroad. In an effort to increase the national revenues, the nitrate fields were taken over by the government.

On February 6, 1873, a treaty of alliance and recognition of each other's territories was signed with Bolivia.

The War of the Pacific. A dispute over the boundary between Chile and Bolivia in the Atacama region resulted in the occupation of the coast of Antofagasta, Cobija, and Tocopilla by Chilean troops. Peru endeavored to bring about a peaceful settlement of the dispute. But Chile not only refused the Peruvian good offices, but demanded that the treaty of alliance between Peru and Bolivia be abrogated. When this was refused, Chile declared war upon both countries (April 5, 1879). The better-armed Chilean forces defeated the allied troops, captured Lima, and destroyed a great deal of civilian property in Peru.

When President Pardo left for Europe, presumably to secure help, Nicolás de Piérola arose against the government and assumed the dictatorship of Peru, but was soon overthrown. A provisional government headed by Francisco García Calderón attempted to negotiate peace with Chile, but failed. Anarchy reigned throughout the country. In 1882 Colonel Miguel Iglesias was given full powers by the congress to negotiate with the Chilean authorities. The "War of the Pacific" between Chile and Peru finally ended with the signing of the Treaty of Ancón in 1883. This treaty was ratified by both nations the following year. In August, 1884, the Chilean troops withdrew from Peruvian territory.

The Question of the Pacific. The Treaty of Ancón gave rise to a long controversy between Peru and Chile, known as the "Question of the Pacific," which was not settled until 1929. One of its provisions declared that the province of Tarapacá was to be ceded by Peru to Chile in perpetuity; the department of Tacna was to be occupied by Chile for ten years, and at the end of that period a plebiscite was to decide to which of the two nations it would belong. The country receiving the province would pay the other 10 million pesos. In 1898 an agreement was signed (Billingshurst-Latorre) whereby the question of whether the plebiscite should be held or not was to be submitted to the arbitration of the Spanish Crown. This agreement was not ratified by Chile, and Tacna continued to be governed by Chilean authorities. In 1910 Peru severed diplomatic relations with Chile. Twelve years later the two governments accepted the mediation of the United States and decided to submit the question of the plebiscite to the arbitration of the President of the United States. President Coolidge, in 1925, decided that a plebiscite should be held; but it was not possible to hold it because of the unrest that prevailed in the disputed area. Diplomatic relations having been re-established in 1928 at the suggestion of Secretary Kellogg, the following year a plan was adopted by the two countries whereby Chile was to receive the department of Arica and that of Tacna was to go to Peru. Chile further agreed to pay to Peru six million dollars and to build port facilities in Arica for Peru. The treaty was ratified on July 28, 1929.

The Aftermath of the War of the Pacific. After the War of the Pacific a period of anarchy followed in Peru. In 1886 General Andrés Avelino Cáceres was elected president. He ruled with dictatorial powers, curtailing government expenditures and entering into an agreement with foreign bondholders whereby the income of the national railroads was pledged to them for sixty-six years. Civil war spread to the whole country in 1894–95. The conflict ended with the assuming of the executive power by Nicolás de Piérola.

The Rule of Leguía and the Revolution of 1930. From 1908 to 1912, and again from 1919 to 1930, Augusto B. Leguía ruled as absolute dictator. In 1920 a liberal constitution was adopted, but Leguía disregarded it entirely. Although many economic improvements took place during his rule, the country was dissatisfied.

In 1909 the President of Argentina issued his award in the Peruvian dispute with Bolivia over the boundary line. Although the decision was favorable in the main to Bolivia, the people of that country protested against it. Relations between Peru and Bolivia thereupon became strained, and war was avoided only by the exchange of certain portions of territory. The dispute over the boundary with Ecuador almost led to war between the two countries in 1910, but the conflict was averted by the intervention of the United States, Brazil, and Argentina.

The opposition to President Leguía resulted in a military revolt in 1930. Leguía was compelled to leave the country, and Luis Sánchez Cerro, leader of the revolt, became chief executive. The political situation in the country was rendered more acute by the economic depression. Strikes, rioting, and military uprisings led to the resignation of Sánchez Cerro the following year. But he was regularly elected to the presidency soon after that.

In the latter part of 1931 the president arbitrarily arrested Víctor

Raúl Haya de la Torre, leader of the party known as APRA (*Alianza Popular Revolucionaria Americana*), and deported other members of that party. On April 30, 1933, Sánchez Cerro was assassinated, presumably by an *Aprista,* and General Oscar Raimundo Benavides, a strong conservative, was elected by a constituent assembly to govern the country.

Benavides' Dictatorship. At first Benavides showed a tendency to be conciliatory. But during the presidential elections of 1936 he not only caused the name of the APRA candidate, Haya de la Torre, to be stricken from the ballot, but when the *Aprista* substitute candidate (Luis Antonio Eguiguren) appeared to have received a majority of votes, the president annulled the elections. A short time afterwards he assumed dictatorial authority, and his term of office was prolonged for three years. Attempts to overthrow President Benavides were unsuccessful.

President Prado y Ugarteche. At the presidential elections held in 1939, Manuel Prado y Ugarteche, a banker and anti-militarist liberal was chosen. Inaugurated on December 8, 1939, President Prado was considerably handicapped in his efforts to restore the country to normalcy by the lack of foreign exchange. President Prado freed all political prisoners jailed during Benavides' administration, and endeavored to promote the development of the national resources.

Former President Benavides' influence was still strongly felt in the country although he had left Peru after the expiration of his term to become Peruvian Ambassador to Spain. By a series of last-minute decrees just before his term expired, he launched a huge program of public works and increased the pay of the military and police forces.

Political Developments since World War II. Peru and Chile agreed on the joint defense of their Pacific coastline February 7, 1941. At the Rio Conference of Foreign Ministers (January, 1942), Peru and Ecuador settled an old boundary dispute peacefully. Diplomatic relations between Peru and the three main Axis powers were broken on January 24, 1942; relations with Vichy France were ended on January 26, 1943. A state of war with Germany and Japan was proclaimed on February 12, 1945. In the same year Peru became a charter member of the United Nations. During World War II, agreements with the United States provided for substantial credits to assist Peruvian rubber production and public works. Reciprocal trade concessions were made, and the United States agreed to purchase all surplus Peruvian rubber and cotton.

Dr. José Luis Bustamante y Rivero, a liberal and leftist candidate, was elected president, June 10, 1945, to succeed President Prado. In June, 1948, President Bustamante instituted government by decree to deal with serious economic and political problems. Rightist revolts in July and October induced the government to outlaw the *Aprista* Party and later (November 2) the Communist Party. A second revolt at Arequipa in October compelled President Bustamante to leave the country. General Manuel A. Odría became provisional president and named an all-military cabinet to draft a statute of government which was instituted on January 7, 1949. There was another violent outbreak in Arequipa, in which 250 persons were killed. Finally, in July, 1950, General Odría was regularly elected for a six-year term.

In 1955, President Odría announced his intention to retire and to hand over the government to the victor at the election to be held in June, 1956. Former President Prado y Ugarteche, candidate of the Moderate Conservative Party, received the majority of votes and was inaugurated on July 28, 1956. On the same day, the Peruvian Congress legalized the *Aprista* Party, which had been suppressed since 1948.

The economic situation of Peru improved considerably in 1960 during the administration of President Prado. A favorable trade balance benefited the economic conditions of the nation, currency was stabilized, and the rise in the cost of living was greatly reduced. President Prado visited the United States in September, 1961.

In the June 10, 1962, elections no candidate received the required one-third vote, and the new congress, convened on July 28, was charged with the election of the president. Alleging fraud, the military leaders overthrew the government on July 18 in a bloodless coup. President Prado was jailed and a military junta took over the government. Congress was dismissed and the constitution was suspended. Major General Ricardo Pérez Godoy was sworn in as junta leader and president. New elections were scheduled for June 9, 1963. Víctor Raúl Haya de la Torre, the APRA candidate, fled the country. The United States and other countries suspended diplomatic relations with Peru. On March 3, 1963, Pérez Godoy was replaced by General Nicholas Lindley López.

Fernando Belaúnde Terry, a candidate of the Popular Action and Christian Democratic parties, won the election of June 9 and was inaugurated as president on July 28 for a six-year term.

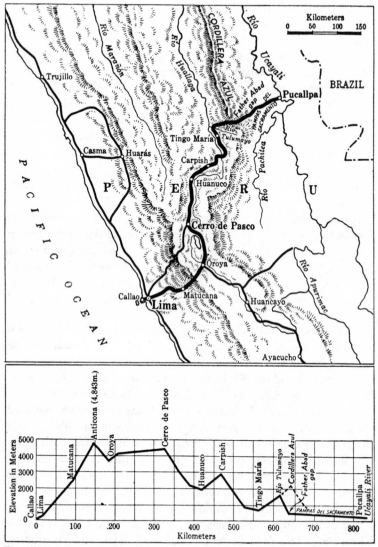

Fig. XVIII–1. An Example of Highway Building in Peru. (Chart from *Bulletin of the Pan American Union*, March, 1940. Map supplied by Miss Julia MacLean of the Pan American Union.)

Economic, Social, and Cultural Development:

ECONOMIC DEVELOPMENT. Although the basic industry of Peru is agricultural, the mining industry is also important. The country has rich deposits of petroleum, copper, silver, gold, lead, vanadium, zinc, iron, uranium, mercury, and tungsten. Guano deposits, used since pre-Columbian days, are still important as a source of fertilizer, now chiefly for local farmers. Agricultural products consist of sugar, cotton, flax, rice, cacao, wheat, tobacco, maize, potatoes, coffee, and fruits. Manufacturing of woolen textiles made from sheep, alpacas, vicuñas, and llamas is important. Smelting of copper, lead, zinc, etc., and the manufacturing of steel (begun in 1945) are of increasing importance. Increased electric power production in recent years has made possible industrial growth, while the continuing construction of highways has facilitated the internal exchange of products.

SOCIAL AND EDUCATIONAL DEVELOPMENT. The population of Peru, an Indian country, is estimated at more than 10 million, of which only about 10 per cent are pure white. Many Chinese came to Peru in the late nineteenth century. Generally, the Indians remain segregated in small villages, where many do not receive an education and know no Spanish. In recent years the government has attempted to remedy this condition, but inadequate finances and the lack of teachers has had a retarding influence on the project. The education system is headed by the famous University of San Marcos in Lima. Other schools of higher learning are the Catholic University in the capital and universities in Cuzco, Trujillo, and Arequipa. There are a number of good professional schools, including schools of music and fine arts.

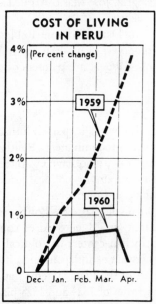

FIG. XVIII–2. Cost of Living in Peru. Chart illustrates how Peru's cost of living was stabilized after the sharp rise in 1959. (From *The New York Times,* June 21, 1960.)

CULTURAL DEVELOPMENT. The literature of Peru is very rich. Among the most notable writers are the following: Felipe Pardo y Aliaga (1806–68), who wrote comedies;

Ricardo Palma (1833–1919), who wrote interesting chronicles, his *Tradiciones peruanas* being a classic of Latin American literature; Pedro Paz Soldán y Unánue (1839–95), one of the country's greatest poets, author of *Cuadros y episodios peruanos*—poetic descriptions of everyday events; Clorinda Matto de Turner (1854–1909), a novelist and the author of *Aves sin nido,* calling attention to the condition of the natives; Mercedes Rabello de Carbonero, also a novelist, author of *Las Consecuencias* and *El Conspirador;* José Santos Chocano (1875–1934), one of the leading poets of Latin America, of virile inspiration; Francisco García Calderón (1834–1905), a historian and essayist; Enríque López Albújar, a modern novelist of native inspiration and the author of *Matalaché;* César Vallejo, poet and novelist, author of *Tungsteno;* César Falcón, a novelist and the author of *Pueblo sin Dios;* José Gálvez, a poet; Jorge Guillermo Leguía, Raúl Porras B. (b. 1897), Jorge Basadre (b. 1903), historians; Julio C. Tello (b. 1880), archaeologist; Eduardo Núñez, critic; Manuel González Prada (b. 1844), an essayist and literary critic; Ciro Alegría, José Mario Argüedas, and José Díez-Canseco, contemporary novelists.

In Daniel Alomía Robles, Peru has one of the greatest musical composers of modern Latin America. Francisco Laso (1823–68) and José Sabogal are painters of great merit.

BOLIVIA

Bolivia is a sparsely inhabited country where the aboriginal element predominates. Politics have been controlled by the Creole minority, who have exploited the government in their own interest. Rivalry among political leaders has resulted in endless wars, revolutions, and dictators.

In colonial days Bolivia formed part of the Viceroyalty of Peru. Lima and Buenos Aires continued for a long time to be the two principal centers of political attraction. In fact, for a while during the wars of independence, it appeared as if Bolivia would become a part of the Plata system; but the prestige of Bolívar and his military victories of 1824 and 1825 placed in his hands the government of the country. On August 6, 1825, an assembly gathered at Chuquisaca (now Sucre) declared the independence of Alto Peru. In honor of the Liberator the assembly changed the name of the country to "Bolívar," and declared the Liberator "Father, Protector, and First

President." It also provided that the country's capital, which was to be chosen later, would be named after General Sucre, the victor of Ayacucho.

The Rule of Bolívar. Bolívar assumed the government of Alto Peru as part of Peru proper, and disregarding the national assembly of Chuquisaca, entered into negotiations with foreign capitalists for the sale of the Potosí mines. He also agreed to cede to the United Provinces of the La Plata River, the province of Tarija, contrary to the wishes of the inhabitants of that region, who remained loyal to the Bolivian government.

The Liberator then proceeded to draft a constitution for the new state, the name of which was changed to "Bolivia" at his request. This constitution was a highly theoretical instrument of government, providing for the election of the executive for life and for the establishment of a tricameral legislature made up of Censors, Senators, and a House of Tribunes. With slight changes, this constitution was accepted by the Chuquisaca Congress and promulgated on November 6, 1826.

As the Liberator wished to return to Colombia, General Sucre was elected president on December 9, 1826.

The National Revolution against Sucre. Antagonism toward Bolívar and Sucre had developed because of the suspicion that the former wanted to annex Bolivia to Great Colombia. When, in 1828, a Colombian battalion stationed at Chuquisaca mutinied, a Peruvian army under the command of General Gamarra invaded Bolivia under the pretext of restoring order. General Sucre was compelled to resign and to leave the country. The Colombian troops were dismissed. The Peruvian General Andrés Santa Cruz, who was then absent in Chile, was elected president by the assembly. Returning to Bolivia (1829), Santa Cruz undertook to restore peace. Bolívar's constitution was discarded, and a new one was adopted, providing for the usual division of powers and election of the executive for a term of four years.

The Peru-Bolivian Confederation. Santa Cruz, who had served under Bolívar in Peru and had been president of the government council left by the Liberator in charge of that country, favored the union of the two countries and planned to become their only ruler. An identical ambition seems to have been entertained by General Gamarra, chief executive of Peru. The rivalry between the two executives was aggravated by commercial rivalry between the ports of Arica, in Peru, and Bobija, in Bolivia, the latter having been made a free port by Santa Cruz in 1830. A treaty of commerce signed between the two nations in 1832 settled the controversy for the time being.

General Santa Cruz continued to scheme for the union of the two nations. Taking advantage of a state of anarchy in Peru, where Generals Orbegoso and Gamarra were fighting for the control of power, Santa Cruz decided to intervene in that country to promote his own interests. In 1835 Bolivian troops invaded Peru. After defeating the two rival factions, Santa Cruz assumed control of the government, reorganized the country into two provinces, and joined them to Bolivia as a confederation. Santa Cruz became Protector of the union, appointing José Miguel de Velasco president of Bolivia, General Orbegoso president of North Peru, and Pío Tristán president of South Peru. On May 1, 1837, the pact of the Confederation was approved by an assembly of representatives of the three provinces.

The Confederation did not last long. Chile, then under the strong rule of Portales, and Argentina, where Rosas ruled, disapproved of the formation of a strong state near their own territories. With armies sent against Santa Cruz they defeated him and compelled the Protector to leave the country. Retiring to Guayaquil, Santa Cruz endeavored several times to regain power, but failed and left for Europe, where he died in 1865.

Restoration of Independence. Even before the defeat of Santa Cruz was known in Bolivia, a revolution led by Generals José Miguel de Velasco and José Ballivián had declared the Confederation abolished. A congress met and adopted a liberal constitution, electing Velasco as president in 1839.

Thereupon Ballivián revolted against the government. Civil war followed in which General Santa Cruz also took a part. In 1841 General Gamarra of Peru invaded Bolivia, but the warring factions in Bolivia united against him, and Gamarra was killed in battle. Peace between the two countries was signed on June 7, 1842. That same year the region along the coast where guano was found became an administrative province of Chile under the name of Atacama. Bolivia protested, alleging that the province was under her own sovereignty, but the Chileans continued to control the region despite the protests of Bolivia.

Meanwhile, anarchy in Bolivia increased. Among the many dictators, one, General Manuel Isidoro Belzú, distinguished himself for his tyranny. In his struggle to keep himself in power (1848–55), he had many people executed, others imprisoned, and still others exiled. However, he restored to the Indians their communal lands and re-established the municipal governments throughout the country. The worst of these rulers was Mariano Melgarejo, an extremely cruel man who ruled (1865–71) as an absolute tyrant through his General Secretary, Mariano Donato Múñoz. He devaluated the currency by issuing quantities of paper money, sold the Indian communal lands at public auction, and signed with Chile a boundary treaty (1866) highly unfavorable to Bolivia and the following year another with Brazil equally unfavorable to his country. Eventually, indignation over these treaties led to revolution, during which Melgarejo was overthrown. He was followed by Agustín Morales (1871), who in a fit of insanity insulted and beat several officials of his entourage and was killed by one of them.

In 1873 Adolfo Ballivián became president. He signed a treaty of alliance (February 6, 1873) with Peru. In 1874 a new treaty was signed, with Chile recognizing the 24th parallel as the boundary between the two countries and providing for joint ownership for twenty-five years of the guano deposits found between the 23rd and 24th parallels. Bolivia also agreed not to tax Chilean industry in the region between the two parallels mentioned.

The War of the Pacific. Despite the Treaty of 1874 the Bolivian Congress in 1878 established a tax of ten centavos per quintal (100 lbs.) of nitrate exported. The concessionaires, mostly Chileans, refused to pay this tax, and when the Bolivian authorities took measures to enforce the law, they appealed to the Chilean government for protection. At once Chilean troops occupied Antofagasta (February, 1879).

An offer from Peru to mediate was rejected by the Chilean government. War was declared by Chile against Bolivia and Peru on April 5, 1879. Despite the bravery of the Peruvian and Bolivian troops, Chile won most of the engagements. After the Battle of Tarapacá, which was won by the Chileans, the defeated General Hilarión Daza, President of Bolivia, abandoned Tacna and fled to Bolivia proper. Denounced as a traitor and a coward, he was overthrown by a military uprising in Arica.

Peru signed a treaty of peace with Chile in 1883. The following year Bolivia signed a truce with Chile providing that the territory occupied by Chile and claimed by Bolivia was to continue in the hands of Chile until the final negotiation of peace terms. Commercial relations between the two nations were to be restored at once.

The Settlement of the Dispute with Chile. In 1891, when relations between Argentina and Chile were strained on account of a boundary dispute between them, Bolivia attempted to secure the help of Argentina in the negotiation of a peace treaty with Chile. In exchange for this help, Bolivia promised seriously to consider annexation of her territory to Argentina. Under the circumstances, Chile was induced to sign a treaty (1895) recognizing Bolivia's right to a strip of land on the Pacific Ocean; Chile was to provide harbor facilities for Bolivia within two years. But since this provision was not carried out, the treaty was considered abrogated. Eventually, in 1904, Bolivia formally surrendered to Chile the province of Atacama, and Chile agreed to build a railroad from Arica to La Paz, the capital of Bolivia, and to build port facilities on the Pacific for the use of Bolivian trade. The ownership of both the railroad and the port was to be transferred to Bolivia fifteen years after the construction of the road. Chile was also to pay an indemnity of 300,000 pounds sterling to Bolivia and to assume the claims of Chilean citizens against Bolivia. The Arica-La Paz railroad was finished in 1912. In later years Bolivia has endeavored to secure a revision of the treaty, but without success.

The Chaco War and Its Aftermath. In 1879 a treaty was signed between Paraguay and Bolivia recognizing as the boundary between them a line due west from the mouth of the Apa River to the Pilcomayo River, but this treaty was not ratified. Various other attempts to settle the question failed. In 1927 the two countries came close to settling the dispute, thanks to Argentina's mediation. But a clash between Paraguayan and Bolivian forces in December, 1928, led to armed conflict which became serious by July, 1932. War was declared the following year. By 1935 Paraguayan troops had occupied most of the disputed territory. Thanks to the efforts of all the other nations of the Hemisphere, the dispute was finally settled by a treaty of peace and friendship signed at Buenos Aires, on July 9, 1938, dividing the disputed territory between the two countries.

Presidents and revolutions have continued to succeed each other at close intervals to the present time. In 1936 President José Luis Tejada Sórzano was overthrown, and a junta headed by Colonel David Toro assumed the government. Toro was later elected president. He announced a program of socialistic reforms, including the abolition of all monopolies, the granting of suffrage to women, the promotion of education, the adoption of social legislation, and other measures. These reforms led to a new uprising in 1937, when General Germán Busch, Chief of Staff, took over the government.

On August 23, 1939, President Busch died, having been mysteriously shot after a quarrel with a cabinet member at a drinking party. On March 10, 1940, General Enrique Peñaranda de Castillo was elected to the presidency. Inaugurated the following month, he showed dictatorial tendencies. Certain army officers were dissatisfied and conspired against President Peñaranda, whose conservative principles they disliked.

Political Developments since World War II. The Peñaranda administration severed diplomatic relations with the Axis powers on January 26, 1942. On December 4, 1943, Bolivia declared war on Germany, Italy, and Japan. Lend-lease agreements with the United States provided funds to help Bolivia purchase defense materials and construct a 225-mile highway. The United States agreed to buy Bolivia's total rubber output from 1942 to 1947. The Bolivian government co-operated closely with the United States during the war, and Bolivia became a charter member of the United Nations.

On December 18–19, 1943, President Peñaranda was overthrown by a revolution led by Major Gualberto Villarroel, who assumed control of the government. Major Villarroel was the head of the National Revolutionary Party, which was opposed to big business and strongly in favor of nationalist policies. He promised to promote the welfare of the people and struggle against the big tin interests. The Villarroel revolution caused some anxiety in the United States and in other countries. Although Argentina recognized the new regime, the United States did not extend recognition to Villarroel until June, 1944.

On July 21, 1946, President Villarroel was, in turn, overthrown by a revolution. He was seized by the revolutionists, thrown from a balcony of the Palace, and shot to death on the street; his body was stripped and hung on a lamp post. During four days of fighting over one thousand persons were killed. A provisional government headed by Dr. Nestor Guillén, senior judge of the Supreme Court, assumed control of the country.

The presidential election of 1947 resulted in victory for Enrique Hertzog, who served until October 22, 1949, when illness forced his temporary retirement. He was replaced by Mamerto Urriolagoitia as acting president. The following year, Urriolagoitia proclaimed a state of siege to forestall an alleged revolution by a Fascist group.

At the general elections held on May 6, 1951, Dr. Víctor Paz Estenssoro, a partisan of former President Villarroel and in exile in Buenos Aires since 1946, seemed to have received the majority of votes. He favored the nationalization of the tin industry and of public utilities, and was opposed to American mining interests. An outbreak of violence on the streets of La Paz led Acting President Urriolagoitia to proclaim a state of siege and to hand over the government to a junta of army officers. The junta, in turn, installed General Hugo Ballivián Rojas as president *ad interim*.

Paz Estenssoro returned from exile and was inaugurated president on April 16, 1952. By decree of July 21, 1952, his government conferred the franchise upon all Bolivian citizens twenty years of age or older, whether literate or not. On October 31, the tin mines were nationalized. Due to a dangerous deterioration of the Bolivian economy, it was announced that the United States government would send to Bolivia agricultural products valued at 5 million dollars, besides extending to the Bolivian government credits of 4 million dollars to purchase essential commodities and services.

The presidential election of 1956 was won by Hernán Siles Zuazo, candidate of the National Revolutionary Movement Party. He was inaugurated on August 6.

In December, 1956, it was announced that the Bolivian government, after consultation with the International Monetary Fund, had decided to abolish the multiple-foreign-exchange-rate system. The Fund granted a stand-by credit of 7.5 million dollars to Bolivia. Credits of an identical sum were extended by the U. S. Treasury and the U. S. International Co-operation Administration.

By July, 1957, left-wing influence on the government seemed to have been eliminated. However, relations between the United States and Bolivia were considerably strained by derogatory remarks published in an American weekly magazine in March, 1959, concerning Bolivia and attributed originally to an American diplomat stationed in La Paz. During a three-day anti-American demonstration an American flag was burned, Point IV headquarters were stoned, and a U. S. library was destroyed.

During 1959 two attempts were made to overthrow President Siles. The precarious situation of the Bolivian economy led to violent anti-administration demonstrations in La Paz and elsewhere. Troops loyal to the government were able to suppress them.

On August 6, 1960, Víctor Paz Estenssoro, leader of the National Revolutionary Movement, became president after comparatively orderly elections. In mid-1961, after a thwarted Communist plot against the government, Paz placed Bolivia under a state of siege. Paz was re-elected in 1964; on November 3, 1964, he was overthrown by a coup led by the Vice-President, General René Barrientos Ortuño, who became co-President with General Alfredo Ovando Candía. On July 3, 1966, General Barrientos Ortuño was formally elected President.

On June 17, 1963, Bolivia withdrew from the council of the Organization of American States in protest against its handling of the dispute over the use of the Bolivian Lauca River, which has its sources in Chile.

Economic, Social, and Cultural Development. Bolivia is largely a mining country, but the exploitation of minerals is hindered by

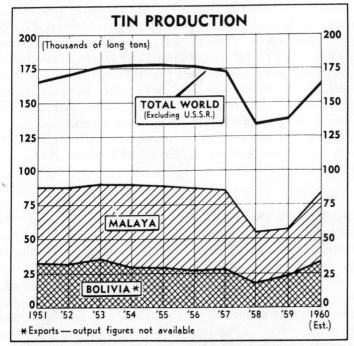

Fig. XVIII–3. Tin Production. World tin output in 1960 rose to 163,000 long tons, due mainly to lifting of export quotas in last three months. (From *The New York Times,* January 22, 1961.)

lack of adequate labor, capital, and transportation. It has large deposits of tin, copper, silver, lead, zinc, tungsten, and antimony. Petroleum is in limited production. Rice, wheat, sugar, and fruits are grown chiefly for local consumption. Cacao, coffee, and rubber are exported. Cattle raising, encouraged by the government, is on the increase. Manufactured articles are made for home purchase. Tin comprises about 70 per cent of the total exports of the country. Since Bolivia has no harbor of its own, many products must be shipped by air, or by railroad or highway, both of which are extremely costly to build in so rugged a country.

The population of Bolivia is nearly 3.5 million people, all but some 8 per cent of which are Indian. The Indians live, for the most part, in isolated rural communities and do not speak Spanish. Education efforts are extremely expensive and not very effective. Higher learning is provided in universities located in La Paz, Sucre, Cochabamba, and elsewhere. Primary and secondary education are unsatisfactory.

Among the writers of Bolivia, the following have distinguished themselves: Benjamín Lens (1836–78), Nesto Galindo (1830–65), and Daniel Calvo (1832–80)—all poets; Rosendo Villalobos (b. 1860), also a poet of note; Ricardo Jaime Freyre, an associate of Rubén Darío and a distinguished modernist poet; Armando Chirveches, a novelist; Franz Tamayo, considered by some the greatest Bolivian poet, author of *La Prometheida, Nuevos rubayatas,* and *Scherzos;* and Fernando Díez de Medina, poet and essayist of note.

Among the painters may be mentioned Cecilio Guzmán de Rojas, Arturo Reque Meruvia, Jenaro Ibáñez, Víctor Pabón, and Jorge de la Reza.

CHILE

Chile is today one of the leading nations of Latin America. The Chileans are, relatively speaking, a homogeneous people, mostly of European origin. They have evinced throughout their history strong and aggressive nationalistic characteristics.

The history of Chile may be divided into four main periods. During the first period (1811–31) the partisans of a strong and centralized government clashed with those who favored a more democratic system; in the second period (1831–61) a highly centralized government was established under the Constitution of 1833, and Chile became a strong and well-integrated nation; in the third period (1861–91) liberalism was in control, local government gained more freedom of action, and the national congress became more influential in national politics; finally, from 1891 to the present, democracy was gradually strengthened, the parliamentary system was abolished, and the president lost a great deal of his power and influence in local politics.

Autocratic Versus Democratic Government (1811–31)

The first national congress of Chile met on July 4, 1811, in Santiago. Three main currents of opinion were apparent at once: that of the moderates, who wished to bring about certain reforms but who were not opposed to the continuation of the Spanish domination; that of the reactionaries, who wanted the restoration of royal control; and that of the *exaltados,* or radicals, a small group of patriots who wanted outright independence at once. Among the latter were Manuel de Sales, Bernardo O'Higgins, and Juan Martínez de Rozas.

A governing junta of three was appointed by the congress. But the patriot group, wishing to bring about independence at once, revolted under the leadership of the Carrera brothers (José Miguel, Juan José, and Luis), overthrew the junta, and replaced it with a junta of their own. A new constituent congress was then called.

This congress abolished the slave traffic and declared free all children born thereafter of slaves. But shortly after its inauguration, José Miguel Carrera overthrew the ruling junta (of which he was not a part), and replaced it with still another one under his own presidency.

On January 1, 1818, a Declaration of Independence was issued by Bernardo O'Higgins, and one year after the victory of Chacabuco, on February 12, 1818, independence was publicly proclaimed throughout the nation.

O'Higgins as Supreme Director. Meanwhile, Bernardo O'Higgins had been made Supreme Director of the country, with dictatorial powers. At once rivalry between his party and that of the Carrera brothers developed. Juan José and Luis Carrera attempted to overthrow O'Higgins, but failed and took refuge in Argentina, where they were arrested and shot (April 8, 1818). The third brother, José Miguel Carrera, who had gone to the United States on a diplomatic mission, was also shot in Argentina three years after his return.

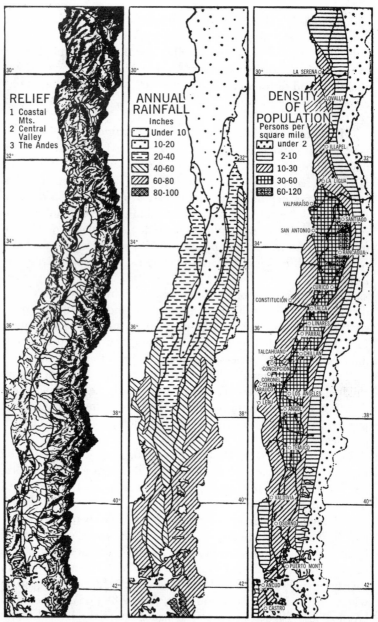

Fig. XVIII–4. Middle Chile. (Reprinted with permission from *South America,* by Clarence F. Jones, published by Henry Holt and Company, New York, 1930.)

O'Higgins endeavored to organize the country. He created a navy, which at first was under the command of the Argentine Manuel Blanco Encalada and later of the British adventurer Lord Thomas Alexander Cochrane. Education was promoted, the *cabildos* and the convents being ordered to open schools throughout the country.

The Supreme Director became unpopular because of his dictatorial tendencies, his disregard for the Catholic Church, and his vindictive attitude toward his political enemies. A constituent assembly called by him under pressure of public opinion drafted a constitution in 1822 granting broad powers to the executive and extending his authority for ten years. After several uprisings, O'Higgins decided to resign and transferred the executive authority to a junta on January 28, 1823. Shortly afterward, he left the country and lived in Peru until his death in 1842.

The Rule of Freire. General Ramón Freire, a liberal, then assumed the executive office. He called a constituent assembly, which drafted a new constitution, promulgated in 1823, providing for the usual division of powers with a bicameral congress, and regulating minutely the life of the people. Slavery was abolished. Education was to be promoted by a special board. However, a few months after its promulgation, this constitution was abolished by Freire. Two other congresses were called and dissolved amidst general indignation. In 1826 Freire called still another congress and resigned.

The Congress of 1826 organized the country as a federal republic. Francisco Antonio Pinto, who as Vice-President had assumed the government after Freire's resignation, abolished the federal regime and called a new constituent assembly. The constitution adopted by this assembly in 1828 embodied the most advanced liberal principles, providing for the division of powers of government, with an executive elected for five years and a bicameral legislature. Pinto was elected president under this constitution. But the conservatives, in turn, revolted against the government, under the leadership of General Joaquín Prieto, and overthrew Pinto.

The Autocratic Regime (1831–61)

At this time there appeared on the political stage of Chile a young conservative named Diego Portales, who more than anyone else contributed to the stability of government in the country. As a very young man, Portales had been in business. During the strug-

gles between the liberals and the conservatives he sided with the latter and was appointed Minister of the Interior. Because of his extraordinary gifts of leadership he soon became practical dictator of
Chile, exercising the broad powers granted him by the congress.
Convinced that militarism was responsible for the disorders in the
country, he ousted from the army all officers who had taken part in
any uprising and dismissed from public office all liberals, replacing
them with members of his own party. Those who revolted against
him were tried by special courts and summarily condemned to death
or to exile.

The Constitution of 1833. After the country was pacified, a constituent congress met and drafted a new constitution which established the Catholic Church as the official church, prohibited other
religious organizations within the national territory, and organized
the country under a highly centralized government. This constitution, promulgated in 1833, remained in effect, with slight changes,
until 1925.

The Governments of Prieto, Bulnes, and Montt. In 1831 Joaquín
Prieto became the chief executive. During his administration the
financial and commercial problems of the republic received considerable attention. Manuel Rengifo, Minister of the Treasury, was
responsible for the adoption of measures curtailing government expenditures, the adoption of a new tariff law, the development of
Valparaíso's port facilities, and the organization of a national merchant marine.

The commercial rivalry between Valparaíso in Chile and Callao
in Peru and fear of the creation of a strong state close to the Chilean
territory resulted in war (1836) against the Peru-Bolivian Confederation organized by General Santa Cruz.

At the outset of this war a military uprising broke out under the
leadership of an army officer named José Antonio Vidaurre. Portales fell into the hands of the revolutionists and was killed by them
(June 6, 1837). Thereafter the rebellion was quickly suppressed by
the government.

Despite Portales' death, the war against the Confederation of
Santa Cruz continued. A Chilean army landed in Peru near the
port of Callao. At the same time Argentine troops invaded Bolivia.
In 1838 Santa Cruz was decisively defeated and compelled to resign.

Prieto was followed by Manuel Bulnes in 1841. During his administration there was general peace and prosperity in the country.

In 1843 Chile took possession of the Strait of Magellan by establishing a fortress and a settlement there. Immigration was promoted, particularly in the southern region. In 1851 the first railroad was opened in Chile. Public education received a good deal of attention, particularly under the direction of Manuel Montt as Minister of Education. In 1842 the University of Chile was established in the capital. A steamship line was opened between the port of Valparaíso and Panama in 1840.

Popular antagonism to the Catholic Church resulted in the adoption of legislation allowing non-Catholics to be married outside the Church and giving the government supervision over the priesthood in Chile. The liberal campaign for more individual freedom and democratic government resulted in the closing of several of the political clubs by the government and in the exile of many liberal leaders.

In 1851 Manuel Montt became president. During his ten-year administration the country continued to prosper. New railroads were built, savings banks were established, immigration was promoted, and many schools were opened.

The liberals revolted against the government several times, but they were quickly suppressed. However, owing to the abolition of the rights of primogeniture and to certain laws restricting the power of the Church, many conservatives (known as *pelucones,* "bigwigs") joined with the liberals in opposition to the government, and at the next presidential elections José Joaquín Pérez, a liberal, was elected.

Liberalism (1861-91)

Inaugurated in 1861, Pérez showed himself conciliatory toward the conservatives. But the liberals were not satisfied, and the most extreme among them formed a Radical Party, which favored an increase of local autonomy. Gradually the municipalities received more freedom of action in local matters.

During Pérez's administration, the Araucanian Indians, who inhabited the southern region of the republic, rebelled against the authorities. It took the government troops several years to quell the rebellion.

In 1871 Federico Errázuriz Zañartu became president. He was a liberal who was strongly opposed to autocratic government. Adopting a strictly impartial attitude toward the presidential elections of 1880, he announced that he favored no candidate. Aníbal

Pinto was elected. Errázuriz was the first president of Chile who was not re-elected.

During Pinto's administration (1876–81) the country suffered a severe economic depression due to decreased production of silver and copper. Chile was also confronted by boundary disputes with Argentina, Peru, and Bolivia. The quarrel with Argentina had to do with sovereignty over the Strait of Magellan and Patagonia. In 1881 a treaty was signed between the two governments providing for recognition of Chilean sovereignty over the Strait and of Argentine sovereignty over Patagonia.

The controversy with Bolivia and Peru resulted in the War of the Pacific, which lasted from 1879 to 1883. Neither the treaty with Peru, signed in 1883, nor the truce with Bolivia, signed the following year, definitely settled the disputes with those countries. However, the war increased Chile's territory by more than one third.

In 1881 Domingo Santa María became president. During his administration laws were adopted making compulsory the civil registration of marriages, births, and deaths. Burial places were taken away from the control of the Church. Antagonism between the Government and the Church was aggravated in 1883 over the appointment of the archbishop of Santiago. Legislation curtailing still more the power of the Church was adopted. At about the same time the suffrage was extended, and powers of the executive were decreased.

José Manuel Balmaceda was the next president, inaugurated in 1886. His administration was characterized by an increase in the public revenues and general prosperity. This permitted the government to undertake a vast program of public works, including means of communication, schools, harbors, and public buildings. Despite general prosperity, Balmaceda's administration ended in civil war.

Having quarreled with the congress, Balmaceda dismissed his cabinet. But the next cabinet did not last long, and the president then appointed a new cabinet with elements from the congressional conservative minority. Meanwhile, the congress had adjourned without appropriating money for government expenditures during the following year, and the president decided to put into effect the budget of the previous year.

A revolution broke out at once (1891). The national fleet sided with the congress. President Balmaceda was deposed, and a governing junta was created composed of Jorge Montt, Commander of the Fleet; Waldo Silva, Vice-President of the Senate; and Ramón Barros

Luco, President of the Chamber of Deputies. The army remained loyal to President Balmaceda. But the government forces were defeated (battles of Concón and La Placilla in 1891), and Balmaceda transferred the executive authority to General Manuel Baquedano González, took refuge in the Argentine legation, and a few days later committed suicide.

The Democratic Regime (1891–1941)

With the defeat of Balmaceda ended the period of presidential predominance in Chile. Up to then, under the Constitution of 1833, the presidents had been able to intervene in local politics and control the election of members of the congress, as well as to dictate their own successors. The revolution established local autonomy and electoral freedom by the promulgation of a new law of municipalities (1891). These reforms introduced what is called by Chilean historians "the parliamentary regime," under which the executive is subject to the will of the majority of the congress.

After the victory of the revolution, the congress met again and elected Jorge Montt as president (1891–96). He was followed in 1896 by Federico Errázuriz Echaurren, who governed until 1901 and was responsible for the peaceful settlement of the boundary dispute with Argentina.

The Boundary Dispute with Argentina. The Treaty of 1881 between Chile and Argentina had provided that any dispute concerning the boundary which might arise between the two contracting parties would be settled by arbitration. In 1898, after negotiations over the line in the Andes region, a protocol was signed submitting the question to the arbitration of the British Crown, and the controversy over the boundary in Puna de Atacama was submitted to the arbitration of the United States Minister to Argentina, William Buchanan. The latter question was settled in 1899, but the former, owing to delay in the decision, almost led to war between the two nations in 1901. The problem was solved with the signing of the Pacts of May, in 1902, providing for the arbitration of all disputes, for the limitation of armaments and equality of naval strength of the two countries, and for the neutrality of each nation in regard to conflicts involving the other. The boundary line in Patagonia was finally defined by the British king's arbitral award in 1902.

Political Affairs from 1901 to 1920. From 1901 to 1906 Germán Riesco was president. During his administration the treaty of peace with Bolivia was signed (1904) providing that the northern section of Antofagasta was to become Chilean territory. There were serious strikes among the workers of Valparaíso, Antofagasta, and Santiago due, in the main, to the high cost of living. The government created special committees in all provinces to promote the construction of low-priced homes for workers.

Pedro Montt was the next president. He carried out an extensive program of public works. In 1907, because of unsatisfactory living conditions among the laborers employed by the great nitrate companies, there was a strike which resulted in many bloody encounters between the workers and the police. Montt died abroad in 1910 while seeking medical assistance for his ailments. From 1910 to 1915 the country was governed by Ramón Barros Luco, and from 1915 to 1920, by Juan Luis Sanfuentes. During these two administrations new schools were built, aviation was promoted, and the national railroads became an autonomous administrative unit. Labor legislation was adopted, including compensation for labor accidents, a six-day working week, and other provisions favorable to the workers. For the first time in the history of Chile, members of the Democratic Party were appointed ministers of state.

In the 1920 elections there were many conflicts and complaints. No candidate received the required majority of votes. From the two principal candidates, the congress chose Arturo Alessandri as president. Alessandri was the candidate of the Liberal Alliance, a party with a large popular backing.

Alessandri's First Administration. President Alessandri was inaugurated during a period of great economic depression in Chile. This condition was due in part to the decrease in exports of nitrates, copper, and wool.

Alessandri's victory at the polls was resented by the conservatives. In the Senate they consistently refused to co-operate with him, and the national budget was for several years approved after a great deal of delay. Meanwhile, the economic situation became worse and the gold conversion of the currency was suspended. In 1924, as a means of increasing the government's revenues, an income tax was adopted by the congress.

The general unrest was increased by attempts to raise the pay of the army and navy, and to provide salaries for members of the congress, who until that time had received no material compensation for their services. New elections brought to the congress a working majority favorable to the administration, and several important laws were adopted, including one that increased the pay of the armed forces.

But soon after that, conflict developed between the president and the military, who requested that the president devaluate the national currency in order to alleviate the economic difficulties of the population. President Alessandri refused to do this and resigned. The congress, however, did not accept the president's resignation; instead, it authorized him to absent himself from the country for six months. On September 10, 1924, he left the capital and went to Europe. Meanwhile, a military junta headed by General Luis Altamirano assumed the government of the country.

A few months later, however, the military junta was overthrown by army officers of the capital's garrison under the pretext that Altamirano had not carried out the reforms he had promised. A new junta was appointed, and Alessandri was invited to return at once to Chile. Arriving in Santiago on March 20, 1925, he was received with great popular acclaim and again assumed the executive office. The president then secured legislation from the congress creating a central bank and called a constituent assembly to amend the constitution.

The Constitution of 1925. The assembly adopted a constitution, which was approved by a plebiscite on August 30, 1925. This constitution provided for separation of Church and State, guaranteed complete religious liberty, declared the rights of property subject to the maintenance and progress of social order, made primary education compulsory, and provided that a member of the congress could not at the same time be a member of the president's cabinet. The president's term was increased to six years. The executive was to be elected by direct popular vote. The cabinet members were to be appointed by the president in a manner similar to that provided by the United States Constitution, thus doing away with the parliamentary system until then in effect in Chile. A new electoral law was also adopted at about the same time.

Other Governments until 1932. Because of a quarrel with the Minister of War, Colonel (later General) Carlos Ibáñez del Campo, President Alessandri resigned again and before leaving the government appointed Minister of the Interior Luis Barros Borgoño as acting president. As such, Barros Borgoño assumed the executive office provisionally. Ibáñez resigned from the cabinet. But the same year (1925) Emiliano Figueroa Larraín was elected to the presidency, and Ibáñez again became Minister of War. Later he was put in charge of the Ministry of the Interior and as such controlled the government with the backing of the army.

Soon afterward, President Figueroa Larraín resigned. In the elections that followed, Ibáñez, the only possible candidate, was elected by a great majority. He was inaugurated on July 21, 1927. Once in power, Ibáñez ruled as virtual dictator, suppressing revolutionary plots with extreme severity. Despite the unrest, the new president undertook a notable program of reforms. A new territorial division of the country was established, reducing the number of provinces from 23 to 16, and establishing two territories—Aysén and Magallanes. The question of Tacna and Arica was settled with Peru by the Treaty of Lima (June 3, 1929). The University of Santiago was made autonomous. Libraries and schools were established throughout the country. The government departments were reorganized with a view to curtailing expenditures. A vast program of public works was put into effect to alleviate unemployment. To solve the nitrate situation, a government-controlled corporation, the *Compañía Salitrera de Chile* (Cosach) was organized with a monopoly on exports of nitrates.

Despite all these measures, the economic condition of the country became progressively worse. Foreign bankers refused to lend any more money, and the government found itself unable to continue its enormous expenditures. There were rioting and revolutionary plots everywhere. On July 26, 1931, Ibáñez resigned, transferring the government to Pedro Opazo Letelier, President of the Senate, who in turn resigned. Juan Esteban Montero, Minister of the Interior, became chief executive in provisional character at first, and later, as regularly elected president.

Inaugurated on December 4, 1931, Montero was unable to restore peace in the nation. On June 4, 1932, a military revolution broke out, the government was overthrown, and a military junta composed of General Puga, Eugenio Matte, and Carlos Dávila, assumed the executive power. One of the leaders of this revolution was Colonel Marmaduque Grove Vallejo, who favored the establishment of a socialistic republic.

The junta dissolved the congress and decreed that the government loan bank (*Caja de Crédito Popular*) return to their respective owners all objects of primary necessity that had been pawned. This increased the popularity of the junta for the time being. But plots and revolutions succeeded each other. Eventually, the armed forces demanded that the government be restored to those who should administer it under the constitution. On October 2, 1932, Abraham Oyanedel Urrutia, as President of the Supreme Court, assumed the executive power. Soon after, elections were held and Arturo Alessandri was elected again by a vast majority.

Alessandri and His Successors to 1941. Alessandri was inaugurated on December 24, 1932. He at once reorganized the nitrate industry, abolishing Cosach. Measures were taken to improve conditions in agriculture and industry. New schools were opened. Public order was restored throughout the nation. In the elections of 1938, Pedro Aguirre Cerda, the candidate of the Popular Front, a coalition of Radicals, Socialists, and Communists, was elected by a small majority. He was inaugurated on December 24, 1938. In the early part of 1940 several cabinet members resigned as a consequence of quarreling among the various groups forming the Popular Front coalition.

In January, 1940, a disastrous earthquake aggravated the already precarious economic condition of Chile. In August of the same year the government announced a vast industrialization plan involving the expenditure of some 24 million dollars. A loan of 12 million dollars was granted by the U. S. Export-Import Bank.

Political Developments since World War II

In 1942 Chile, having declared a policy of neutrality in the war against the Axis powers, was accused of harboring subversive agents for the Axis. Shortly thereafter, economic difficulties and popular pressure induced the government to sever relations (January 20, 1943) with Germany, Italy, and Japan. Chile declared war on Japan April 11, 1945, and in that year became a charter member of the United Nations.

A controversy with Great Britain over the ownership of the Palmer Peninsula and of islands off the lower tip of South America led Argentina and Chile to join hands in pressing their claims against the British.

President Aguirre Cerda, who resigned because of ill health in November, 1941, died shortly thereafter, and in the election held in February, 1942, Juan Antonio Ríos, of the Radical Party, was elected. He served until 1946, when he too became ill and died. The leftist candidate, Gabriel González Videla, defeated his opponent in the September, 1946, election and was inaugurated on November 3. His coalition cabinet included several Chilean Communists. In 1948 the administration, accusing the Communists of obstructionism and violence, enacted a law (with the backing of conservatives, radicals, liberals, and socialists) to curb the influence of the Communist Party by denying Communists the right to hold public office and the right to be active in trade union affairs. A few months before, Chile had broken diplomatic relations with the Soviet Union and with Czechoslovakia on account of alleged interference by Communist agents in labor strikes in the country.

In preparing for the 1952 elections, the congress approved legislation extending the franchise to women. Former President Carlos Ibáñez del Campo was declared elected by the congress in 1952 for the constitutional term of six years. Ibáñez's administration was beset by difficult economic and financial problems.

In the election of 1958 no candidate received a clear majority, although Senator Jorge Alessandri Rodríguez led all other candidates. In October, the congress declared Senator Alessandri elected. He was inaugurated on November 3, for the regular six-year term.

On March 22, 1960, the governments of Chile and Argentina announced that they had requested Queen Elizabeth II of Great Britain to arbitrate in a frontier dispute concerning a 35-mile stretch in the southern Andes, in the area submitted to the arbitration of King Edward VII in 1902. The request was accepted and the two governments set themselves to preparing their respective cases for presentation to the arbiter.

President Alessandri's plans to check inflation and to stabilize the country's economy were given a severe setback by serious earthquakes, tidal waves, and volcanic eruptions in May, 1960. About 10,000 persons were killed, the homes of some 2 million people were destroyed, and 50 per cent of the land under cultivation was affected. The losses were estimated at about 500 million dollars. The government acted promptly to alleviate the situation. Help was received from the United States and other nations. Fortunately, no major industrial center had been seriously affected. The copper, tin, nitrate, and steel industries continued to operate normally.

In January, 1961, a 10-year development program was announced by the government. Assistance from the World Bank and the International Development Bank was assured.

In 1964, Eduardo Frei was elected president. Inaugurated in November of that year, he immediately announced a plan to nationalize the copper industry. In 1965, he visited several countries of Europe and successfully negotiated for certain commercial and financial advantages for Chile.

Economic, Social, and Cultural Development

Economic Development. The nitrate industry has been the source of great wealth for Chile. Between 1880 and 1929, for example, the government collected some billion dollars from the taxes on nitrates and iodine. Copper is of great importance in the Chilean economy, with most of the industry controlled by United States corporations. Other mineral products are gold, salt, sulfur, manganese, cobalt, borate of lime, silver, coal, and iron. Since World War II the iron and steel industry has developed rapidly, and the country is almost self-sufficient in coal production. Petroleum production has developed chiefly since 1945, with wells located in Tierra del Fuego. Increased use of hydroelectric power has helped to expand manufacturing in leather, textiles, and foodstuffs.

Agriculture has always been important in Chile, largely because of its wide range of climate. Among these products are wheat, corn, rye, oats, beans, potatoes, lentils, forage crops, sugar, tobacco, and hemp. Grapes for making wine are diverse and excellent. The cattle industry is of great importance, and wool production is increasing. Interior roads and railways make transportation of people and produce quite satisfactory. The country is served by several airlines.

Social Development. The population of Chile is more than 7 million, and most of the people are of European origin with about half of them living in urban communities. The Araucanian Indians live chiefly in the south. The government in recent years has taken an effective interest in public health and welfare and "state socialism" has been an accomplished political objective.

Education. Illiteracy is relatively low in Chile. The National University and the Catholic University in Santiago head the list of institutions of higher learning. There are many special and professional schools of all types, and primary and secondary education is quite adequate.

Literary and Artistic Development. During its early years the literary life of Chile was dominated by the great Andrés Bello (1781–1865), a Venezuelan by birth, who devoted the best part of his life to the service of education and culture in Chile. A man of en-

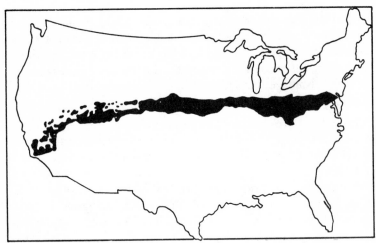

FIG. XVIII–5. Comparative Areas of Chile and the United States.

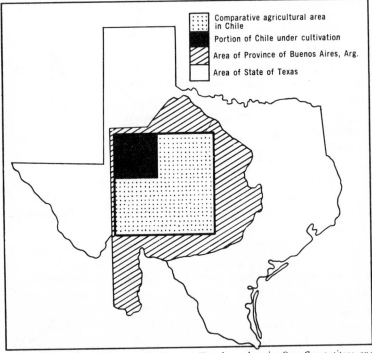

Comparative agricultural area in Chile

Portion of Chile under cultivation

Area of Province of Buenos Aires, Arg.

Area of State of Texas

FIG. XVIII–6. Comparisons with Texas. (Based on data in *Our Competitors and Markets,* by Arnold W. Lahee, published by Henry Holt and Company, New York, 1924.)

cyclopedic mind, he wrote poetry, drafted a civil code for Chile, wrote extensively on international law, education, and other subjects, and was the author of one of the best Castilian grammars in existence. Other writers of note in Chile are: José Victoriano Lastarria (1817–88), who wrote on philosophy and politics; Miguel Luis Amunátegui (1828–88), a historian; Benjamín Vicuña Mackenna (1831–86) and Diego Barros Arana (1830–1907), both historians, the latter of whom was one of the greatest in Latin America, author of a monumental work in sixteen volumes, *Historia general de Chile;* José Joaquín Vallejo (1809–58), who wrote on traditions and customs of Chile; Daniel Barros Grez (1834–1904), a master of historical fiction; Alberto Blest Gana (1830–1922), a novelist; Eusebio Lillo (1826–1900), a poet, author of the national anthem of Chile; Valentín Letelier, rector of the University of Santiago, who wrote on many subjects; Gonzalo Bulnes (b. 1851), author of the *Historia de la Guerra del Pacífico;* Tomás Guevara, author of *La Civilización de la Araucania;* José Toribio Medina (1852–1930), one of the most outstanding bibliographers in the Western Hemisphere; Eduardo Barrios (b. 1884), a novelist, author of *El Hermano asno;* Joaquín Edwards Bello, a novelist and author of *El Roto, El Chileno en Madrid, Criollos en París,* etc.; Gabriela Mistral (1899–1956), a great poet well known throughout the world of letters; Pablo Neruda, Daniel de la Vega, Pedro Prado, Amanda Labarca, Inés Echeverría de Larraín (Iris), Elvira Santa Cruz (Roxane), and many others.

Among the painters may be mentioned Rafael Correa, Pedro Subercaseaux, and Pedro Lira; among the sculptors, Virginio Arias, Nicanor Plaza, and Rebeca Matte de Iñíguez; and among the musicians, Humberto Allende, Alfonso Leng, Enrique Sono, and Luis Sandoval.

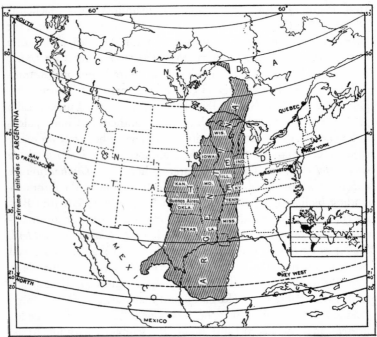

F<small>IG</small>. XIX–1.   Location of the Argentine Republic if Placed at the Corresponding Latitudes in the Northern Hemisphere.   (Courtesy of the Pan American Union.)

CHAPTER XIX

THE RIVER PLATA STATES

T HE RIVER PLATA BASIN is one of the most important centers of political, as well as economic and cultural, development in Latin America. On either side of the River Plata are to be found two leading Latin American capitals, Buenos Aires and Montevideo. The former is the third largest city in the Western Hemisphere. Further north, on the banks of the Paraguay River, a tributary of the Paraná, is Asunción, capital of the republic of Paraguay. These three states, Argentina, Uruguay, and Paraguay, have always been intimately connected politically, and at the time of independence they came very near to uniting into a single nation. Regional jealousies and foreign intervention, particularly in Uruguay, prevented this union from taking place.

ARGENTINA

In many ways Argentina is today one of the leading nations of Latin America. Her steady economic development, the increasing orderliness of her political life, her relative racial homogeneity, and the favorable climate of much of her territory have contributed to the formation of a progressive people, proud of their history and conscious of their destiny.

The history of Argentina may be divided into four main periods. During the first period (1810–20) Buenos Aires became the center of political activity and its leaders endeavored to organize the new nation, including Paraguay and the Banda Oriental (Uruguay), under its sway despite the strong opposition of the provinces; after the Battle of Cepeda (1820), when the aristocratic element of Buenos Aires was decisively defeated, and until the fall of Rosas (1852), the nation was ruled by crude and greedy *caudillos,* who often clashed with each other and with foreign powers. This resulted in general internal disorder and a succession of debilitating wars. A period of national reorganization followed (1852–80) under the federal Constitution of 1853; and finally, with the federalization of the municipality of Buenos Aires (1880), there began a new period, during which modern Argentina, as a well-integrated and strong nation, emerged from the chaos and the turbulence of the previous years. This orderly progress was interrupted briefly by the war and the Perón dictatorship (1946–55) and its aftermath.

Federalism Versus Unitarianism (1810–20)

With the overthrow of the Spanish authorities on May 25, 1810, and the establishment of a governing junta under the leadership of General Cornelio Saavedra, the emancipation of Argentina had its inception. But it was not until July 9, 1816, that a formal declaration of independence was issued. During the intervening years the revolution spread to other sections of the Spanish colonies in southern South America, expeditions being sent out from Buenos Aires to Alto Peru (Bolivia), to Paraguay, and to the Banda Oriental (Uruguay).

Attempts to Organize a Government in Buenos Aires. From the beginning the members of the Buenos Aires junta quarreled among themselves on matters of policy. The troublesome question of federalism versus unitarianism made its appearance. On April 5 and 6, 1812, the provincial delegates demanded to be incorporated in the junta and forced the resignation of Mariano Moreno, secretary of that body, who was one of the most influential leaders of the unitarian faction. The following August, the junta was replaced by a triumvirate. When the provincial delegates conspired to overthrow the triumvirate, the latter ordered them to leave the capital. An uprising took place in which the grenadiers of San Martín joined with the Masonic lodges to demand from the *cabildo* the dissolution of the triumvirate and of the assembly, the appointment of a new government, and the calling of a constituent assembly within three months.

The *cabildo* complied with the popular requests. On January 31, 1813, an assembly meeting in the capital provided for the freedom of children born of slaves after that date, abolished titles of nobility, declared the state independent from foreign religious organizations, and abolished the Indian tribute. But it did not declare national independence, nor did it adopt a constitution.

The assembly also quarreled with José Gervasio Artigas, leader of the patriots in the Banda Oriental (Uruguay), by refusing to recognize the delegates sent to represent that province. This was done because Artigas had instructed his representatives to demand provincial autonomy.

The assembly abolished the triumvirate, replacing it by a single executive under the name of "Supreme Director of the United Provinces," appointed for two years and advised by a council of state consisting of nine members. On January 31, 1814, Gervasio Antonio Posadas was appointed first Director. Before long, he was replaced by Carlos María de Alvear.

In the meantime, Artigas had crossed the River Plata and threatened to attack Buenos Aires. When Alvear left that city at the head of an army, an uprising took place (April 15, 1815) in his absence, and the *cabildo* dissolved the assembly, deposed the directory, and created a "Junta of Observation," with the specific duty of calling a national congress to adopt a constitution.

The Tucumán Congress of 1816 and the War between the Provinces. On March 24, 1816, the national congress called by the junta met at Tucumán, with representatives from all the provinces except those siding with Artigas (Corrientes, Entre Ríos, Santa Fe, Córdoba, and Montevideo). The conflict between Buenos Aires and the River Plata provinces had resulted in general anarchy. Elsewhere in Spanish America, the cause of independence seemed lost with the defeat of the patriots in Mexico, in northern South America, and on the Pacific coast. The royalist forces threatened to invade the River Plata region from Alto Peru. In Spain, Ferdinand VII had returned to the throne.

The congress appointed as Supreme Director, General Juan Martín de Pueyrredón. At the suggestion of San Martín, Belgrano, and other leaders, and in order to raise the spirits of the people, the delegates adopted on July 9, 1816, a resolution declaring the "United Provinces of South America" independent of Spain.

After that, they discussed plans for a national government. The monarchist element predominated in the congress. Some of the most influential leaders, including San Martín, Belgrano, Rivadavia, and Alvear, favored some sort of attenuated monarchy. The congress had not yet decided this fundamental question when it was adjourned to meet again in Buenos Aires early the following year. When the congress reconvened, a committee was appointed to negotiate with Brazil a treaty of recognition incorporating the declaration that the River Plata provinces had abandoned the idea of establishing a republic and wished to create a constitutional monarchy, possibly under a Brazilian prince. While the congress discussed what form of government to adopt, anarchy spread to the whole country.

General Pueyrredón, unable to restore the public order, resigned as Director, and General José Rondeau was appointed to take his place in 1819. The new Director ordered all Argentine troops, including those fighting under General San Martín on the Pacific coast, to return at once to Buenos Aires to restore public order. San Martín disregarded these orders. At the end of 1819 civil war broke out between the provinces and Buenos Aires. Francisco Ramírez, the *caudillo* of Entre Ríos, and Estanislao López, the *caudillo* of Santa Fe—instigated by the Chilean José Miguel Carrera and the Argentine Carlos de Alvear—declared war against Buenos Aires, issuing a proclamation giving as their aims the removal of the despots in Buenos Aires, the restoration of the liberty of the provinces, and the suppression of the Portuguese-Brazilian invasion in the Banda Oriental. The provinces of Córdoba, San Luis, San Juan, and Mendoza adhered to this movement. An army sent against them by Rondeau revolted and supported the cause of the provinces; their commander, General Juan Bautista Bustos, assumed the governorship of Córdoba. Another army gathered by the Director was defeated in the Battle of Cepeda (February 1, 1820). In the war of the provinces against the efforts of the aristocrats of Buenos Aires to impose upon them their domination, the latter were decisively defeated.

Anarchy and Tyranny (1820–52)

The Constitutional Project of 1819 and Provincial Anarchy. Meanwhile, unable to decide what form of government to adopt, the congress of Buenos Aires issued "provisional regulations for the direction and administration of the State." Two years later a constitution was promulgated (April 22, 1819), providing for a centralized form of government. This constitution was at once rejected by the provinces.

As a consequence of the victory of Cepeda, Ramírez and López demanded the dissolution of the Buenos Aires congress and the abolition of the directory; this demand was met by the *cabildo*. A few days later Manuel Sarratea was appointed governor and captain general of the Buenos Aires province. A treaty of peace was then signed by Buenos Aires and the provincial *caudillos,* providing that a general congress of the provinces should meet to draft a federal form of government. This treaty was rejected by the people of Buenos Aires.

The state of anarchy continued. On one single day three different persons occupied the governorship of Buenos Aires: Alvear, who was backed by López and Carrera, was overthrown by Manuel Dorrego, who in turn was overthrown by Martín Rodríguez. As governor of the Buenos Aires province, Rodríguez signed a treaty of peace with López on November 24, 1820, providing for the calling of a general congress which met the following year in Córdoba but did not bring about the desired unification of the nation.

Meanwhile, Artigas had been defeated by the Portuguese in the Banda Oriental and had retreated to Argentina. He requested the help of the *caudillos* of Entre Ríos, Corrientes, and Misiones to continue the war against the Portuguese. Ramírez, Governor of Entre Ríos, not only refused, but turned against Artigas and with the help of López defeated him. Artigas then took refuge in Paraguay, and Ramírez, in turn, quarreled with López, who defeated and killed him.

Reforms in Buenos Aires. After peace was restored, Martín Rodríguez endeavored to reorganize the administration of Buenos Aires. Aided by Bernardino Rivadavia, one of the most capable statesmen Argentina has ever had, many reforms were undertaken. The *cabildo,* the old municipal government, was abolished; a loan was negotiated in London; and harbor facilities were built. A bank of discount was created. The army was reorganized. The Church's special courts of justice were abolished. On August 12, 1821, the University of Buenos Aires was inaugurated. Primary and secondary education was promoted, and public welfare was fostered by a private organization, the *Sociedad de Beneficencia,* under the auspices of Rivadavia.

The General Constituent Congress of 1824. On December 16, 1824, a general congress met at Buenos Aires with representatives from fourteen provinces. The congress created the executive power of the United Provinces of the River Plata and elected Bernardino Rivadavia its first president. Immediately thereafter, Buenos Aires was declared the capital of the United Provinces, despite certain opposition from the inhabitants of that city, who feared the loss of their provincial autonomy.

The congress also, on July 19, 1826, adopted a unitarian constitution, which, like the previous one, was rejected by the provinces.

War with Brazil. The renewed conflict between the provinces and Buenos Aires was aggravated at this time by war with Brazil. Anarchy in the Banda Oriental had, as has been mentioned, resulted in an invasion of that province by Portuguese-Brazilian troops. Artigas and José Fructuoso Rivera, the two principal patriot leaders in Uruguay, were defeated, and on February 20, 1817, the Portuguese entered Montevideo. On July 18, 1821, a congress met in that city under the auspices of the Portuguese governor, General Carlos Frederico Lecor, and it declared the Banda Oriental incorporated in the United Kingdom of Portugal, Brazil, and the Algarves, under the name of "Cisplatine Province."

But this last Brazilian domination of the Banda Oriental did not last long. On April 19, 1825, Juan Antonio Lavalleja and a few patriots landed there and proclaimed war against foreign domination. In August of the same year, independence was proclaimed by a congress meeting at Florida (Uruguay). Lavalleja was made governor, and the incorporation of that province with the United Provinces of the River Plata was approved. This incorporation was accepted by the general congress then gathered at Buenos Aires, and war broke out between Buenos Aires and Brazil, which had, in 1822, become independent from Portugal.

This war ended with the virtual destruction of the Brazilian navy by the Argentine fleet under the command of Admiral William Brown on February 10, 1827. On land, the Argentine forces gained a decisive victory at Ituzaingó on February 20 of the same year. A treaty of peace was signed on September 5, 1828, providing for the recognition of the independence of the Banda Oriental by both countries.

The Tyranny of Rosas. After the war with Brazil, the provinces and Buenos Aires continued their struggle with each other for national supremacy. Rivadavia resigned the presidency of the United Provinces in 1827. The *caudillos* became supreme in their respective provinces and made war against each other. Rivadavia was followed by Manuel Dorrego in the presidency of the Union. But in 1828 the troops returning to Buenos Aires from the Banda Oriental set up one of their officers, Juan Lavalle, as chief executive. Dorrego fled the capital in December, 1828, but a few days later he was seized and executed. Then Lavalle began a war against the provinces, whose troops were led by Estanislao López. In April of the following year Lavalle was defeated.

This general disorder prepared the way for Juan Manuel de Rosas. He was born of a good family in Buenos Aires on March 30, 1793. At the age of thirteen he joined the patriot troops against the British invasion of 1806. Two years later he became a rancher in the pampa. During 1820 he took part in the wars against the *caudillos* of other provinces and rose to a leading position because of his personal valor. He took part in the Buenos Aires campaign and later joined López in war against Juan Lavalle.

After the defeat of Lavalle, Juan José Viamont was made provisional governor of Buenos Aires. He immediately called a provincial assembly which elected Rosas governor and captain general. Inaugurated with broad powers, on December 8, 1829, Rosas proceeded to rule with the enthusiastic support of the population as a whole. At the end of his term, Rosas was replaced by Juan Ramón Balcarce. In 1833 Rosas led an expedition against the rebellious southern Indians, during which more than 6,000 natives were killed or enslaved.

Meanwhile, Balcarce quarreled with the partisans of Rosas and was overthrown. Upon his return to Buenos Aires, Rosas was received with great honors and again elected governor of the province. After rejecting the office four times, he accepted it and was inaugurated in March, 1835, with dictatorial powers and for a term of years as long as he considered necessary to restore peace and order. This appointment was confirmed by a plebiscite at the request of Rosas.

Thus began the long rule of Rosas, which gradually developed into one of the worst tyrannies ever seen in Latin America. Rosas governed by violence. The *Mazorca,* an organization established during Balcarce's government to promote Rosas's return to the government, committed all sorts of violence against those who dared to criticize the tyrant. A literary society called the *"Salón Literario,"* formed by Esteban Echeverría, Juan María Gutiérrez, Juan Bautista Alberdi, Vicente Fidel López, and Miguel Cane, was dispersed by the police and its members persecuted under the pretext that they had conspired against the government. As a result, some of them organized a secret society similar to the revolutionary Italian societies of that time. This society, called *"Asociación de Mayo,"* or *"Joven Argentina,"* promoted the return of freedom.

Many uprisings took place against the tyrant. At the same time his government was harassed by complications with foreign powers.

The Falkland (Malvinas) Islands. These islands, off the coast of Argentina, in the South Atlantic, had been occupied by Spain and were claimed by Argentina after independence. In 1831 United States ships took reprisals against the local authorities because they endeavored to enforce the prohibition of fishing by foreign ships in the territorial waters of the islands. Buenos Aires requested an explanation from the U. S. government, but none was given. In 1833 a British ship landed troops on the islands, which were declared occupied by Great Britain. The government of Rosas protested, but Great Britain has continued to occupy the islands ever since.

The Quarrel with France. In 1837 Rosas sided with Chile in a war against the Peru-Bolivian Confederation created by General Santa Cruz. A French citizen residing in Buenos Aires was suspected of being a spy in the service of Santa Cruz and was imprisoned. When he died a short while afterward, the French consul demanded redress in such terms that Rosas expelled him from Buenos Aires. A French fleet then blockaded the River Plata, and at the same time French agents negotiated with Rivera and Lavalle in Uruguay, furnishing them help in their war against Rosas. The difficulties with France ended with an agreement signed between Rosas and French representatives on October 29, 1840, whereby Rosas recognized the French claims.

The Dispute with Chile. In 1847 a dispute arose with Chile, when that country occupied the Strait of Magellan. Rosas protested, claiming that during colonial days the Strait had been under the jurisdiction of Buenos Aires. Chile, however, refused to recognize the Argentine rights to that region. The question was not settled until 1902, as pointed out in the chapter on Chile.

The Quarrel with Paraguay. At the same time Rosas quarreled with Carlos Antonio López, the ruler of Paraguay, because of alleged help furnished to Corrientes when that province had revolted against him. Commerce between Buenos Aires and Paraguay was prohibited by Rosas.

The "Great War" and the Fall of Rosas. Rosas nursed the plan of annexing Uruguay to Buenos Aires, partly to prevent it from continuing to be a base of supply and place of refuge for his enemies. In the civil war then raging in the Banda Oriental, Rosas sided with Manuel Oribe, one of the leaders of the *Blanco* Party. In 1842

Oribe, at the head of an Argentine army, laid siege to Montevideo. Despite protests from Great Britain, France, and Brazil, Rosas ordered the port of Montevideo blockaded by the Argentine fleet under the command of Admiral Brown.

The difficulties of Rosas were increased at this time by the declaration of General Justo José de Urquiza, Governor of Entre Ríos, inviting the other provinces to join him in war against Rosas (May 25, 1851). The legislature of Entre Ríos passed a law accepting the resignation of Rosas as Director of Foreign Relations of the United Provinces, a position for which he had been elected under the Treaty of 1831 and which he had no intention of giving up. A few days later, a treaty against Rosas was signed in Montevideo between Urquiza, the Uruguayan patriots of the *Colorado* Party, the province of Corrientes, and representatives of Brazil.

Urquiza then crossed to the Banda Oriental and compelled Oribe to raise the siege of Montevideo, which had lasted for nearly nine years. Returning to Argentina at the head of an army of some 30,000 men, Urquiza defeated the forces of Rosas decisively on February 3, 1852, in the Battle of Monte Caseros. Rosas then resigned and left Argentina with his daughter on board a British ship. He died in Southampton on May 14, 1877.

National Reorganization (1852–80)

General Urquiza, immediately after the Battle of Monte Caseros, devoted himself to organizing the nation on a stable basis. At a meeting of the provincial governors held in San Nicolás, an agreement was signed on May 31, 1852, providing for the calling of a federal congress to draft a constitution. Urquiza was also granted broad powers to restore order anywhere within the nation.

This agreement was not well received in Buenos Aires, and the provincial legislature refused to ratify it. On September 11, Buenos Aires arose in arms against Urquiza, who was unable to subdue it. The province adopted a constitution of its own on April 12, 1854.

The Federal Constitution of 1853 of the United Provinces. On November 20, 1852, a constituent congress with delegates from the thirteen outlying provinces met at Santa Fe, as agreed upon at San Nicolás. A treatise on the political conditions of the nation was at this time circulated among the delegates. Written by Juan Bautista Alberdi, one of the most distinguished political thinkers of his time, it studied in detail the basis for the political organization of the nation. On May 1, 1853, a constitution was adopted, which was promulgated by General Urquiza on the 25th of the same month. It recognized provincial autonomy to a certain extent, but at the same time provided for a strong central government. The executive was to be elected for six years indirectly by an electoral college. The congress was to be bicameral.

Under this constitution Urquiza was elected first president. During his administration, treaties were signed with Great Britain, the United States, and France, opening the Paraná and Uruguay rivers to the navigation of the world. Public education was promoted. The University of Córdoba was nationalized. Immigration was fostered. The survey for a railroad connecting Rosario with Córdoba was begun in 1854, and the trans-Andine railway project was approved the following year.

Buenos Aires Joins the Confederation. The separation of Buenos Aires from the Confederation was only transitory. In 1854 and 1855 treaties of peace and commerce were signed between the Confederation and that province. But owing to economic and financial difficulties, the Confederation adopted a law in 1856 establishing certain duties on foreign goods introduced into the provinces through the port of Buenos Aires. This law was interpreted by the people of Buenos Aires as a menace to their economic dominance, and in 1859 they took reprisals.

The Paraná Congress then authorized Urquiza to force the annexation of Buenos Aires to the Confederation. Buenos Aires prepared for war by appointing General Bartolomé Mitre commander of her troops. At Cepeda, on October 23, 1859, Mitre was defeated. An agreement was then signed, on November 11, incorporating Buenos Aires in the Confederation, under the condition that within twenty days a provincial congress would meet in Buenos Aires to propose any amendments to the Constitution of 1853 that it might consider necessary.

The following year the delegates from Buenos Aires to the national congress were refused recognition because they had not been elected in accordance with the electoral provisions of the Constitution of 1853. Buenos Aires resented this and declared the Treaty of 1859 abrogated.

Thereupon war broke out again between Buenos Aires and the Confederation. But at the Battle of Pavón, on September 17, 1861, General Mitre remained in control of the field. As a consequence, the national congress appointed Mitre provisional president of the Confederation. Argentina was for the first time a united nation.

Mitre's Administration. The first question taken up by the congress was that of the national capital. A law was adopted providing for the federalization of the entire province of Buenos Aires, but that province refused to give its consent to this move. Eventually a "Law of Compromise" was adopted, establishing the capital of the Confederation in Buenos Aires for five years. On October 5, General Mitre was elected president of Argentina.

Mitre's administration was characterized by many progressive reforms and general progress in education, foreign relations, and commerce. However, the Paraguayan War, which broke out at this time, prevented further development.

The Paraguayan War. Relations between Argentina and Paraguay had not been friendly for many years. In 1842 Rosas had refused to recognize Paraguayan independence, and in retaliation President Carlos Antonio López had given help to the province of Corrientes, then in revolt against Rosas. The Argentine tyrant in turn prohibited all commerce with Paraguay. In 1849 Paraguayan troops occupied the territory of Misiones, and the Buenos Aires legislature authorized Rosas to bring about the annexation of Paraguay to the Argentine Confederation. During the war against Rosas, Paraguay sided with his enemies.

When the Confederation established its capital at Paraná, Argentina, after the downfall of Rosas, the independence of Paraguay was recognized. In 1862 Carlos Antonio López died, and his son, Francisco Solano López, assumed the executive office in Paraguay. That country had by then accumulated a substantial war chest and possessed a large and well-trained army. Its defenses had been improved. Flushed with ambition, Francisco López entertained dreams of becoming the ruler of an extensive empire in the heart of South America.

When Brazilian troops, in 1864, invaded Uruguay in an effort to restore order in that country, Francisco López immediately protested and broke off diplomatic relations with Brazil. A Paraguayan army invaded the Brazilian province of Mato Grosso. In January, 1865, López requested from Argentina permission to cross the province of Corrientes to attack the Brazilian province of Rio Grande do Sul. President Mitre refused, and López at once declared war against Argentina.

On May 1, 1865, a treaty of alliance was signed at Buenos Aires between Argentina, Uruguay, and Brazil against López of Paraguay. General Mitre was made the commander-in-chief of the allied armies.

The war lasted longer than expected. After forcing the pass of Humaitá in 1868, the allied forces compelled López to evacuate most of the fortifications and to withdraw toward the north. On January 2, 1869, the allied troops entered Asunción. On March 1, 1870, López was killed near Aquidabán, and in June peace was signed between the allies and a provisional government set up at Asunción. The boundary question between Paraguay and Argentina was settled in a treaty signed six years later.

Mitre's *Testamento Político*. The presidential election of 1868 was hotly contested. President Mitre had the strength of character to remain neutral, declaring in a letter to a friend, since then known as his *"Testamento Político,"* that in his opinion the executive should not influence the election of his successor.

Domingo Faustino Sarmiento was elected president and inaugurated on October 12, 1868. Sarmiento was a sociologist, educator, and statesman of great ability. During his administration public education was vigorously promoted, new railroads were built, and immigration was fostered.

The peace negotiations after the Paraguayan War resulted in some ill feeling between Argentina and Brazil. These difficulties disappeared with the visit, in 1872, of General Mitre to Rio de Janeiro. The treaties of peace and limits with Paraguay were signed by Argentina in 1876.

After Sarmiento's term of office expired, Nicolás Avellaneda governed the country. His administration was disturbed by a revolution led by General Mitre. This uprising, which was suppressed by the government forces, was a protest against the custom, followed generally by the executive, of influencing the election of his successor.

Buenos Aires Becomes the National Capital. In 1880 Carlos Tejedor, a candidate for the presidency, rose against the government in the province of Buenos Aires to defend the autonomy of that province from the encroachments of the national government, but the revolution was quickly suppressed. On September 20, the congress adopted a law federalizing the municipality of Buenos Aires, which became the permanent capital of the nation. With this act the organization of Argentina as a nation was at last accomplished.

Argentina from 1880 to 1940

Roca and His Successors. In 1880 General Julio A. Roca, who had distinguished himself in a campaign against rebellious southern Indians, became president. Roca sent new expeditions against the Indians, gaining considerable territory for settlement and cultivation. Foreign trade increased very rapidly, its total amount almost doubling between 1880 and 1886. Railway mileage more than doubled, and immigration, which in 1880 was 41,561, rose to about 108,000 in 1885. During the six-year term of Roca, 483,000 immigrants settled in Argentina.

The next president was Miguel Juárez Celman, who triumphed at the polls in 1886 with the backing of the administration. At once a severe financial and economic crisis developed in the country owing to overexpansion during the previous years. A new party, the *Unión Cívica*, was formed, and about the middle of 1890 its members rose in rebellion against the government in the capital. Although the rebels were defeated by government troops, Juárez Celman resigned. He was replaced by the Vice-President, Carlos Pellegrini. The economic situation did not improve, and the government had to resort to the issue of paper money in order to be able to pay its own debts. The public lost confidence in the banks, and both the national bank and the provincial bank of Buenos Aires were closed, with a considerable loss to their depositors. The government endeavored to remedy the situation by creating a new bank, the *Banco de la Nación,* on December 1, 1891.

In 1892 Luis Sáenz Peña was elected president by a coalition of the *Unión Cívica* and the National Party. His administration was characterized by general unrest. During the first nine months of his term there were twenty-three different cabinets. Radical agitation in the provinces became alarming, and the central government was compelled to intervene in several of them to restore public order. Unable to cope with the situation, President Sáenz Peña resigned and was replaced by the Vice-President, Dr. José Evaristo Uriburu, in 1895.

During Uriburu's administration a national convention met in 1898 and amended the constitution, increasing the national representation in the congress and reorganizing the ministries, the number of which was increased to eight. In 1898 General Roca was again elected to the presidency. A labor code was adopted. At this time Argentina expounded through her Minister of Foreign Affairs,

Luis M. Drago, the doctrine since then known as the "Drago Doctrine," whereby debts of states were not to be collected by force of arms. In 1899 the currency was stabilized by the guarantee of its conversion to gold at a fixed rate. In 1902, during President Roca's second administration, the amicable settlement of the boundary dispute with Chile took place.

In 1904 Dr. Manuel Quintana became president. The following year a radical revolution broke out which was suppressed by the government with difficulty. The president died in 1906, and the vice-president, Dr. José Figueroa Alcorta, assumed the executive office. He restored peace, promoted public education, and established the first rural schools in Argentina. In 1912 Roque Sáenz Peña was elected to the presidency. During his administration the electoral laws were reformed in order to allow greater participation of the people at large. The secret ballot was adopted, and voting became compulsory for those eligible. Because of ill health, the president was replaced by the vice-president, Victorino de la Plaza. With the outbreak of World War I, Argentina's exports were curtailed, unemployment increased, and a severe economic and financial depression was felt throughout the country.

Radical Administrations. As a result of the adoption of the new electoral laws, the radicals won the presidential election of 1916, and Hipólito Irigoyen became president. Argentina remained neutral during the war. Public education was promoted by the new president, more than 1,000 new schools being opened throughout the nation. The universities were reformed. Social legislation was enacted in favor of the working classes.

In 1922 another radical, Marcelo T. de Alvear, was elected to the presidency. Six years later Irigoyen returned to the executive chair, but the conservatives revolted and an attempt was made to assassinate the president on December 24, 1929. One year later the situation was aggravated by labor strikes and rioting in the capital. On September 5, 1930, President Irigoyen resigned and was arrested, and the following day, General José Félix Uriburu, a conservative leader, assumed the executive power. He ruled as dictator, arresting many members of the Radical and Socialist parties, and exiling many others.

Uriburu, who had assumed the presidency in a provisional character, delayed the elections as long as possible. Forced by public opinion, he finally ordered elections held on November 8, 1931. The

National Democrats and the anti-Irigoyen Radicals merged and elected General Agustín P. Justo.

Although civil liberties were restored by President Justo, who was inaugurated on February 20, 1932, several members of the Radical Party, including Irigoyen and Alvear, were exiled. President Justo endeavored to steer clear of both the Fascist and Socialist factions, but ruled dictatorially and interfered in the elections and general politics of the provinces. In the congressional elections of 1936 the Radicals won a majority representation, despite the administration's interference. A "popular front" was organized in opposition to the Fascist groupings.

In 1937 Roberto M. Ortiz was elected president. He was inaugurated on February 20, 1938. Poor agricultural conditions and a 40 per cent decline in exports were reflected in diminishing government revenues and poor business conditions throughout the whole country. This situation was aggravated by the new European war. President Ortiz refused to devaluate the currency, as some suggested, and instead cut government expenditures. Barter agreements with Italy and Germany reduced the wheat surplus, held mostly by the government. Agreements with Spain and Great Britain also tended to improve general economic conditions.

In July, 1940, President Ortiz, who had been ill for some time suffering from diabetes, took sick leave. The presidency was occupied by Vice-President Ramón S. Castillo, a strong conservative leader who proceeded to undermine President Ortiz's influence in the government. To avert a cabinet crisis President Ortiz resumed his duties in August.

Political Developments since World War II

President Ortiz resigned August 22, 1942, after a Senate inquiry and debate on a land-sale scandal involving the Minister of War and other cabinet members. He was succeeded by Vice-President Ramón S. Castillo, whose regime was ousted in June, 1943, by a *coup d'état* which placed General Pedro P. Ramírez in the presidency.

In September another serious political crisis developed following the refusal by the United States government to permit the sale of arms to Argentina. The American government alleged that Buenos Aires had failed to implement the provision of the 1942 Rio de Janeiro agreement to the effect that all American nations should break relations with the Axis powers.

A bitter discussion ensued. The public in general and some of the most influencial newspapers demanded an alignment with the United States and the other American nations. The breaking of relations with the Axis was opposed by a group of army officers known as *Grupo de Oficiales Unidos* (GOU) which had played an important role in the overthrowing of Castillo.

Although President Ramírez had declared that Argentina would maintain its neutrality in the war, evidence submitted by the British government of widespread Axis espionage in Argentina led to the breaking of relations with the Axis early in 1944. Ramírez resigned on March 10 and was replaced by the Vice-President, General Edelmiro Julián Farrell, who annulled all anti-Axis measures previously taken.

On July 7, Colonel Juan Domingo Perón, one of the most influential leaders of GOU, was appointed Vice-President and Minister of Labor and Social Welfare. A few days later the United States issued a declaration to the effect that Argentina had violated the pledge of co-operation with, and support of, hemispheric defense policies. Finally, on March 27, 1945, Argentina declared war on Germany and Japan. In April she signed the Charter of the United Nations.

Unrest continued throughout the country. On October 9, after violent public demonstrations in Buenos Aires, Colonel Perón resigned. He was detained on an island in the River Plata, but soon thereafter he was ordered released. This was done mainly on account of widespread protests by the workers, who had gained considerable advantages through legislation introduced by Perón as Minister of Labor.

In the elections held on February 24, 1946, Perón was a candidate for the presidency backed by nationalist elements and by the labor unions. The United States accused Argentina of protecting Nazi interests, but this criticism failed to prevent Perón's victory at the polls. He was installed on June 4, and promptly adopted a five-year plan for the development of industry, transportation facilities, public works, and education. Legislation was adopted nationalizing the banking system and extending the franchise to women. Labor legislation of a very progressive character was also adopted, including social insurance, and increased participation of the workers in the ownership and direction of corporations.

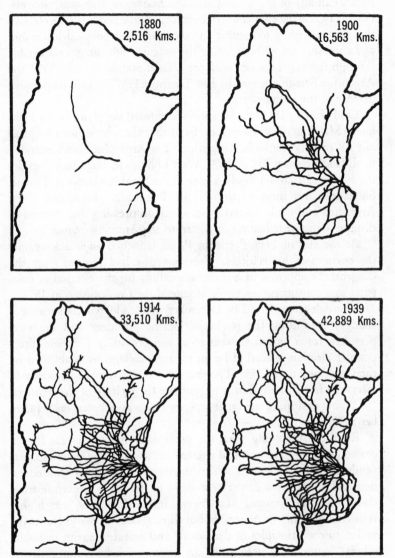

Fig. XIX–2. Development of Argentine Railways, 1880–1939. (Courtesy of *Informaciones Argentinas,* June–July, 1941. From *Argentina Económica,* 1940, by Emilio Llorens and Rafael García Mata.)

Although President Perón declared in 1947 that Argentina would fight as an ally of the United States in case of another war, the relations between the two countries continued strained. It was obvious that Perón wished to assume the economic and political leadership of Latin America without losing the potential advantages obtainable through friendly relations with the United States. In July, 1950, the Argentine Senate ratified the Rio Treaty of 1947 for the co-operative defense of the Hemisphere.

On February 18, 1948, Argentina reaffirmed her claim to the Falkland (Malvinas) Islands and declared that she would not recognize any European colonies in Antarctica. The Argentine claim extended to all land between 25° and 74° West Longitude, including (besides the Falkland Islands) South Georgia, the South Orkneys and South Shetlands, and most of the Palmer Peninsula. In March, 1948, Argentina and Chile agreed to act jointly in pressing their territorial dispute with Great Britain in regard to the Antarctic region.

At the end of 1948, President Perón launched an attack against the enemies of his reforms. Previously, he had secured from the congress the approval of a resolution calling for the election of delegates to a constituent assembly to amend the Constitution of 1853.

The delegates elected in December, 1948, adopted constitutional changes permitting the re-election of the president and the vice-president for a second six-year term and providing for their direct popular election instead of by an electoral college, as established by the Constitution of 1853. The executive was given the authority to intervene in private industry to promote the welfare of the workers.

A new and quite stringent security law was adopted on September 8, 1950.

Early the following year, the great daily newspaper *La Prensa* ceased publication after it had rejected demands from the newspaper-vendors' union (affiliated with the Argentine General Confederation of Labor) for a 20 per cent share in the paper's revenue from classified advertisements. *La Prensa,* founded in 1869, was highly respected not only in Argentina but throughout the world for its devotion to the principles of democracy and moral integrity in public affairs. After some rioting and an investigation by a congressional committee, legislation was adopted expropriating *La Prensa.* Its chief editor, Dr. Alberto Gainza Paz, escaped to Uruguay. On November 19, 1951, the paper reappeared under the direction of the government-controlled General Confederation of Labor.

On September 28, 1951, a serious military uprising broke out at the Campo de Mayo base and the Palomar and Punta Indio airfields. The revolt was led by retired Generals Arturo Rawson and Benjamín Menéndez, who accused Perón of bringing about the ruin of the nation. The uprising was promptly suppressed by Perón; some of the military leaders escaped to Uruguay, and several of the civilian leaders, including Dr. Arturo Frondizi, were arrested. At a press conference (October 1), President Perón accused the United States Ambassador, Spruille Braden, of having inspired the revolt. Other American citizens, including John Griffith, former American Embassy attaché at Buenos Aires, were also accused of complicity.

At the presidential elections of November 11, 1951, Perón was re-elected.

In an effort to tighten Argentina's relations with neighboring nations, Perón visited Chile in February and Paraguay in October, 1953. Relations with Uruguay remained strained, in part because of alleged disregard for Argentina's claims over the Falkland Islands on the part of Uruguay in a trade agreement signed with Great Britain.

In April, 1953, rioting, arson, and mob violence broke out in Buenos Aires after two bombs exploded while Perón was addressing a mass meeting in the Plaza de Mayo. The meeting had been called by the General Confederation of Labor to express support for the president's campaign against "profiteering." Perón was unhurt, but six people were killed and close to one hundred injured.

Although President Perón denied that any economic, political, or social crisis existed in Argentina, the country was going through difficult times. Prices soared, the cost of living was 600 per cent higher in 1953 than in 1943, and livestock production, the country's basic industry, declined rapidly.

Perón now became involved in a serious quarrel with the Roman Catholic hierarchy. On November 10, 1954, he publicly accused certain churchmen of attempting to infiltrate the trade unions and of engaging in intrigues against the state. Several priests were arrested. At a mass meeting of the *Peronista* Party and the General Confederation of Labor in the capital, protests were voiced against the alleged clerical infiltration. Catholic groups also staged counter-demonstrations. The president then signed decrees abolishing the Church's control of religious education in the public schools and legalizing divorce. Several months later (February 10, 1955), the government withdrew its subsidies from eighty Roman Catholic schools and dismissed some two hundred priests and nuns from their posts as teachers or inspectors in state-subsidized schools. On May 18–19, legislation was adopted by the congress disestablishing the Church. The Roman Catholic Church had been the official church since 1810. Legislation was also adopted making the property of the Church, of convents, and of other ecclesiastical organizations liable to taxation.

There followed more arrests of Catholic leaders and the deportation of two leading Roman Catholic dignitaries. The Holy See retaliated by excommunicating those responsible for the violation of the Church's rights in Argentina. In defiance of the government's ban, mass demonstrations were staged throughout the country against the president's policies. Finally, on September 16–19, Perón's regime was overthrown by a military and civilian revolt. Perón resigned and took refuge on a Paraguayan gunboat. General Eduardo Lonardi, leader of the revolution in Córdoba, was installed as provisional president on September 23.

Lonardi promised immediate restoration of civil liberties, including freedom of the press. All signs of Perón and Eva, his wife (who had died on July 26, 1952), were torn down in Buenos Aires and other cities. Admiral Isaac Rojas, who commanded the naval forces during the uprising, was made vice-president on September 25.

General Lonardi's regime did not last long. On November 13, he was replaced by General Pedro Eugenio Aramburu, Chief of General Staff, in a bloodless revolt in which both military and civilians of liberal principles took part. They criticized Lonardi's overtolerant attitude towards Perón's followers and his appointment of ultra-Catholics to the cabinet.

A call for a general strike by the General Confederation of Labor was only partially successful. Government troops occupied the Confederation's headquarters in Buenos Aires, and the strike was called off within a few days (November 17).

Perón's followers continued to plot against the government. In June, 1956, forty supporters of Perón were arrested and executed. President Aramburu announced that general elections would be held late in 1957.

Meanwhile, the economic and financial position of Argentina continued to decline. Early in 1957, in the attempt to improve conditions, the government adopted the Verrier Plan. Based on the assumption that the country was undercapitalized, badly equipped, and in debt though enormously rich, the plan advocated the freezing of wages and a simultaneous increase in prices. This plan had to be set aside because of strong opposition from many quarters.

On September 17, 1956, the U. S. Export-Import Bank extended to Argentina much-needed credits totaling 100 million dollars.

A constituent assembly met at Santa Fe on September 1, 1957, to amend the Perón Constitution of 1949. This assembly discontinued its work a few weeks later after the withdrawal of a large majority of the delegates because of irreconcilable disagreement on fundamental principles. However, the assembly approved a resolution re-establishing the 1853 constitution as the basic law of the nation.

President Aramburu then issued a decree on November 18, 1957, calling for general elections (to be held on February 23, 1958), under the electoral law of Sáenz Peña. The provisional government would hand over the administration to the new constitutional president on May 1, 1958. Despite widespread unrest and strikes, the election was held as planned. Ten parties presented candidates for the electoral college which would elect the president and the vice-president, and for a new congress, provincial legislatures, provincial governors, and municipal councils.

The election was reputed to have been free and orderly. The *Unión Cívica Radical Intransigente,* Dr. Arturo Frondizi's party, won a majority both in the electoral college and in the two houses of congress, as well as in all provincial councils. Declared elected by the electoral college, Dr. Frondizi was inaugurated as constitutional president of Argentina on May 1, 1958. Immediately he had to contend with the labor, economic, and financial problems created by the Perón regime. Elections in March, 1960, gave Frondizi a narrow majority in the Chamber of Deputies. Political disturbances led to a declaration of a state of emergency on March 15. The army was given authority to maintain order, and hundreds of Peronists were arrested. On October 13 ten top army officers resigned in protest against the president's decision to retain General Rodolfo Larcher as Secretary of War. The crisis stemmed from the army's conflict with the president over his acceptance of Peronist support in the election. In September, and again in December, 1961, President Frondizi visited the United States at the invitation of President Kennedy.

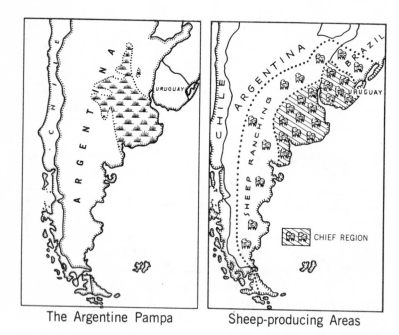

The Argentine Pampa

Sheep-producing Areas

CHIEF REGION

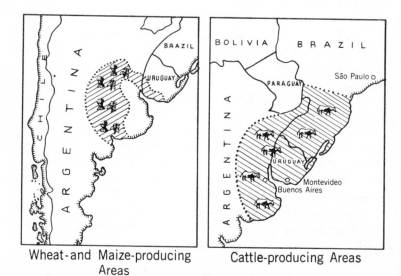

Wheat-and Maize-producing
Areas

Cattle-producing Areas

Fig. XIX–3. Agricultural Maps of Argentina and Uruguay.

In the Chamber of Deputies election of March 18, 1962, Peronists won a majority in several provinces and the next day the president took over control of the provinces to "protect the republican system." But on March 29 the army imprisoned Frondizi, replacing him with President of the Senate José María Guido, who canceled the election results on April 24, recessed congress for a year, and dissolved all parties. Under pressure from the military, presidential elections were held on July 31, 1963. Dr. Arturo Illia, backed by the Popular Radical Party, won the election. He was inaugurated on October 12, 1963. Frondizi was released on July 31.

Economic, Social, and Cultural Development

Economic Development. Argentina's chief source of wealth is agriculture and cattle raising. The rich soil and varied climate favor both temperate and tropical products: grains and cereals, livestock, and all kinds of fruits. Wheat, meat, hides, and wool are leading exports. Dairy products abundantly supply local needs. Meat packing has long been an important industry. Argentina is self-sufficient in textiles, leather, cement, certain chemicals, agricultural machinery, and some iron and steel products. Quebracho extract and wood are widely produced and exported. Steamship and air lines connect with all parts of the world, and domestic highway and rail communications are adequate.

After World War II, Argentina increased her trade with European countries by extending credits to them for purchase of Argentine products, particularly cereals, meats, and raw materials such as wool and hides. This effort was aided by the European Recovery Program initiated by the United States to help European nations resume large-scale trading. Argentina had an annual trade surplus from 1937 to 1947, when this surplus was sharply reduced through increased imports. Industries developed rapidly during the war. From 1937 to 1944, manufacturing increased 51 per cent, cotton-textile production 157 per cent. In 1947 agricultural production was 12 per cent above the prewar level. But most of these gains were lost because of Peron's socio-economic policies.

Social Development. The population of Argentina is estimated at more than 20 million; the people are almost all of Italian and Spanish origin. The few Indians are found in the extreme south or the extreme north. Standards of living are like those in the United States for similar localities, with many large centers of population.

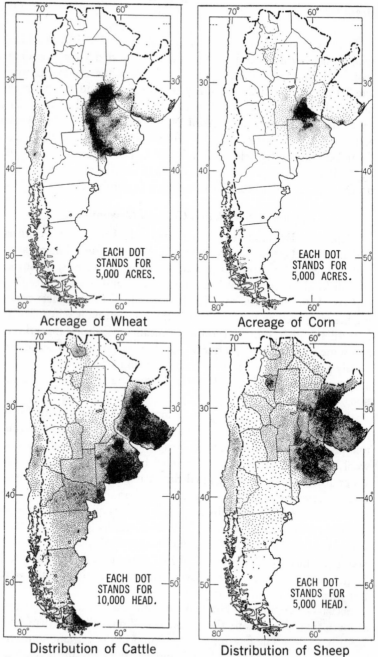

Acreage of Wheat

Acreage of Corn

EACH DOT STANDS FOR 5,000 ACRES.

EACH DOT STANDS FOR 5,000 ACRES.

EACH DOT STANDS FOR 10,000 HEAD.

EACH DOT STANDS FOR 5,000 HEAD.

Distribution of Cattle

Distribution of Sheep

Fig. XIX–4. Agricultural Maps of Argentina and Uruguay. (Courtesy of the United States Department of Agriculture.)

Buenos Aires is one of the great capitals of the world and compares favorably with Paris or New York. The government has long been interested in public health and social welfare, with the result that all levels of society have benefited. Labor legislation is of the highest order, and business and labor get along quite well together despite numerous strikes.

Education. There are six national universities: in Buenos Aires, La Plata, Tucumán, Córdoba, Cuyo, and the Litoral. There are also many industrial and professional schools preparing students for all types of skills and professions. Primary and secondary education are adequate for the country's educational needs, and normal schools, dating from the time of Sarmiento, provide a continuing supply of teachers.

Literary and Artistic Development. Among the early Argentine writers may be mentioned Vicente Fidel López (1815–1903), historian and author of the national anthem; Esteban de Luca, a poet who sang of the Revolution; and Juan Cruz Varela (1794–1839), who celebrated the liberal reforms of Rivadavia's time. During the Rosas regime there appeared a brilliant group of writers, among them: Esteban Echeverría (1805–51), sociologist, historian, poet, and one of the greatest prose writers of Argentina, author of *Profecía de la Plata, Elvira,* and *La Cautiva;* José Rivera Indarte (1814–45), a poet; José Mármol (1818–71), who wrote the epic *Cantos del peregrino* and the novel *Amalia,* which is popular even today; Juan María Gutiérrez (1809–78), a poet and a historian of great merit; Olegario V. Andrade (1841–82), an inspired nationalist poet; Estanislao del Campo (1834–80), author of *Fausto;* José Hernández (1834–86), author of *Martín Fierro,* the most famous of all poems of the gaucho type in Argentina; Domingo Faustino Sarmiento (1811–88), statesman, educator, poet, and prose writer—the author of *Facundo,* a socio-political biography of the lieutenants of Rosas; Bartolomé Mitre (1821–1906), statesman, poet, journalist, and one of the leading historians of Latin America. Other important writers are: Rafael Obligado (1851–1920), author of the very popular poem *Santos Vega el payador,* celebrating the legendary gaucho hero and popular poet of that name; V. Pedro Palacios ("Almafuerte") (1854–1914), a great poet of biblical inspiration; Rubén Darío (1867–1916), born in Nicaragua but a resident of Buenos Aires for many years—author of *Azul* and other notable books of poems, and founder of the modernist school in Latin America; Leopoldo Lugones (1869–1938), one of the greatest Latin American poets, author of *Lunario sentimental, Romancero,* and other works both in verse and in prose; Carlos Octavio Bunge (1875–1918), an essayist, novelist, and sociologist; José Ingenieros (d. 1925), a poet, journalist, sociologist, and one of the great intellectual leaders of Latin America; Manuel Ugarte (b. 1878), a writer who has had a great influence upon Latin American youth because of his hostile criticism of the United States; Manuel Gálvez (b. 1882), a popular novelist, author of *La Maestra normal* and *La Sombra del convento;* Enrique Rodríguez Larreta (b. 1875), author of the well-known novel *La Gloria de Don Ramiro,* depicting life in Spain, and of *Zogoibi,* about life in Argentina; Benito Lynch (b. 1885), novelist, author of *El Inglés de los güesos;* Hugo Wast (whose real name is Gustavo Martínez Zuviría) (b. 1883), author of many popular novels; Ricardo Güiraldes (1882–1927), author of one of the best-known novels of the pampa, *Don Segundo Sombra;* Alfonsina Storni and Luisa Luisi, poetesses; Ricardo Levene (b. 1886), Emilio Ravignani (b. 1886), and Enrique de Gandía (b. 1906), historians; Ricardo Rojas (b. 1882), historian, poet, and dramatist.

Argentina has had many painters of merit, including Gramajo Gutiérrez, A. Ballerini, Cupertino del Campo, Ernesto de la Cárcova, Jorge Bermúdez, Pablo Tosto, and Eduardo Sivori; and sculptors, among whom are Rogelio Irurtia, Francisco Caffareta, and Troiano Troiani.

PARAGUAY

Among all the Latin American nations, Paraguay has had, undoubtedly, one of the most tragic histories. The mass of the people are of Indian blood, belonging to the warlike Guaraní stock, which in pre-Columbian days occupied a vast region in southern South America. The Guaraní language is still spoken by most Paraguayans, and Spanish is habitually spoken only by the very small educated class. The government of the country has always been in the hands of dictators. Some of these dictators have ruled in the most tyrannical manner for long periods, such as Francia (1814–40) and the two López, father and son (1844–70); others have lasted for shorter periods. The country has had to fight two long and bloody wars, the Paraguayan War (1865–70), which reduced the population of Paraguay to less than half, and the Chaco War (1932–35), during which Paraguay lost some thirty or forty thousand men.

The history of Paraguay may be roughly divided into four main periods. From 1811 to 1814 an independent government was established; from 1814 to 1840, Francia ruled as absolute dictator; after a few years of chaos, the country was ruled from 1844 to 1870 by Carlos Antonio López and his son Francisco Solano López. Since then the country has been governed by lesser dictators.

National Organization (1811–14)

After the revolution of May 14, 1811, a congress met at Asunción and appointed a governing junta of five members under the presidency of Fulgencio Yegros. An alliance with the Buenos Aires patriots was also decided upon, provided that they recognized Paraguayan independence.

This decision of the congress was communicated to the Buenos Aires government, which appointed Manuel Belgrano and Vicente Anastasio de Echeverría commissioners to negotiate the annexation of Paraguay to Buenos Aires. Failing to bring this about, Belgrano and Echeverría, on October 12, 1811, signed a treaty of alliance with Paraguay, guaranteeing the latter's independence.

The junta's efforts to organize the country were hindered from the beginning by the interference of army officers. José Gaspar Rodríguez Francia, one of the leading members of the junta, resigned as a protest against this interference but was later persuaded to resume his duties in the junta. Francia, however, quarreled with the other members of the junta about whether a new congress should be called; Francia favored such an action, whereas the other members opposed it for fear of new disturbances.

Quarrel with Buenos Aires. At this time a dispute arose between the Paraguayan governing junta and the government of Buenos Aires over the interpretation of the treaty of alliance signed in 1811. Buenos Aires requested the help of Paraguay in the war against the royalists, but the government of Asunción refused the request. On the other hand, Paraguay was lending help to José Gervasio Artigas, the Uruguayan *caudillo*, in the latter's attempt to establish an independent state in the Banda Oriental. Early in 1813 this quarrel resulted in the severing of diplomatic relations between Asunción and Buenos Aires. Nevertheless, the Paraguayan government insisted upon sending delegates to the general assembly of the Plata provinces then meeting at Buenos Aires.

The Constitution of 1813. A congress met in the latter part of 1813 in Asunción and adopted a constitution, which was drafted in the main by Francia. This instrument of government, called the "*Reglamento de Gobierno,*" provided for a government of two consuls who were to alternate with each other in the exercise of the powers of government. The command of the national army was to be divided between the two consuls. Francia and Yegros were elected consuls, the former to rule for the first four months.

This congress also affirmed the absolute independence of Paraguay from Spain and all other countries. The alliance with Buenos Aires was abrogated.

The First Consulate. The two consuls reformed the administration, endeavored to establish commercial relations with Europe, reorganized the army, and took measures against the corruption of the clergy, then very prevalent in Paraguay. Laws were also adopted limiting the privileges of the Spaniards living in Paraguay. Their marriage with Paraguayan white women was prohibited, but they were allowed to marry Indian or Negro women.

The Dictatorship of Francia (1814–40)

When another congress met in October, 1814, Francia secured the adoption of a law providing for one chief executive instead of two consuls. The congress then appointed Francia head of the government for five years.

Francia has been pictured as a bloody, heartless despot. As a matter of fact, very little is known about him today. There is no doubt, however, that as a dictator he ruled the country with an iron hand and kept the state from the disorders and perpetual revolutions characteristic of the other Latin American states. He considered himself above all other persons and expected to be revered as a king. He also considered his country above all others, and in consequence he cut off all communication between Paraguay and the rest of the world.

Once in power, Francia devoted himself to consolidating his control of the government. He reorganized the administration and strengthened the national defenses. He prohibited the export of gold and silver coin and bullion, and increased import duties. Commerce with Brazil was authorized only at certain ports. The exporting of lumber became a government monopoly. Means of communication were improved, and agriculture was fostered. Religious communities were declared independent of outside organizations, and the Inquisition was suppressed.

On June 1, 1816, Francia was appointed dictator for life. The national congress was to meet only when the dictator considered it necessary.

As absolute ruler of Paraguay, Francia prohibited all public gatherings except at certain specified religious feast days; maintained defenses against the wild Indians; cultivated friendly relations with Brazil; severely punished dishonesty in public service; and instituted strict economy in all government expenditures. He also assumed the right to approve all Church appointments and abolished the monastic orders, allowing the secularization of the friars and confiscating the property of the monasteries. All marriages celebrated without his special permission were declared without legal effect.

Francia became a tyrant, punishing all criticism of his rule with imprisonment or death. In 1820 a serious conspiracy was discovered. Several prominent persons involved, including former consul Yegros, were either shot, imprisoned, or exiled, and their property was confiscated by the government. No foreigner was allowed to enter the country; those who went to Paraguay despite this prohibition were not allowed to leave. Paraguay became a hermit nation.

Fearing new conspiracies in which the Spaniards living in the country might participate, Francia imprisoned many of them and did not allow them to return to their homes until they paid a heavy fine.

Foreign Relations. In 1820 Francia quarreled with the Portuguese government of Brazil, claiming that it had instigated the Indians to attack Paraguayan settlements. Trade with Brazil was prohibited. In 1824, when Brazil had achieved independence, he received a diplomatic representative of that country; but since his claims as a result of the Indian depredations were not recognized, he again broke off relations with Brazil and prohibited all commerce with it.

Later Francia permitted trade with Brazil through Itapua, the dictator personally supervising all trade, approving prices, establishing duties to be paid, and specifying all the details. Traders who went to Itapua needed a special license from the dictator. Commerce was carried on through barter, no money being allowed to leave the country.

The End of Francia's Regime. On September 20, 1840, Francia died at the age of seventy-four, without having made any arrangement as to the future government of the country. His rule was beneficial in many respects: he was honest, was a good administrator, defended the country against foreign encroachments, promoted agriculture, and maintained internal peace. But his cruelty, despotism, and paranoid suspiciousness obstructed the political and cultural development of Paraguay.

After Francia's death, Policarpo Patiño, his secretary, endeavored to assume the government of the country. But a military revolution broke out the same day, and a governing junta was appointed. A few days later, a meeting of the municipal council was called, at which Manuel Antonio Ortiz was chosen president to govern the country with the help of four other members of the junta. No other changes were made in the government as established under Francia. Patiño was chosen first secretary of the junta, but later he was ousted and thrown into prison, where he committed suicide.

The junta was not well received by the public, and on January 22, 1841, a military revolution deposed it. A general congress was then elected to draft a new constitution and to elect a government. Before it met, a new revolution headed by Carlos Antonio López and Mariano Roque Alonso occurred.

The Restoration of the Consulate. On March 12 the new congress finally met at Asunción under the presidency of López. The consulate was restored, with López and Mariano Roque Alonso as consuls to govern the country jointly. The *cabildo* of the capital was re-established.

The two consuls at once freed all political prisoners; restored relations with the outside world; signed a treaty of friendship, commerce, and navigation, and another of limits with the Argentine province of Corrientes; and took measures promoting public education, establishing a secondary school in the capital, restoring relations with the papacy, and freeing the children of slaves born thereafter. On November 26, 1842, the congress reaffirmed the declaration of independence of Paraguay.

The Rule of the López Family (1844–70)

The Congress of 1844. On March 13, 1844, another congress met in the capital and approved a new constitution providing for a republican form of government, with the usual division of powers, the president to be elected for ten years. A council of state, appointed by the president, was to advise him on important matters. The following day López was made first president of the republic.

The congress also authorized the sending of six young Paraguayans to study abroad at the expense of the government, and the bringing of foreign professors of medicine to Paraguay. Several foreign nations recognized the new government, thanks, in great measure, to the good offices of Brazil.

The Administration of Carlos Antonio López. One of the first acts of López was to create an official newspaper. He promoted friendly relations with foreign countries; improved the national defenses, fearing an attack from Rosas, then ruling in Buenos Aires; abolished the Indian communities, a heritage from colonial times; and in general promoted the economic development of the country.

On December 25, 1850, López signed with Brazil a treaty under which the territory in dispute between the two countries was to be evacuated by the citizens of both parties until settlement of the boundary took place.

In 1851 Paraguay sided with Brazil and Uruguay against Rosas, the dictator of Buenos Aires, and after the fall of the tyrant, Paraguayan independence was recognized in a treaty signed by the United Provinces and Paraguay on July 15, 1852. During the same year, agents of France and the United States arrived at Asunción and signed treaties of friendship, commerce, and navigation with the Paraguayan government. López sent his son, Francisco Solano, to Europe as diplomatic representative to various courts.

In 1854 the congress met and re-elected López for another term of ten years; it also adopted slight changes in the constitution so as to permit the president to appoint the vice-president and to reduce the number of national representatives in the congress. López accepted the re-election only for three years.

International Complications. At this time the relations of Paraguay with the United States were strained by the complaints of an American citizen named Edward A. Hopkins, who was consul in Asunción and whose exequatur López annulled after a quarrel with him. The question was aggravated by an incident with the *Water Witch,* an American vessel visiting the River Plata at the time with a scientific expedition. The commander of the vessel sided with Hopkins against López. He also attempted to force the entrance of the upper Paraná without the authorization of the Paraguayan authorities. This dispute was settled later in a treaty, signed on February 4, 1859, whereby the question was to be submitted to arbitration. In the main the arbitral award was favorable to Paraguay.

On April 27, 1855, López was compelled by a display of force to sign a treaty of limits with Brazil. A treaty with Argentina on the boundary question was refused ratification in 1852, and a new one was negotiated in 1856. But the final settlement of the boundary disputes between Paraguay and these two nations took place only after the Paraguayan War.

Francisco Solano López as President. In 1857 the congress re-elected López for another term of ten years. But on September 10, 1862, he died, having previously appointed his son, Francisco Solano López, vice-president of the republic. Francisco López assumed the executive office at once. Later, the congress elected him for the legal term of ten years.

Francisco López assumed the government of Paraguay at a difficult period, requiring the utmost tact, a quality which he did not possess. Both Argentina and Brazil had postponed the final settlement of their boundary disputes with Paraguay until a more opportune moment. His father had left the country in excellent economic and military condition, with a strong and well-disciplined army, a strong navy, and efficient defenses. Francisco López continued to improve the armed forces of the country and conceived grandiose dreams of empire and military glory.

The Paraguayan War. For some time both Argentina and Brazil had been intervening in the internal politics of Uruguay, where they favored the party headed by Flores against the government. On August 30, 1864, Paraguay notified Brazil that she disapproved of Brazilian interference in Uruguay and that her government was disposed to intervene if Brazilian forces were to invade that country. When Brazilian forces did enter Uruguayan territory, Paraguay broke off diplomatic relations with Brazil, prohibited the navigation of the Paraná and Paraguay rivers to Brazilian shipping, captured a Brazilian vessel, the *Marquês de Olinda,* then in Paraguayan waters, and ordered an expedition to invade the Brazilian province of Mato Grosso. On January 14, 1865, López requested from Argentina permission to cross the province of Corrientes to attack the Brazilian province of Rio Grande do Sul, and upon refusal, he declared war upon Argentina.

Meanwhile, on May 1, 1865, at Buenos Aires, a treaty of alliance had been signed between Brazil, Argentina, and Uruguay. This treaty declared that the war was to be carried on against López until his downfall, that Paraguay should be compelled to pay a war indemnity, that the Paraguayan defenses should be destroyed, and that the boundary disputes with the allied powers should be finally settled. Although secret, the treaty became known throughout the world soon after its signature.

The war lasted longer than was expected, owing to the determined resistance of the Paraguayan people and the strategic advantages of Paraguay. The brunt of the attack fell on Brazil. Despite jealousy and lack of co-operation between the allied commanders, the Paraguayan defenses were gradually broken down. On June 11, 1865, the Paraguayan fleet was destroyed in the Battle of Riachuelo. Slowly the allied troops under the command of President Mitre of Argentina advanced into Paraguayan territory. On February 19, 1868, the Brazilian fleet forced the dangerous passage of Humaitá on the Paraguay River. The fortresses of Humaitá fell a few months later. In 1868 General Mitre left the command of the allied forces in the hands of the Brazilian Baron of Caxias, who on January 2, 1869, entered Asunción at the head of Brazilian, Argentine, and Uruguayan troops. López withdrew toward the north. On March 1, 1870, he was attacked near Cerro Corá and killed. With his death the war ended. This conflict, one of the bloodiest ever fought in the Western Hemisphere, lasted six years and resulted in the death of about half the population of Paraguay.

Provisional Government. In 1869, after the capital fell into the hands of the allies, a provisional government was set up. The following year a treaty of peace was signed providing for the payment of a heavy war indemnity by Paraguay. An army of occupation remained in the country until 1876.

In the negotiation of boundary treaties with the allies, Paraguay did not lose as much territory as might have been expected, because of quarrels among the allied governments. The treaty with Argentina, signed in 1876, provided that the boundary line between the Pilcomayo and the Verde rivers was to be determined by arbitration of the President of the United States. In 1878 President Hayes issued the arbitral award, which was, in the main, favorable to Paraguay.

Political Events from 1870 to 1940

The Constitution of 1870. In 1870 a constituent congress met and adopted a modern constitution providing for a bicameral congress, the executive to be elected for four years.

There followed a period of dictators and revolutions until 1912, when President Eduardo Schaerer was able to serve out his full term. In 1916 a member of the Radical Party, Manuel Franco, was elected president. He was followed in 1920 by Manuel Gondra, a distinguished jurist. But one year later a revolution overthrew him, and Eusebio Ayala became chief executive. Ayala resigned in 1923, and the congress elected Eligio Ayala to succeed him. In 1928 José Patricio Guggiari became president. He was succeeded by Eusebio Ayala, who was deposed by the army in 1936.

The Chaco War. A treaty of limits signed in 1879 between Paraguay and Bolivia provided that the boundary between the two countries should be a line due west from the mouth of the Apa River to the Pilcomayo River; but this agreement was not ratified by either country. In later years (1887, 1907, 1913) other treaties were negotiated but failed to receive ratification by either one or both nations. In 1927, at the invitation of Argentina, delegates from both nations met in Buenos Aires to discuss the matter. Unfortunately, in December, 1928, a clash between Bolivian and Paraguayan soldiers led to a break in diplomatic relations between the two countries. Preparations for war followed. Despite all efforts of the other American nations and of the League of Nations to prevent an armed conflict, serious fighting broke out in the middle of 1932. The following year Paraguay declared war, intending to bring into play against Bolivia an embargo on sales of arms from neutrals. But Bolivia continued to purchase arms in Chile, which led to a protest and the breaking of diplomatic relations between Paraguay and Chile.

In 1933 the Inter-American Conference, meeting at Montevideo, secured the signing of a truce between Bolivia and Paraguay. Another truce was agreed upon in the middle of 1935. In August, 1937, the two countries renewed diplomatic relations. Finally on July 21, 1938, they signed a treaty of peace and friendship at Buenos Aires, formally ending the conflict. Credit for the re-establishment of peace was due, in great measure, to the constant efforts of the six neutral delegates to the Chaco Peace Conference, representing Argentina, Brazil, Chile, Peru, the United States, and Uruguay. The treaty provided for the arbitration of the boundary between the sixty-second meridian and the Paraguay River. By October 10, 1938, the arbitral college, made up of delegates of the same countries, had rendered its decision, which was accepted by the two parties.

Presidents from 1936 to 1940. Early in 1936 President Eusebio Ayala, who favored a conciliatory policy toward Bolivia, exiled Colonel Rafael Franco, the leader of a group of young army officers who wished to continue the war until the complete defeat of Bolivia. Franco, a national hero, rose against the government and overthrew Ayala. His program of government included labor legislation and the distribution of land among the poor, as well as the nationalization of the natural resources and main industries of the country. With the carrying into effect of some of these reforms, there was unrest throughout the nation. On August 13, 1937, Franco was overthrown and a more conservative man, Dr. Félix Paiva, was made president, at first in a provisional character and later (October 10, 1938) as constitutional executive for an indefinite term. On April 30, 1939, however, General José Félix Estigarribia was elected president for a four-year term. Inaugurated on August 15, 1939, President Estigarribia assumed dictatorial powers and embarked on a program of public works and aid to agriculture, industry, and commerce. He favored the enactment of minimum wage laws, protection of labor unions, and the guarantee of political freedom in the country.

By a presidential decree of February 18, 1940, a committee was appointed to draw up a new constitution. This instrument, which followed the fundamental lines of the 1870 constitution but gave the government extensive powers over the nation's economic life, was adopted and went into effect on July 10, 1940.

On September 7, 1940, President Estigarribia was killed in an airplane accident, and General Higinio Moríñigo, Minister of War, assumed the presidency in a provisional character, appointed by the cabinet.

In 1940, the U. S. Export-Import Bank granted a credit of 3 million dollars to Paraguay to help the country free itself from financial dependency on Argentina.

Political Developments since World War II

Paraguay broke off diplomatic relations with the three principal Axis powers on January 28, 1942, and declared war on Germany and Japan on February 7, 1945; she became a charter member of the United Nations in April. During the war there were many industrial strikes. On July 1, 1946, the Moríñigo government recognized the Communist Party, which had previously been outlawed. Paraguay stood firmly on the side of the democratic nations after the war, and in July, 1950, the Chávez administration pledged aid against the North Korean Communists.

Under the new Constitution of 1940, General Moríñigo assumed full powers of government on December 7, 1940. He ruled as a dictator and dissolved the Liberal Party for alleged subversive activities. An army revolt against the president, which broke out early in 1944, was suppressed by loyal forces. Another and more serious rebellion broke out in March, 1947. Headed by Colonel Rafael Franco, the revolutionists called for the immediate election of delegates to a constituent assembly to amend the constitution. After months of fighting, the insurgents were defeated by the government forces, and Colonel Franco fled to Argentina.

Elected president in 1948, Dr. Juan Natalicio González was deposed on December 30 by an army coup led by General Raimundo Rolón, who was, in turn, deposed on February 27, 1949, when Dr. Felipe Molas López became provisional president with army support. Although regularly elected to the office in April, he resigned in September. Dr. Federico Chávez ruled in a provisional character for almost five years; he retired, May 5, 1954. Tomás Romero Pereira then served as president *ad interim*. General Alfredo Stroessner won the July elections. Re-elected in 1958, he declared his intention to restore constitutional government.

On February 10, 1963, General Stroessner, backed by the *Colorado* Party, defeated his sole rival, Dr. Ernesto Gavilán, candidate of the *Renovacionista* Party (a dissident group of the Liberal Party), and was re-elected for a third term. He was inaugurated on August 15, to serve for a six-year term.

Economic, Social, and Cultural Development

Paraguay produces good tobacco, cotton, Paraguayan tea (yerba mate), and some fruit. Oil of petitgrain, extracted from the leaves and twigs of native bitter-orange trees, is exported, as is quebracho wood used for tanning purposes. The livestock industry is growing slowly. There is no mining industry, although some iron deposits and petroleum are found in the country. Interior transportation is by rivers, a few miles of railroads, and inadequate roads. Air connections with other countries in South America are fairly satisfactory.

The population of Paraguay is more than 1.5 million people, the majority being of mixed or Indian blood. The settlement of Mennonites from Canada and the United States, and of Germans, Russians, and Middle Europeans has been encouraged by the government. The average standard of living is low.

Education is provided by the National University at Asunción, and by a small number of primary and secondary schools. Education is now compulsory for children up to the age of fourteen. Illiteracy is high. A large number of the people speak Guaraní rather than Spanish.

Among the most important writers the following may be mentioned: Alejandro Guanes, a poet; Casaccia Bibolini, a novelist; Juan Stefanich, an essayist; and Juan E. O'Leary, a poet.

URUGUAY

Uruguay is the smallest South American nation, and has been one of the most progressive. Its history may be divided into four main periods. From 1811 to 1821, the Uruguayan people, under the leadership of Artigas, endeavored to establish an independent government of their own; from 1821 to 1828, the country was first under Portuguese and Brazilian domination as the "Cisplatine Province," and later under the domination of Argentina; from 1828, when both Brazil and Argentina recognized the independence of Uruguay, until 1904, the country was in perpetual chaos. Civil war ended and political stability was established during the presidency of José Batlle y Ordóñez, who was able to enter into an agreement with his enemies (September 20, 1904). Since then the country has progressed very rapidly.

Efforts to Establish an Independent Government (1811–21)

At the outset of independence in the River Plata region, Uruguay (or the "Banda Oriental," as it was then known) remained at first loyal to the Spanish government. The revolution did not begin until February, 1811, when José Gervasio Artigas, a captain in the Spanish army, joined the patriots in Buenos Aires. From then to 1820 Artigas was recognized as leader of the movement for independence in the Banda Oriental.

The war against the royalists in the River Plata region ended only with the surrender of the Spanish authorities in Montevideo on June 20, 1814. By the end of 1812 most of the territory of the Banda Oriental was under the control of Artigas.

On April 4, 1813, Artigas gathered at his home representatives of the people to elect delegates to the general constituent assembly recently inaugurated in Buenos Aires. At this time Artigas was chosen military governor of Uruguay and president of the provincial government. The delegates sent to Buenos Aires were instructed to demand, among other things, that absolute independence be declared at once by the United Provinces, and that a confederate government be established allowing to the Banda Oriental autonomy of government.

Upon refusal of the Buenos Aires congress to recognize the Uruguayan delegates on this basis, another provincial assembly met on December 8, 1813, and chose new delegates. At the same time Artigas was deposed from office as military governor.

Under the circumstances, Artigas broke with the Buenos Aires government and abandoned the siege of Montevideo, which was still in the hands of the royalists. Crossing into Argentina, he proclaimed war against the Buenos Aires government in the name of the principles of autonomy and civil, religious, and commercial liberty. His authority was recognized at once by the provinces of Corrientes, Entre Ríos, Santa Fe, and Córdoba.

After the fall of Montevideo in 1814, the Banda Oriental was ruled by agents sent by the Buenos Aires government until 1815, when Fructuoso Rivera, a supporter of Artigas, defeated the Argentine troops and compelled them to evacuate Montevideo.

Artigas and the Federal League. From his headquarters at Hervidero, on the east bank of the Uruguay River, Artigas ruled the Banda Oriental and the four Argentine provinces which had recognized his authority. These provinces, and the territory of Misiones, between the Paraná and the Uruguay rivers, formed a "Federal League" against Buenos Aires. In 1816 Artigas organized Uruguay into six administrative provinces or departments. The same year, the first public library was opened in Montevideo under the auspices of a distinguished scholar, Father Damaso A. Larrañega. A few primary schools were organized.

The Portuguese Invasion of 1816. The Portuguese court, then established in Rio de Janeiro, had for some time endeavored to extend its control as far as the River Plata. Under the pretext of protecting its territory from the raids of Artigas' irregular troops (called *montoneras*), a Portuguese-Brazilian army was sent in August, 1816, into the Banda Oriental under the command of General Carlos

Frederico Lecor. Artigas and Rivera were defeated, and on January 20, 1817, Lecor entered Montevideo, where the *cabildo* accepted the Portuguese rule.

Indignant at the lack of help from Buenos Aires, Artigas declared war against the Argentine government. But he was defeated by the governor of Entre Ríos and was compelled to take refuge in Paraguay. Received by Francia, dictator of Paraguay, Artigas died in that country on September 23, 1850. Six years later his remains were taken to Montevideo and interred in the National Pantheon. Artigas is honored by his compatriots as the founder of Uruguayan nationality.

Foreign Domination (1821–28)

Brazilian Domination. On July 18, 1821, a congress convened in Montevideo and declared the annexation of Uruguay to the United Kingdom of Portugal, Brazil, and Algarves, under the name of the "Cisplatine Province." When, in 1822, Brazil became independent of Portugal, General Lecor in Montevideo sided with Dom Pedro, first Emperor of Brazil. After a short conflict between the partisans of Portugal and those of Dom Pedro, the Cisplatine Province was annexed to Brazil on May 9, 1824.

The War of Independence. On April 19, 1825, a group of thirty-three Uruguayans led by Juan Antonio Lavalleja, and known as "The Thirty-three," crossed from Argentina into the Banda Oriental and raised the flag of rebellion against the Brazilians. On June 14, 1825, a provisional government was set up under the direction of Manuel Calleros, and on August 25, a declaration of independence was issued. Lavalleja was elected governor and captain general of the province, and the Banda Oriental was declared incorporated in the United Provinces of the River Plata.

The Brazilians were defeated in the battles of Rincón and Sarandí. An Argentine army joined the Uruguayan patriots in January, 1826. At the same time the Argentine fleet under the command of Admiral Brown defeated the Brazilian fleet in the River Plata in February, 1826, and again in February, 1827. In December, 1826, Argentine forces invaded southern Brazil. The following February 20, the Brazilian troops were decisively defeated in the Battle of Ituzaingó. Peace was signed on August 27, 1828, both Argentina and Brazil recognizing and guaranteeing the independence of Uruguay.

Anarchy and Caudillaje (*1829–68*)

On September 10, 1829, a constitution was adopted by a constituent and legislative assembly, providing for the establishment of a representative republic under the name of "República Oriental del Uruguay." The assembly had elected provisionally (1828) and later confirmed General José Rondeau as president of the republic.

Meanwhile, a quarrel had developed among the Uruguayan patriots. Two factions appeared, one called the *Blancos,* led by Lavalleja, and another the *Colorados,* under the leadership of Rivera. On April 25, 1830, Lavalleja became provisional president after Rondeau had resigned. But he soon afterward assumed dictatorial powers and removed Rivera from his post as commander of the army. War between the two factions seemed inevitable when, thanks to the efforts of several patriots, among them particularly Father Larrañega, a conciliation pact was signed between Rivera and Lavalleja on June 16, 1830. The following October, Rivera was elected first constitutional president of the republic by the national legislative assembly.

The peace between the *Blancos* and *Colorados* did not last long. On July 3, 1832, a revolution aiming at the overthrow of Rivera broke out in Montevideo. Although defeated at first, the *Blancos,* helped by Rosas, the tyrant of Buenos Aires, invaded Uruguay in 1834. Again defeated by the government forces, their leader, Lavalleja, was compelled to take refuge in Brazil.

In 1835 General Manuel Oribe was elected president, with the support of both parties. His government was peaceful at first. But in consequence of the president's apparent friendship with the *Blancos* and with Rosas, the followers of Rivera arose in rebellion (July, 1836) against the government. An Argentine army under Lavalleja crossed into Uruguay to help Oribe. In the decisive Battle of Palmar (June 15, 1838), the government forces were defeated. Oribe resigned and sailed to Buenos Aires.

In 1839 Rivera again became president and signed treaties of alliance with the governor of Corrientes and with the French against Rosas. War broke out, and Argentine forces under the command of Oribe laid siege to Montevideo on February 16, 1843. This siege, known as the *"Guerra Grande,"* lasted nearly nine years, until October, 1851, despite the efforts of Great Britain, France, and Brazil to put an end to the conflict. It ended with the defeat of Oribe at the hands of General Justo José de Urquiza, Governor of Entre Ríos, who revolted against Rosas in 1851 and signed a treaty of alliance against the tyrant with the Uruguayan patriots and with Brazil.

From 1852 to 1853 Juan Francisco Girón was president. He was compelled to resign in consequence of a revolution headed by César Díaz and León Palleja. A triumvirate composed of Lavalleja, Rivera, and Venancio Flores was established to govern the country in a provisional character. But soon after, Lavalleja and Rivera died and Flores was elected to complete Girón's unfinished term of office.

Flores was, from the beginning, opposed by a group of the *Colorado* Party called *Conservadores,* who feared that the new president intended to perpetuate himself in power. A revolution broke out in the capital on August 28, 1855. Flores was overthrown, and Manuel P. Bustamante was elected provisional president.

The civil war continued with short intervals of peace. In 1860 Bernardo P. Berro became president. On April 19, 1863, Flores, who had taken refuge in Buenos Aires, invaded Uruguay at the head of an army composed for the most part of members of the *Colorado* Party. This invasion is known as the *"Cruzada Libertadora."*

As a consequence of losses suffered by Brazilian citizens living in Uruguay and the constant raids into southern Brazil by the warring factions, Emperor Dom Pedro II of Brazil endeavored to bring about peace in Uruguay. For this purpose he sent José A. Saraiva to Montevideo. Failing to restore peace, Saraiva presented an ultimatum to the Uruguayan government demanding compensation for the losses suffered by Brazilian citizens. Upon rejection of this ultimatum, Brazilian troops, in December, 1864, joined the army of Flores in war against the government of Atanasio C. Aguirre, then President of Uruguay. The allied forces entered Montevideo on February 21, 1865, after defeating the government army in several battles. Flores assumed once more the government of the country.

During the Paraguayan War, Flores, who had signed the Treaty of the Triple Alliance against López, co-operated personally as commander of a section of the allied armies.

On February 15, 1868, Flores was replaced by Pedro Varela as president. Four days later Flores was assassinated in the streets of the capital by a fanatic belonging to the *Blanco* Party.

Uruguay from 1868 to 1940

From 1868 to 1903 there were many presidents, who were usually overthrown by revolutions. Little progress could have been

made under the circumstances. In 1903 José Batlle y Ordóñez became the chief executive. At once a revolution broke out. But the
president was able to suppress it by signing an agreement with his
enemies on September 20, 1904, which put an end to civil war in Uruguay. During the remainder of the term of Batlle y Ordóñez some
economic progress took place. This progress continued during the
administration of Dr. Claudio Wílliman, who was president from
1907 to 1911. Railroads were built and the harbor works were completed. In 1909 Brazil granted to Uruguay the right of joint control over the Yaguarón River and Lake Mirim.

Dr. Wílliman was followed by Batlle y Ordóñez (1911–15), Dr.
Feliciano Viera (1915–19), and Dr. Baltasar Brum (1919–23). The
latter was the first president to govern under the Constitution of
1919.

The Constitution of 1919. This constitution, a very advanced instrument of government, provided for the establishment of a unitary
republic, with the usual division of powers. The executive power
was to be exercised by a president, elected by direct popular vote for
four years, together with a National Council of Administration of
nine members, chosen for six years by the people and by ministers of
state, appointed by the National Council of Administration. The
legislature was bicameral, and a permanent commission of seven
members was to sit while the congress was not in session. Local
government was strengthened by the restoration of the powers of
government of the municipalities.

Dr. Brum's administration was enlightened and progressive. He
was followed by José Serrato (1923–27), Juan Campísteguy (1927–
31), and Gabriel Terra (1931–38).

Subsequent Administrations to 1940. When President Terra was
inaugurated, the country was suffering from a serious economic and
financial depression. He put into effect a vast program of public
works to reduce unemployment and improve business conditions.
A dispute arose between the president and the Administrative Council as to matters of policy, and the president's enemies in the congress
attempted to impeach him. At the same time an aggressive Communist minority created unrest throughout the nation.

President Terra took measures to suppress this unrest by force,
and these measures created opposition. He then dissolved the Council and the congress. Former President Brum, who was president of
the Council, killed himself, fearing violence from the government

forces. The president called a constituent assembly, which adopted a new constitution in 1934.

The new constitution provided for the establishment of a representative, democratic, republican form of government. It had some unusual features, such as the provision for the establishment of autonomous industrial organizations to be owned by the state; the regulation of labor conditions in industry and commerce; social insurance; protection and aid to children; compulsory primary education; and woman suffrage. It required that all international treaties to which the nation becomes a party must include a clause providing for the arbitration or other peaceful settlement of all disputes arising between the contracting nations. The president was to be assisted by a Council of Ministers, composed of nine members chosen by the president from the two political parties polling the greatest number of votes at the presidential elections. Six were to be selected from the majority party.

Under this constitution, Terra was re-elected in 1934, but unrest and plotting continued. In 1935 a military revolution was suppressed by the government.

In 1938, General Alfredo Baldomir was elected to the presidency. Inaugurated on June 19, 1938, President Baldomir clashed with the congress on a bill he strongly favored, providing for national military conscription. Despite popular opposition to the measure, this bill became law in July, 1940. It was said that much of the opposition to the bill had been inspired by Nazi and Fascist agents. A law was passed by the Chamber of Deputies empowering the Minister of Interior to declare illegal any organization spreading antidemocratic ideas, and to control or suppress Nazi and Fascist propaganda.

The U. S. Export-Import Bank granted a loan of 7 million dollars to Uruguay in 1940.

Political Developments since World War II

Uruguay broke off diplomatic relations with Germany, Italy, and Japan on January 25, 1942, and with Vichy France on May 12, 1943. On February 15, 1945, the Montevideo government declared war on Germany and Japan and later became a charter member of the United Nations.

Reacting to the opposition of pro-Axis members of the national congress, President Baldomir dissolved that body on February 21, 1942, postponed the presidential election indefinitely, and set up a

Council of State to act on legislation. However, elections were held on November 29, 1942, and Dr. Juan José Amézaga, the candidate of the liberal anti-Axis coalition, was elected president for the term ending March 1, 1947. A popular referendum approved a new constitution drafted during President Baldomir's administration. In the election of November 24, 1946, Tomás Berreta received the majority of votes. However, he died soon after inauguration and was succeeded (August 2, 1947) by Vice-President Luis Batlle Berres. The 1950 election was won by Andrés Martínez Trueba, who pledged continuance of the democratic policies of the previous administration.

On December 16, 1951, a proposal approved by the congress to abolish the presidential system was submitted to a plebiscite. With the endorsement of the majority of the electorate, the new scheme of government went into effect on March 1, 1952. The one-man executive was superseded by a nine-member National Council of Government (on the model of the Swiss Federal Council), which included six members selected by the congress from the majority party and three from the minority party. President Martínez Trueba, of the *Colorado* Party, became the chairman of the first Council. Under the new scheme, each one of the six majority-party members was to be the chairman of the Council for one year. In 1958, for the first time in 93 years, the *Blanco* Party won the general elections and, consequently, a majority in the National Council of Government.

After serious rioting on January 10, 1961, between anti- and pro-Castro factions, police raided Communist headquarters and arrested 131 persons. The Soviet Ambassador and the First Secretary of the Soviet Embassy were accused of instigating the riots and expelled. On February 15, 1962, the Executive National Council voted to maintain diplomatic relations with Castro.

Economic, Social, and Cultural Development

Economic Development. A very high percentage of the land of Uruguay is devoted to stock raising. In 1864 the first meat-packing plant was established, and fresh and jerked beef (*tasajo*) are exported. In 1905 the first freezing plant (*frigorífico*) was built. Since then the number of cattle and sheep has increased steadily, and wool production has become more and more important. The principal crops are wheat, corn, oats, barley, linseed, fruits, and vegetables. Manufacturing is chiefly limited to the use of local products. Interior transportation by roads and railroads is fairly adequate. Airlines provide connections with other South American countries.

Social Development. The population of Uruguay is more than 2.5 million people, largely of European descent, the majority of whom live in urban communities. The standard of living is high, due in part to advanced social legislation.

Education. Illiteracy is relatively low in Uruguay, and education is provided by a well-regulated system of primary, secondary, and technical (including normal) schools. The National University in Montevideo provides adequate education at the advanced level.

Literary and Artistic Development. The patriarch of Uruguayan literature is Francisco Acuña de Figueroa (1790–1862), a monarchist who satirized the movement for independence. Other writers of note are: Adolfo Berro (1819–41), a romantic poet; Pedro P. Bermúdez (1806–60), author of *El Charrúa,* a drama on colonial wars with the Indians; Francisco X. de Achá (1828–88), a poet and dramatist; Heraclio C. Farjado (1833–67), who wrote dramas and poetry; Alejandro Magariños Cervantes (1825–93), a novelist, author of *La Estrella del sur, Caramurú* (his best novel, dealing with gaucho life), and several plays; Wáshington P. Bermúdez (b. 1847), a poet; Juan Zorrilla de San Martín (1857–1931), an original poet who wrote *Tabaré,* which is considered the masterpiece of Uruguayan literature; Santiago Maciel (b. 1867), who wrote notable poems on the war between Chile and Peru; Carlos Roxlo (1860–1927), a literary critic; Eduardo Acevedo Díaz (b. 1851), the greatest Uruguayan novelist, author of *Brenda, Ismael, Nativa,* and many other novels; Manuel Bermúdez (b. 1867), a realistic novelist, author of *Las Hermanas Flammary;* Carlos Reyles (1868–1938), a versatile novelist and author of *El Embrujo de Sevilla, Historias primitivas,* and many other works of merit; and José Enrique Rodó (1872–1918), poet, essayist, and one of the most influential writers in all Latin America —the author of *El Mirador de Próspero, Ariel,* and other works.

Uruguay has produced several painters of renown, including Juan and Nicanor Blanes, father and son, and Joaquín Torres-García, a very influential artist. In music, Professor Francisco Curt Lange, of the National University, ranks among the most influential authorities on folklore in the whole Hemisphere; also Eduardo Fabini and Luis Cluzeau Mortet have contributed much to the music field.

Fig. XX–1. Comparison of the Areas of Brazil and the United States.

Fig. XX–2. Comparison of the Latitudes of Brazil and the United States.

CHAPTER XX

BRAZIL

Among the Latin American nations, Brazil is the greatest in territory and also has the largest population. Its historical development has been quite different from that of the other Latin American countries. In the first place, the early settlers were Portuguese instead of Spanish, and the Brazilians are today a Portuguese-speaking people. In the second place, Brazil was the only Latin American nation to adopt for any length of time a monarchical form of government. The monarchy lasted in Brazil from the declaration of independence in 1822 until the republican revolution in 1889, and is divided into two periods: the reign of Dom Pedro I (1822–31), and the reign of Dom Pedro II (1831–89). The republican period may, in turn, be divided into two parts: the "Old Republic" (1889–1930) and the "New Republic" (1930 to the present).

THE FIRST EMPIRE (1822–31)

After the declaration of independence in 1822 by Dom Pedro, most Brazilians and many Portuguese living in the country sided with the Autonomist Party. José Bonifácio de Andrada e Silva (commonly known as José Bonifácio), a scientist of aristocratic family educated in Europe, contributed largely to the success of the independence movement. He was made premier of the cabinet appointed by Dom Pedro a few months before the declaration of independence and was one of the few organizers of the revolutionary governing junta in the São Paulo province in the latter part of the previous year.

Government Organization. Dom Pedro was acclaimed first Emperor of Brazil on October 12, 1822, and was solemnly crowned in the chapel of the royal palace on December 1. Among his first acts was the signing of a decree granting amnesty to all political prisoners

Fig. XX–3. Geographical Divisions of Brazil. (Based on data from *Economic Geography of South America,* by R. H. Whitbeck, published by McGraw-Hill Book Company, Inc., New York, 1926.)

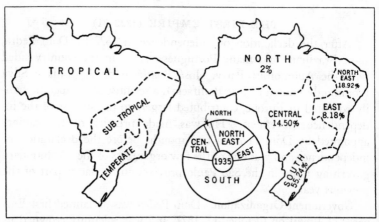

Fig. XX–4. Climatic Regions of Brazil and Percentage of Agricultural Production. (From *Brazil—Statistics, Resources, Possibilities,* Rio de Janeiro, 1938. Courtesy of Ministry of Foreign Affairs.)

and expelling from Brazil certain Portuguese known to be declared enemies of the independence cause.

In order to obtain the recognition of Brazilian independence by Great Britain, France, and the United States, Dom Pedro sent agents to those countries.

The war of independence lasted until 1825, when Portugal, through the mediation of Great Britain, recognized Brazil's independence. It was waged mostly in the northern provinces of Pará, Maranhão, Ceará, and Bahia, where the Portuguese element was stronger.

At this time, at the suggestion of José Bonifácio, Lord Thomas Alexander Cochrane, a British adventurer, entered the service of Brazil after having helped in the organization of the patriots' navy in Chile and Peru. Cochrane organized the Brazilian navy and defeated the Portuguese fleet in several encounters. The Brazilian land forces were commanded by a French soldier named Pedro Labatut.

In the Cisplatine Province (Banda Oriental), the Portuguese loyalists were defeated by General Carlos Frederico Lecor, who sided with the cause of independence. That province was annexed to Brazil on May 9, 1824.

The Constitution of 1824. The first general constituent and legislative assembly was called by Dom Pedro and met in Rio de Janeiro on April 17, 1823. This assembly was under the control of a conservative faction headed by José Bonifácio and his brothers, Antônio Carlos and Francisco Ribeiro de Andrada e Silva. The latter, as members of a drafting committee, prepared a rather conservative project. While the committee was at work, antagonism developed between the Andrada brothers and the Emperor. Dom Pedro ousted them from his cabinet and appointed another one with members of the liberal faction. The Andrada brothers then organized an opposition party. Through the press, particularly the newspapers *O Tamoyo* and *A Sentinela,* they accused Dom Pedro of being more friendly toward the Portuguese than toward the native Brazilians. The situation was aggravated by quarrels between Portuguese-born army officers and Brazilians.

In November, the assembly declared itself in permanent session. Dom Pedro dissolved it at once, arrested the Andrada brothers and other members of the opposition, and exiled them. The following month a committee appointed by the Emperor presented a draft of a constitution based on the previous draft and on the French and

Fig. XX–5. Brazil's Advancing Frontier. (Prepared by Wayne D. Rasmussen. Reprinted from the *Land Policy Review*, October, 1941, with permission of the United States Bureau of Agricultural Economics.)

Portuguese constitutions of that time. This constitution was sent to all the municipal governments throughout the country for criticism and suggestions. Approved in the main by them, it was publicly sworn to in the capital on March 25, 1824. It remained in effect, with slight changes, until 1889. It provided for the establishment of a hereditary and limited monarchy; the emperor was to exercise the executive power, with the aid of a ministry and a privy council appointed by him; and there was to be a bicameral legislature composed of a senate (the members appointed for life by the emperor from lists chosen by indirect popular vote) and a house of representatives (the members selected by electors chosen by popular vote). The legislature was given the power of voting in a new dynasty at any time.

The Confederation of the Equator. As a result of dissatisfaction with Dom Pedro's government, a revolution broke out in the northern provinces in 1824 with the purpose of forming a federal republic separated from the empire. The proposed state was to be called the "Confederation of the Equator." But the uprising was quickly suppressed by forces sent from the capital under the command of General Francisco de Lima e Silva.

The Loss of the Banda Oriental. At this time an uprising also broke out in the Banda Oriental (Uruguay). In April, 1825, Lavalleja and his followers landed in that province and incited the inhabitants into rebellion against the Brazilian authorities. On August 25, the independence of the Banda Oriental was declared by the patriots, who also solicited annexation to the United Provinces of the River Plata. Buenos Aires sent an army to help Lavalleja. The Brazilian troops were decisively defeated in several encounters, and the Brazilian fleet was destroyed by the Argentine navy under the command of Admiral Brown. On August 27, 1828, a treaty was signed with the government of Buenos Aires whereby Argentina and Brazil recognized and guaranteed the independence of Uruguay.

Important Legislation. A law granting freedom of the press was adopted in 1823. The slave traffic was abolished in 1826, although the law was not put into effect until 1850. A criminal code was adopted in 1830. Primary education was promoted by the creation of schools in all cities, towns, and important settlements. In 1827 law faculties were created in São Paulo and Olinda.

Dom Pedro's Abdication. Partly owing to the defeat of the Brazilian forces in the River Plata region, and to his irregular family relations, Dom Pedro became very unpopular. On March 10, 1826, his father, King John VI, died in Portugal. Dom Pedro, heir to the Portuguese throne, was confronted with the problem of choosing between Portugal and Brazil, as he could not be king of both countries at the same time. He decided to abdicate the Portuguese throne in favor of his little daughter, Dona Maria da Glória. But his enemies in Brazil spread the rumor that he wanted to unite the two kingdoms again under his own rule.

In April, 1831, a military revolt broke out in Rio de Janeiro because of the dismissal by the Emperor of the liberal cabinet. As the population sided with the rebels, Dom Pedro, on April 6, abdicated in favor of his little son, Dom Pedro de Alcântara. A week later he and his wife sailed for Europe.

THE SECOND EMPIRE (1831–89)

On April 13, 1831, Dom Pedro de Alcântara was acclaimed second Emperor of Brazil. He was born on December 2, 1825, in Brazil, of his father's first wife, Dona Maria Leopoldina, who had died while he was still an infant. Before leaving Brazil, his father asked José Bonifácio to be the tutor of the young Emperor.

The Regency. The April revolution resulted in the election by the legislature of a Council of Regency of three members (José Joaquim Carneiro de Campos, General Francisco de Lima e Silva, and Senator Nicolau Pereira de Campos Vergueiro). The liberal ministry, dismissed by Dom Pedro I, was recalled by the Regency at once, and public order was restored.

The rule of the Regency constitutes a very important period in the history of Brazil. Despite many regional uprisings, it showed the capacity of the Brazilian people for self-government and prepared the way for the long, unified, and prosperous reign of Dom Pedro II after 1840.

The first Regency governed from April 7 to June 17, 1831. It took measures to restore public order and to suppress several uprisings in the northern provinces as well as in Minas Gerais and Rio Grande do Sul.

The Andrada brothers, who had been allowed to return to Brazil just before the abdication of Dom Pedro I, became again centers of political activity with a view to securing the return of the first Emperor. The political situation was aggravated by a severe economic depression due in great measure to the lack of capital and labor for the development of the country. Various political parties appeared at this time. One of the most important was founded by Evaristo da Veiga, a moderate liberal newspaperman whose influence in national politics contributed largely to prevent the disintegration of the country.

On June 17, the Regency was declared permanent during the minority of the Emperor. José Bonifácio was confirmed as the young Emperor's tutor.

Public order was restored by the energetic action of Father Diogo Antônio de Feijó, Minister of Justice during the first Regency. He severely punished any disturbance of the peace. Another element contributing to the restoration of peace was the adoption of the so-called *"Ato Adicional,"* promulgated on August 12, 1834, as an appendix to the Constitution of 1824 and granting a certain measure of autonomy to the provinces. It also reduced the number of regents to one.

The influence of the Andrada brothers decreased with the dismissal of José Bonifácio in 1832 as tutor of the Emperor for alleged participation in a revolutionary plot. The death of the former Emperor in Portugal in 1834 also discouraged the reactionary movement headed by the Andrada brothers. Many of their followers later adhered to the Conservative Party, headed by Bernardo de Vasconcelos.

The regencies created a national guard; abrogated the ancient decrees of war against the Indians; freed the slaves brought from foreign countries; reorganized professional education; established a bank of deposit and issue; established the municipal district of the court, later changed into the federal district; and aided the construction of the first railroad, which had been begun in 1854 by private initiative.

The Regencies of Feijó and Araújo Lima. In 1835 Feijó was elected regent. Between April, when he was elected, and October, when he was inaugurated, the country was governed by General Lima e Silva because, of the two other regents, one had died and the other had resigned. The same year the Farrapos War broke out in the province of Rio Grande do Sul in the extreme south of the country. The rebels were commanded by Bento Gonçalves da Silva, and their purpose was to establish a federal republic. The following year Bento Gonçalves was proclaimed president of the rebel government; the name *"República de Piratini"* was adopted for the proposed state.

The war lasted for ten years. On September 19, 1837, Regent Feijó, unable to suppress the revolution, resigned and was replaced by Pedro de Araújo Lima.

During Araújo Lima's regency the model secondary school Colégio Pedro II was established in the capital; the Brazilian Historical and Geographical Institute was organized; and an agricultural school was created. Also at this time the two-party system was established in Brazil with the alternation of the Liberal and Conservative parties in the cabinet. Several uprisings took place, but they were suppressed by the government.

Dom Pedro Declared of Age (1840). As a means of restoring public order in the provinces, the liberals advocated the idea of declaring the Emperor of age at once. Dom Pedro was not yet fifteen years old and the legal age was eighteen, but the movement received the adherence of many leaders throughout the country. On July 23, 1840, therefore, Dom Pedro II was declared of age by the imperial Parliament, and the Regency was discontinued.

Dom Pedro II was crowned in July, 1841. A short time afterward he married Teresa Cristina Maria, daughter of the King of Naples.

During the reign of Dom Pedro II, Brazil became one of the best-governed countries in the Western Hemisphere. The Emperor ruled wisely and promoted public education, commerce, means of communication, immigration, and agriculture. The parliamentary system was effectively established in Brazil with the alternation of the liberals and conservatives in power. The Emperor's moderating power was exercised conservatively. Dom Pedro did not tolerate dishonesty in the public administration. Revolutionary movements in the provinces were suppressed by General Luís Alves de Lima e Silva, later Baron and finally Duke of Caxias, the outstanding military man of his time in Brazil. He also put an end to the Farrapos War in Rio Grande do Sul in 1845.

The War against Rosas. The period from 1850 to 1870 was characterized by general prosperity, internal reforms, and foreign complications. In 1851 the Brazilian government came to the conclusion that it would be necessary to overthrow Rosas, the tyrant of Buenos Aires, to prevent his annexing the territory of the Banda Oriental to Argentina. An alliance was negotiated by the Brazilian Empire with the liberals of Uruguay and General Urquiza, leader of the opposition to Rosas in the Argentine provinces of Entre Ríos and Corrientes. By October, 1851, General Oribe, commander of the Argentine troops in Uruguay, was compelled to raise the siege of Montevideo, which had lasted since 1843. Finally, at the Battle of Monte Caseros on February 3, 1852, Rosas' last resistance was broken. The tyrant then resigned and left the country.

At this time several important measures were taken. The Bank of Brazil was reorganized; a manual arts school was created; and the country was divided into twenty-one provinces and one neutral municipal district.

Other Foreign Complications. In 1862 a British ship, the *Prince of Wales,* was shipwrecked near the coast of the Rio Grande do Sul province. William D. Christie, British consul, dissatisfied with the inquiry of the Brazilian officials, demanded that a British naval officer be included in the investigating board. A short while before, another diplomatic question had arisen between the two countries because of the disorderly conduct of several British sailors in the Brazilian capital and their arrest by the local police. Christie violently demanded reparation, and when his demand was not heeded, he severed relations with the Brazilian government. Immediately thereafter, reprisals were taken by British ships against Brazilian vessels. Brazil protested, and the matter was submitted to arbitration. The award of King Leopold I of Belgium, the arbiter, issued on June 18, 1863, was in the main favorable to Brazil. Relations between Brazil and Great Britain were resumed a year later, thanks to the mediation of the King of Portugal.

At this time Brazil was compelled to intervene in Uruguay. For years the Brazilian government had complained against depredations and assassinations of Brazilian citizens in Uruguay and across the border in Brazilian territory by Uruguayan irregulars fighting in the civil wars of that country. These complaints were always ignored. In 1864, when Aguirre assumed the presidency of Uruguay, these depredations increased because of support given by Brazilians to Flores, the other Uruguayan *caudillo*.

The Emperor sent to Montevideo, José Antônio Saraiva, one of the ablest Brazilian statesmen of all times, to try to bring about a settlement. After futile negotiations, he presented an ultimatum to Aguirre on August 4, 1864, and when this was not heeded a Brazilian army invaded Uruguay. In the short war that followed, the troops of Aguirre were defeated. Flores, helped by the Brazilian troops, laid siege to Montevideo, which surrendered in February, 1865.

The Paraguayan War. After his inauguration in 1862 as President of Paraguay, Francisco Solano López entertained dreams of extending his territorial domain. With this in view, he increased the army, the navy, and the general defenses of the country.

In November, 1864, López protested against Brazilian intervention in Uruguay. As his protest had no effect, he held a Brazilian ship, the *Marquês de Olinda,* then in Paraguayan waters, closed the Paraguay and Paraná rivers to Brazilian shipping, and sent an army into the Mato Grosso province of Brazil.

On May 1, 1865, Brazil signed with Uruguay and Argentina a treaty of alliance against López. The war lasted longer than expected, but with the death of López on March 1, 1870, near Cerro Corá, the conflict ended. A treaty of limits was signed between Brazil and Paraguay on March 27, 1872.

The Slavery Question. African slaves were first brought to Brazil about 1532. By the middle of the nineteenth century sentiment against slavery developed in Europe, particularly in Great Britain. In 1845 the British Parliament adopted the Aberdeen Act, by which all ships suspected of carrying slaves were to be pursued by British cruisers even within the territorial waters of foreign countries. If captured, the traders were to be tried under British laws.

This procedure was a breach of international law, and when several Brazilian slave traders were arrested by British cruisers, public opinion throughout Brazil became strongly antagonistic to Great Britain. However, on November 14, 1850, the Brazilian parliament adopted a law abolishing the slave traffic, as provided by the law of November 7, 1831, promulgated in accordance with the agreement with Great Britain signed in 1825, at the time when the latter recognized Brazil's independence.

In 1848 about 60,000 slaves had been landed at Brazilian ports. After the adoption of the 1850 law, the number of slaves introduced into the country decreased rapidly, and by 1855 the traffic was almost extinct. Anti-slavery sentiment also increased throughout the country, and many bills were introduced in the parliament providing for the abolition of slavery. The Emperor was in favor of abolition, but he held that it should be carried out slowly and with compensation to the owners. On September 28, 1871, the Rio Branco Law (named after Viscount Rio Branco, who was responsible for its approval by the assembly) was adopted, freeing the children of slaves who were born after that date. On September 28, 1885, another law freed slaves sixty years old or more. Dom Pedro declared at this time in the Council of Ministers that he would rather lose his crown than allow slavery to continue in Brazil much longer. Finally, on May 13, 1888, a law was adopted abolishing slavery in the whole country. No compensation was provided, however, for the owners. At the time of abolition the number of slaves existing in Brazil was about 740,000.

Among the principal leaders of the abolitionist movement were Joaquim Nabuco de Araújo, José do Patrocínio, Afonso Celso Junior, João Alfredo Correia de Oliveira, and Antônio Prado. Princess Isabel, who occupied the Regency of the country in the absence of the Emperor, signed the Law of 1888. For this reason she is known in Brazilian history as "Isabel the Redeemer."

Republican Propaganda. After 1870 republican ideals spread throughout the country under the benevolent rule of Dom Pedro II. That year a few young men formed a Republican Club, and a newspaper, *A República,* appeared as an organ of propaganda of republican ideals. Among the members of the Republican Club were Saldanha Marinho, Arístides Lobo, and Quintino Bocayuva. On December 3, 1870, a republican manifesto to the nation was issued, and a few months later a republican convention met in São Paulo. Republican ideals spread among army officers, particularly in the military school, where a strong republican, Benjamin Constant Botelho de Magalhães (commonly known as Benjamin Constant), was professor of mathematics. In the election of 1885 the republicans were able to elect three deputies.

Dissatisfaction with the Emperor. Republican propaganda against the Emperor found fertile ground among those who complained of his too great interference in the details of the administration.

Between 1873 and 1875 certain church officials headed by the Bishop of Olinda quarreled with the Masons in Pará and Pernambuco over the attempted expulsion by the Catholics of Masons from the religious organizations known as *irmandades.* Instead of remaining neutral, the government took the side of the Masons and imprisoned two bishops. This act caused many of the Catholics to become opposed to the Emperor.

Dissatisfaction also existed in certain military circles because of the tendency of the government to disregard what the army officers considered as their prerogatives and to punish certain officers who criticized the government through the press. One of the leaders of the discontented army officers was General, later Marshal, Manuel Deodoro da Fonseca, a hero of the Paraguayan War and at the time Governor of the Rio Grande do Sul province.

After the abolition of slavery many plantation owners who had been impoverished by the loss of their slaves also sided with the enemies of the Emperor.

The Overthrow of the Empire. By the middle of 1889 the conservative ministry in power was being strongly criticized for its handling of various national problems, and the Viscount of Ouro Prêto was entrusted with forming a new ministry, under which the suffrage was broadened, religious freedom was established, import duties were lowered, and the Council of State and the civil code were reformed.

Despite this broad program of reforms, dissatisfaction in the army increased. In November, 1889, rumors spread that the government would soon transfer certain battalions from the capital to the far regions of the country. A few army officers met at the home of Marshal Deodoro, then in the capital, and when, in the afternoon of November 14, rumors spread that Deodoro da Fonseca and Benjamin Constant had been arrested, a revolt broke out in the barracks. The next day, Deodoro da Fonseca seized control of the chief government departments and arrested the members of the ministry. In the evening of the same day, decrees were published in the name of the army, the navy, and the nation proclaiming a republic in Brazil, appointing a provisional government under the leadership of Deodoro da Fonseca, and banishing Dom Pedro and his family. The next day the Emperor was notified of his banishment, and soon he and his family sailed for Europe. He died in a second-rate hotel in Paris on December 5, 1891, having refused a donation of money from the revolutionary government of Brazil.

THE "OLD REPUBLIC" (1889–1930)

The republican regime established in Brazil in 1889 has become known, since the Revolution of 1930, as the "Old Republic" to distinguish it from the new regime established in that year.

The provisional government headed by Deodoro da Fonseca adopted decrees establishing universal manhood suffrage, separation of Church and State and freedom of religion, a new civil code, abolition of corporal punishment in the armed forces, secularization of the cemeteries, and other reforms.

A committee was appointed to prepare a draft of a new constitution, which was adopted provisionally on June 22, 1890. A constituent congress was then called, and the proposed constitution was adopted with slight changes on February 24, 1891. In general, this constitution was similar to that of the United States, providing for a representative federal republic under the name of "Estados Unidos do Brasil" with the customary separation of powers—the chief executive, to be elected by direct vote for a term of four years, a bicameral legislature, and a federal judiciary. The states were authorized to adopt constitutions of their own in harmony with the federal constitution. An extensive bill of rights was also included in the constitution.

Early Presidents. Under this constitution, Deodoro da Fonseca was elected first president, with Marshal Floriano Peixoto as vice-president. Deodoro da Fonseca soon quarreled with the congress and dissolved it on November 3, 1891, assuming dictatorial powers. A few weeks later the navy revolted against him under the command of Rear Admiral Custódio José de Melo. Deodoro da Fonseca resigned, and Vice-President Peixoto assumed the presidency.

There now followed a period of unrest and civil war. The new president called the national congress in special session. But on March 31, 1892, a manifesto signed by thirteen generals was published demanding new presidential elections at once. At the same time war broke out in the southern provinces, and part of the fleet in the Bay of Guanabara revolted on September 6, 1893, under the leadership of Rear Admirals Custódio José de Melo and Luís Felipe de Saldanha da Gama. After severe fighting between land forces loyal to the government and the ships which had revolted, the rebellion was suppressed. By the end of the following year, public order had been re-established throughout the country, except in parts of the extreme South, where peace was restored only in 1895.

Later Presidents. On November 15, 1894, Prudente José de Morais Barros was inaugurated president. He was the first civilian chief executive of the republic. He granted amnesty to all political prisoners and endeavored to restore order throughout the country. After four years of fighting, the rebellion led by the religious fanatic Antônio Vicente Mendes Maciel, commonly known as "Antônio Conselheiro," in the interior of the state of Bahia, was suppressed in June, 1897. Disruption of the economy by the republican revolution and succeeding uprisings resulted in a critical financial situation.

The next president, Manuel Ferraz de Campos Salles, inaugurated in 1898, was able to improve the financial situation of the country, thanks to a loan secured from European bankers. During his administration, disputes with Bolivia and France, the latter over the boundary with French Guiana, were brought to a satisfactory end by peaceful settlement.

Francisco de Paula Rodrigues Alves, inaugurated in 1902, was the next president. During his administration the capital was beautified, sanitary conditions in various cities were improved, and other reforms were undertaken. President Rodrigues Alves chose as Minister of Foreign Relations the distinguished diplomat Barão do Rio Branco, who negotiated with Bolivia the boundary agreement known as the Treaty of Petrópolis (November 17, 1903). By this agreement the serious dispute in regard to the territory of Acre was satisfactorily settled. A dispute with Great Britain over the Guiana boundary line was brought to an end by arbitration in 1904. Two years later the boundary question with the Netherlands in regard to its remaining Guiana territory was also satisfactorily settled by direct negotiation between the two countries.

The next president was Afonso Augusto Moreira Pena, inaugurated in 1906. He improved the currency situation by creating a conversion bureau which fixed the rate of exchange and guaranteed the redemption of paper money in gold. Immediately the economic and financial situation of the country improved. President Pena died in 1909, and the Vice-President, Nilo Peçanha, became president. He negotiated the Treaty of 1909 with Uruguay, granting that country joint sovereignty over Lake Mirim and the Yaguarón (or Jaguarão) River. A service of protection to the Indians was organized under the direction of General Cândido Mariano Rondón.

In 1910 Marshal Hermes da Fonseca became president. He reorganized the armed forces, suppressed several naval uprisings, and endeavored to improve the financial situation, which had been unfavorably affected by the falling prices of coffee and rubber. Hermes da Fonseca was followed by Wenceslau Brás Pereira Gomes in 1914. During his administration there was some improvement in the economic and financial situation of the country, owing to a rise in the price of coffee and to an increase in exports to Europe during World War I. The sinking of Brazilian vessels by German submarines led to the breaking of diplomatic relations between Brazil and Germany, and later to a declaration of war.

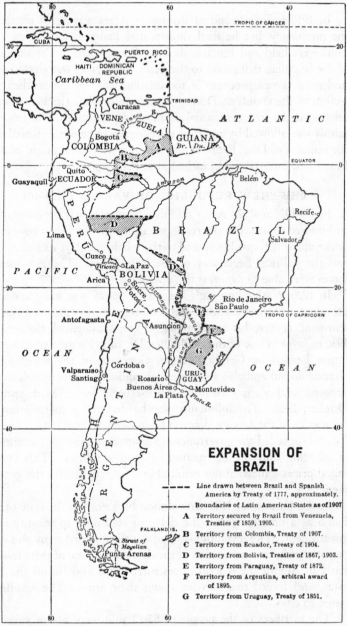

FIG. XX–6. Territorial Expansion of Brazil through Boundary Settlements. (Reproduced with permission from *History of Latin America,* by Hutton Webster, published by D. C. Heath and Company, Boston 1924.)

In 1918 former President Rodrigues Alves was again elected to the presidency, but he died shortly after inauguration. New elections were held and Epitácio da Silva Pessoa, then in Paris as head of the Brazilian delegation to the peace conference, was elected. He undertook a vast program of reclamation work in the northeastern section of the country. During his administration (in 1922) Brazil celebrated the first centennial of her independence. The imperial family was allowed by an act of the congress to return to Brazil, and the remains of Dom Pedro II and his empress were brought back to Brazil and interred in the cathedral at Petrópolis.

THE "NEW REPUBLIC" OF VARGAS (1930–40)

From 1922 to 1926 Artur da Silva Bernardes was president. He endeavored to improve the economic situation. In 1924 a revolution broke out which quickly spread to the whole country; its aim was to end the political hegemony of the large states. The government forces were able to suppress the uprising.

In 1926 Washington Luís Pereira de Souza was inaugurated as president. He carried into effect a program of reforms. But resentment against his interference in the presidential elections of 1930 in favor of one of the candidates, Dr. Júlio Prestes, led to a revolution headed by Getúlio Vargas, Governor of the state of Rio Grande do Sul and also a presidential candidate. The president was deposed, and Vargas assumed the executive power as dictator in October, 1930. The following year he declared a moratorium on the service of the foreign debt. The world-market situation for coffee and sugar led the government to adopt a program of curtailment of planting and the destruction of crop surpluses. This system raised prices somewhat but resulted in a large deficit for the government.

In the summer of 1932 a revolution broke out in the state of São Paulo as a protest against the delay in returning to constitutional government. The revolutionists had a well-equipped army and were defeated only in consequence of the defection of one of their leaders. Early in August the federal forces surrounded and cut off the Paulistas, and forced them to lay down their arms. The revolution lasted 83 days.

The sacrifices of the people of São Paulo were not in vain. In 1934 a constituent congress gathered in the capital and adopted a strongly nationalistic constitution, which was promulgated on July 16 of that year. It contained many provisions which aimed at the improvement of the social and economic conditions of the common people. Certain provisions also curtailed the privileges of foreigners in Brazil. The form of government remained essentially the same as that provided by the Constitution of 1891. Women, however, were given the right to vote and to hold public office. Vargas was elected president under the new constitution.

On November 10, 1937, because of general unrest throughout the country, Vargas set aside the 1934 constitution and resumed the dictatorship. A new instrument of government, extending the powers of the executive and curtailing those of the states, was promulgated by President Vargas, subject to a plebiscite. Later the president dissolved by decree the *Integralista* Party, a Fascist organization. On May 11, 1938, the *Integralistas* revolted, but the revolt was quickly suppressed by the government. After that, President Vargas maintained his strong rule despite unrest in certain regions. During the latter part of 1940 it was said that President Vargas was planning to carry out the constitutional provisions for a plebiscite. Meanwhile, the president had publicly expressed his sympathy with the Nazi-Fascist regimes. But when the Washington government showed surprise and alarm, Vargas sent a message to President Roosevelt (June 15, 1940) to the effect that Brazil would not fail him in loyalty towards the United States.

On September 27, 1940, Brazil and the United States signed an agreement whereby American assistance would be given to Brazilian plans to establish a large steel industry in the country. An initial credit of 20 million dollars was extended to Brazil by the Export-Import Bank for the purchase of the required machinery in the United States. The Volta Redonda steel plant, the largest in Latin America, was 80 per cent completed by the middle of 1960.

POLITICAL DEVELOPMENTS SINCE WORLD WAR II

During World War II, Brazil was officially neutral until the 1942 Conference of Foreign Ministers of the American States of Rio de Janeiro, when President Vargas severed diplomatic relations with the Axis powers. The Brazilian government had assisted the United Nations by censoring German- and Italian-language publications, freezing non-American bank deposits, and supplying strategic materials to the United States. On August 22, 1942, following Axis attacks on Brazilian shipping, Brazil declared war on Germany and

Italy and mobilized its armed forces until they reached a maximum of 200,000 men. Relations with Vichy France ended on November 13, 1942. The Brazilian Air Force had primary responsibility for the defense of the South Atlantic. Expeditionary forces were sent to Italy in 1944. War on Japan was formally declared on June 6, 1945.

A number of agreements were signed with the United States providing for "lend-lease" aid and for the purchase of war supplies. In November, 1946, an Agricultural Development Corporation was set up in Brazil as a subsidiary of the American International Association for Economic and Social Development to make available to the Brazilian people technical and managerial experience and needed capital. In 1947 a joint Brazil-United States technical commission was set up to assist in the economic recovery of the nation.

Brazil participated in the Chapultepec Conference of 1945, adhered to the United Nations Declaration, and was represented in the United Nations Conference on International Organization held in San Francisco in 1945.

During the war, President Vargas, who had pursued with increased firmness his policies of nationalism and centralization of power, promised that he would not seek re-election. In March, 1945, he called for national elections to be held on December 2. The political campaign was carried out amidst considerable enthusiasm and, in many cases, bitter denunciations. On October 30, Vargas' fifteen-year dictatorship came to an end in a bloodless coup headed by General Goes Monteiro, Minister of War. The uprising was precipitated by Vargas' appointment of his brother as chief of police in the capital. There were demonstrations on a large scale by troops stationed in Rio. General Goes Monteiro called a meeting at the war ministry attended by the two principal presidential candidates, the chiefs of the armed forces, President Vargas, and Judge José Linhares, President of the Supreme Court. Early in the morning a proclamation was issued to the effect that President Vargas, to avoid major trouble, would leave the government and hand over the presidential powers to Dr. Linhares. After being detained a few hours, Vargas was set free and left Rio for his farm in southern Brazil.

Judge Linhares was sworn in as president *ad interim* on October 30, to hold office until the election of a new president. The presidential election was held, as scheduled, on December 2, 1945, and Major General Eurico Gaspar Dutra, the candidate of the Social Democratic Party, won by a large majority.

A new constitution, adopted in 1946, affirmed the basic rights to universal suffrage and the secret ballot but maintained wide government authority over social and economic institutions, including the power to ban any political party considered antidemocratic. In May, 1947, the Communist Party was declared illegal, and a few months later the Chamber of Deputies voted to oust all Communist legislators. The three major political parties (Social Democratic Party, National Democratic Union, and the Republican Party) pledged their support to President Dutra's drive against the Communists. In 1949 and 1950 there were revolutionary attempts inspired by Communist agents. An extensive economic development program, known as the SALTE plan, was adopted by the congress in 1948; it provided for the development of agriculture, transportation facilities, public health, and education.

Former President Vargas won the 1950 election by a plurality. He was backed by a coalition of the Brazilian Labor Party and the Social Progressive Party. Inaugurated on January 31, 1951, Vargas declared that his would be a government of evolution and not of revolution. But on August 24, 1954, the president shot and killed himself following a political crisis during which there was an unsuccessful attempt against the life of Deputy Carlos Lacerda by elements connected with Vargas' entourage. In a typewritten letter signed by himself, Vargas declared: "To the hatred of my enemies I bequeath my death. I regret I was unable to do for the humble all I wanted."

Vice-President Café Filho assumed the presidency. On November 8, he took sick leave, having suffered a heart attack a few days before. The same day, Carlos Coimbra da Luz, Speaker of the Chamber of Deputies, became Acting President, under the constitution. Three days later he was deposed by a *coup d'état* led by the Minister of War, General Henrique Baptista Duffles Teixeira Lott. Senator Nereu Ramos, President of the Senate, became Acting President, to serve until January 31, 1956.

At the election of October 3, 1955, Dr. Juscelino Kubitschek de Oliveira, backed by the Labor Party and the Social Democratic Party, received a majority of the votes. Vice-President Café Filho, having recovered his health, declared he would resume the presidency; however, at a special meeting held November 22, the Cham-

ber of Deputies disqualified him and confirmed Nereu Ramos as
Acting President until installation of President-elect Kubitschek.

Duly inaugurated on January 31, 1956, President Kubitschek introduced in the congress a five-year plan of economic development,
to provide an increase in electric-power production, a rise in agricultural and livestock production, the establishment of an automobile industry, the construction of shipyards, and the improvement
of transportation facilities. Despite continued economic and financial problems, owing largely to reduced exports and inflation,
President Kubitschek continued to carry out his program.

On September 20, 1956, a law was signed by the president authorizing the federal government to take adequate measures to
transfer the federal capital to a new site in the interior of the state
of Goiás. One year later, the president set April 21, 1960, for the
inauguration of the new capital, Brasília. The design and construction of the necessary public buildings was carried out on the basis of
an elaborate plan prepared by well-known Brazilian architects.

In 1958, President Kubitschek, in a letter addressed to President
Eisenhower, proposed that the United States government seriously
consider the adoption of a comprehensive economic and financial
program of assistance to Latin America. This proposal, known as
"Operation Pan America," was later studied at special conferences
held in Washington April–September, 1958, under the auspices of
the Organization of American States.

Brazil was one of the promoters of the Mexico City agreement of
1957 for the stabilization of coffee prices. This agreement was subsequently enlarged by another one signed in Washington (1958)
for the purpose of controlling coffee exports.

Relations between the United States and Brazil were somewhat
strained in the middle of 1959 by the refusal on the part of the International Monetary Fund to approve a loan of 300 million dollars
badly needed by Brazil to offset a deficit in the country's balance of
payments. The Fund authorities had insisted that certain fiscal
measures be taken by Brazil before any loan could be authorized.
The Washington government insisted that without the Fund's approval no loan could be granted to Brazil.

The presidential elections of October 3, 1960, were bitterly contested. The principal candidates were Jânio Quadros, former governor of São Paulo, and Milton Campos, former governor of Minas
Gerais, for president and vice-president, respectively, both backed

by the National Democratic Union; and Marshal Henrique Teixeira Lott, former Minister of War, and João Goulart, leader of the Brazilian Labor Party and incumbent vice-president, for president and vice-president, respectively, both supported by the labor unions and the Social Democratic Party. Quadros was elected president by a large plurality, with Goulart re-elected as vice-president.

The new administration, inaugurated January 31, 1961, was faced with problems of heavy foreign indebtedness, official corruption, mounting inflation, and large-scale smuggling. President Quadros persuaded the United States government to reschedule the payment of loans due in 1961, 1962, and 1963 and to grant new loans.

In foreign affairs, President Quadros opposed intervention in Cuba. He also declared that he would send missions to Communist nations to improve trade relations. Bitter opposition to the president's stand on Communism led to his resignation on August 25. Because of the opposition of some military leaders to Vice-President Goulart's assuming the presidency as provided by the constitution, the congress adopted an amendment to the constitution providing for a parliamentary government, with many former presidential powers to be exercised by a premier who was to be president of the Council of Ministers. On September 7, 1961, João Goulart was sworn in as president for the remainder of Quadros' term. Dr. Tancredo Neves, a conservative Social Democrat, was made premier. In November, 1961, despite strong anti-Communist feeling, Brazil renewed diplomatic relations with Soviet Russia.

In January, 1963, the constitutional amendment adopted in 1961 was repealed and the country returned to a presidential regime as provided by the constitution of 1946. Because of his insistence on radical reforms, Goulart was ousted by a military coup early in April, 1964. He was temporarily replaced by Paschoal Ranieri Mazzilli, president of the Chamber of Deputies. Congress then elected General (later Marshal) Humberto de Alencar Castelo Branco and José Maria Alkmim as interim president and vice-president. They were installed on April 15 for the remainder of Goulart's term (to end January 31, 1966). New elections were scheduled for October, 1965, but in July, 1964, the congress approved a constitutional amendment providing, among other things, that the presidential elections should be postponed until October, 1966, and extending President Castelo Branco's term of office to March 15, 1967. The presidential term of office was shortened to 4 years.

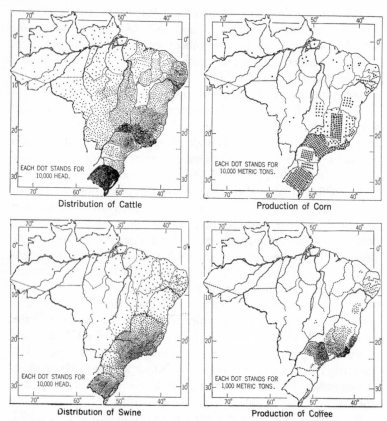

Fig. XX–7. Agricultural Maps of Brazil. (Reproduced with permission from *Southern Lands,* by H. H. Barrows, E. P. Parker, and M. T. Parker, published by Silver, Burdett & Company, New York, 1937.)

ECONOMIC, SOCIAL, AND CULTURAL DEVELOPMENT

Economic Development. Agriculture is the most important source of wealth in Brazil. Coffee is cultivated on about five million acres in various states, especially São Paulo, Minas Gerais, Paraná, Rio de Janeiro, Espírito Santo, Bahia, and Pernambuco. Other important agricultural products are sugar, cacao, Paraguayan tea, rubber, rice, corn, wheat, fruits, and cotton. Brazil's forests are among the world's richest. Stock raising is an important industry.

The mineral wealth of the country is very great. Manganese is exported to the United States. The state of Minas Gerais alone is estimated to have deposits of some 11 billion metric tons of this mineral. Large deposits of manganese are now being exploited in the territory of Amapá, north of the Amazon River. Deposits of iron are also very rich, it being estimated that the country has about 23 per cent of the world's supply, much of it of high quality. Petroleum is being extracted in several regions, particularly in the state of Bahia. Coal deposits are extensive but of inferior quality. Gold,

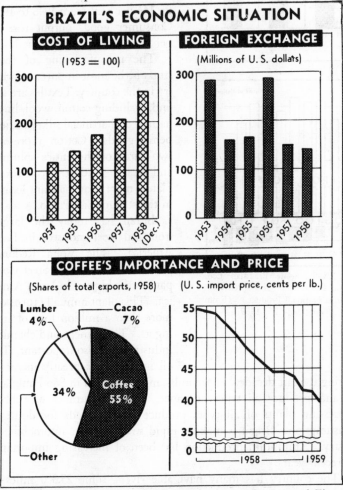

FIG. XX–8. Brazil's Economic Situation, 1959. (From *The New York Times*, May 10, 1959.)

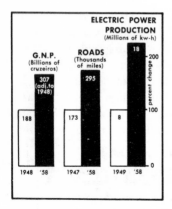

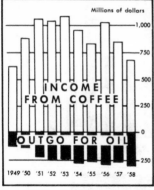

Fig. XX–9. Some Brazilian Economic Facts, 1948–58. ("G.N.P." is Gross National Product.) (From *Time*, May 25, 1959.)

diamonds, and other precious and semiprecious stones are mined in considerable quantities, mainly in the state of Minas Gerais.

The industrial development of the country since 1946 has been rapid. The biggest gains have been in capital goods industries— up 144 per cent from 1946 to 1954. Consumer goods output rose 52 per cent in the same period.

The manufacturing of foodstuffs is the most important industry in the country. Textiles are second, including cotton, wool, linen, natural and artificial silk, jute, and hemp goods. Cotton represents two-thirds of the entire spinning and weaving industry. Of textile plants, more than half are located in the state of São Paulo.

Brazil has today the largest iron and steel industry in Latin America. The Volta Redonda plant of the National Steel Company is the biggest in Latin America. This plant annually turns out more than a million tons of steel ingots. The cement and chemical industries are also important. The oil industry has greatly increased during the last decade. Paper mills, mostly located in São Paulo and Paraná, produce all types of paper. A large number of rubber-processing plants of all types produce rubber goods for domestic consumption. Brazil is making rapid strides in the automobile industry. Aluminum production has been of increasing importance in recent years.

The country has many navigable rivers, some 25,000 miles of railroads, and a constantly increasing mileage of good highways. Air connections with many parts of the world are extensive.

Social Development. The population of Brazil is estimated at more than 62 million people, the majority of whom are of mixed blood and nominally Roman Catholic. In the southern states there are many people of European—especially, Portuguese, German, Italian, and Spanish—descent. After World War I Japanese immigration was encouraged by the Brazilian government. There are several large cities in Brazil with rapidly increasing population. Brasília, the new capital, has developed phenomenally since its inauguration in 1960. Social welfare and labor legislation has received much governmental attention.

Education. Brazil has eleven universities in several states and the Federal District. There are a number of excellent technical and professional schools, while elementary and secondary schools, although inadequate, are found in all parts of the country.

Literary and Artistic Development. Brazilian literature is rich and varied. Among the most distinguished writers are: Domingos José Gonçalves de Magalhães (1811–82), poet, author of *A Confederação dos Tamoios;* Antônio Gonçalves Dias (1823–64), a poet, author of poems about Indians, such as *Os Timbiras* and *Canção do Tamoio;* Manuel Antônio Alvares de Azevedo (1831–52), a very popular poet inspired by Byron, de Musset, and Shelley; Laurindo Rebelo (1826–64), a poet of great inspiration; Casimiro de Abreu (1839–60), a writer of sentimental poetry; Luís Nicolau Fagundes Varela (1841–75), a very versatile poet inspired by Byron, author of the lyric and descriptive *Evangelho das selvas;* Antônio Castro Alves (1847–71), author of poetry of social protest such as *O Navio negreiro* and *Vozes d'Africa;* Tobias Barreto (1839–89), a more universal poet; Joaquim Manuel de Macedo (1820–82), a very popular novelist; José Martiniano de Alencar (1829–77), writer of novels about Indians, such as *O Guarani* and *Iracema;* Manuel Antônio de Almeida (1830–61), author of historical novels such as *Memórias de um sargento de milícias;* Bernardo da Silva Guimarães (1827–84), a novelist and poet; A. de Escragnolle Taunay (1843–99), author of a very popular novel, *Inocência,* and a historical book, *A Retirada da laguna,* of great merit; Francisco Adolfo Varnhagen (1816–78), historian and author of *História geral do Brasil;* João Manuel Pereira da Silva (1817–98), historian, author of *A Fundação do Império Brasileiro.* More recent important writers are: José Isidoro Martins Junior (1860–1903), and Luís Guimarães (1847–98), poets; Joaquim Maria Machado de Assis (1839–1909), novelist, poet, essayist, and one of the greatest writers of the Portuguese language; Teófilo Dias (1857–89), a poet, author of _Cantos tropicais;_ Raimundo Correia (1860–1911), author of fine poetry such as _Noites de inverno;_ Olavo Bilac (1865–1918), one of the greatest poets of Brazil; Alberto de Oliveira (1859–1937), a poet; Aluísio Azevedo (1857–1913), author of realistic novels, such as _O Mulato, A Casa de pensão,_ and _O Cortiço;_ José Joaquim Medeiros e Albuquerque (1867–1934), essayist; Joaquim Aurélio Nabuco (1849–1910), historian, essayist, and author of _Um Estadista do Império,_ an excellent study on the political life of the Second Empire; Sílvio Romero (1851–1914) and José Veríssimo (1857–1916), both outstanding literary critics; João Ribeiro (1861–1934), grammarian and historian; Manuel de Oliveira Lima (1867–1928), publicist, historian, and author of _Dom João VI no Brasil;_ Afonso Arinos (1868–1916), a novelist; José Pereira Graça Aranha (1868–1931), a modernist novelist, author of _Canaã;_ Afrânio Peixoto (1876–1947), Agripino Grieco (b. 1888), Humberto de Campos (1886–1934), Ronald de Carvalho (1893–1935), João Bento Monteiro Lobato (1882–1948), José Lins do Rêgo (1901–57), Jorge de Lima (1895–1953), Gilberto Freyre, Erico Veríssimo, and many others.

Brazil has produced many painters of merit, including Victor Meirelles de Lima, Almeida Reis, Pedro Américo, Rodolfo Amoedo Bernardelli, Georgina de Albuquerque, Pedro Bruno, Henrique Cavaleiro, Leopoldo Potozzo, Oswaldo Teixeira, and Paulo Rossi. Among sculptors may be mentioned J. Figueira and Leão H. Velloso. Among the leading musicians are Carlos Gomes, author of many operas, especially _Il Guarani,_ Henrique Oswaldo, Luciano Gallet, J. Octaviano, Alberto Nepomuceno, and Heitor Villa-Lobos (d. 1960), who is considered one of the outstanding composers of Latin America.

CHAPTER XXI

THE CARIBBEAN INSULAR STATES

THERE ARE ONLY THREE independent states in the islands of the Caribbean—Haiti, the Dominican Republic, and Cuba. The first one is a French-speaking country; the other two are Spanish in language and culture. A third island of Spanish cultural background, Puerto Rico, has been a dependency and is now a free commonwealth within the political framework of the United States. The other islands of the Caribbean are colonies or dependencies of Great Britain, France, the Netherlands, or the United States.

THE ISLAND OF HISPANIOLA BEFORE 1844

The island of Santo Domingo, or Hispaniola (*Española* in Spanish), was the center of Spanish colonization in the New World for many years. It early became almost depopulated because of the extinction of the natives and as a consequence of the organization of many expeditions of white settlers to the mainland. Negro slaves were brought over to replace the native workers. At one time the Spanish government offered bounties to the settlers who remained on the island and even had to prohibit emigration in order to keep the island sufficiently populated for the purpose of defense.

The island was frequently attacked by freebooters and adventurers. In 1585 Drake captured the city of Santo Domingo, withdrawing only after the payment of ransom. In 1630 buccaneers took the western part of the island, where they established several settlements. A fort was built at Port-au-Prince by French settlers shortly afterward. Eventually, by the Treaty of Ryswick (1697), the western section of the island was ceded to France. In this manner there appeared two colonies on the island: one Spanish and the other French. The island became known as Saint-Domingue to the French, and as Santo Domingo, Española, or Haiti to the Spaniards.

The Struggle for Independence. When the French Revolution broke out in 1789, the whites of the French settlement were admitted to the privileges of French citizens. Deprived of the same rights, the Negroes rose in rebellion on October 23, 1790, headed by an educated mulatto named Jacques Vicente Ogé. The uprising was severely suppressed, and the leaders were executed. On May 16, 1791, the French Assembly decreed that all colored persons born of free parents in French territory should be free. The whites protested, and the decree was not enforced. This caused another rebellion of the colored people of the island. During the revolt, Spanish and British forces attacked the French section by land and by sea, and in August, 1793, in order to put an end to the civil conflict, the French authorities declared slavery abolished. The Spanish and British invaders were expelled with the help of the Negroes under the leadership of Toussaint L'Ouverture, a pure-blooded Negro of considerable military ability. By the Treaty of 1795, France received the whole island. Meanwhile, Toussaint had established himself as the ruler of the island, promulgating a constitution on July 1, 1801. This constitution provided that the Catholic Church would be the official church, commerce was to be free from all restrictions, and blacks and whites were to be equal before the law. The island was also declared an independent nation, and Toussaint was made president for life.

Napoleon endeavored to reconquer the island. He sent an expedition under the command of General Victor Emanuel Leclerc, which was nearly wiped out by guerrilla warfare and yellow fever. Leclerc won over Jean Jacques Dessalines and Henri Christophe, and agreed with Toussaint to call a representative assembly to decide upon the future government of the island. When this assembly met on May 1, 1802, Toussaint was seized by the French and later sent as a prisoner to France, where he died in a dungeon in 1803. War broke out again on the island. Finally, on December 2, 1802, Leclerc died of yellow fever. His successor hunted down revolutionists with bloodhounds. But despite these ruthless measures, the French were defeated and compelled to surrender at the end of 1803. The following year independence was declared once more, and Dessalines became the president of the Republic of Haiti.

Dessalines' Empire. Soon after, Dessalines declared himself emperor of the island, under the name Jacques I, ordering all the French inhabitants to be executed. On October 17, 1806, he was assassinated, and Christophe made himself the ruler, under the name of Henri I. But at Port-au-Prince, Alexandre Pétion led a revolution and established himself as ruler, disputing with Christophe the supreme authority over the island. In 1818 Pétion died, and two years later Christophe committed suicide. General Jean Pierre Boyer, in 1822, became the ruler of the western part of the island. In 1825 the French acknowledged the independence of Haiti.

Meanwhile, in 1806 the Spaniards had regained control over their half of the island. But in 1821 its independence from Spain was declared, under the protection of Great Colombia. However, in January, 1822, General Boyer of Haiti conquered the Spanish section of the island, uniting it with Haiti under a single government to form the Republic of Haiti. It was not until 1844 that the Spanish section of Haiti became free again.

THE REPUBLIC OF HAITI

Early Presidents. General Boyer ruled Haiti until 1842, when he was overthrown. Five years later General Faustin Élie Soulouque was elected president. On August 26, 1849, he proclaimed himself emperor, under the title of Faustin I. He amended the constitution and created a nobility. In 1850 he was crowned with great pomp. But his despotism led to revolution, and in 1859 he was overthrown by General Fabre Geffrard—who was himself overthrown in 1867. There followed a period of anarchy, with many presidents.

In 1869 the United States appointed Ebenezer Don Charles Basset, a Negro, as minister resident and consul general in Haiti, this being the first appointment of a colored American to a diplomatic post. In 1874 and 1875 two large loans of three million and twelve million piastres, respectively, were secured from France, burdening the country unnecessarily. Around 1900 the first railroad was constructed from Cap Haitien to the Grand Rivière du Nord. German capitalists also received several concessions for the construction of railroads. Toward the end of the century many Cubans emigrated to Haiti on account of the severity of Spanish rule in Cuba. Most of them were excellent workers and made a valuable contribution to the economic life of Haiti.

Foreign Intervention. In 1904, during Nord Alexis' administration, there were several attacks by natives upon French and German citizens living in Haiti. These attacks resulted in foreign intervention. Unable to maintain order, Alexis was overthrown. In 1913

Michel Oreste became the first civilian president of Haiti. He surrounded himself with ministers of ability, and one of his first acts was to introduce measures to reduce military expenditures. But gradually he became despotic, and a revolt broke out against his government, compelling him to resign. In 1915 Vilbrun Guillaume Sam became president, but shortly afterwards a massacre of political prisoners took place at Port-au-Prince, and the president, considered the author of this massacre, was assassinated. The situation in the country became such that United States troops were landed to restore order. On August 12, 1915, Sudré Dartiguenave was chosen president in an election supervised by American officials. But unrest continued. On September 16, the United States, under the provision of a treaty with the Haitian government, took over the administration of the customs and the finances of the country for a ten-year period. At the same time a force of United States Marines was stationed on the island to maintain order.

On June 12, 1918, after a plebiscite had approved it, a new constitution went into effect. But the following month a revolution broke out in protest against the American occupation; this revolution was suppressed by the United States forces.

The End of United States Intervention. In 1922 President Dartiguenave was replaced by Louis Borno, an able executive who was re-elected in 1927. But his administration was not popular, and there were plots and uprisings against him. On December 4, 1929, mobs attacked the customs house at Port-au-Prince and other places. There followed clashes with the United States forces. On December 7, President Hoover sent a commission of inquiry to the island to survey the situation. This commission recommended that the Treaty of 1915 remain in effect until 1936; that the number of United States Marines stationed on the island be reduced; that a national guard be organized to maintain public order; that the American military high commissioner be replaced by a civilian; and that new elections be held on the island to choose a chief executive.

President Vincent. Following these recommendations, on May 15, 1930, Eugène Roy became temporary executive, followed on November 18, by Stenio Vincent, regularly elected by the national assembly. The American occupation of Haiti ended by an agreement between President Roosevelt and President Vincent signed on August 14, 1934. The Garde d'Haiti, trained by United States officers, took over the policing of the country. A fiscal representative, appointed by the President of Haiti on recommendation of the President of the United States, became the supervisor of the customs on behalf of foreign bondholders. As a part of the financial reconstruction of the republic, the National City Bank of New York sold to the Haitian government its local branch bank for one million dollars.

In 1935 President Vincent was re-elected. The same year a trade agreement was signed between the United States and Haiti granting mutual concessions. In the early part of 1940 President Vincent publicly declared that he would retire after the expiration of his term on May 15, 1941.

Political Developments since World War II. Haiti declared war on Japan on December 8, 1941, and on Germany and Italy four days later. Diplomatic relations with Vichy France were broken off on November 10, 1942. Haiti became a charter member of the United Nations in 1945.

World War II caused immense difficulties by cutting off European markets; however, several trade agreements signed with the United States aided the national economy during that critical period.

In 1941, the Haitian Chamber of Deputies voted unanimously to extend President Vincent's term of office for an additional four years, but the president persisted in his determination to retire at the end of his first term. The national assembly then elected Élie Lescot, who was at the time Haitian Minister to the United States. Lescot served as president until deposed by a military junta on January 11, 1946. The army leaders promised free elections and, on August 16, Dumarsais Estimé, a leader of the Democratic Party, was declared elected by a general constituent assembly. In May, 1950, the cabinet resigned following a dispute over the question of the re-election of President Estimé. A military junta again assumed control of the government and called a general election.

On October 8, Colonel Paul Magloire, a member of the junta, was regularly elected president. He resigned on December 12, 1956, following widespread disorder and strikes in protest against his efforts to prolong his rule. There followed six months of almost continuous political disturbances. The country was ruled by successive provisional presidents, all of whom were ousted after a few weeks in office.

In the middle of 1957, the army took over the government. Presidential elections were finally held in September of the same year, Dr. François Duvalier being declared elected. Sworn in on

October 22, he decreed general amnesty for political prisoners and began to restore a democratic regime. However, in April, 1961, he dissolved the bicameral legislature and replaced it with a 58-member single chamber. Although his term was to run another two and a half years, presidential elections were announced for April 30. Dr. Duvalier was elected (without opposition) to another six-year term. He set up a virtual dictatorship, purging the army of officers unfriendly to him and creating a palace guard, the "People's Militia." He ruled mainly by decree, at times under martial law. United States aid of 12 million dollars a year prevented collapse of all organized government, but on May 17, 1963, the United States suspended diplomatic relations and canceled the aid program. In August, 1963, two attempted invasions by Haitian refugees from the Dominican Republic failed. Haiti requested the Organization of American States to prevent new invasions and threatened to appeal to the United Nations. On June 14, 1964, Dr. Duvalier was elected "President for life."

Social, Economic, and Cultural Development. The population of Haiti is estimated at about 3.5 million people, most of whom are black or mulatto. Standards of living are extremely low and many groups may be classed as primitive.

The chief products are agricultural, including sugar, coffee, cotton, sisal, tobacco, cacao, fruits, and logwoods. Manufacturing has developed very little. Roads are few and poor, but the country has international connections by air.

The University of Haiti was founded in 1944, but instruction at all levels is unsatisfactory. Illiteracy is the highest of all the Latin American countries. French is the official government language, but Creole and local dialects are widely spoken by the people.

Among the principal writers of Haiti the following may be mentioned: Éméric Bergeaud, novelist; Massillon Coiçon, writer on political matters; Frédéric Marcelin, essayist; Fernand Hibbert, novelist; Georges Sylvain, a very popular poet and critic; and Dantès Bellegarde, who has produced some good historical studies. Recently Haiti's "primitive" painters have become internationally famous.

THE DOMINICAN REPUBLIC

Early Presidents. On November 6, 1844, the Dominican Republic was established as an independent country, with a constitution under which General Pedro Santana was elected first president.

Constant unrest and a series of invasions from Haiti beset Santana's administration, and his despotic rule created many enemies.

In 1848 General Manuel Jiménez, Minister of War, was elected to succeed Santana. Meanwhile; war with Haiti broke out and, taking advantage of the situation, Santana caused Santiago Espaillat to be elected to the presidency. But when the latter refused to take office, Colonel Buenaventura Báez was chosen chief executive.

President Báez reorganized the army, opened schools, and endeavored to give the country an honest administration. In 1853 Santana was elected again and immediately took steps to exile Báez and to decrease the power of the clergy. The following year he had the constitution amended to provide for the election of a vice-president.

In 1856 General Regla Mota was elected president with the backing of Santana, but soon after his inauguration he resigned and General Báez was chosen to replace him. Santana opposed the new president, accused him in the congress of having taken unconstitutional measures, and caused him to be overthrown in 1857. But the next president, General José Desiderio Valverde, also incurred the antagonism of Santana, who revolted against him and was made chief executive again in 1858.

Spanish Rule. Between March 18, 1861, and May 3, 1865, Spain assumed control over the eastern section of the island of Hispaniola at the invitation of Santana. The latter was made governor and captain general, as well as Senator of Spain and Marqués de Las Carreras. In 1862, however, he resigned, disgusted with the preference given to Spaniards in government positions. Revolts occurred in several places. With the help of Haiti, war against the Spanish authorities broke out under the leadership of General J. A. Salcedo and Juan Pablo Duarte. As a result of pressure from the United States government, Spain decided to withdraw from Santo Domingo, and eventually (May 3, 1865) the annexation was annulled by the Spanish Cortes. On February 27, 1865, a national convention at Santiago again declared the independence of the eastern section of the island, adopted the old republican constitution, and elected General Pedro A. Pimental president of the republic.

The Second Republic. Pimental refused to move the capital from Santiago back to Santo Domingo, persecuted his enemies, and tolerated corruption in the administration of public affairs. A revolution broke out, and the president was overthrown within a few months of his inauguration. His substitute, José María Cabral, a hero of the War of Restoration, was also deposed by revolution and on December 8, 1865, General Báez again became chief executive.

The new president was unable to restore order in the country. The following year, a triumvirate composed of Generals Gregorio Luperón, Pedro Antonio Pimental, and Federico de Jesús García assumed the executive power. Then José María Cabral was once more elected chief executive, but Santana revolted against him. In 1871 Báez, who was again in power, sent a commission to Washington to arrange to have his country annexed to the United States. This scheme failed, and in 1873 Báez was succeeded by Ignacio González. Between 1882 and 1899 General Ulises Heureaux was president, suppressing numerous revolutions. In 1899 he was assassinated and Juan Isidro Jiménez gained control of the government. Shortly afterward, he was deposed by General Horacio Vásquez.

United States Intervention. In 1905, during the administration of President Carlos F. Morales, the United States took over, under the provision of a *modus vivendi,* the collection and administration of the customs of the republic to prevent trouble with foreign nations. In 1906 a treaty between the two countries gave the United States a fifty-year right to collect the customs duties in the republic; this arrangement was ended by treaty in 1940.

On August 27, 1914, after a succession of revolutions, a provisional government with Ramón Báez as executive was established under United States protection. In elections supervised by American officials, Juan Isidro Jiménez was elected. In 1915 American forces were sent to the republic to help maintain order, but the president was nonetheless overthrown in April, 1916.

On November 29, 1916, the United States took over full control of the state and maintained a military government under the direction of the Navy Department. In 1919 no president or congress existed in Santo Domingo; Rear Admiral Thomas Snowden of the United States Navy administered the affairs of the country. In 1922 J. B. Vicini Burgos was installed as provisional president. In 1924 the government of the republic was turned over completely to the national authorities. On March 19 of that year, Horacio Vásquez was elected president for four years. In September, the United States forces were withdrawn from the country.

The Dictatorship of Trujillo. In 1927 a new constitution was adopted, the presidential term being changed to six years. In February, 1930, Vásquez was overthrown, and Rafael Estrella Ureña assumed the executive power. The same year General Rafael Leónidas Trujillo Molina was elected president. From then on until August, 1938, when he decided to retire, Trujillo ruled as absolute dictator. The Vice-President, Dr. Jacinto B. Peynado, became chief executive when Trujillo retired. In 1936 the name of the capital was changed to Ciudad Trujillo; it was renamed Santo Domingo in 1961. On March 7, 1940, President Peynado died and was replaced by Vice-President Manuel de Jesús Troncoso de la Concha.

United States control of the Dominican customs was ended by a treaty signed between the two governments on September 24, 1940.

Political Developments since World War II. The Dominican Republic sided with the democratic nations against the Axis during World War II and against Communism after the war. The government declared war on Japan, December 8, 1941, and on Germany and Italy three days later. On November 11, 1942, the Trujillo regime broke off diplomatic relations with the Vichy French government. In April, 1945, the Dominican Republic became a charter member of the United Nations.

General Trujillo was again elected president on May 16, 1942. Re-elected in 1947, he took a firm stand against Communist influences in the Americas. In 1947 and in 1949 his administration put down revolts which he attributed to plotters from Guatemala, Cuba, and Costa Rica, although those countries denied his charges. President Trujillo announced in 1948 that he would not be a candidate in the 1952 election. His brother, General Héctor Trujillo Molina, was elected president and was re-elected in 1957.

During 1959 relations between the Dominican Republic and the other American nations, especially in the Caribbean area, became increasingly tense. In June of that year, an invasion of the Dominican territory by Dominican exiles from Cuba, Venezuela, and Puerto Rico was thwarted by government troops. The Dominican government accused Fidel Castro of instigating the invasion. In reply, Cuba broke diplomatic relations with the Dominican Republic on the grounds that the latter had refused to extradite former dictator Batista and had failed to return the planes in which Batista and his assistants had fled to the Dominican Republic.

The Santiago (Chile) meeting of the foreign ministers of the American nations (August 14–20, 1959) convened to consider the tensions in the Caribbean area, adopted a declaration reaffirming the principle that governments should be based on free elections and charged the Inter-American Peace Committee to recommend means to prevent activities abroad designed to overthrow the established governments in the Hemisphere.

The oppressive political conditions in the Dominican Republic were reflected in a pastoral letter signed by six Catholic bishops and read throughout the nation on January 25, 1960, requesting the government to stop the arrest and execution of civilians on political grounds. A report issued by the Inter-American Peace Committee on June 8, 1960, confirmed the rumors of political violence in the republic and accused the Dominican government of "flagrant and widespread violation of human rights."

On August 3, 1960, General Héctor Trujillo resigned as president and was succeeded by Dr. Joaquín Balaguer, elected vice-president in 1957. Attempts were made to relieve the oppressive conditions; a bill introduced in the congress provided for general amnesty for political prisoners and permitted exiles to return.

After an unsuccessful bomb attempt was made on President Betancourt of Venezuela (June 24, 1960), the Dominican government was accused of complicity. Charges brought before the OAS in Washington resulted in a special meeting of the foreign ministers of the American nations at San José, Costa Rica (August 16–28, 1960). The meeting heard a special report on the matter submitted by the Inter-American Peace Committee and adopted a resolution condemning the Dominican government for acts of aggression and complicity in the attempt against the life of President Betancourt. It also called upon all OAS members to break off diplomatic relations with the Dominican Republic and to impose partial economic sanctions.

Five countries—Venezuela, Cuba, Colombia, Ecuador, and Peru—had already broken relations with the Dominican government. Others—Argentina, Chile, Costa Rica, Guatemala, Haiti, Honduras, Mexico, Nicaragua, Paraguay, Uruguay, and the United States—did likewise immediately after the San José meeting. Brazil closed her embassy in Ciudad Trujillo but did not break off relations. On January 4, 1961, limited economic sanctions were imposed by the United States and other American nations.

On May 30, 1961, Generalissimo Rafael Leónidas Trujillo Molina was assassinated. His eldest son, Major General Rafael Trujillo, Jr., was then appointed by President Balaguer as Chairman of the Joint

Chiefs of Staff of the Armed Forces and as such controlled the situation. On June 5, 1961, the OAS Council decided to send a mission to the Dominican Republic to investigate alleged acts of violence against civilians. At the same time the Dominican government requested that diplomatic relations with the other American nations be re-established to avoid a total breakdown of law and order. The OAS investigating committee confirmed the accusation against the Dominican authorities and did not recommend an immediate renewal of diplomatic relations.

In November, 1961, serious disturbances compelled members of the Trujillo family to flee the country. On January 1, 1962, a council of government headed by President Balaguer was formed, with the understanding that he would step down as soon as the sanctions imposed by the OAS on the Trujillo government were removed. On January 4, the Council of the OAS voted to remove the sanctions, and two days later the United States renewed diplomatic relations with the Dominican Republic. Other Latin American governments took similar action. However, on January 16, General Pedro Rodríguez Echavarría seized power. But within a few days air force officers arrested General Rodríguez Echavarría, and Rafael Bonnelly, Vice-President under Balaguer, was named president.

In the elections of December 20, 1962, Juan Bosch, leftist, anti-Communist candidate of the Dominican Revolutionary Council, won a majority of votes. He was inaugurated on February 27, 1963, but on September 25, he was ousted by the armed forces. The legislature was dissolved, the July constitution was abolished, and the Communist Party was outlawed. The following day a three-man civilian junta headed by Donald J. Reid Cabral was inaugurated. On April 24, 1965, the junta was overthrown by a revolt headed by Colonel Francisco Caamaño Deñó. Former president Bosch was invited to return from exile to serve the remainder of his constitutional term but did not do so. A so-called "loyalist" military force headed by Brig. General Antonio Imbert Barreras was organized to fight the rebels. On April 29, the United States sent troops for the declared purpose of protecting American citizens on the island. As fighting between rebels and "loyalist" forces continued, more American troops landed, this time with the avowed purpose of preventing a take-over of the country by Communists. While the OAS, United Nations, and U. S. President Johnson's special envoys tried to restore peace, an Inter-American Peace Force was created

by the OAS with troops supplied by member states. This force occupied strategic points in the capital and endeavored to keep the two
warring factions apart. By mid-1965, all efforts to restore peace had
apparently failed.

Social, Economic, and Cultural Development. The population of
the Dominican Republic is estimated at about 3 million people,
mostly of mixed European and African blood. Standards of living
are still low although they have improved since 1930. The chief
agricultural products are sugar, cacao, coffee, and tobacco. Cattle
raising is little developed. The mining industry is still undevel-
oped, although bauxite is becoming increasingly important. Some
traces are found of gold, copper, iron, salt, coal, and petroleum.
The country is well provided with highways, but railroads are inadequate. Airlines connect the country with many parts of the
Americas.

Illiteracy has declined somewhat in recent years, but is still high.
The educational system is headed by the University of Santo Domingo, but primary and secondary schools do not meet the requirements of the island.

Many writers of merit have been born in the Dominican Republic. Among these the following may be mentioned: Félix María del
Monte (1819–99), a poet and intellectual leader; Javier Angulo
Guridi (1816–84), a writer of Indian legends in poetry and prose;
Salomé Ureña (1850–97), poetess of great merit and founder of the
first school for young ladies in Santo Domingo; José Joaquín Pérez
(1845–1900), a poet; Francisco Gregorio Billini (1844–98), a prose
writer who portrayed local life; César Nicolás Pensón (1855–1902),
author of historical tales; Manuel de Jesús Galván (1834–1911), author of *Enriquillo,* a well-known historical novel; Federico Henríquez y Carvajal (b. 1848), poet and dramatist; Américo Lugo
(b. 1871), literary critic and writer of short stories; Fabio Faillo
(b. 1865), popular poet and prose writer; Tulo M. Cestero (b. 1877),
modernist writer; Federico García Godoy, historical novelist; and
Pedro and Max Henríquez Ureña, both writers of great merit.

CUBA

At the time of the wars of independence in Spanish America,
Cuba remained loyal to Spain. In 1810 the island sent deputies to
the Spanish Cortes, and two years later the Spanish constitution of
that year was proclaimed throughout its territory. This does not

mean, however, that the Spanish American revolutions for independence did not have some repercussions in the island. Secret societies were organized, and political independence was discussed at their sessions. A plot originating in a secret society called *"Los Soles y Rayos de Bolívar"* was discovered by the Spanish authorities and suppressed in 1826. The leaders, Francisco de Agüero and Andrés Manuel Sánchez, who were hanged, are today venerated in Cuba as precursors of the island's independence. Another conspiracy, known as the *"Conspiración del Águila Negra,"* and centering in the Mexican Masonic lodges, was also discovered and suppressed. At one time Simón Bolívar, the liberator of northern South America, entertained the idea of sending an expedition to free the island from the Spanish domination. But this was never carried into effect, owing in part to diplomatic pressure from the United States.

The island progressed, thanks in part to the patriotic activity of its citizens, who formed a *Sociedad Económica de Amigos del País* to promote public education and culture. In 1841 certain reforms were undertaken by the Spanish authorities, including the secularization of the University of Havana. In general, however, the Spanish rule was harsh and autocratic.

The Beginning of the Struggle for Independence. By the middle of the nineteenth century the Cuban people had decided that they could not put up with the Spanish regime any longer. The movement for independence on the island was aided in many cases by American citizens. Many expeditions against the Spanish domination were outfitted in the United States, and many Cuban patriots persecuted by the Spanish authorities took refuge in this country.

The first serious effort to overthrow the Spanish regime took place in 1849, when the Venezuelan general Narciso López tried to bring about a revolution on the island. He failed and fled to the United States. Once in this country, he secured the help of many American friends and Cuban exiles and organized another expedition, which left New Orleans and landed in Cuba on May 19, 1850. But again he failed for lack of support from the inhabitants of the island and had to return to the continent. The following year another revolutionary outbreak took place, led by Joaquín de Agüero, who, on July 4, proclaimed the independence of Cuba in Camagüey. But this revolution also was suppressed by the Spanish authorities.

As the Spanish rule increased in harshness, the desire for independence among the Cubans increased. On August 12, 1851, Nar-

Fig. XXI-1.   Political Divisions of Cuba.   (Courtesy of Farrar & Rinehart, Inc.)

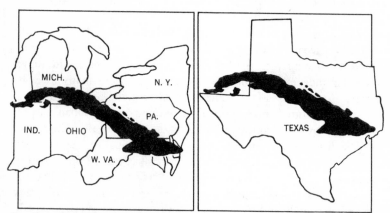

Fig. XXI-2.   Length and Area of Cuba in Comparison with Portions of the United States.   (Reproduced with permission from *Our Competitors and Markets,* by Arnold W. Lahee, published by Henry Holt and Company, New York, 1924.)

ciso López made still another attempt to free the island. This time he fell into the hands of the Spanish authorities and was shot. A plot against the authorities led by Ramón Pintó, a distinguished Spanish educator of liberal convictions, was discovered a little later, and Pintó and other leaders were shot.

At this time, sentiment in favor of the annexation of Cuba developed in the United States. But the outbreak of the American Civil War prevented any action being taken to that effect.

The Ten-Year War. Despite economic progress, dissatisfaction with Spanish rule did not abate. On October 10, 1868, a revolution broke out in Yara, led by Carlos Manuel de Céspedes, a lawyer of great prestige and wealth. He was joined by other patriots, including Francisco Vicente Aguliera, Máximo Gómez, and Vicente García, and the revolution spread to many sections of the country. Help was received from the United States. In April, 1869, a popular assembly met in Guáimaro (Camagüey) and adopted a constitution providing for a republican government. Céspedes was elected first president. But the patriots were defeated in the Battle of Jimaguayú on May 11, 1873, and Ignacio Agramonte, one of their most capable leaders, was shot. An expedition organized in the United States and traveling on board the *Virginius* failed when the Spanish authorities boarded the ship and arrested the revolutionists, took them to Cuba, and tried and shot many of them.

Meanwhile, the patriots were quarreling among themselves. Céspedes was replaced by Salvador Cisneros y Betancourt in 1873. Shortly afterward, Céspedes was killed by the Spaniards. Then General Vicente García refused to acknowledge the authority of the revolutionary government, and Cisneros y Betancourt resigned, his place being taken by Juan Bautista Spotorno, who in turn was replaced soon after by Tomás Estrada Palma.

At this time the Spanish government sent to the island General Arsenio Martínez Campo to restore order. He was able to negotiate with the rebels the Pact of Zanjón, on February 12, 1878, whereby they were permitted to return to their homes and occupations without further action against them from the Spanish authorities. A few patriots led by Antonio Maceo refused to recognize the pact and continued to fight for independence. But they were compelled to leave the island, and peace was restored.

One year later, however, war broke out again because the reforms promised by the Spanish authorities had not been carried into effect. The leader of the new revolution was General Ramón Blanco. He received help from the Cuban exiles in the United States, where Calixto García Iñíguez co-operated with the revolutionaries. This uprising, known in Cuban history as the *"Guerra Chiquita,"* was quickly suppressed.

Spanish Reforms. As a result of all these uprisings, the Spanish government effected some reforms in the colonial government. In 1879 the right of representation in the Spanish Cortes at Madrid was granted to the Cuban people, and two years later the Spanish constitution was extended to the island. On October 7, 1886, slavery was abolished. In 1895 a Council of Administration was created to advise the government of Cuba, half of its members being Cubans. These reforms, however, did not satisfy the inhabitants of the island.

The Revolution of 1895. The tyranny of Spain led many Cubans to emigrate to the United States. In New York City a central committee was established, with branches in other parts of the United States, to promote the liberation of the island from Spanish rule. The man who did more than anyone else to bring about unity among the Cuban patriots residing in the United States was José Martí, one of the greatest poets of Latin America.

In 1895 a revolution was planned to break out at the same time in several parts of Cuba. In March of that year, General Máximo Gómez issued a manifesto inviting all Cubans to unite in war against the Spanish authorities. Several patriot expeditions landed on the island. In May, the revolutionary leaders issued a call for the election of representatives to meet in a constitutional convention. This assembly met in September and declared Cuba independent, adopted a provisional constitution, elected Salvador Cisneros y Betancourt president, and chose Máximo Gómez as commander of the patriot army.

The Spanish government sent to the island as governor, Valeriano Weyler y Nicolau, who endeavored to quell the revolution by cruelty and who became known as the "Butcher." He ordered the rural population to concentrate in certain towns in order to be better guarded by the militia, an action which resulted in great misery for the population. In 1897 Weyler was replaced by a more conciliatory man, General Ramón Blanco y Arenas, who reformed the administration and established an autonomous government. But this conciliatory policy came too late. The revolution in Cuba involved Spain in war with the United States.

The Spanish-American War. Disturbances in Havana led to the request by the American consul that a United States war vessel be sent to that port to protect the lives of American citizens. On February 15, 1898, the battleship *Maine,* which had been sent by the American government as requested, was blown up in the harbor of Havana by an explosion, apparently from a mine. On April 19, the United States Congress recognized that the people of Cuba were and ought rightfully to be free and independent. The Spanish government interpreted this as a declaration of war and on April 21 severed diplomatic relations with the United States, following this with a formal declaration of war on April 24. The next day the United States declared war on Spain.

The Spanish fleet under the command of Admiral Cervera was soon defeated by the United States fleet under the command of Admiral Sampson. An American expedition landed on the island and captured the city of Santiago. Peace negotiations started soon after, and by August, a protocol containing the terms of peace was signed between the two belligerents. By the treaty of peace, signed in Paris on December 10, 1898, Spain renounced sovereignty over Cuba. The government of the island was transferred to the American forces of occupation on January 1, 1899.

The United States Occupation. The American forces occupied Cuba, and a military government was established which restored peace throughout the island, helped the population, reorganized the public services, promoted public education, and undertook a census of the inhabitants.

In November, 1900, General Leonard Wood, the United States military governor, assembled a constituent convention at Havana which on February 21, 1901, adopted a constitution providing for the establishment of a republican government. On June 12, the provisions of the Platt Amendment were incorporated in the Cuban constitution. The United States was thereby authorized to intervene in the island to guarantee its independence and Guantánamo Bay and Bahía Honda were leased to the United States. Later, the territory of the lease was increased and Bahía Honda was relinquished by the United States.

Cuban Presidents from 1902 to 1940. On May 20, 1902, Tomás Estrada Palma, a conservative, was inaugurated as the first president of the Republic of Cuba, and the American military governor turned over to him the administration of the island. In 1906 he was re-elected. But a revolution broke out and the president resigned. The congress was unable to decide upon a new executive. General unrest resulted in the intervention of the United States. The government of the island was assumed on September 29, 1906, by William Howard Taft, who later was replaced by Charles E. Magoon. The latter undertook many reforms and spent the resources he found in the Cuban treasury. He called elections, and José Miguel Gómez was chosen president, being inaugurated on January 28, 1909. The American troops were withdrawn.

The next president was the conservative, Mario García Menocal, who was inaugurated on May 20, 1913. He attempted to eliminate graft from the government and reformed the finances. In 1916 a military revolt resulted in a new intervention by the United States. In elections supervised by the U. S., Menocal was re-elected. In 1920 Alfredo Zayas, backed by the National League of Conservatives and Liberals, was chosen president. Ill feeling against the United States caused the American government to send General Enoch Herbert Crowder to the island. He suggested several reforms to be undertaken by the Cuban government in order to prevent a new intervention by the United States; these reforms were undertaken by President Zayas.

In 1924 a revolution broke out against Zayas's re-election. General Gerardo Machado y Morales was elected with the backing of the liberals. He was inaugurated on May 20, 1925. At this time the United States (March 13, 1925) definitely relinquished its claim to the Isle of Pines, and Cuba assumed sovereignty over the island.

President Machado's administration was beset by economic and financial crises. Rebellions led to strong repressive measures by the government. Machado asked the congress to extend his term by two years. In April, 1928, the term of the president was changed to six years, and Machado was re-elected without apparent opposition for a term ending in 1935. Fears that Machado intended to rule as dictator led to many uprisings and plots. On August 12, 1933, Machado was overthrown by a revolution known as the "Revolt of the Six Sergeants," headed by Sergeant Fulgencio Batista y Zaldívar. A period of disorder followed, during which several executives backed by Batista followed each other in rapid succession.

On June 12, 1934, a new constitution was adopted. Elections took place in January, 1936, and Dr. Miguel Mariano Gómez y Arias was elected president by a large majority. Amnesty was granted to all political prisoners and exiles, except those charged with terrorism. Social legislation of advanced character was adopted.

A new treaty was signed with the United States, superseding that of 1903; and the Platt Amendment, which gave the American government the right to intervene in the island, was abrogated. This treaty was ratified by the United States Senate on May 31, 1936.

In December, 1936, President Gómez was impeached and removed from office by the congress, under the influence of Batista, now a colonel, whose sway in Cuban politics became all-powerful after the fall of Machado. Federico Laredo Bru, the Vice-President, became chief executive with the backing of Batista.

First Presidency of Batista. The next presidential elections, which should have taken place on February 28, 1940, were postponed until March 28, and later until July 14, on account of political unrest. At this time two congresses claimed the right to represent the nation. One, regularly elected, was favorable to Colonel Batista's presidential candidacy; the other, a constituent assembly elected on November 15, 1939, to draft a new constitution for the nation, was led by former President Dr. Ramón Grau San Martín. Batista, candidate of the Socialist-Democratic coalition, won in an election in which it is said about 70 per cent of the electorate cast their votes. President Fulgencio Batista was inaugurated on October 10, 1940.

The new constitution, approved on June 8, 1940, and put into effect on September 15, was a long and detailed document with 318 articles. It provided for a semiparliamentary regime, the president to appoint a sort of prime minister who can be removed when he fails to obtain a vote of confidence in the chamber. The president was to be elected for a four-year term, by direct popular vote. Extensive social provisions were included in the new constitution.

Relations between Cuba and the United States were somewhat strained in 1939 by Cuba's default on payments on gold-obligation public works bonds, and a new tax which affected particularly United States insurance companies. On the other hand, the suspension of sugar quotas on the part of the United States hit the Cuban sugar industry very hard. Eventually, on December 27, 1939, a new reciprocal trade agreement was signed between the two countries restoring the sugar-quota system.

Political Developments since World War II. During President Batista's administration, Cuba co-operated closely in the Allied drive against the Axis powers. Cuba declared war on Japan on December 9, 1941, and on Germany and Italy two days later. Agreements with the United States provided for "lend-lease" aid for the purchase of defense materials, reciprocal trade concessions on imports from the United States and on Cuban exports thereto, as well as military bases and facilities for their use by the United States armed forces. The air bases were returned to Cuba after the war. In 1945 Cuba became a charter member of the United Nations.

Former President Ramón Grau San Martín, whose candidacy was supported by the Liberals, the Democrats, and the Popular Socialists, was elected president in June, 1944, to succeed President Batista; he was inaugurated on October 10. His administration was beset by industrial strikes and a plot to assassinate him. This situation resulted in a reorganization of the army whereby many officers were retired from service and others, accused of conspiring against the government, were discharged outright.

Grau San Martín was succeeded by Senator Carlos Prío Socarrás, elected on June 1, 1948. His policies included a firm opposition to Communism (both in domestic and in foreign affairs), vigorous action against inflation, the establishment of a national bank, and the organization of labor courts to decide industrial disputes.

On March 10, 1952, the president was overthrown by a military uprising led by former President Batista. It was alleged by the revolutionists that Prío Socarrás had plunged the country into violence in order to suspend the presidential elections scheduled for June 1 and to install his own candidate in the presidency. General Batista then assumed the powers of chief of state on March 11.

On July 26, 1953, an attack on the army barracks of Santiago de Cuba was led by a young lawyer named Fidel Castro. The revolutionists were driven back by the government forces and Castro was captured. Sentenced to fifteen years' imprisonment, he was released after eleven months under a general amnesty decreed by President Batista.

The presidential election was finally held in November, 1954, and General Batista was once more elected. However, the plotting against his regime continued. Fidel Castro, who had taken refuge in Mexico, landed in Oriente province on December 2, 1956, with a small group of armed followers. Hiding in the hills, they carried on guerrilla warfare with the government forces. On March 17, 1958, the revolutionists declared total war on the Batista regime. However, a call for a general strike was only partially heeded.

From 1957 on, constitutional guarantees were suspended by Batista. In March, 1958, the Catholic hierarchy appealed to the president to form a coalition government in order to put an end to violence in the country. Batista rejected this appeal and intensified the war against the rebels.

The presidential election of 1958 was won by Andrés Rivero, with Batista's backing. But on January 1, 1959, before the new president could be installed, the Batista administration collapsed and former Judge Manuel Urrutia was proclaimed provisional president. Batista and his family fled to the Dominican Republic. The bearded revolutionists, headed by Fidel Castro, made their triumphal entrance into the capital on January 8. There followed, soon, a series of trials and executions of Batista's followers which shocked the world.

On January 27, the United States military mission to Cuba was withdrawn at Castro's request. Several attempts at counterrevolution were speedily suppressed. In July, 1959, Urrutia was replaced by Osvaldo Dorticós Torrado. Fidel Castro, the real ruler of the country, held the office of prime minister.

Cuba was accused of aiding in the invasion of the Dominican Republic and Haiti by political exiles and Cuban Communists. At the request of the Dominican government, a meeting of the foreign ministers of the American republics was held in Santiago de Chile (August, 1959) to consider measures to stop the conflict.

One of the most criticized acts of the Castro regime was the land-reform decree, which went into effect June, 1959. Estates larger than 995 acres were to be expropriated and divided among some 300,000 landless peasants, each to receive 66 acres. The decree excepted sugar cane, rice, and cattle farms of less than 3,316 acres. The owners of the expropriated land would receive payment in 20-year 4 per cent bonds. Interest on these bonds must be reinvested in Cuba. Foreigners were barred from buying or inheriting land on the island. United States citizens were said to own about 1.6 million acres in Cuba.

In January, 1960, Soviet First Deputy Premier Anastas I. Mikoyan visited Cuba. During his visit he concluded several agreements with Fidel Castro's government providing for the purchase by the U.S.S.R. of Cuban sugar, for loans and technical assistance, and for the resumption of diplomatic relations, broken off since 1952. Later on, similar agreements were concluded with Poland, Czechoslovakia,

Eastern Germany, and the Chinese People's Republic (with which diplomatic relations were established on September 25). Cuba also established diplomatic relations with North Korea.

Relations with the United States became increasingly tense. On March 7, 1960, a French ship loaded with munitions from Belgium exploded in Havana harbor. The Cuban authorities attributed the explosion to American agents. This was emphatically denied by Washington. Shortly after, President Eisenhower asked the American Congress for authority to cut Cuba's quota of the United States sugar market. Under the Sugar Act of 1934, domestic and foreign producers were assigned quotas of the American market and received prices 2 to 3 cents above the world market price. Cuba's quota for 1960 was 3,119,000 tons, one-third of the United States requirements. The value of the price differential paid to Cubans was estimated at 150 million dollars.

On October 19, 1960, the United States government reluctantly declared an embargo on exports to Cuba of all commodities except medicines, medical supplies, and certain food products. This was done in reply to the increased campaign of hostility and slander on the part of the Cuban authorities as well as to measures levying restrictive taxes on American exports, discrimination against American trade, and the seizure of private American property without proper compensation. After the embargo, all the remaining American-owned property in Cuba—estimated at about 250 million dollars —was seized. Earlier seizures were valued at 1.25 billions, including many sugar mills, two petroleum refineries, the Cuban Electric Co., the Cuban Telephone Co., and three banks.

The United States Ambassador to Cuba, Philip W. Bonsal, was recalled on October 20. A few weeks later, President Eisenhower warned Cuba that the United States would take whatever steps seemed appropriate to defend its naval base at Guantánamo. He added that the United States would not agree to the abrogation or modification of the Treaty of 1903 in regard to the base. Meanwhile it became known that Cuba was receiving MIG jet fighters and tanks from the U.S.S.R. and other armaments and munitions from "iron curtain" countries. Bitter denunciation of American alleged unfriendly acts towards Cuba before the UN General Assembly and the Cuban demand that the staff of the United States embassy in Havana be reduced to eleven persons, led Washington to break diplomatic relations with Cuba on January 3, 1961.

After Fidel Castro assumed power in Cuba, a large number of Cuban citizens took refuge in the United States, particularly Florida. These Cuban refugees organized themselves into loose groups for mutual aid, political action, and training for an eventual invasion of their fatherland. Guerrillas had been in training since May, 1960, at camps in Guatemala under the supervision of an American army officer. These forces joined others from Louisiana and Florida early in April, 1961. An invasion of Cuba planned for April 10 took place seven days later. About 1,500 men took part in landings at the Bahía de Cochinos. Most of them were killed or captured by Cuban loyal forces. The invasion had been badly planned. There were dissensions among the leaders and at the last minute air cover promised by the American authorities failed to materialize. Moreover, there was no attempt to rally support in Cuba.

Although President Kennedy assumed the responsibility for the failure of the invasion, it is to be presumed that it was due in large measure to faulty evaluation of conditions on the island. Since President Kennedy had, on April 12—just a few days before the invasion—given a firm pledge that U.S. armed forces would not intervene in Cuba, the attempted invasion damaged United States prestige in the eyes of the other American nations, where it was considered contrary to existing inter-American agreements of non-intervention.

There followed an attempt on the part of Fidel Castro to capitalize on American sympathy towards the anti-Castro Cubans by offering to exchange 1,200 prisoners for 500 agricultural tractors. The offer, at first accepted by a private committee organized to raise the necessary funds, failed when the Cuban premier raised his demand to equipment worth 62 million dollars.

Attempts on the part of Argentina and Brazil to mediate in the dispute between the United States and Cuba were rejected. In the latter part of 1961, documents stolen from the Cuban embassy in Buenos Aires and published in the United States seemed to link Fidel Castro to a plot to overthrow the government of President Frondizi, in Argentina. The support of the Cuban regime by Brazilian President Jânio Quadros was dealt a severe blow with the Quadros resignation in August, 1961.

The Cuban problem was considered in August, 1961, at Punta del Este (Uruguay) by the Inter-American Economic and Social Council. In January, 1962, at Colombia's proposal, a special conference of foreign ministers of the American nations was called to deal with the Cuban problem. On January 30, a resolution was adopted to exclude Cuba from the inter-American system because of the incompatibility of its Communist regime with democratic principles; to put into force a hemispheric arms embargo on Cuba; and to exclude Cuba from all proceedings of the Inter-American Defense Board in Washington. Argentina, Bolivia, Brazil, Chile, Ecuador, and Mexico abstained from voting. At the end of the year 13 American nations had no diplomatic relations with Cuba.

In September the attacks on the part of the authorities against the Catholic Church were increased. Priests and nuns were accused of plotting to overthrow the regime of Premier Fidel Castro, acting as agents for the United States intelligence service.

On December 2, 1961, Castro declared publicly that he was, and would continue to be until the last day of his life, a Marxist-Leninist.

A buildup of Russian missile weapons and bases occurred in Cuba in September and October, 1962. On October 22, after intensive U. S. photographic air surveillance, President Kennedy announced that Russian missiles capable of destroying American cities were being rapidly installed at a number of Cuban bases. The president ordered a "quarantine" of the island by U. S. naval and air forces, and he moved Army and Marine personnel into southern Florida and elsewhere, to be ready for any emergency.

Premier Khrushchev protested the blockade, but when he realized that the U. S. intended to enforce it, he offered to dismantle the bases and ship the weapons back to Russia. It was agreed that the Secretary General of the United Nations should visit Cuba with a party of experts to make sure that the dismantling of the weapons occurred.

Though Premier Castro refused to permit UN inspection of missile sites, U. S. aerial photographs indicated that the bases had been dismantled, and Premier Khrushchev agreed to permit U. S. naval forces to observe the missiles on Russian ships leaving the island. The blockade had been suspended while UN representatives were in Cuba, but on November 2 it was reinstituted.

Social, Economic, and Cultural Development. The population of Cuba is estimated at some 6.5 million people, largely of mixed blood and of Spanish origin. The products are chiefly agricultural, including sugar, tobacco, coffee, cacao, and a variety of fruits. Stock raising has steadily increased in recent years, as has the poultry industry. Known minerals are coal, iron, copper, manganese, gold, mercury, zinc, lead, silver, antimony, and some petroleum, asphalt, and asbestos. Highways, including a Central Highway completed in 1931, are adequate. Railroads are important, and numerous airlines connect the country with various parts of the Americas.

There are large universities in Santiago and Havana; the National University, in Havana, was founded in 1721. Numerous technical and professional schools have been founded in recent years. Under Batista and Castro many new primary and secondary schools were established in rural communities. Illiteracy is much lower than in other Caribbean countries.

Cuba has produced many writers of merit, among whom the following may be mentioned: José María de Heredia (1803–39), a fine poet who spent most of his life abroad and who is the author of many works including *Himno del desterrado* and a poem about Niagara Falls; Juan Clemente Zenea (1832–71), a poet, author of *Cantos de la tarde* and *En Días de esclavitud,* a collection of patriotic poems; José Martí (1853–95), an inspired poet and essayist and the "Apostle of Cuban Independence"; Gertrudis Gómez de Avellaneda (1814–73), a poetess; Enrique José Varona (b. 1849), a journalist, philosopher, and sociologist; Jesús Castellanos (1879–1912), writer of short stories and literary critic; Ramón de Palma y Romay (1812–60), a teacher and dramatist as well as a poet; Carlos M. Trelles (b. 1866), a historian and bibliographer of note; Dulce María Borrero de Luján, a recent poetess of great inspiration; Juan Marinello (b. 1899) and Félix Lizaso (b. 1891), literary critics; Fernando Ortiz, historian, ethnologist, jurist, and linguist; and Jorge Mañach (1898–1961), historian.

Among Cuban painters of note are: Miguel Melero, José Arbury Morell, Miguel Angelo, Armando Menocal, Leopoldo Romañach, and Esteban Valderrama.

RECENT DEVELOPMENTS IN
LATIN AMERICAN HISTORY

Guatemala. In March, 1966, Julio César Méndez Montenegro was elected President by the congress. He was inaugurated on July 1, 1966.

Honduras. Colonel Osvaldo López Arellano, leader of the bloody revolt that overthrew Villeda Morales, was elected President by a Constituent Assembly which met in March, 1965.

Colombia. After a four-year term, Guillermo León Valencia was succeeded as President by Carlos Lleras Restrepo, who was inaugurated on August 7, 1966.

Panama Canal. After the Canal Zone incidents of 1963, the Canal Treaty was revised, and the new version was signed in September, 1965. It recognizes Panama's sovereignty over the Canal territory as well as the United States' right to maintain a military and naval base and to provide for the defense of the Zone. It also makes both countries partners in the operation of the Canal.

Argentina. Following the internal turmoil of recent years, President Illia was overthrown on June 28, 1966, by a military coup, and a provisional government headed by General Juan Carlos Onganía was installed.

Uruguay. On November 27, 1966, the National Assembly held a public referendum on whether to continue or to abolish the nine-member National Council, after more than 800,000 citizens signed a petition against the system.

Dominican Republic. After prolonged negotiations, an Act of Conciliation was signed between the warring forces on August 31, 1965. Hector García Godoy was then installed as provisional President; Joaquín Balaguer was later elected President and was inaugurated on July 1, 1966. All foreign troops were withdrawn by September of the same year.

PART FOUR

INTERNATIONAL RELATIONS
SINCE INDEPENDENCE

PART FOUR

INTERNATIONAL RELATIONS
SINCE INDEPENDENCE

D<small>URING NEARLY A CENTURY</small> and a half the international relations of the Latin American countries have passed through a series of stages in which the United States of America has played an ever increasing and dominating role. Today no one can consider the diplomacy of any one Latin American country without considering also its influence upon hemispheric relations and the attitude and reactions of the United States regarding it. In this section the foreign relations of the Latin American countries will be studied under four main headings: Inter-Latin American Relations; Latin America and the United States; the Pan American System; and Latin America and Non-American Nations.

Fig. XXII–1. Latin America Today. (Courtesy of Farrar & Rinehart, Inc.)

CHAPTER XXII

INTER–LATIN AMERICAN RELATIONS

EARLY RELATIONS

FROM THE BEGINNING of the independence movement in Latin America, attempts were made to unite the Spanish colonies in their struggle against the mother country. Francisco de Miranda, a Venezuelan, suggested such a union about 1797. He founded in London a political society called *"Gran Reunión Americana,"* designed to co-ordinate efforts in favor of the liberation of the Spanish colonies of America. Many future leaders of the Spanish American independence movement, among them Bernardo O'Higgins, Simón Bolívar, and José de San Martín, belonged to this society.

The revolution of May, 1810, in Buenos Aires had a general continental purpose, and one of its leaders, Mariano Moreno, suggested the organization of a great La Plata state, to include Brazil. In Chile, during the same year, a "Declaration of the Rights of the Chilean People" was published by Juan Martínez de Rozas, advocating a South American Union, and the following year Juan Egaña suggested the calling of a general Spanish American congress for self-defense and co-operation.

In their struggle for independence, the South American patriots soon became convinced that they would have to expel all Spanish soldiers from the continent before their efforts could be successful. Bolívar's armies marched as far south as Bolivia; San Martín crossed the Andes into Chile and marched northwards to Peru. From Buenos Aires armies were sent into the Banda Oriental (Uruguay), Paraguay, and Upper Peru (Bolivia). In 1817 Argentina and Chile signed a treaty of alliance against Spain. The idea of co-operation in the struggle against Spanish domination was discussed by the two most prominent military leaders of the patriots, San Martín and Bolívar, in their interviews at Guayaquil in 1822. It is possible that they also discussed the establishment of a great Spanish American state, to include all the former Spanish colonies in the New World. This idea had already been discussed by others, including Pueyrredón in Argentina. In 1821 Colombia had suggested the creation of a South American union, and the following year, in a treaty signed with Chile, a provision was included for the calling of a continental congress of all the former Spanish colonies.

These efforts to consolidate the former Spanish colonies into one or two large states were not welcomed everywhere. In Paraguay all attempts by the Buenos Aires government to induce the people of that province to join the United Provinces of the River Plata were a failure, and even resulted in the abrogation of the treaty of alliance between the two countries signed on October 12, 1811. In Uruguay, Artigas and his followers fought against the annexation of that province to Buenos Aires. The Argentine troops of occupation were defeated in the Battle of Guayabos (February 10, 1815) and evacuated Montevideo a few weeks later. The repeated efforts of the Buenos Aires government to annex Upper Peru (Bolivia) also failed.

Bolívar in northern South America and Iturbide in Central America were more successful than the Buenos Aires leaders, but not for long. The state of Great Colombia, the creation of Bolívar, including Venezuela, New Granada, and Ecuador, lasted only until 1830. Central America was united to the Mexican Empire of Iturbide from January 5, 1822, to June 24, 1823. The Peru-Bolivian Confederation established by General Santa Cruz in 1837 lasted only a little over a year. The United Provinces of Central America lasted from 1823 to 1838.

THE PANAMA CONGRESS OF 1826

While a refugee in Jamaica during the wars of independence, Bolívar wrote, on September 6, 1815, what has since been called his "prophetic letter," expressing the wish that some day in the future the representatives of the republics, kingdoms, and empires of America might meet in the Isthmus of Panama to discuss peace and war with the nations of other parts of the world. To this idea the Liberator devoted a good deal of attention during the following years. Finally, on December 7, 1824, while he was at the head of the Peruvian government, he sent invitations for such a congress to Colombia, Mexico, Central America, Brazil, and the United Provinces of the River Plata. At first, the United States of America was not invited. Later, however, at the suggestion of Mexico, Colombia, and Central America, a verbal invitation was extended by the representatives of Mexico and Colombia at Washington.

In all, ten meetings of the congress were held (June 22 to July 15, 1826), with the attendance of representatives from Colombia, Central America, Peru, and Mexico. The Buenos Aires government did not accept the invitation and did not send representatives; Chile accepted, but did not send representatives; Brazil was not represented; and the representative of the United States arrived too late to participate in the sessions of the congress. The delegates agreed that a congress should meet every two years at Tacubaya, Mexico, where the climate was more favorable than in Panama, and signed a treaty of union and of perpetual confederation and a convention providing for an army of 60,000 troops, to be furnished proportionately from the several states, for the defense and support of the union. Restriction of European expansion in the Western Hemisphere was discussed. Colombia was the only state that ratified the agreements of the congress.

OTHER LATIN AMERICAN CONGRESSES

On March 13, 1831, the government of Mexico invited the other Latin American states to send delegates to a congress to meet either in Panama, Tacubaya, or Lima, but the invitation was accepted by only a few of the states, and the congress was not held. The Mexican government again issued invitations for a congress on December 18, 1838, August 6, 1839, and April 2, 1840. But nothing came of these efforts.

In 1844 Juan Bautista Alberdi, of Argentina, suggested the creation of a Latin American league of states to discuss and settle any disputes arising between those states and to promote their common interests. This idea was not carried out. Three years later, however, Bolivia, Chile, Ecuador, New Granada, and Peru decided to establish closer relations among themselves and met in a congress at Lima, Peru. Nineteen meetings were held from December 11, 1847, to March, 1848. Treaties of confederation, commerce, and navigation, as well as a postal treaty and a consular convention, were signed; but New Granada was the only state that ratified any of the agreements.

On September 15, 1856, delegates of Peru, Chile, and Ecuador met at Santiago, Chile, and signed a treaty known as the "Continental Treaty," providing for the establishment of a "great American family" union. The other American nations, except the United States of America, were invited to adhere to the treaty. No results of any value came of this move.

On November 14, 1864, at the invitation of the Peruvian government, delegates from Bolivia, Chile, Ecuador, Colombia, Guatemala, Peru, the Argentine Republic, and Venezuela met in Lima, to discuss plans to accomplish a Latin American union. But again, nothing of practical value came of the conference.

On September 3, 1880, the governments of Colombia and Chile signed a treaty of arbitration providing that in case of a dispute between the contracting parties which could not be settled by direct negotiation, the question should be submitted to the arbitration of the president of the United States. On October 11, Colombia invited all the other Latin American states to send delegates to a congress to be held in Panama in September, 1881, for the purpose of securing the adherence of all to the agreement of September 3. Although most of the American states accepted this invitation, the congress could not be held because of the War of the Pacific between Chile, Bolivia, and Peru.

From August 25, 1888, to February 18, 1889, there met at Montevideo, a South American Jurists' Congress to discuss and negotiate treaties on matters of private international law. Thirty-five meetings took place, and treaties were signed on international law, civil law, commercial law, penal law, law of procedure, literary and artistic property, and trade marks and patents.

The similarity of race, culture, language, and customs of the peoples of Latin America has inspired many gatherings to promote closer social and cultural relations among these countries. Such meetings have taken place in Montevideo (1908), Buenos Aires (1910), Lima (1912), Mexico (1921 and 1930), and other cities. Buenos Aires has been an important center of this movement. A society known as the *"Unión Latino-Americana"* was founded there in 1922. Periodicals such as *Nosotros,* published in Buenos Aires, and *Genio Latino,* published in Mexico, have promoted this movement. At times Latin American solidarity has taken the form of antagonism to the United States.

Scientific co-operation in Latin America has resulted in a series of congresses, the first of which took place in Buenos Aires in 1898. Other congresses of this type were held at Montevideo in 1901 and at Rio de Janeiro in 1905. The fourth of the series, held at Santiago de Chile in 1908, became the First Pan American Scientific Congress, with the attendance of delegates from the United States.

In recent years several regional conferences have taken place. The Inter-American Conferences of the Caribbean were held at Havana, Cuba, in 1939, at Ciudad Trujillo, Dominican Republic, in 1940, and at Port-au-Prince, Haiti, in 1941. To the Third Inter-American Conference the Mexican delegation offered a plan for an "Inter-American Union of the Caribbean." This project was objected to on the ground that it would duplicate the work of the Pan American Union at Washington and result in still other regional groups. The word "Union" was eliminated from the project, which in its essence was referred to the several governments for consideration. No agreement was reached, however, in regard to the matter. Twelve countries, including the United States, participated in these conferences.

The River Plata Regional Economic Conference was held at Montevideo from January 27 to February 6, 1941. Delegates from Argentina, Bolivia, Brazil, Paraguay, and Uruguay attended the conference. Observers also attended from Peru, Chile, and the United States.

The purpose of this conference was to develop commerce among the participating nations in order to offset the heavy losses they had suffered through the wartime disruption of their commerce with Europe. A special convention was adopted providing that the signatory nations should renounce most-favored-nation treatment for themselves for a period of ten years. Other conventions provided for the development of petroleum resources and the adoption of a regional parcel-post system. Nine conventions and seventeen resolutions were approved. A permanent regional office of economic information and study was set up in Buenos Aires to co-operate with the Pan American Union, the International Labor Office, and Economic and Financial Consultative Commissions in each of the participating countries.

THE ATTEMPTED UNION OF CENTRAL AMERICA

After the disintegration of the Central American Confederation in 1838, several attempts were made to re-establish the union of the Central American nations. On March 17, 1842, El Salvador, Honduras, and Nicaragua sent delegates to Chinandega, in Nicaragua,

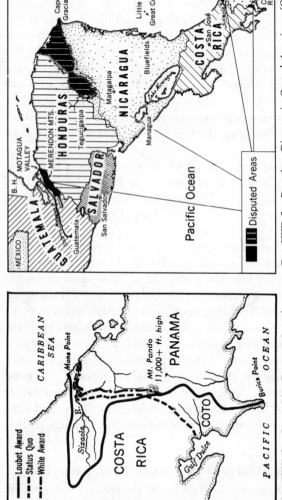

Fig. XXII-2. Costa Rica-Panama Boundary Dispute. (Courtesy of Farrar & Rinehart, Inc.)

Fig. XXII-3. Boundary Disputes in Central America. (Courtesy of Farrar & Rinehart, Inc.)

to a congress which adopted a treaty providing for the establishment of a confederation. The federal government was to consist of a council of four, one representative for each state, and one supreme delegate. A supreme court was to be selected by the legislatures of the states. In 1844 the Confederation came to an end, when Honduras and El Salvador attacked Nicaragua. On April 4, 1845, El Salvador and Guatemala signed a treaty agreeing to meet at a congress to study methods for the maintenance of peace in their respective territories and to co-operate in foreign affairs. The other Central American countries were to be invited to adhere. But the plan did not work out. In 1847 a meeting at Nacaome, in Honduras, adopted resolutions to call a congress of representatives of El Salvador, Nicaragua, and Honduras to study plans for union. This attempt, however, also failed.

In November, 1849, the same three states signed a treaty of federation at León, Nicaragua, providing for co-operation in matters of defense and foreign affairs. In January, 1852, the delegates of the three states met at Tegucigalpa, Honduras, selected a president, and a little later drafted a constitution. But Nicaragua and El Salvador refused to ratify the instrument of union.

A new attempt was made in 1862 by Nicaragua, with the co-operation of Honduras and El Salvador. But this attempt, like the previous one, was unsuccessful. In 1876, at the suggestion of President Justo Rufino Barrios of Guatemala, delegates from all the Central American states met at Guatemala City to consider projects for a new union. But war broke out between Guatemala and El Salvador, and the plan was given up. On February 28, 1885, President Barrios announced that he would become the commander of the troops of a Central American Confederation and asked the other states to send delegates to Guatemala City. But war ensued between Guatemala and the other states, and Barrios was killed. Other attempts were made in 1886 by Guatemala, and in 1889 by a congress meeting at San Salvador, but these attempts were also unsuccessful.

In 1895, Nicaragua, El Salvador, and Honduras sent representatives to Amapala, Honduras, and signed a treaty providing for the establishment of a joint commission to be in charge of the conduct of all relations between the three contracting parties and foreign countries. Plans were to be studied for the organization of the "Greater Republic of Central America." But the whole scheme came to an end when the government in El Salvador was overthrown.

In 1907 José Santos Zelaya, of Nicaragua, attempted by force to unite the states of Central America into a confederation. But the other states resisted, and Mexico and the United States intervened to restore peace. Later in the same year, all the Central American states were persuaded to send delegates to a conference which was held in Washington. Several treaties were signed at Washington, the most important of which provided for the maintenance of peace and the compulsory judicial settlement of all disputes, neutralized Honduras, and established a Central American Court of Justice. The Court functioned until 1918.

On January 19, 1921, the states of Guatemala, Honduras, El Salvador, and Costa Rica reached an agreement at San José, Costa Rica, for a union to be called the "Federation of Central America." Costa Rica, however, rejected this pact. A revolution in Guatemala upset the Central American equilibrium and by March 7, 1922, the union had been abandoned.

Again, in 1951, an attempt was made to unite the Central American states for common action to solve problems affecting them all. On the initiative of El Salvador, a conference of delegates from Costa Rica, Guatemala, Honduras, Nicaragua, and El Salvador met at San Salvador from October 10 to 14. A new regional organization was set up under the name of "Organization of Central American States," to promote, by group action, the strengthening of fraternal bonds among the Central American republics and to serve as an instrument for the study and solution of common problems. The five nations were to send delegates to periodical meetings to study measures to be taken. No action was taken at this time on a Nicaraguan proposal for political union.

In May, 1955, an agreement was signed by the five Central American governments to set up a center for technological research in Guatemala with the assistance of the United Nations.

The ministers of finance of the five countries met at Guatemala City (February 24, 1957) to study two draft treaties prepared by experts of the United Nations Economic Committee for Latin America, to create a free-trade area in Central America and a system of regional industries. The free-trade, or common-market, agreement was ratified by three of the Central American governments and went into effect on January 8, 1959.

On April 28, 1958, an agreement was signed by Guatemala and Honduras known as the "Charter of San Pedro Sula," providing for the integration of the two countries' transportation systems, the exchange of raw materials, the abolition of double taxation, and guarantees for capital investments.

In October, 1959, at a meeting in San Salvador, a recommendation was made by representatives of the defense ministers of the five countries to establish a Central American Defense Council.

During 1960 negotiations among the Central American nations led to the signature of three economic integration (common market) treaties by El Salvador, Guatemala, Honduras, and Nicaragua. Although it participated in the negotiations, Costa Rica decided not to join for the time being, considering the treaties detrimental to its economy. These agreements, signed on December 13, included: a general treaty of economic integration for 20 years; a protocol on the equalization of tariff rates; and an agreement for the establishment of a Central American Integration Bank. The treaty on economic integration provided that at the end of 5 years all goods would be allowed free entry into the participating nations. The Central American Integration Bank was to be capitalized at 16 million dollars (4 million to be contributed by each member state). The United States government also pledged 10 million dollars assistance to the bank.

INTER–LATIN AMERICAN BOUNDARY DISPUTES AND SETTLEMENTS

There have been numerous boundary disputes between the various Latin American countries, and in several cases these disputes have led to war. At the time of independence, no definite boundaries existed between the various Spanish colonies in America or between these and the Portuguese colony of Brazil. The patriot governments agreed to accept in principle the *uti possidetis* of 1810 in their future negotiations regarding the boundaries of their respective territories. But the interpretation of this provision was not always an easy one since colonial boundaries in 1810 were not well marked.

Argentina and Bolivia signed treaties regarding boundaries in 1868, 1889, and 1925. The latter treaty has not yet been ratified by Argentina. The line in Puna de Atacama remains undefined. With Brazil, Argentina had a long controversy over the boundary in the Misiones region. In 1889 the two countries signed a treaty providing for the arbitration of the question by the United States. On

Fig. XXII–4.   Territorial Cessions to Argentina and Brazil Following the Paraguayan
War.   (Courtesy of Farrar & Rinehart, Inc.)

February 6, 1895, President Grover Cleveland issued his arbitral award, deciding in favor of the Brazilian claim. Other sections of the boundary were defined under the provisions of treaties between the two countries signed in 1900, 1910, and 1927. Two difficult boundary questions were peacefully settled by Argentina and Chile: the section in Los Andes was decided under the terms of the treaties of 1893, 1896, and 1898, the last providing for the negotiations to be carried on in Buenos Aires with the co-operation of a commission of ten, or, if this did not prove satisfactory, of a commission of three, one for each of the two countries and the third to be the United States minister in Buenos Aires. The section in Patagonia was defined under the terms of several treaties signed in 1881, 1893, 1895, and 1896, the last providing for arbitration of the dispute. King Edward VII of Great Britain issued the arbitral award in regard to the case on November 20, 1902. The dispute between Argentina and Paraguay was settled by treaties of 1856, 1865, and 1876, the last providing for the arbitration of a certain section of the boundary. President Rutherford B. Hayes acted as arbitrator and on November 12, 1878, issued an award in favor of Paraguay. With Uruguay, Argentina has had a long dispute over the sovereignty of the island of Martín García. There is a treaty of unconditional arbitration of disputes between the two countries signed in 1899.

Bolivia and Brazil signed treaties of limits in 1867 and 1903, the latter providing for the cession by Bolivia to Brazil of the territory of Acre. To Chile, Bolivia relinquished the territory of Antofagasta under the terms of the treaties of 1895 and 1904. Bolivia has endeavored to secure the revision of the Treaty of 1904, so far without results. The dispute over the Chaco between Bolivia and Paraguay, although the subject of several treaties (1879 and 1887), was settled only in 1938, after years of negotiation and armed conflict. The boundary between Bolivia and Peru was the subject of treaties signed in 1826, 1831, 1847, 1886, and 1902. Under the 1902 treaty, a section of the boundary was submitted to the arbitration of the President of Argentina in 1904. The award, issued in 1909, was not well received in Bolivia but was later accepted by that country.

Brazil and Colombia signed a boundary treaty in 1907, which was supplemented by another one signed in 1928. Brazil and Ecuador signed a treaty in 1904, defining the boundary between their respective territories in case they were to be adjacent to one another as a result of a settlement favorable to Ecuador of disputes with

Fig. XXII–5. The Paraguay-Bolivia Boundary Dispute. (Courtesy of the American Geographical Society of New York.)

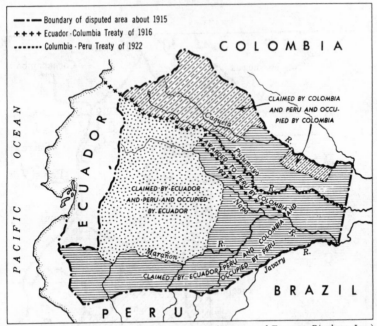

Fig. XXII–6. Boundary Disputes of Ecuador. (Courtesy of Farrar & Rinehart, Inc.)

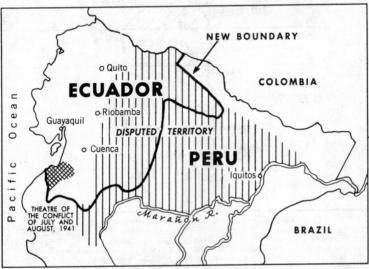

Fig. XXII–7. The Peru-Ecuador Boundary Dispute, 1941–42.

Fig. XXII-8. Chilean Expansion Northward.
A. Original Chile-Bolivian boundary. B. Claimed by Chile in 1842. a. Established by treaty in 1866, but in A–B nitrate revenues were divided equally. C. Original Peru-Bolivian boundary. D. Boundary of Chile as a result of the War of the Pacific, 1883, with D–E to be occupied by Chile ten years. d. Chile-Peruvian boundary by settlement of 1929. (Reproduced with permission from *Tacna and Arica*, by W. J. Dennis, published by Yale University Press, New Haven, 1931.)

Colombia and Peru. With Paraguay, Brazil signed a treaty of limits in 1872. Brazil and Peru signed treaties of limits in 1851, 1874, 1904, and 1909. The boundary between Brazil and Uruguay, defined in the Treaty of 1851, was modified by the agreements of 1857 and 1909, the latter ceding to Uruguay joint rights of control over Lake Mirim and the Yaguarón River. The boundary between Brazil and Venezuela was defined under the terms of treaties of 1852, 1859, 1905, and 1928.

The Tacna-Arica dispute between Chile and Peru was finally settled by the Treaty of 1929. Colombia and Ecuador signed a treaty of limits in 1916 ending their long dispute over the boundary in the eastern section. Colombia also settled her dispute with Peru in 1922. A dispute arising from the occupation of Leticia (a small port on the Amazon River) by Peruvian civilians in 1932, was finally settled by negotiation in 1934. Colombia and Venezuela signed treaties of limits in 1811, 1833, and 1845. Under the 1845 treaty, the dispute over a section of the boundary was submitted to the arbitration of the Spanish crown. The decision was issued in 1891 and was accepted by both countries. Other treaties on the matter were signed in 1896, 1898, and 1916, the last providing for arbitration of the dispute over the Arauca-Yávita region. This arbitration took place in 1922, the Swiss Federal Council being the arbitrator. A treaty defining the boundary between Colombia and Venezuela was signed on April 6, 1941.

Ecuador and Peru signed boundary treaties in 1860, 1887, and 1890. In 1934 they requested permission to send delegates to Washington to discuss the boundary question. In 1936 the two countries signed a protocol providing for the submission of their dispute to the arbitration of the President of the United States in case they could not reach a satisfactory agreement by direct negotiation. In the winter of 1940–41 there were clashes between Ecuadorian and Peruvian border patrols; by midsummer these had developed into an undeclared war. Peruvian forces invaded, occupied, and administered territory long governed by Ecuador. Hostilities were suspended thanks to the efforts of Argentina, Brazil, and the United States. The settlement of the dispute was finally agreed upon during the Rio Conference of Foreign Ministers and a treaty between Ecuador and Peru was signed on January 29, 1942, under which Ecuador was to get about 80,000 square kilometers of land in the Suzumbio zone and Peru was to withdraw its troops from the occupied territory within fifteen days. Again, in 1956, at the request of Ecuador, the Organization of American States met at Washington to consider charges against Peru over the massing of Peruvian troops at the frontier between the two countries. An investigating committee sent by OAS to the region reported that it had found no signs of such troops.

In his inaugural address of September 1, 1960, President Velasco, of Ecuador, declared that the agreement for the demarcation of the boundary with Peru was unjust and had been imposed by force. At the request of Peru, the representatives of the four guarantors of the Treaty of 1942—United States, Brazil, Argentina, and Chile—met in Rio de Janeiro (October, 1960), to study the implications of Ecuador's denunciation of the treaty. They recommended further direct negotiations between Peru and Ecuador with a view to reaching a mutually satisfactory settlement of the dispute. No settlement has, as yet, been reached.

Chile and Argentina announced on March 22, 1960, that they had decided to request Queen Elizabeth II of Great Britain to arbitrate in a frontier dispute concerning a 35-mile stretch in the southern Andes, in the area subjected to the arbitration of King Edward VII in 1902. The request was accepted but no decision has yet been announced.

The Central American countries have submitted several of their boundary disputes to arbitration as follows: Honduras and Salvador in 1880; Costa Rica and Colombia in 1880; Costa Rica and Nicaragua in 1886 and 1896; Honduras and Salvador in 1886; Guatemala and Mexico in 1892; Honduras and Nicaragua in 1894; Honduras and Guatemala in 1895; Honduras and Salvador in 1895; Nicaragua and Honduras in 1904; and Costa Rica and Panama in 1910. The boundaries between Guatemala and Honduras, between Honduras and Nicaragua, and between Costa Rica and Panama remain unsettled.

In February, 1960, Guatemala protested against the inclusion of British Honduras (Belize) in the British Commonwealth. Guatemala has, for years, claimed this territory or parts of it and in 1962 asked the United States government to assist in settling the dispute.

CHAPTER XXIII

LATIN AMERICA
AND THE UNITED STATES

Fᴿᴼᴹ ᴛʜᴇ ʙᴇɢɪɴɴɪɴɢ of the independence movement in Latin America, a sympathetic interest was shown by the government and citizens of the United States. President Madison, in 1811, adopted a policy of watchful waiting in regard to the Spanish colonies then at war with their mother country. Many United States citizens gave aid to Mexican and Venezuelan patriots and even joined in the war against Spain under the revolutionary flags of Mexico, Buenos Aires, New Granada, and Venezuela.

The Spanish American revolutionists early sought recognition by the United States, sending for that purpose numerous commissioners to this country. The United States also sent observers to Latin America. In 1810 the American government sent Robert K. Lowry to Venezuela and Joel Roberts Poinsett to Buenos Aires as agents. In 1817 Theodorick Bland, John Graham, Caesar Augustus Rodney, and Henry Mane Brackenridge were sent as special commissioners to South America.

At this time Henry Clay became the champion and advocate of the recognition by the United States of the independence of the new South American governments. Clay opposed the strict enforcement of the neutrality laws against the South American patriots and urged that diplomatic agents be sent to the independent governments of South America. On March 8, 1822, President Monroe recommended to Congress that the independence of the former Spanish colonies be recognized. On May 4, 1822, a bill was passed appropriating money for the purpose of sending representatives to those states. As a result of this act, diplomatic agents were appointed to Colombia (1823), Argentina (1824), Chile (1824), Mexico (1825), Central America (1825), and Peru (1826). Recognition was extended also to New Granada (1832), Uruguay (1834), Venezuela

(1835), Ecuador (1838), Bolivia (1848), and Paraguay (1852). The United States extended recognition to Brazil in 1824, when an agent of that country was received by President Monroe.

THE MONROE DOCTRINE

The fundamental idea of the Monroe Doctrine was conceived in principle by statesmen of both North and South America before its declaration by Monroe. In 1808 Thomas Jefferson, in a letter to Governor Claiborne of Orleans Territory, affirmed that the interests of certain Spanish American countries were identical with those of the United States and that they should "exclude all European influence from this hemisphere." Monroe crystallized the ideas of his time into fixed formulae to meet the situation as it then existed in Europe. The original expression of the Monroe Doctrine was contained in the message of President Monroe to Congress on December 2, 1823. It comprised two statements. The first of these was concerned with the prevention of the further expansion of Russia on the northwest Pacific coast and proclaimed that "the American continents, by the free and independent condition which they have assumed and maintain, are henceforth not to be considered as subjects for future colonization by any European powers."

The second statement concerned Latin America and was aimed at the Holy Alliance and its plans in respect to the Western Hemisphere: ". . . We should consider any attempt on their part to extend their system to any portion of this hemisphere as dangerous to our peace and safety. With the existing colonies or dependencies of any European power we have not interfered and shall not interfere. But with the governments who have declared their independence and maintained it, and whose independence we have, on great consideration and just principles, acknowledged, we could not view any interposition for the purpose of oppressing them, or controlling in any other manner their destiny, by any European power in any other light than as the manifestation of an unfriendly disposition toward the United States."

EXTENSIONS OF THE MONROE DOCTRINE
BEFORE 1936

The Monroe Doctrine has been variously interpreted and extended by the United States during the years that have followed its enunciation.

In 1825 Secretary of State Clay notified the French government that the United States would not consent to the occupation of Cuba and Puerto Rico "by any other European Power than Spain, under any contingency whatever."

During the Mexican War the government of Yucatan proclaimed its independence from Mexico and appealed to the United States, to England, and to Spain for annexation to one of these powers. In 1848 President Polk suggested that in order to keep the territory from falling into foreign hands the United States should assume the burden of annexation. Nothing, however, was done about this suggestion.

In 1870 President Grant declared that "hereafter no territory on this continent shall be regarded as subject to transfer to a European Power," not even from one European power to another.

In 1880 President Hayes declared that the United States would not consent to see a canal built and controlled by any other power than the United States for the reason that "it would be a great ocean thoroughfare between the Atlantic and Pacific shores, and virtually a part of the coast line of the United States."

In 1895 Secretary of State Olney said: "To-day the United States is practically sovereign on this continent, and its fiat is law upon the subjects to which it confines its interposition."

In 1905 President Roosevelt negotiated a treaty with Santo Domingo, ratified in 1907, for the purpose of administering the customs of that country in order to pay the debts due Europeans.

In 1912 Senator Henry Cabot Lodge drew up a resolution aimed at preventing the acquisition of a military base by Japan on Magdalena Island, asserting that "when any harbor or other place in the American continents is so situated that the occupation thereof for naval or military purposes might threaten the communication or the safety of the United States, the government of the United States could not see without grave concern the possession of such a harbor or other place by any corporation or association which has such relations to another government not American as to give that government practically power of control for naval or military purposes." This resolution was not accepted by President Taft.

Under the Monroe Doctrine, President Wilson, in 1913, protested against the acquisition by a British concern of a large oil concession from the government of Colombia, carrying with it the right of the company to improve harbors and to dig canals.

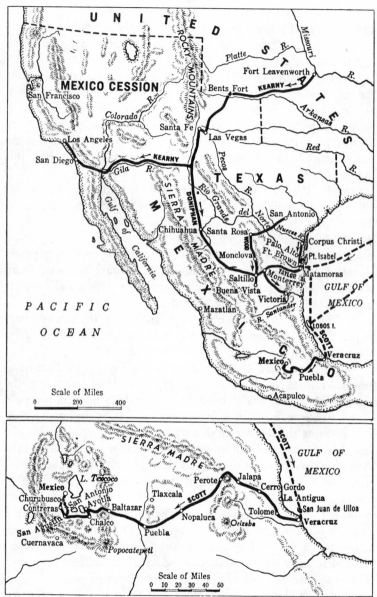

Fɪɢ. XXIII–1. Campaign Routes of United States Forces during the War with Mexico. (Courtesy of Farrar & Rinehart, Inc.)

In 1927 President Coolidge gave other nations to understand that the United States would pursue a different and more active policy north of Panama from that south of the Isthmus in regard to international obligations.

A modification of the Monroe Doctrine to include as its guarantors all the independent nations of the Western Hemisphere, was suggested at various times. In 1920, Dr. Baltazar Brum, President of Uruguay, suggested that all the states of the Western Hemisphere should unite and agree to go to the aid of any of them if any should be attacked by a foreign power. He further suggested the organization of an American league of nations. This latter proposal has also been made at various times by the governments of Latin American countries, and projects embodying that idea have been presented to several Pan American conferences.

Some of the principles of the Monroe Doctrine have been expanded by the signing of the Convention for the Maintenance, Preservation, and Re-establishment of Peace, in 1936, at the Inter-American Conference for the Maintenance of Peace, held at Buenos Aires.

THE UNITED STATES IMPERIALISTIC POLICY TOWARD LATIN AMERICA

About the middle of the nineteenth century the people of the United States began to feel that it was their "manifest destiny" to dominate the Western Hemisphere and to control and guide the destinies of the other American nations. This imperialistic attitude led to war with Mexico (1846–48) as a result of the admission of Texas to the American Union; to the acquisition of California and New Mexico under the terms of the Treaty of Guadalupe-Hidalgo (1848); and to the Gadsden Purchase (1853). It also resulted in the Spanish-American War (1898), the annexation of Puerto Rico and the Philippines, and the imposition of the Platt Amendment on Cuba (1901); in the recognition of the independence of Panama (1903) and the securing of full sovereign rights over the Panama Canal Zone; and in President Theodore Roosevelt's statements of 1903 and 1904 to the effect that ". . . chronic wrong-doing, or an impotence which results in a general loosening of the ties of civilized society, may in America . . . force the United States . . . to the exercise of an international police power." It likewise led to the intervention of the United States in the Dominican Republic and the assumption of control over the customs houses of that country for the purpose of adjusting its obligations with foreign creditors (1904); to the occupation of Nicaragua in 1909, of Haiti in 1915, and of the Dominican Republic in 1916 to maintain public order; and to intervention in Cuba and Central America on several occasions.

This imperialistic attitude of the United States toward Latin America, known under various names such as "Manifest Destiny," "Elder Sister Policy," "Big Stick Policy," and "Dollar Diplomacy," created ill feeling and distrust toward the "Colossus of the North" in Latin America.

THE RENEWAL OF GOOD WILL

During Theodore Roosevelt's second term a change of attitude toward Latin America was noticeable in this country. In 1906 Elihu Root, while still Secretary of State, visited South America and attended the Third Pan American Conference, held that year at Rio de Janeiro. He tried to convince Latin Americans that the United States was not interested in any further territorial expansion and wished the friendship of the other nations of this Hemisphere. In 1912 Secretary Knox visited the Caribbean states. The following year President Wilson, in a speech at a commercial convention held at Mobile, declared that his policy was to deal justly with the other American states and to promote constitutional liberty. In 1913 treaties were signed by the United States with various Latin American countries providing for the creation of international commissions of investigation to help in the peaceful settlement of any disputes arising between the contracting parties. In 1915 President Wilson also accepted the good offices of Argentina, Brazil, and Chile (the "ABC powers") in the dispute between the United States and Mexico.

This policy of good will was continued by succeeding administrations. With the inauguration of President Franklin D. Roosevelt it became known as the "Good Neighbor Policy." In 1933 President Roosevelt declared at various times that the United States wished to act toward the other American nations as a good neighbor. At the Seventh Pan American Conference, held in Montevideo in December, 1933, Secretary of State Cordell Hull emphasized this "Good Neighbor Policy" and declared further that ". . . no government need fear any intervention on the part of the United States under the

Roosevelt administration." President Roosevelt himself declared a few days later that ". . . the definite policy of the United States from now on is one opposed to armed intervention."

In pursuance of this policy, the Platt Amendment was abrogated in May, 1934; in August of the same year, the last marines were withdrawn from Haiti; and in March, 1936, a treaty was signed (ratified by the United States Congress in 1939) with Panama, whereby the United States surrendered its right to intervene in the internal affairs of that country and no longer guaranteed the independence of Panama. On January 30, 1936, President Roosevelt invited the other American nations to send delegates to a conference to consider their joint responsibility in preventing armed conflicts in the Western Hemisphere and to further the cause of permanent peace.

This Inter-American Conference for the Maintenance of Peace met at Buenos Aires December 1–23, 1936. President Roosevelt attended the formal opening of the conference and addressed the delegates, emphasizing once more the good will of the United States toward its neighboring nations. He also visited other Latin American nations en route to and from the conference.

As a consequence of these various moves, relations between the United States and Latin America became more friendly.

At the Eighth Pan American Conference, held at Lima in 1938, a certain antagonism toward the United States project of implementing continental solidarity was apparent. This, however, did not affect the friendly relations existing between the United States and Latin America as a whole. The new era of good will was reflected in Latin America in the changed attitude towards the United States on the part of leaders such as Víctor Raúl Haya de la Torre, Luis Alberto Sánchez, and others. Haya de la Torre, leader of the *Alianza Popular Revolucionaria Americana* (APRA) and an avowed enemy of "Yankee imperialism," in 1941 publicly urged all Latin American liberals to co-operate with the United States in the defense of democracy against totalitarianism.

As it became apparent during 1940 that the Western Hemisphere might become involved in the new European war, the United States adopted a more definite policy of friendly co-operation with Latin America with a view to preventing foreign intervention in the Americas. Latin American chiefs of staff toured United States camps and arms plants at the invitation of the American General Staff, and the Export-Import Bank considered the lending to Latin American governments of some 300 million dollars for armaments. Informal negotiations for naval and air bases were conducted during 1940 in South America as well as in the Caribbean area, and a proposal was presented that all the bases thus established, as well as those secured from Great Britain by the United States, be opened to the military and naval forces of all the American republics. On September 7, 1940, it was officially announced that the government of the United States had made available all bases secured from Great Britain to the naval forces of Latin America.

In pursuance of this policy the government of the United States also consistently supported all existing Latin American governments against any revolutionary attempts from disgruntled elements.

Several new U. S. government agencies were created to promote and strengthen economic and cultural relations with Latin America. In August, 1940, a Co-ordinator of Cultural and Commercial Relations between the American Republics (later known as the Co-ordinator of Inter-American Affairs) was appointed in the Council of National Defense. Several conferences were held at Washington under the auspices of the Division of Cultural Relations of the Department of State to consider ways and means of promoting cultural relations with Latin America. United States "lend-lease" funds for the American republics during the period from March, 1941, to July, 1945, totaled $262,762,000.

In the realm of economics, a project was announced at Washington prior to the gathering of the Havana Conference of Foreign Ministers (1940) for the establishment of a Hemisphere Trade Cartel with a view to making the United States the clearinghouse for all Western Hemisphere commerce. This plan was opposed by some of the Latin American governments and was dropped.

Trade relations between the United States and Latin America increased during World War II. In 1937 and 1938 the United States took about 31 per cent of Latin American aggregate exports. In 1940 this rose to 43.7 per cent, and during the first six months of 1941 to 54.3 per cent. The United States furnished about 35 per cent of total Latin American imports in 1938. But the percentage rose to 54.6 per cent in 1940 and to 60.5 per cent during the first six months of 1941.

Heavy American purchases in Latin America during 1941 resulted in a trade balance favorable to Latin America for the first time in many years—a balance of $106,000,000, and the net imports of gold and silver from Latin America by the United States amounted to $112,903,000.

DEVELOPMENTS SINCE WORLD WAR II

The friendly relations and the co-operation which existed during the war years between the United States and Latin America tended to disappear after 1945. A feeling of bitter disappointment and resentment was expressed throughout those countries because of American financial and economic aid to Europe and other parts of the world to the exclusion of the nations of the Western Hemisphere.

This feeling was evident at the Bogotá Conference (1947) and at other inter-American gatherings. It was particularly noticeable during the good-will visit of United States Vice-President Richard Nixon to Argentina and seven other nations of South America, in April-May, 1958. In Peru and Venezuela, Mr. Nixon was the victim of various indignities from enraged mobs which broke police controls.

Alarmed at this situation, President Eisenhower sent his brother, Dr. Milton S. Eisenhower, President of Johns Hopkins University, on an investigative visit to some of the Latin American countries. In his report, presented to President Eisenhower on December 27, 1958, Dr. Eisenhower urged that immediate steps be taken by the United States government to improve relations between the United States and the other American countries. He pointed out that the masses of people in those countries no longer accept low standards of living as inevitable. They look towards the United States for assistance; not financial grants, but public and private credits, stable trade relations, greater stability of prices for the raw materials which they export, and technical assistance.

Dr. Eisenhower specifically recommended a program of: (1) closer co-operation with the OAS; (2) an improvement of the existing information services among the American nations; (3) the extension of adequate public and private credits; (4) the establishment of an inter-American bank; (5) the improvement of housing facilities throughout the Hemisphere; (6) the establishment of a common market for Central America and for Latin America in general; (7) aid to the coffee-producing countries by the stabilization of prices; (8) the organization of a Joint Council on Inter-American

Affairs; and (9) the revision of the United States' attitude towards dictators and democracies.

Latin American dissatisfaction with United States policy was further expressed in a letter addressed on May 28, 1958, by President Juscelino Kubitschek, of Brazil, to President Eisenhower. The Brazilian President declared that "the hour has come for us to undertake jointly a thorough review of the policy of mutual understanding in this hemisphere." President Eisenhower's reply, dated June 5, delivered in Rio de Janeiro by Roy R. Rubottom, Jr., Assistant Secretary for Inter-American Affairs, expressed agreement that "our two governments should consult together as soon as possible" on the problems of inter-American relations.

President Kubitschek, in a radio-TV address to the nation on June 20, proposed a meeting of an inter-American conference on the highest political levels, to seek solutions for the "disease of underdevelopment." Kubitschek added that Latin America found itself in "a neglected economic position" because the United States had given its major attention during the past thirteen years to East-West disputes. He proposed: (1) intensifying investments in backward areas; (2) doubling technical assistance; (3) stabilizing prices for basic products; and (4) liberalizing the lending policies of international financing organizations.

U. S. Secretary of State John Foster Dulles visited Rio de Janeiro in August, 1958, to discuss plans for a meeting of representatives of the twenty-one American republics to study President Kubitschek's proposals, which became known as "Operation Pan America."

As a result of President Kubitschek's proposals, a conference was held in Washington under the auspices of the OAS, in September, 1958. After lengthy discussions two main resolutions were approved setting up an Inter-American Development Bank, with a capital of one billion dollars, and a Fund for Special Operations, of 150 million dollars. The United States government was to contribute 40 per cent of the Bank's capital and 100 million dollars for the Special Fund. The latter was to make socially useful loans which were not necessarily self-liquidating. Both agencies were to be set up as soon as the agreements were ratified by countries whose subscriptions represented 85 per cent of the authorized capital.

The agreement on the part of the United States government to assist in the setting up of the Bank represented a radical change in Washington's policy towards Latin America, which, until 1958, opposed any such schemes on the ground that private banks, the World Bank, the U. S. Export-Import Bank, and similar institutions were able to provide adequate credits for sound development projects.

It seems proper to call attention here to the Final Report adopted by the Sixteenth American Assembly which met in October, 1959, at Arden House, Harriman, N. Y., under the auspices of Columbia University. The Assembly was called to discuss the general topic "The United States and Latin America." The following are among the most significant—and logical—conclusions reached by the Assembly:

1. Latin America is important to the United States from the political, economic, and cultural points of view. The American republics are bound together by geography, historical ties, and many common ideas and aspirations.

2. Unless the United States participates wholeheartedly in determined attacks on continued widespread poverty among the Latin American peoples, the relatively advanced standard of living and the democratic way of life of the United States will be seriously threatened.

3. The Latin American countries constitute the most important investment and trading area of the United States today. The two-way trade is estimated at 8 billion dollars a year, which makes each of us (the United States and Latin America) the other's largest trading partner. U. S. private investments in Latin America total more than 9 billion dollars, and U. S. government investments in the same area exceed 2 billion dollars.

4. Part of this trade comprises some thirty strategic materials. In a nuclear war, inter-American co-operation would be vital to the survival of Western civilization.

5. North Americans must realize that Latin America differs from the United States in many respects—social, economic, political. Even among themselves, Latin American nations differ greatly. Latin America is now undergoing great economic, social, and political changes. Its population is increasing rapidly. The industrial revolution is speeding up in many areas. North Americans need to study and understand Latin Americans if we are to have closer relations. To accomplish that, we need to develop the proper means of mass information both in this country and in Latin America.

The resolution of the American Assembly included recommendations quite similar to those submitted by Dr. Milton S. Eisenhower, as mentioned above, in which he said that the peoples of the American nations "know that low standards of living are neither universal nor inevitable." These peoples were, in Dr. Eisenhower's opinion, impatiently insisting on remedial action and the United States should take the lead in urging the OAS to take effective measures to develop true co-operation among all the nations of the Western Hemisphere.

From February 23 to March 3, 1960, President Eisenhower visited Brazil, Argentina, Chile, and Uruguay on a good-will tour. This visit was considered a distinct success despite some anti-American demonstrations by students and other antagonistic elements in the countries visited. Joint declarations were signed in the various countries, including a Declaration of Brasília (February 23), reaffirming the traditional solidarity between the two nations and their determination to defend the democratic freedoms and fundamental rights of man as well as to implement the principles of political and economic solidarity; the Declaration of San Carlos de Bariloche, Argentina (February 28), reaffirming the determination of the two countries to foster improved living standards for the peoples of the Americas; the Declaration of Santiago, Chile, of March 1, reaffirming the determination to collaborate in international organizations, to realize common purposes; the Declaration of Montevideo (March 3), emphasizing respect for human rights, the support of institutions and organizations for international co-operation and the promotion of economic, social, and cultural co-operation.

In July, 1960, in reply to threats from Premier Khrushchev of retaliation against the United States if the latter intervened in Cuba, President Eisenhower declared that the United States would never permit the establishment of a regime dominated by international Communism in the Western Hemisphere. This declaration was followed by a statement from the Department of State at Washington reaffirming the United States' determination to uphold the principles of the Monroe Doctrine.

After his inauguration, President Kennedy sent several fact-finding and good-will missions to Latin America, including those headed by Ambassador Adlai E. Stevenson and Co-ordinator for Latin American Affairs Adolf Berle, Jr.

On March 13, President Kennedy outlined a broad development program for Latin America (*Alianza para Progreso*) at a reception for Latin American diplomats at the White House. It included: a vast 10-year plan for economic and financial assistance; the calling of a special Inter-American Economic and Social Conference to study details for the implementation of this plan; the request for 500 million dollars from the United States Congress for immediate aid to Latin America; the support for the economic integration of the area; the co-operation in individual commodity market problems (coffee, cotton, cacao, etc.); a program of distribution of foodstuffs through the Food for Peace agency; a plan to assist Latin American scientists in the preparation for an expanded plan of scientific education; assistance for technical training; a pledge to defend any American nation whose independence is threatened; and an invitation to Latin America to contribute to the enrichment of life and culture of the United States.

The following day, President Kennedy requested from Congress appropriations totaling 600 million dollars for aid to Latin America (500 millions for the Inter-American Fund for Social Progress and 100 millions for aid to the Chilean victims of the 1960 earthquakes and tidal waves). The fund was to be administered by the Inter-American Development Bank, which had opened for business in October, 1960.

The Inter-American Economic and Social Conference which President Kennedy had proposed met at Punta del Este, Uruguay, August 5–17, 1961, with the attendance of delegates from all the 21 American nations. The United States sent a strong delegation headed by Secretary of Treasury C. Douglas Dillon. A "Declaration to the Peoples of America on the Alliance for Progress" (Charter of the Alliance for Progress) was signed on August 17 by all the delegations except the Cuban. In it, Secretary Dillon promised in the name of his government, at least 20 billion dollars, principally in public funds in financial assistance to Latin America from the United States and other Western nations, over the next ten years. On the other hand, Latin America promised to undertake fundamental land, taxation, and other essential reforms.

The Declaration of Punta del Este ended on an optimistic note. A new era in inter-American relations was about to begin, said the Declaration, when Latin America will supplement its "institutional, legal, cultural and social accomplishments with immediate and concrete actions to secure a better life, under freedom, for the present and future generations." The inclusion of an anti-Cuban political clause suggested by Peru and backed by several other nations was voted down by the conference.

By September, 1961, close to 100 loans, totaling more than 960 million dollars, had been granted to Latin America by the United States and U.S.-supported institutions, including the Inter-American Development Bank, the U. S. Development Loan Fund, the Export-Import Bank, the International Monetary Fund, and the World Bank.

The second annual review meeting of the Alliance held in São Paulo, Brazil, November 11–16, 1963, created an Inter-American Committee to recommend financial and other measures for carrying out the program. To date, the Alliance for Progress has not resulted in as much financial and economic cooperation between the United States and Latin America as some had expected. Nevertheless, more loans (totaling 450 million dollars) were made by U. S.-supported institutions to various Latin American countries during the first six months of 1964 than in all of 1963.

Despite past errors and miscalculations such as the deplorable involvement in the Cuban invasion of April, 1961, and the landing of U. S. troops in the Dominican Republic without previous consultation with the other members of the OAS, the relations between the United States and Latin America seemed, in general, to be regaining the ground lost during the previous years of negative policy.

RECENT DEVELOPMENTS

In his address on the Dominican Republic crisis, U.S. President Johnson declared (May 2, 1965) that "revolution in any country is a matter for that country to deal with," however adding that it calls for hemispheric action only "when the object is the establishment of a Communist dictatorship."

This hemispheric cooperation policy was somewhat weakened when the U.S. House of Representatives endorsed (September 20, 1965) the unilateral use of force by the United States or any other western hemisphere nation to prevent a Communist takeover in the hemisphere. The Latin American reaction to this declaration was unfavorable.

CHAPTER XXIV

THE PAN AMERICAN SYSTEM

THE PAN AMERICAN MOVEMENT, in counterdistinction to the inter-Latin American movement, aims at eliciting the participation of all the independent states of the Western Hemisphere in all forms of American co-operation. Before the first Pan American conference met in 1889, numerous suggestions were made for the establishment of closer relationships among all the American nations. As early as 1820, Henry Clay outlined a plan for the organization of "a human freedom league in America." In 1824, upon being officially received by President Monroe, José Silvestre Rebello, the Brazilian envoy, suggested the organization of "a concert of American powers to sustain the general system of American independence." In the middle of the nineteenth century, Stephen A. Douglas suggested "a general union for commercial purposes" to embrace "all the various political communities of the American continent and the adjacent islands." But it remained for James Gillespie Blaine, Secretary of State of the United States, to carry this idea into effect.

PAN AMERICANISM

In July, 1881, President Garfield, at the suggestion of Secretary Blaine, decided to call a congress of the American states to convene at Washington, and the invitations were sent out on November 29. The aim of the congress was to seek "a way of permanently averting the horrors of a cruel and bloody combat between countries, oftenmost of one blood and speech, or the even worse calamity of internal commotion and civil strife. . . ." Before any answer could be received, however, Secretary Blaine was replaced by Frederick Frelinghuysen, and in August, 1882, the invitations for the congress were canceled.

On May 24, 1888, however, a bill providing for a conference of

American nations was passed by the Congress of the United States. Invitations were sent out on July 13, 1888, by Secretary of State Thomas Francis Bayard. The conference was to take place at Washington in October, 1889. Among the questions to be discussed were: the promotion of peace; the formation of an American customs union, with a uniform system of customs regulations; the adoption of a uniform system of weights and measures and a common silver trade coin; and the formulation of a plan of arbitration.

In all, eighteen countries were represented at the conference, which met on October 2, 1889. After a period of traveling throughout the United States, the delegates parted company on April 19, 1890. Many agreements were signed, but few ever received the ratification of more than a small percentage of the signatory governments. The most important achievement of the conference was the establishment at Washington, D. C., of the Bureau of American Republics, later known as the Pan American Union.

Other conferences, called International Conferences of American States, have been held at the following places: Mexico City (1901–2), Rio de Janeiro (1906), Buenos Aires (1910), Santiago, Chile (1923), Havana (1928), Montevideo (1933), Lima (1938), Bogotá (1948), and Caracas (1954). At the 1910 Buenos Aires Conference, the Bureau of American Republics was reorganized. A convention on the reorganization of the Bureau, which was to be called the Pan American Union, was referred for study to the following conferences and was finally signed at Havana in 1928. Many resolutions and agreements have been adopted on such matters as the construction of an intercontinental railway; private, civil, and commercial international law; arbitration, conciliation, and good offices; co-operation for the protection of industry, agriculture, and commerce; patents, trademarks, and copyright; arbitration of pecuniary claims; exchange of official, scientific, literary, and industrial publications; sanitary police regulations; promotion of the interchange of professors and students; simplification of passports and adoption of a standard form for them; arbitration of commercial disputes; and uniformity of nomenclature for the classification of merchandise.

The Ninth Inter-American Conference, which met in Bogotá from March 30 to May 1, 1948, is of particular importance. The United States was represented by a strong delegation led by Secretary of State Marshall and including Secretary of Commerce Harriman and the Chairman of the Export-Import Bank. The principal items on the agenda were the drafting of an organic pact for the inter-American system and the problem of foreign-inspired subversive activities in the Western Hemisphere. Other questions discussed were U. S. economic aid to Latin America and the status of European colonies in this hemisphere.

The need for a "Marshall Plan" for Latin America was urged by the delegates of several nations, who criticized the United States for being absorbed in Europe and ignoring the needs of the American nations. The U. S. delegation endeavored to justify the United States policy of economic aid to Europe by pointing out that trade between Latin America and Europe, disrupted by the war, would only be re-established if Europe were to recover economically. This recovery would only be possible through American aid.

On the colonial question, the U. S. representatives adopted a conciliatory attitude in regard to proposals calling for an end of all European colonial possessions in the Hemisphere.

Regarding an organic inter-American pact, opposition soon developed among certain delegations to collective interference in the internal affairs of any American nation.

The proceedings of the conference were interrupted on April 9 by a violent popular uprising in Bogotá, following the assassination of a prominent liberal leader. The mob violence was attributed to the activities of international Communist agents.

The conference continued after a short interruption and closed its work on May 1 with the signing of the Charter of the Organization of American States. This charter gave permanent legal form to the hitherto loosely and indefinitely organized Pan American system. It formally organized the American nations' union under the United Nations, with a specific declaration of the rights and duties of the American states.

The Charter of the Organization of American States (OAS) provided for the pacific settlement of disputes, collective security, and economic, social, and cultural co-operation. The organs of the OAS were declared to be: (1) the Inter-American conferences; (2) the consultative meetings of the member nations' foreign ministers; (3) the Council of OAS; (4) the Pan American Union at Washington; (5) specialized conferences; and (6) specialized organizations set up by the various organs.

The Tenth Inter-American Conference met at Caracas, Venezuela, March 1–28, 1954. The conference, among other resolutions, adopted a Declaration of Solidarity for the Preservation of the Political Integrity of the American States against international Communism; and a Declaration of Caracas, reaffirming the principles and aims of the Charter of OAS and reiterating the recognition of the inalienable right of each state to choose freely its own institutions. A Convention for the Promotion of Inter-American Cultural Relations was signed during the conference.

The Eleventh Inter-American Conference, scheduled to meet at Quito, Ecuador, in 1960, was postponed because of the disturbed conditions in inter-American relations.

THE PAN AMERICAN UNION

The Pan American Union, with headquarters in Washington, is the central permanent organ and general secretariat of the OAS. It performs a wide variety of general and technical services for all the other organs of the OAS, as well as for the governments and peoples of the member states. The Union is under the direction of the Council of the OAS, in which every member state is represented by a special ambassador; and of a Secretary-General and an Assistant Secretary-General selected by the Council for ten-year terms.

The OAS has created the following other organs: an Inter-American Economic and Social Council, an Inter-American Council of Jurists, and an Inter-American Cultural Council.

SPECIALIZED INTER–AMERICAN CONFERENCES

Between the main inter-American conferences, many other special conferences have taken place to discuss commercial, industrial, scientific, agricultural, financial, juridical, sanitary, and other matters. Among these, the following meetings are of particular importance.

The Inter-American Economic Conference, which met in Rio de Janeiro November 22–December 2, 1954, reaffirmed the common bonds of friendship and co-operation among the various American nations and expressed the determination of all member states to speed up the progress of each nation, within the framework of freedom and justice, by intensifying inter-American economic, financial, and technical co-operation.

The American Presidents' Meeting of Panama, July 21–22, 1956, was called to commemorate the 130th anniversary of the First Panama Congress (1826). A Declaration of Panama was signed by all the presidents, setting forth the political, economic, and financial principles of the American nations.

At the suggestion of President Eisenhower, an Inter-American Committee of Presidential Representatives came into existence, to make recommendations for rendering the OAS more effective in its work. This committee met in Washington in September, 1956, and again in January and in May, 1957. It adopted a series of 27 recommendations on economic and financial matters, on co-operation in agriculture, education, public health, technical development, and other activities.

The Buenos Aires Economic Conference of August–September, 1957, decided to strengthen the Economic Council of the OAS as a co-ordinating organ for official inter-American economic and social activities. An Economic Declaration was adopted by the delegates to the effect that it was the firm intention of the American states to strengthen the conditions which promote the maximum economic growth of each American country.

The Seventh Pan American Highway Congress of Panama, August, 1957, was called to consider ways to improve the highways of the Hemisphere, particularly the Pan American Highway, through the co-operation of all the American nations.

The most significant of these specialized inter-American conferences to date was the Inter-American Economic and Social Conference which met August 5–17, 1961, at Punta del Este, Uruguay, to implement President Kennedy's Alliance for Progress. As noted above, the conference adopted a "Declaration to the Peoples of America on the Alliance for Progress," which was signed, on August 17, by all the participating nations except Cuba.

Inspired by the principles consecrated in the Charter of the OAS, in "Operation Pan America," and in the Act of Bogotá, the American republics declared their agreement to establish an Alliance for Progress to bring about a better life for all the people of the Hemisphere. The Alliance was established on the basic principle that free men working through the institution of representative democracy can best attain man's aspirations, including those for work, home and land, health, and schools. To that purpose, the following goals were established: to improve and strengthen democratic institutions through the application of the principle of self-determination; to accelerate the economic and social development of the nations of the Hemisphere; to carry out urban and rural housing programs; to encourage programs of comprehensive agrarian reform; to wipe out illiteracy; to press forward with programs of health and sanitation; to assure fair wages and satisfactory working conditions to all workers; to reform tax laws; to maintain monetary and fiscal policies which will protect the purchasing power of the people; to stimulate private enterprise; to find a quick and lasting solution to the problems created by excessive fluctuation in the prices of basic exports; to accelerate the integration of Latin America so as to stimulate the economic and social development of all.

In the Declaration, the American nations expressed the conviction that these changes could come only through self-help efforts of each country. The United States pledged its efforts to supply financial and technical co-operation, providing a major part of a minimum of 20 billion dollars, principally in public funds over the next 10 years; also to provide from public funds an immediate contribution of more than one billion dollars during the twelve months which began March 13, 1961, when the Alliance for Progress was first announced. The United States promised to supply development loans on a long-term basis running up to 50 years at very low or zero rates of interest. Latin America, on the other hand, agreed to devote a steadily increasing share of its own resources to economic and social development, and to take the necessary steps to bring about the needed reforms. Each Latin American country was to formulate a comprehensive national program for the development of its own economy. Experts were to be made available to help in formulating these programs.

The Declaration of Punta del Este and the pledged assistance of the United States government were received with enthusiastic approval throughout Latin America, but the problem of implementing the Alliance for Progress remained an extremely difficult and complicated one.

Of some importance also was the Inter-American Conference of Bogotá, held September 5–13, 1960, with the attendance of delegates from all the American nations except the Dominican Republic. The conference called upon the countries of Western Europe to facilitate the importation of Latin American products and recommended closer relations with European economic organizations. The United States delegation to the conference emphasized the need to raise the living standards of the great masses of people in Latin America and pledged United States assistance to that effect.

THE INTER–AMERICAN COFFEE AGREEMENT
OF 1958

Coffee is either the principal export or one of the most important exports of fifteen Latin American countries, with the United States as the main consumer market. For a number of years, the producing countries, led by Brazil, have endeavored to stabilize coffee prices by controlling production and exports.

In 1940 fourteen Latin American coffee-producing countries entered into a three-year agreement with the United States under which the latter would purchase from Latin America about 15.5 million bags of coffee a year, and not more than 11.5 million bags from other regions of the world.

In 1940 the Inter-American Financial and Economic Advisory Committee prepared a plan fixing export quotas on coffee, which was signed at Washington under the name of "Inter-American Coffee Agreement," on November 28, 1940, between the United States and fourteen coffee-producing Latin American countries (Brazil, Colombia, Costa Rica, Cuba, the Dominican Republic, Ecuador, El Salvador, Guatemala, Haiti, Honduras, Mexico, Nicaragua, Peru, and Venezuela). Later an Inter-American Coffee Board, with headquarters in Washington, was set up as an enforcing agency.

After World War II, Africa increased its coffee production and became a serious competitor of Latin America in the world markets. In 1957 seven Latin American countries (Brazil, Colombia, Mexico, El Salvador, Guatemala, Costa Rica, and Nicaragua) responsible for 80 per cent of the world's coffee production met in Mexico City to discuss measures to stabilize coffee prices and to control exports.

As a result of this meeting, a conference of *all* coffee-producing countries was then called to be held in Rio de Janeiro in 1958. At the Rio conference a proposal to establish an international organization for controlling coffee production and stabilizing prices was adopted. However, the agreement embodying that resolution had failed to receive the ratification of the necessary number of countries by the end of the year. Brazil and Colombia then made a joint declaration on coffee policies and agreed to fully support the International Coffee Organization set up at Rio de Janeiro. And on September 27, 1958, an agreement was signed at Washington by the Latin American coffee-producing countries providing for the control of their respective exports of the product. This agreement, signed by fifteen countries, replaced that adopted at Mexico City in 1957.

The signatory countries were: Brazil, Colombia, Costa Rica, Cuba, Dominican Republic, Ecuador, El Salvador, Guatemala, Haiti, Honduras, Mexico, Nicaragua, Panama, Peru, and Venezuela.

THE INTER–AMERICAN SYSTEM OF PEACE AND SECURITY

The following is a list of the general agreements for the peaceful settlement of disputes among the American republics and for mutual defense: Treaty to Avoid or Prevent Conflicts between the American States (Gondra Treaty), signed May 3, 1923; General Treaty of Inter-American Arbitration and Additional Protocol of Progressive Arbitration, signed January 5, 1929; General Convention of Inter-American Conciliation, signed January 5, 1929; Additional Protocol to the General Convention of Inter-American Conciliation, signed December 26, 1933; Anti-War Treaty of Non-Aggression and Conciliation, signed October 10, 1933; Convention to Expand the Commission of Investigation and Conciliation, signed October 10, 1933; Convention to Co-ordinate, Extend, and Assure the Fulfillment of the Existing Treaties between the American States, signed December 23, 1936; Inter-American Treaty on Good Offices and Mediation, signed December 23, 1936; Treaty on the Prevention of Controversies, signed December 23, 1936; Declaration of the Principles of Solidarity of America, signed December 23, 1938; Declaration on Improvement of the Procedure of Consultation, signed December 24, 1938; Declaration of Reciprocal Assistance and Co-operation for the Defense of the Nations of the Americas, issued at the Havana Conference of Ministers of Foreign Affairs, held in July, 1940; the Declaration of Solidarity and Mutual Consultation of the Rio Conference, January, 1942; the Act of Chapultepec, providing for reciprocal assistance and inter-American solidarity, signed at the Conference on Problems of War and Peace, which met in Mexico City February 21–March 3, 1945; and the Treaty of Rio de Janeiro for Collective Action against Aggressors, signed during the Petrópolis Conference, in September, 1947.

The Convention for the Maintenance, Preservation, and Reestablishment of Peace, signed at Buenos Aires in 1936, introduced the principle of consultation into the inter-American peace organization, providing for mutual consultation among the American states with a view to arriving at a method of peaceful collaboration in the event of a war between American states; and in the event of a war outside America which menaces the peace of the American republics, providing for consultation to determine what measures to adopt to preserve the peace of the Hemisphere. An additional protocol was signed declaring inadmissible the intervention of any of the signatory nations in the internal or external affairs of any other of the contracting parties. In August, 1938, President Franklin D. Roosevelt extended the Monroe Doctrine to include Canada, when he declared at Kingston, Ontario, that the United States would not stand idly by if Canada were threatened by any other nation.

The principles of the Buenos Aires Convention of 1936 were reaffirmed and broadened during the Lima Conference of 1938 by the adoption of the Declaration of Lima whereby the American nations agreed that any problem that involves the peace and security of any one of them will immediately become the problem of them all. Furthermore, they pledged themselves to solve future problems of this kind by consultation. When it is deemed advisable and at the initiative of any one of the American governments, the ministers of foreign affairs of the American nations will meet in their several capitals by rotation, and without protocolary character, to facilitate this consultation.

In accordance with the Lima Declaration (1938), the ministers of foreign affairs of the twenty-one American republics met in conference at Panama September 23–October 3, 1939, to consider the consequences of the new European war on the Western Hemisphere. The most important resolution of the Panama meeting was the so-called "Panama Declaration," establishing a 300-mile neutrality zone intended to isolate the Western Hemisphere from warlike operations and to permit uninterrupted commerce between American nations. An Inter-American Neutrality Committee—a continuing body consisting, when finally constituted, of seven members, one each from Argentina, Brazil, Chile, Costa Rica, Mexico, the United States, and Venezuela—was also set up to study and formulate recommendations with respect to the problems of neutrality. The committee had its headquarters at Rio de Janeiro, Brazil, and its first meeting was held in that city on January 15, 1940.

The Panama meeting also created an Inter-American Financial and Economic Advisory Committee, which met continuously at the Pan American Union in Washington. Composed of one representative from each American republic, the committee was established primarily to consider the financial and economic problems arising

FIG. XXIV-1. The Second World War Line-up in Latin America. (Courtesy of *The New York Times*, February 1, 1942.)

out of the war. This committee negotiated a convention for an Inter-American Bank, which was signed on May 1, 1940, by an insufficient number of countries to enable the bank to be established.

When, later on, events in Europe threatened to jeopardize the security of the American nations, a second meeting of the foreign ministers of the American republics was held at Havana, from July 21 to 30, 1940. This conference adopted a Declaration of Reciprocal Assistance and Co-operation for the Defense of the Nations of the Americas, known as the "Act of Havana," which marked a considerable advance over the mere expression of common concern contained in the Lima Declaration of 1938. This declaration did not create a true system of collective security, but it set up a legal framework for effective co-operation, authorizing bilateral or even unilateral action by the American states for the purpose of implementing the declaration, thus avoiding delay and other difficulties. Confronted with the possibility that changes in the political situation in Europe might result in the transfer of colonies in America from one European power to another, the representatives of the American republics declared that they would not recognize such transfers and agreed that if any were to take place they themselves would assume the administration of such colonies and possessions. For this purpose an Emergency Committee on the Administration of European Colonies and Possessions in America was created. In April, 1941, the United States established a protectorate over Greenland for the duration of the war, under an agreement with the Danish government-in-exile. In November it sent a military expedition to Surinam (Dutch Guiana) to protect that colony's bauxite mines.

After the attack on Pearl Harbor, several nations declared war on Japan. By December 12, nine Latin American states had declared war on Japan, Germany, and Italy: Costa Rica, Cuba, Dominican Republic, El Salvador, Guatemala, Haiti, Honduras, Nicaragua, and Panama. Colombia, Mexico, and Venezuela severed diplomatic relations with the Axis powers. Argentina did not declare war or sever relations with the Axis powers but stated that it would not regard the United States as a belligerent and allowed United States warships to use Argentine ports. Peru froze Japanese funds but did not break diplomatic relations. Uruguay stated that it would not consider any American nation engaged in war with a non-American nation as belligerent and would allow all such American nations to use Uruguayan ports. Chile adopted a policy of neutrality.

To clarify the meaning of the Declaration of Reciprocal Assistance of 1940, the foreign ministers of the twenty-one nations met at Rio de Janeiro, January 15–28, 1942. The agenda topics included protection of the Western Hemisphere and economic solidarity. A resolution offered by Colombia, Mexico, and Venezuela calling for immediate severance of diplomatic relations with the Axis was adopted, with modifications suggested by Argentina and Chile.

As adopted, the resolution declared that the American republics, in accordance with the procedures established by their own laws and in conformity with the position and circumstances obtaining in each country, recommended the breaking of their diplomatic relations with Japan, Germany, and Italy, since Japan had attacked and the other two nations had declared war on an American country. This resolution was made effective by the nineteen Latin American republics that had either declared war on, or severed relations with, the Axis. Argentina took this action later on.

Other resolutions of the Rio meeting of foreign ministers included the establishment of a Committee on Continental Defense at Washington; the adoption of a co-operative continental system designed to safeguard the economic structure of all the nations of this Hemisphere; the assurance of an adequate supply of basic and strategic materials to the countries of this Hemisphere according to plans formulated by the Inter-American Financial and Economic Advisory Committee; the maintenance of domestic economies by equality of access to inter-American commerce and raw materials; increased efficiency of national and inter-American transportation facilities; a conference of representatives of central banks for standardizing procedure connected with bank credits and other financial transactions of citizens of Axis powers; the industrialization of national raw materials; the elimination of espionage, sabotage, and subversive acts, for which purpose an Inter-American Conference on the Coordination of Police and Judicial Measures was to be convened; the recommendation that steps be taken to restrict the operation or use of civil or commercial aircraft and the use of aviation facilities to citizens and enterprises of the American republics; the convening of an Inter-American Technical Economic Conference entrusted with the study of present and postwar economic problems; and the entrusting of the Inter-American Juridical Committee with the study of all matters relative to international organization in the juridical and political fields in the postwar period.

The Pan American Political Defense Committee met for the first time at Montevideo on April 15, 1942, with representatives from the United States, Argentina, Brazil, Chile, Mexico, Uruguay, and Venezuela. Resolutions were adopted with a view to check Communist infiltration in the Hemisphere.

A vital provision of the Act of Chapultepec (1945) stated that aggression against one American state would be considered aggression against all the signatory powers; further, the American states agreed to consult on preventive measures in case of any threat of such aggression. This provision was implemented in the Rio Treaty of August, 1947, and other provisions were carried out at the Ninth International Conference of American States at Bogotá (1948), which produced a charter for the OAS and also the Pact of Bogotá—both documents aimed at the pacific settlement of disputes.

The policy of co-operation with the United States and other democratic members of the United Nations was continued after the war. The struggle against international Communism found the American peoples united in behalf of democratic procedures and the ideal of world peace with justice. On October 21, 1947, Brazil and Chile severed diplomatic relations with Soviet Russia. Colombia did the same in May, 1948.

Meetings of the ministers of foreign affairs of the American nations were held in Washington (1951) and Santiago, Chile (1959). At Washington, in a statement of general principles known as the "Declaration of Washington," the nations declared their intention to stand together spiritually and materially in any emergency.

The meeting of Santiago, Chile, was called to consider the threat to peace arising from the situation of international tension in the Caribbean area, specifically the invasion or threatened invasion of the territories of Haiti, Panama, Nicaragua, and the Dominican Republic by armed bands originating in neighboring nations, especially in Cuba and Venezuela. The delegates adopted resolutions reaffirming the principle of nonintervention in the internal affairs of any American nation and setting forth the functions of the Inter-American Peace Committee in dealing with any crisis. The committee may act in any dispute between American nations either on the request of any government or on its own initiative, but the consent of the affected countries must be obtained before it undertakes any investigation. The committee, with representatives from the United States, El Salvador, Mexico, Uruguay, and Venezuela, was appointed under provisions of the Rio Treaty of 1947. This was the fifth time that the Rio Treaty had been invoked and its provisions applied to settle conflicts between American nations.

Other conflicts successfully settled were those between Nicaragua and Costa Rica in 1949; between the Dominican Republic and Haiti and between Cuba and Guatemala in 1950; between Costa Rica and Nicaragua again in 1955; and between Honduras and Nicaragua in 1957.

The Council of the OAS was requested by the Venezuelan government to take appropriate action against the Dominican Republic for complicity in the unsuccessful bomb plot against President Betancourt of Venezuela on June 24, 1960. A meeting of the foreign ministers of the American nations was held at San José, Costa Rica, August 16–28, 1960, to consider the Venezuelan accusation, as well as the dispute between the United States and Cuba. The meeting condemned the Dominican Republic for acts of aggression and intervention against Venezuela, including complicity in the attempt to kill President Betancourt. It called upon OAS members to break off relations with the Dominican government and to impose partial economic sanctions, implementing the Inter-American Treaty of Reciprocal Assistance (Rio Treaty) of 1947. The conference decided to set up an eleven-man committee to try to reconcile Cuba and the United States. Another resolution condemned any threat of extra-hemispheric intervention in affairs of the American republics.

At a meeting of the American foreign ministers at Punta del Este (Uruguay), January 22-31, 1962, sanctions against Cuba were opposed by Argentina, Bolivia, Brazil, Chile, Ecuador, Mexico, and Panama. However, resolutions were passed to exclude Cuba from the inter-American system and from proceedings of the Inter-American Defense Board and to impose an arms embargo on Cuba.

Under a resolution of the OAS Council, a meeting of the Ministers of Foreign Relations of the American States (the tenth) was held in Washington beginning May 1, 1965, to deal with the Dominican Republic question. On May 4, a call was issued to the members to provide a policing force to replace the U. S. force then on the island. Mexico, Uruguay, Chile, Peru, Ecuador voted against the measure, while Venezuela abstained. Consequently, only a few Latin American nations, besides the United States, contributed with troops to the inter-American peace force.

CHAPTER XXV

LATIN AMERICA AND NON–AMERICAN NATIONS

T HE DIPLOMATIC RELATIONS of the Latin American states with the governments of Europe during the nineteenth century included the attempt of Spain to win back her former colonies culturally, if not politically, and the efforts of other European countries to increase trade and markets in the former Spanish and Portuguese colonies. In the twentieth century Latin America became conscious of the hopes of Japan and China to find markets, while Latin American diplomacy took on new characteristics with the coming of World Wars I and II and the rapid rise of the influence of international Communism throughout the world.

RELATIONS WITH GREAT BRITAIN

After her failure to hold the River Plata region (1806–8), Great Britain decided that she would rather have the friendship of Spain in the war against Napoleon than antagonize the Spanish Crown any more in America. It was not until after the Congress of Verona (1822), when the states of the Holy Alliance decided to aid Spain to regain her former colonies, that the British government felt inclined to recognize the independence of the Latin American nations. In 1823 Canning suggested to the representative of the United States that the two powers jointly protest against the transfer of the former Spanish colonies to any other European power. But the United States decided to act alone (Monroe Doctrine). By the end of the same year British consuls were appointed to the South American nations and finally, on December 14, 1824, the governments of Mexico and Colombia were recognized. The recognition of the other Latin American nations followed shortly.

British trade with Latin America increased very rapidly after the independence of these nations. By 1823 it was nearly 40 million

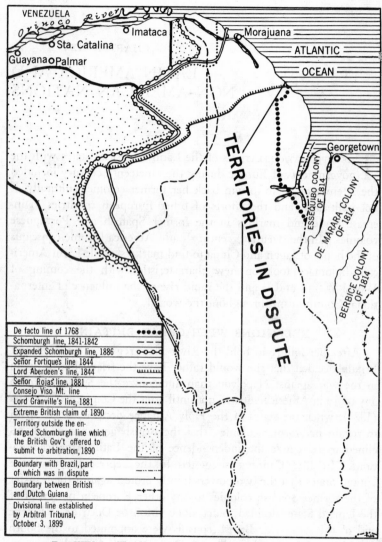

Legend:

De facto line of 1768	••••
Schomburgh line, 1841-1842	– – –
Expanded Schomburgh line, 1886	o–o–o
Señor Fortique's line 1844	
Lord Aberdeen's line, 1844	⊥⊥⊥⊥
Señor Rojas' line, 1881	–·–·–
Consejo Viso Mt. line	
Lord Granville's line, 1881	······
Extreme British claim of 1890	
Territory outside the enlarged Schomburgh line which the British Gov't offered to submit to arbitration, 1890	(stippled)
Boundary with Brazil, part of which was in dispute	
Boundary between British and Dutch Guiana	–+–+–
Divisional line established by Arbitral Tribunal, October 3, 1899	══

Map labels: VENEZUELA, Orinoco River, Imataca, Sta. Catalina, Guayana, Palmar, Morajuana, ATLANTIC OCEAN, Georgetown, TERRITORIES IN DISPUTE, ESSEQUIBO COLONY OF 1814, DE MARARA COLONY OF 1814, BERBICE COLONY OF 1814

Fig. XXV–1. The Venezuelan Controversy with Great Britain.

dollars. British investments in Latin America amounted to almost 200 million dollars in 1830.

In 1826 England signed with Mexico an agreement recognizing British sovereignty over the territory of the River Wallis, or Belize, and Río Hondo, in Central America. In 1831 a similar agreement was signed with Central America. By 1841 England claimed the right to exercise a protectorate over the Mosquito Indians, and in 1850 this territory was made exempt from the provision of the Clayton-Bulwer Treaty between the United States and England with respect to the nonfortification of the region. In 1856, because of diplomatic pressure from the United States, England agreed to withdraw her claims in regard to the Mosquito Indians. Boundary disputes between Britain and Guatemala were settled in 1859. The following year England and Nicaragua signed a treaty recognizing Nicaraguan sovereignty over the territory of the Mosquito Indians. Later (1894), Nicaraguan troops invaded the Mosquito territory. England landed forces at Bluefields at the request of the Indians, and United States Marines also disembarked at Bluefields. On November 20, 1894, a convention was signed in which the Indians were incorporated with Nicaragua, and both the British and United States troops were to withdraw from the country.

The relations of Great Britain with Brazil have been, in the main, quite friendly. The British government assisted Brazil to secure the recognition of its independence from Portugal (1825) and aided the country's economic development.

A dispute arose between the two countries over the unilateral enforcement of antislavery measures by Great Britain (1845). There was also a controversy (1862–63) over the demands of William D. Christie, British diplomatic representative in Rio de Janeiro, in regard to a shipwrecked British ship and British sailors' disorderly conduct in the Brazilian capital. This question was settled by arbitration.

A dispute between the two countries over the boundary line in the Guiana region was satisfactorily settled by arbitration in 1904.

At the Bogotá Conference (1948) several of the Latin American nations advocated taking collective action to end all European sovereignty over continental territories. Guatemala and Mexico have advanced claims on parts of British Honduras.

A boundary dispute between Great Britain and Venezuela in regard to the Guiana region was settled by arbitration in 1899, thanks to the intervention of the United States. In 1902 Great Britain joined with Germany and Italy in an attempt to compel Venezuela to recognize the validity of certain claims held by the citizens of the three nations. By virtue of the intervention of the United States, the Venezuelan government recognized the claims and agreed to arbitrate. In 1903 mixed commissions met at Caracas and decided upon the various claims.

Despite World War I and its aftermath, Great Britain managed to maintain her economic position in Latin America. Her investments were nearly a billion pounds sterling in 1913 and £1,139,-659,470 in 1925. She purchased almost 21 per cent of Latin America's exports in 1913 and about 18 per cent in 1925, while she furnished nearly 24 per cent of Latin America's imports in the former year and a little less than 18 per cent in the latter. Great Britain's Latin American trade was valued at 897 million dollars in 1924. In 1929 and 1930 the British made a vigorous effort to increase their trade with Latin America. In 1933 their share of this trade had increased from 14.9 per cent in 1929 to 18.1 per cent. Later, however, trade between Great Britain and Latin America consistently declined until Latin American purchases in Britain were only 10.5 per cent (about 140 million dollars) of their total value. After World War II, British trade with Latin America again increased.

Among the Latin American countries, Argentina has consistently been the best customer for British manufactured goods, except during the period of the First World War and thereafter until about 1930, and again during World War II. In 1945, because of a dispute on meat prices and exports, the 1936 trade agreement between the two countries was terminated. A new agreement was signed on April 22, 1951.

British investments in Argentina, which amounted to approximately two billion dollars before the Second World War, were almost totally liquidated during the conflict. Argentina, Uruguay, Brazil, and Mexico took advantage of the situation to purchase British-owned public utility services and meat-packing plants which became, in most cases, government-controlled corporations.

Argentina has maintained its claim, based on previous ownership by Spain, to the Falkland (Malvinas) Islands. Both Argentina and Chile have, for several years, advanced claims on parts of the Antarctic region directly south of their respective national territories, a territory which is also claimed by Great Britain. The British government offered to submit the question to the International Court of Justice (1955), an offer which both Argentina and Chile rejected.

In February, 1960, Guatemala protested against the inclusion of British Honduras (Belize) in the British Commonwealth. Guatemala has for years asserted that Belize is part of her territory. The Guatemalan claim was rejected by the British government.

RELATIONS WITH SPAIN

Spain did not recognize the independence of her former colonies for several years. She recognized Mexico in 1836, Ecuador in 1840, Chile in 1844, Venezuela in 1845, Bolivia in 1847, Nicaragua in 1851, Argentina in 1858, Costa Rica in 1859, Guatemala in 1863, Peru and El Salvador in 1865, Paraguay in 1880, Colombia in 1881, Uruguay in 1882, and Honduras in 1894.

In 1864 war broke out between Spain and Peru over the refusal by the Peruvian government to recognize certain claims arising from alleged ill treatment of Spanish citizens in Peru. Ecuador, Bolivia, and Chile joined Peru in the war against Spain. In 1871 a truce was agreed upon between Spain and Peru through the mediation of the United States, and on August 14, 1879, a treaty of peace was signed at Paris.

Between March 18, 1861, and May 3, 1865, Spain held control over the eastern section of Hispaniola at the invitation of General Pedro Santana, dictator of the Dominican Republic.

After the Spanish-American War (1898) Spain became desirous of promoting closer cultural relations with the Spanish-speaking countries of America. In Spanish America many intellectual leaders have also advocated closer cultural relations with Spain. Many clubs have accordingly been organized throughout Spain and Spanish America to foster these relations. An Ibero-American society was organized in Spain, which published a periodical called *Unión Ibero-Americana*. The exchange of professors and students has been carried on to a great extent by special funds raised for that purpose. In 1914 and 1921 congresses of Spanish American history and geography were held, and in 1924 a Spanish American university was opened at Sevilla.

There are today approximately three million Spaniards in Latin America, Argentina having about one million, Cuba 600,000, and Mexico 500,000. Although many of these people are not in sympathy with the Franco regime in Spain, there are everywhere small and well-organized groups called *"Falanges Españolas,"* the purpose of which is to promote sympathy towards the Franco regime and, it is declared, to reconquer Spain's "spiritual empire" in Latin America. In some countries the *Falanges* have been suppressed. On January 8, 1941, a *Consejo de Hispanidad* (Council of Hispanicism) was created by government decree in Madrid. The council consisted of more than sixty charter members, including leaders of the *Falange* and Spanish diplomats in Latin America. Its main purpose was to promote Hispanicism in Latin America.

Hispanicism in Latin America goes by several names (*hispanismo, hispanicismo, hispanidad, falangismo*). Of all these, *falangismo* lays the greatest stress on political objectives, propaganda against the United States, and claim to Spanish hegemony over the Spanish-speaking countries of Latin America.

RELATIONS WITH OTHER COUNTRIES

France. Early relations of Latin America with France were friendly and mostly of a cultural nature. In 1838, however, owing to the refusal of the Mexican government to recognize certain French claims, a French squadron bombarded Veracruz. The incident ended with the recognition of the French claims by the Mexican government.

In 1862 France joined Britain and Spain in the occupation of Veracruz in an effort to force the Mexican government to recognize certain claims on the part of citizens of those countries. Soon afterward it became apparent that the French had ulterior designs in regard to Mexico, and the Spanish and British forces withdrew. The French forces occupied a portion of Mexican territory and carried out the plan of establishing an empire in Mexico under the protection of France. After the end of the Civil War, the United States government protested against the French occupation of Mexico and demanded the withdrawal of French troops from Mexican soil. The French government complied with this demand and Maximilian's empire, without French support, collapsed (1867).

French cultural influence in Latin America has remained extensive. An attempt has been made to promote closer relations between France and Latin America by emphasizing the common cultural background.

Germany. Latin American commercial relations with Germany became important only in the beginning of the present century.

Just before the First World War, Germany had become the largest seller of manufactured goods to Latin America, and after the war it regained very rapidly an important place in the foreign trade of several Latin American nations.

In 1902 Germany joined with Great Britain and Italy in the attempt, already mentioned, to compel Venezuela to recognize certain claims of the citizens of those countries.

During the First World War, eight Latin American nations joined the Allies in declaring war against Germany: Brazil, Costa Rica, Cuba, Guatemala, Haiti, Honduras, Nicaragua, and Panama. Peru and Uruguay did not declare war, but they broke off diplomatic relations with Germany. Bolivia, the Dominican Republic, and Ecuador also severed relations with Germany. Argentina, Chile, Colombia, Mexico, Paraguay, El Salvador, and Venezuela remained neutral.

Germany's total trade with Latin America was valued at 420 million dollars in 1938, that is to say, about 13 per cent of total Latin American foreign trade.

The U.S.S.R. The Union of Soviet Socialist Republics maintained (at the end of 1961) embassies in Argentina, Cuba, and Mexico. It also maintained diplomatic relations with Bolivia, Brazil, Costa Rica, the Dominican Republic, Ecuador, Guatemala, Nicaragua, and Uruguay. However, in all the Latin American countries there are Communist parties, legal or illegal, through which the ideas and the program of Communism are spread. Of late, there has been increasing emphasis on the improvement of trade relations with the Communist countries, especially on the part of Cuba, Mexico, Brazil, and Argentina.

Others. In recent years Italy, China, and Japan have endeavored with considerable success to renew and improve trade relations with the various Latin American nations. Red China, particularly, began in 1959 to spread propaganda and to improve its trade relations with several Latin American governments.

LATIN AMERICA AND THE LEAGUE OF NATIONS

Because of their role in the First World War, thirteen of the Latin American nations were entitled to participate in the Peace Conference. Of these, ten (Bolivia, Brazil, Cuba, Guatemala, Haiti, Honduras, Nicaragua, Panama, Peru, and Uruguay) signed the peace treaty and became members of the League of Nations. In a short

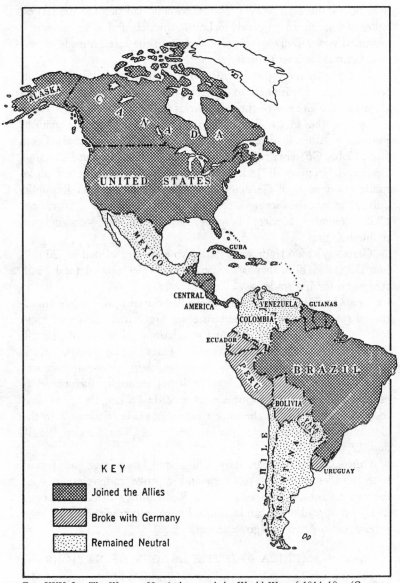

KEY

Joined the Allies

Broke with Germany

Remained Neutral

FIG. XXV–2. The Western Hemisphere and the World War of 1914–18. (Courtesy of Farrar & Rinehart, Inc.)

time all the other states became members of the League excepting Mexico, Ecuador, and the Dominican Republic. Costa Rica, in 1925, and Brazil, in 1926, gave the required two years' notice of withdrawal from the League. Mexico entered in 1931 and the Dominican Republic and Ecuador in 1934. In 1937 Paraguay, offended at League action during the Chaco War, left the organization. In 1936 Guatemala, Honduras, and Nicaragua gave formal notice of intention to withdraw; in 1937 El Salvador and in 1938 Chile and Venezuela also declared their intention to withdraw from the League.

LATIN AMERICA AND THE UNITED NATIONS

The United Nations Declaration of January 1, 1942, was signed by Costa Rica, Cuba, the Dominican Republic, El Salvador, Guatemala, Haiti, Honduras, Nicaragua, and Panama. The following nations adhered to the Declaration later: Mexico (June 5, 1942), Brazil (February 8, 1943), Bolivia (April 27, 1943), Colombia (December 22, 1943), Ecuador (February 7, 1945), Peru (February 11, 1945), Chile and Paraguay (February 12, 1945), Venezuela (February 16, 1945), and Uruguay (February 23, 1945). Argentina was the only Latin American nation which neither signed the Declaration nor adhered to it. For that reason, Argentina was the only Latin American government not invited to send delegates to the United Nations Conference on International Organization, which met at San Francisco on April 25, 1945. On April 30, however, a resolution was approved inviting the Argentine government to send delegates to San Francisco. The Argentine delegation arrived in San Francisco on May 11, and participated in the proceedings which set up the United Nations.

The following Latin American governments offered military and other assistance in support of the UN action in Korea in 1952: Argentina, Bolivia, Brazil, Colombia, Costa Rica, Cuba, Ecuador, El Salvador, Mexico, Nicaragua, Panama, Paraguay, Peru, Uruguay, and Venezuela; only Colombia and Cuba sent troops. Brazil and Colombia were among the ten countries which sent troops to the UN Emergency Force entrusted with the duty of supervising the cessation of hostilities in the Suez Canal zone during the 1956 conflict. All Latin American countries have participated in the activities of the UN and subsidiary bodies.

Premier Fidel Castro attended the UN Fourteenth General Assembly meeting in New York. He addressed the Assembly on

September 26, 1960, for four and a half hours, defending his administration and accusing the United States of aggressive acts towards his country.

The attempted invasion of Cuba in April, 1961, was debated by the Fifteenth General Assembly. A resolution was adopted calling on all the parties to remove the existing tension and referring the matter for proper consideration to the OAS.

In 1962 the OAS condemned the intrusion of the Soviet Union in Cuba and supported the U.S. blockade which compelled the USSR to withdraw its offensive weapons from Cuban territory (November, 1962).

STATUS OF THE COMMUNIST PARTY IN LATIN AMERICA

Legal and a present threat   Legal but under control   Illegal

Country	Population	Communists
Argentina	18,056,000	40,000
Bolivia	3,089,000	2,000
Brazil	55,772,000	60,000
Chile	5,932,000	40,000
Colombia	12,033,000	5,000
Costa Rica	850,000	5,000
Cuba	5,807,000	30,000
Dom. Rep.	2,236,000	Negligible
Ecuador	3,350,000	5,000
El Salvador	2,054,000	1,000
Guatemala	2,890,000	1,000
Haiti	3,200,000	Negligible
Honduras	1,513,000	Negligible
Mexico	28,053,000	5,000
Nicaragua	1,088,000	Negligible
Panama	864,000	1,000
Paraguay	1,464,000	2,000
Peru	9,035,000	10,000
Uruguay	2,353,000	15,000
Venezuela	5,440,000	20,000
British Guiana	444,000	—
Surinam	227,000	Negligible
French Guiana	26,000	—

FIG. S–1. Communist Party Membership in Latin America, 1954. (From *The New York Times,* March 7, 1954.)

URBAN	%
UNITED STATES	64.01
ARGENTINA	62.49
CHILE	60.22
CUBA	57.03
VENEZUELA	53.81
MEXICO	42.59
COLOMBIA	38.69
EL SALVADOR	36.49
BRAZIL	36.16
PERU	36.09
PANAMA	35.97
NICARAGUA	34.93
PARAGUAY	34.61
BOLIVIA	33.57
COSTA RICA	33.50
HONDURAS	31.01
ECUADOR	28.54
GUATEMALA	24.95
DOMINICAN REPUBLIC	23.80
HAITI	12.64

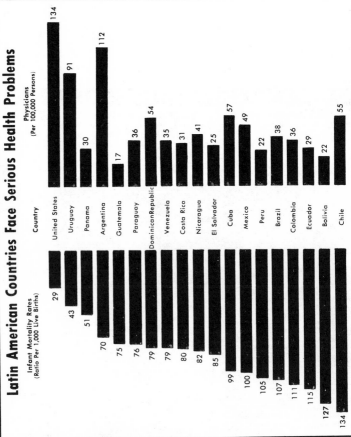

Latin American Countries Face Serious Health Problems

Country	Infant Mortality Rates (Ratio Per 1,000 Live Births)	Physicians (Per 100,000 Persons)
United States	29	134
Uruguay	43	91
Panama	51	30
Argentina	70	112
Guatemala	75	17
Paraguay	76	36
Dominican Republic	79	54
Venezuela	79	35
Costa Rica	80	31
Nicaragua	82	41
El Salvador	85	25
Cuba	99	57
Mexico	100	49
Peru	105	22
Brazil	107	38
Colombia	111	36
Ecuador	115	29
Bolivia	127	22
Chile	134	55

Fig. S–2. Percentages of Urban Population in Latin America. (From *El Analfabetismo en América*, Pan American Union, 1958.)

Fig. S–3. Latin American Countries Face Serious Health Problems. (From *Report to Congress on the Mutual Security Program* for the six months ending June 30, 1954.)

NATIONAL GROSS PRODUCTION PER PERSON

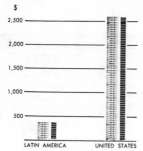

$
2,500
2,000
1,500
1,000
500

LATIN AMERICA   UNITED STATES

POPULATION GROWTH, NORTH AMERICA AND LATIN AMERICA (YEARS 1925-2000)

MILLIONS OF PEOPLE

600
500
400
300
200
100

—— NORTH AMERICA
•••••• LATIN AMERICA

1925   1950   1975   2000

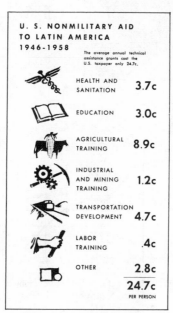

U. S. NONMILITARY AID TO LATIN AMERICA 1946-1958

The average annual technical assistance grants cost the U.S. taxpayer only 24.7c.

HEALTH AND SANITATION	3.7c
EDUCATION	3.0c
AGRICULTURAL TRAINING	8.9c
INDUSTRIAL AND MINING TRAINING	1.2c
TRANSPORTATION DEVELOPMENT	4.7c
LABOR TRAINING	.4c
OTHER	2.8c
	24.7c

PER PERSON

Fig. S–4. Production, Population Growth, and U. S. Aid. (From the AFL–CIO *American Federationist,* May, 1960.)

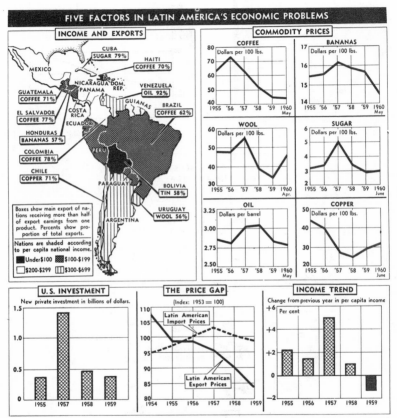

Fig. S–5. Five Factors in Latin America's Economic Problem. (From *The New York Times*, September 11, 1960.)

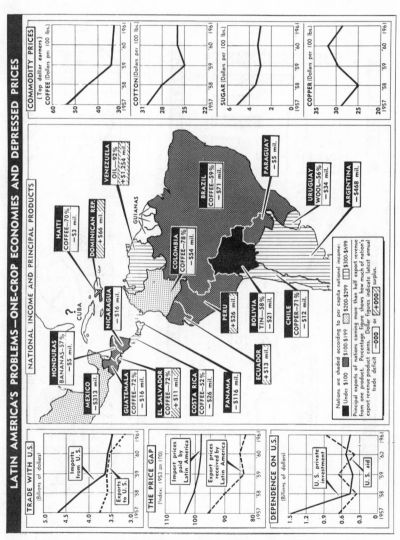

Fig. S–6. Latin America's Problems—One-Crop Economies and Depressed Prices.
(From *The New York Times,* April 29, 1962.)

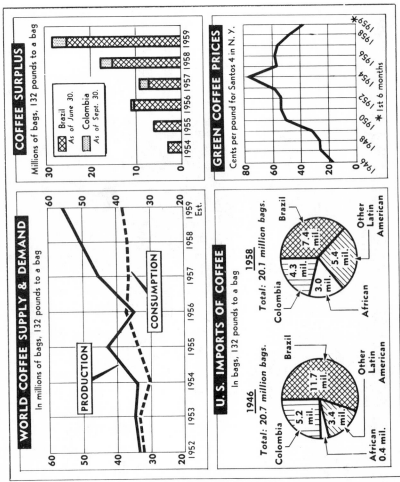

Fig. S–7.   Some Data Concerning Coffee.   (From *The New York Times*, June 28, 1959.)

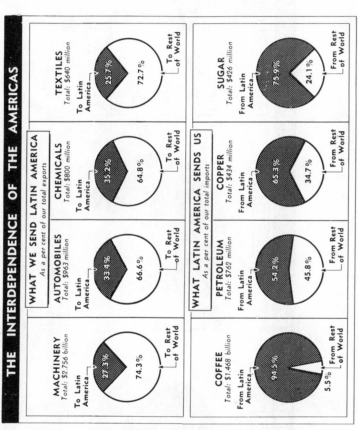

Fig. S–8. The Interdependence of the Americas. (From *The New York Times*, February 28, 1954.)

444

Supplementary Maps and Charts

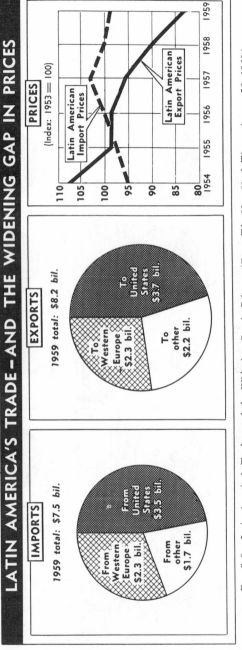

FIG. S–9.   Latin America's Trade—and the Widening Gap in Prices.   (From *The New York Times*, August 28, 1960.)

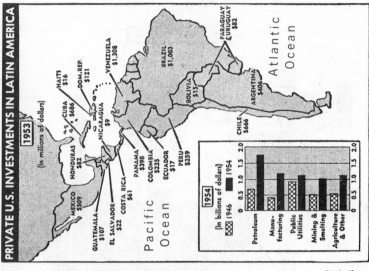

Fig. S–11. Direct U. S. Investments in Latin America. Direct private investments account for $6,200,000,000 of the United States' $7,500,-000,000 stake in Latin America. Holdings of transferable securities make up the rest. (From *The New York Times*, February 27, 1955.)

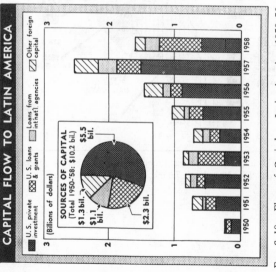

Fig. S–10. Flow of Capital to Latin America, 1950–58. (From *The New York Times*, May 17, 1959.)

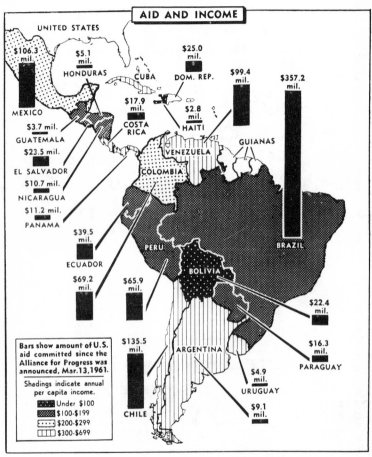

Fig. S–12. U. S. Aid under Alliance for Progress in First Year of Operation.
(From *The New York Times,* April 8, 1962.)

BIBLIOGRAPHY

GENERAL

Alexander, R. J., *Communism in Latin America* (1957).
Apel, P. H., *Music of the Americas, North and South* (1958).
Benjamin, H. R. W., *Higher Education in the American Republics* (1965).
Brandenburg, F. R., *The Development of Latin American Private Enterprise* (1964).
Considine, J. J., *The Church in the New Latin America* (1964).
Form, W. H., and Blum, A. A., *Industrial Relations and Social Change in Latin America* (1965).
Hamill, H. M. (ed.), *Dictatorship in Spanish America* (1965).
Houser, P. M. (ed.), *Urbanization in Latin America* (1961).
James, Preston, *Introduction to Latin America* (1964).
Johnson, J. J., *The Military and Society in Latin America* (1964).
Koth, Marcia N., et al., *Housing in Latin America* (1965).
Lekis, Lisa, *Folk Dances of Latin America* (1958).
Lieuwen, Edwin, *Arms and Politics in Latin America* (1960).
Martz, J. D., *The Dynamics of Change in Latin American Politics* (1965).
Needler, M. C. (ed.), *Political Systems of Latin America* (1964).
Pike, F. B., *The Conflict Between Church and State in Latin America* (1964).
Porter, C. O., Alexander, R. J., *The Struggle for Democracy in Latin America* (1961).
Powelson, J. P., *Latin America: Today's Economic and Social Revolution* (1964).
Schurz, W. L., *Latin America* (1964).
Smith, T. L. (ed.), *Agrarian Reform in Latin America* (1965).
Wilgus, A. Curtis (ed.), *South American Dictators* (1963 ed.).

CHAPTER I: THE AMERICAN BACKGROUND

Baudin, Louis, *Daily Life in Peru under the Last Incas* (1962).
Carlson, F. A., *Geography of Latin America* (3d ed., 1952).
Covarrubias, Miguel, *Indian Art of Mexico and Central America* (1957).
Gallenkamp, Charles, *Maya: The Riddle and Rediscovery of a Lost Civilization* (1959).
Kelemen, Pál, *Medieval American Art* (1-vol. ed., 1956).
Kidder, Alfred, Chinchilla, C. S. (eds.), *The Art of the Ancient Maya* (rev. ed., 1959).
Means, P. A., *Ancient Civilizations of the Andes* (1964 ed.).
Moore, S. F., *Power and Property in Inca Peru* (1958).
Sejourne, Laurette, *Burning Water: Thought and Religion in Ancient Mexico* (1957).
Society of Mexican Architects, *4000 Years of Mexican Architecture* (1957).
Spinden, H. J., *Maya Art and Civilization* (rev. ed., 1957).
Von Hagen, V. W., *Incas, People of the Sun* (1961).
————, *Realm of the Incas* (1957).
————, *The Ancient Sun Kingdoms of the Americas* (1960).
————, *The Aztec: Man and Tribe* (1958).
Wissler, Clark, *The American Indian* (3d ed., 1958).

CHAPTER II: SPAIN AND PORTUGAL IN THE AGE OF DISCOVERY

Ashe, Geoffrey, *Land to the West: St. Brendan's Voyage to America* (1962).
Babcock, W. H., *Legendary Islands of the Atlantic* (1922).
Brandi, Karl, *The Emperor Charles V* (rev. ed., 1954).
Chapman, C. E., *A History of Spain* (1965 ed.).
Chase, Gilbert, *The Music of Spain* (rev. ed., 1960).
Madariaga, Salvador de, *Spain: A Modern History* (1958).
Mariéjol, J. H., *The Spain of Ferdinand and Isabella* (1961).
Moses, Bernard, *The Establishment of Spanish Rule in America* (1965).
————, *The Spanish Dependencies in South America* (2 vols., 1965).

Northrup, G. T., *An Introduction to Spanish Literature* (3d ed., 1960).
Parry, J. H., *The Spanish Sea-Borne Empire* (1966).
Stanislawski, Dan, *The Individuality of Portugal* (1959).
Wilbur, M. E., *The Unquenchable Flame: The Biography of Philip II of Spain* (1952).

CHAPTER III: COLUMBUS AND HIS CONTEMPORARIES

Anderson, C. L. G., *Life and Letters of Vasco Núñez de Balboa* (1941).
Arciniegas, Germán, *Amerigo and the New World: The Life and Times of Amerigo Vespucci* (tr. by Harriet de Onís) (1955).
Columbus, Christopher, *Journals* (ed. Cecil Jane) (1960).
Greenlee, W. B. (ed. and tr.), *The Voyage of Pedro Alvares Cabral to Brazil and India* (1938).
Méndez Pereira, Octavio, *Balboa* (1944).
Morison, S. E., *Christopher Columbus, Mariner* (1955).
Parr, C. M., *So Noble a Captain: The Life and Times of Ferdinand Magellan* (1959).

CHAPTER IV: THE GREAT CONQUERORS

Arciniegas, Germán, *The Knight of El Dorado: The Tale of Don Gonzalo Jiménez de Quesada* (1942).
Braden, C. S., *Religious Aspects of the Conquest of Mexico* (1930).
Cunninghame Graham, R. B., *Pedro de Valdivia, and the Conquest of Chile* (1926).
———, *The Conquest of New Granada* (1922).
Díaz del Castillo, Bernal, *The Discovery and Conquest of Mexico, 1517–1521* (tr. by A. P. Maudslay, ed. by Genaro García) (1956).
Kelly, J. E., *Pedro de Alvarado, Conquistador* (1932).
Madariaga, Salvador de, *Hernán Cortés: Conqueror of Mexico* (2d ed., 1956).
Means, P. A., *The Fall of the Inca Empire* (1964 ed.).
Shay, Frank, *Incredible Pizarro, Conqueror of Peru* (1932).

CHAPTER V: THE GREAT EXPLORERS

Arciniegas, Germán, *Germans in the Conquest of America* (tr. by A. Flores) (1943).
Bolton, H. E. (ed.), *Spanish Explorations in the Southwest, 1542–1706* (1908).
———, *The Spanish Borderlands* (1921).
——— and Marshall, T. M., *The Colonization of North America, 1492–1783* (1920).
Connor, J. T., *Pedro Menéndez de Avilés* (1923).
Cunninghame Graham, R. B., *In Quest of El Dorado* (1923).
———, *The Conquest of the River Plate* (1924).
Day, A. G., *Coronado's Quest* (1964 ed.).
Hallenbeck, Cleve, *Alvar Núñez Cabeza de Vaca* (1939).
Haring, C. H., *The Spanish Empire in America* (1947).
Lummis, C. F., *The Spanish Pioneers and the California Missions* (rev. ed., 1929).
Nowell, C. E., *The Great Discoveries and the First Colonial Empires* (1957).
Priestley, H. I., *The Coming of the White Man, 1492–1848* (1929).

CHAPTER VI: COLONIAL ADMINISTRATION

Aiton, A. S., *Antonio de Mendoza, First Viceroy of New Spain* (1927).
Andrews, K. R., *English Privateering Voyages to the West Indies, 1588–1595* (1959).
Boxer, C. R., *The Dutch in Brazil, 1624–1654* (1957).
Cunningham, C. H., *The Audiencia in the Spanish Colonies* (1919).
Fisher, L. E., *The Intendant System in Spanish America* (1929).
———, *Viceregal Administration in the Spanish-American Colonies* (1926).
Gibson, Charles, *The Aztecs Under Spanish Rule* (1964).
Kemp, P. K., and Lloyd C., *Brethren of the Coast: Buccaneers of the South Seas* (1961),
Lynch, John, *Spanish Colonial Administration, 1782–1810* (1958).
Madariaga, Salvador de, *The Rise of the Spanish American Empire* (1965 ed.).

Moore, J. P., *The Cabildo in Peru under the Hapsburgs* (1955).
Moses, Bernard, *Spanish Dependencies in South America* (1914).
Roscher, W. G. F., *The Spanish Colonial System* (1944).
Zavala, Silvio, *New Viewpoints on the Spanish Colonization of America* (tr. by Joan Coyne) (1943).
Zimmerman, A. F., *Francisco de Toledo, Fifth Viceroy of Peru, 1569–1581* (1938).

CHAPTER VII: THE COLONIAL ECONOMIC SYSTEM

Carse, Robert, *The Age of Piracy* (1957).
Corbett, J. S., *The Successors of Drake* (1933).
Crouse, N. M., *French Pioneers in the West Indies, 1624–1664* (1940).
———, *The French Struggle for the West Indies, 1665–1713* (1943).
Esquemeling, John, *The Buccaneers of America* (rev. ed., 1962).
Hamilton, E. J., *War and Prices in Spain, 1651–1800* (1947).
Hart, F. R., *Admirals of the Caribbean* (1922).
Means, P. A., *The Spanish Main: Focus of Envy, 1492–1700* (1965).
Nesmith, R. I., *The Coinage of the First Mint of the Americas at Mexico City, 1536–1572* (1955).
Newton, A. P., *The European Nations in the West Indies, 1493–1688* (1933).
Pares, Richard, *War and Trade in the West Indies, 1739–1763* (1936).
———, *Yankees and Creoles: The Trade between North America and the West Indies before the American Revolution* (1956).
Schurz, W. L., *The Manila Galleon* (1959).
Simpson, L. B., *The Encomienda in New Spain: The Beginnings of Spanish Mexico* (rev. ed., 1950).
Smith, R. S., *The Spanish Guild Merchant* (1940).

CHAPTER VIII: COLONIAL SOCIETY

Bolton, H. E., *Outpost of Empire: The Story of the Founding of San Francisco* (1931).
Boxer, C. R., *The Golden Age of Brazil, 1695–1750* (1962).
da Costa, L. E., *Rio in the Time of the Viceroys* (tr. by D. H. Momsen) (1936).
González Obregón, Luis, *The Streets of Mexico* (tr. by B. C. Wagner) (1937).
Leonard, I. A., *Baroque Times in Old Mexico* (1959).
Morse, R. M., *The Bandeirantes* (1965).
Moses, Bernard, *Spain Overseas* (1929).
———, *Spain's Declining Power in South America, 1730–1806* (1965).
———, *The Intellectual Background of the Revolution in South America* (1966).
Rojas, A. R., *The Lore of the California Vaquero* (1958).
Whitaker, A. P. (ed.), *Latin America and the Enlightenment* (2d ed., 1961).
Wilgus, A. C. (ed.), *Colonial Hispanic America* (1936).
Wiznitzer, Arnold, *Jews in Colonial Brazil* (1960).

CHAPTER IX: COLONIAL CULTURE

Bolton, H. E., *Rim of Christendom: A Biography of Eusebio Francisco Kino* (1960).
Demarest, Donald, and Taylor, Coley (eds.), *The Dark Virgin: The Book of Our Lady of Guadalupe* (1959).
Dominian, H. G., *Apostle of Brazil: The Biography of José de Anchieta* (1958).
Dunne, P. M., *Black Robes in Lower California* (1952).
———, *Pioneer Jesuits in Northern Mexico* (ed. by H. E. Bolton) (1944).
Geiger, M. J., *The Life and Times of Fray Junípero Serra* (1959).
Goldberg, Isaac, *Brazilian Literature* (1922).
Hague, Eleanor, *Latin American Music, Past and Present* (1934).
Hawthorne, Hildegarde, *California's Missions: Their Romance and Beauty* (1942).
Henríquez Ureña, Pedro, *Literary Currents in Hispanic America* (1945).

Keyes, F. P., *The Rose and the Lily: The Lives and Times of Two South American Saints* (1961).

Lanning, J. T., *The University in the Kingdom of Guatemala* (1955).

Lea, H. C., *The Inquisition in the Spanish Dependencies* (1908).

Leonard, I. A., *Don Carlos de Sigüenza y Góngora, A Mexican Savant of the Seventeenth Century* (1929).

Mecham, J. L., *Church and State in Latin America* (1934).

Moses, Bernard, *Spanish Colonial Literature in South America* (1922).

Rippy, J. F., and Nelson, J. T., *Crusaders of the Jungle* (1936).

Steck, F. B., *Education in Spanish North America during the Sixteenth Century* (1943).

Tibesar, Antonine, *Franciscan Beginnings in Colonial Peru* (1953).

Wethey, H. E., *Colonial Architecture and Sculpture in Peru* (1949).

CHAPTER X: PRELUDE TO COLONIAL INDEPENDENCE

Humphreys, R. A., and Lynch, John, *The Origins of the Latin American Revolutions, 1808–26* (1965).

McAlister, L. N., *The Fuero Militar in New Spain, 1764–1800* (1957).

Moses, Bernard, *South America on the Eve of Emancipation* (1965).

———, *Spain's Declining Power in South America, 1730–1806* (1919).

———, *The Intellectual Background of the Revolutions in South America* (1926).

Mulhall, M. G., *The English in South America* (1918).

Robertson, W. S., *France and Latin-American Independence* (1939).

———, *The Life of Miranda* (1930).

Shafer, R. J., *Economic Societies in the Spanish World, 1763–1821* (1957).

CHAPTERS XI AND XII: INDEPENDENCE OF SPANISH AMERICA

Bushnell, David, *The Santander Regime in Gran Colombia* (1954).

Cunninghame Graham, R. B., *José Antonio Páez* (1929).

Davis, T. F., *MacGregor's Invasion of Florida, 1817* (1928).

Hasbrouck, Alfred, *Foreign Legionaries in the Liberation of Spanish South America* (1928).

Madariaga, Salvador de, *Bolívar* (1952).

Mehegan, J. J., *O'Higgins of Chile* (1913).

Noll, A. H., and McMahon, A. P., *Life and Times of Miguel Hidalgo y Costilla* (1910).

Rippy, J. F., *Rivalry of the United States and Great Britain Over Latin America, 1808–30* (1965 ed.).

Robertson, W. S., *Rise of the Spanish-American Republics as Told in the Lives of Their Liberators* (rev. ed., 1965).

Rojas, Ricardo, *San Martín, Knight of the Andes* (tr. by Herschel Brickell and Carlos Videla) (1945).

Sherwell, G. A., *Antonio José de Sucre* (1924).

Street, John, *Artigas and the Emancipation of Uruguay* (1959).

Trend, J. B., *Bolívar and the Independence of Spanish America* (1948).

Turnbull, A. D., and Van der Veer, N. R., *Cochrane the Unconquerable* (1929).

Vinogradov, A. K., *The Black Consul* (tr. by Emile Burns) (1935).

Wendehake, J. R., *The Master of Bolívar* (1930).

Whitaker, A. P., *The United States and the Independence of Latin America, 1800–1830* (rev. ed., 1962).

CHAPTER XIII: INDEPENDENCE OF BRAZIL

Armitage, John, *The History of Brazil from 1808 to 1831* (1835–36).

Costa, Sérgio Corrêa da, *Every Inch a King: A Biography of Dom Pedro I, First Emperor of Brazil* (tr. by Samuel Putnam) (1950).

Freyre, Gilberto, *The Masters and the Slaves* (tr. by Samuel Putnam) (2d ed., 1956).

Harding, Bertita, *Amazon Throne: The Story of the Braganzas of Brazil* (1941).
———, *Southern Empire: Brazil* (1948).
Haring, C. H., *Empire in Brazil: A New World Experiment with Monarchy* (1958).
Oliveira Lima, Manoel de, *The Evolution of Brazil* ... (1914).
Putnam, Samuel, *Marvelous Journey: A Survey of Four Centuries of Brazilian Writing* (1948).

CHAPTER XIV: LATIN AMERICA AT THE END OF THE REVOLUTIONS FOR INDEPENDENCE

Bryce, James, *South America, Observations and Impressions* (1914).
García Calderón, Francisco, *Latin America: Its Rise and Progress* (tr. by B. Miall) (1913).
Jane, Cecil, *Liberty and Despotism in Spanish America* (1929).
Neely, T. B., *South America, Its Missionary Problems* (1910).
Wilgus, A. C. (ed.), *Modern Hispanic America* (1933).

CHAPTER XV: MEXICO

Braddy, Haldeen, *Cock of the Walk: The Pancho Villa Legend* (1955).
Brandenburg, F. R., *The Making of Modern Mexico* (1964).
Brenner, Anita, *Idols behind Altars* (1929).
———, *The Wind That Swept Mexico: The History of the Mexican Revolution, 1910–1942* (1943).
Brushwood, J. S., *The Romantic Novel in Mexico* (1954).
Callcott, W. H., *Church and State in Mexico, 1822–1857* (1965 ed.).
———, *Liberalism in Mexico, 1857–1929* (1965).
Corti, E. C., *Maximilian and Charlotte of Mexico* (1929).
Flandrau, C. M., *Viva Mexico* (1964 ed.).
González Peña, Carlos, *History of Mexican Literature* (rev. ed., 1945).
Gruening, Ernest, *Mexico and Its Heritage* (1926).
Johnston, Marjorie, *Education in Mexico* (1956).
Lewis, Oscar, *The Children of Sánchez: Autobiography of a Mexican Family* (1961).
Myers, B. S., *Mexican Painting in Our Time* (1956).
Parkes, H. B., *History of Mexico* (rev. ed., 1960).
Paz, Octavio (ed.), *Anthology of Mexican Poetry* (tr. by Samuel Beckett) (1958).
Pinchon, Edgcumb, *Zapata, the Unconquerable* (1941).
Quirk, R. E., *The Mexican Revolution, 1914–1915* (1960).
Ross, S. R., *Francisco I. Madero, Apostle of Mexican Democracy* (1955).
Schmitt, K. M., *Communism in Mexico* (1965).
Scholes, W. V., *Mexican Politics during the Juárez Regime, 1855–1872* (1957).
Scott, R. E., *Mexican Government in Transition* (rev. ed., 1964).
Shipway, Vera and Warren, *The Mexican House, Old and New* (1960).
Simpson, E. N., *The Ejido: Mexico's Way Out* (1937).
Simpson, L. B., *Many Mexicos* (3d ed., 1959).
Tannenbaum, Frank, *Mexico: The Struggle for Peace and Bread* (1950).
Wilgus, A. C. (ed.), *The Caribbean: Mexico Today* (1964).

CHAPTER XVI: THE FIVE REPUBLICS OF CENTRAL AMERICA

Checchi, Vincent, et al., *Honduras: A Problem in Economic Development* (1959).
Kelsey, Vera, and Osborne, Lilly de Jongh, *Four Keys to Guatemala* (rev. ed., 1961).
Martz, J. D., *Central America: The Crisis and the Challenge* (1959).
Osborne, Lilly de Jongh, *Four Keys to El Salvador* (1956).
Parker, F. D., *The Central American Republics* (1964).
Rodríguez, Mario, *Central America* (1965).

Rosenthal, Mario, *Guatemala: The Story of an Emergent Latin American Democracy* (1962).
Silvert, K. H., *A Study in Government: Guatemala* (1954).
Tumin, M. M., *Caste in a Peasant Society* (Guatemala) (1952).
Whetten, N. L., *Guatemala: The Land and the People* (1961).
Wilgus, A. C. (ed.), *The Caribbean: The Central American Area* (1961).

CHAPTER XVII: THE STATES OF NORTHERN SOUTH AMERICA

Alexander, R. J., *The Venezuelan Democratic Revolution* (1964).
Bernstein, Harry, *Venezuela and Colombia* (1964 ed.).
Biesanz, John and Mavis, *The People of Panama* (1955).
Blanksten, George, *Ecuador: Constitutions and Caudillos* (1964).
Eder, G. J. (ed.), *Taxation in Colombia* (1964).
Gilmore, Robert, *Caudillism and Militarism in Venezuela, 1810–1910* (1964).
Lieuwen, Edwin, *Venezuela* (1965).
Linke, Lilo, *Ecuador, Country of Contrasts* (3d ed., 1960).
Shoup, C. S., et al., *The Fiscal System of Venezuela* (1959).
Watters, Mary, *A History of the Church in Venezuela, 1810–1930* (1933).
Wilgus, A. C. (ed.), *The Caribbean: Contemporary Colombia* (1962).
————, *The Caribbean: Venezuelan Development, a Case History* (1963).
Wurfel, S. W., *Foreign Enterprises in Colombia* (1965).

CHAPTER XVIII: PERU, BOLIVIA, AND CHILE

Alexander, R. J., *The Bolivian National Revolution* (1958).
Arnade, C. W., *The Emergence of the Republic of Bolivia* (1957).
Bowers, C. G., *Chile through Embassy Windows: 1939–1953* (1958).
Ford, T. R., *Man and Land in Peru* (1955).
Galdames, Luis, *A History of Chile* (tr. and ed. by I. J. Cox) (1964 ed.).
Gil, Federico G., *The Political Society of Chile* (1966).
Mautner, H. E., *Doctor in Bolivia* (1960).
Mistral, Gabriela, *Selected Poems* (tr. by Langston Hughes) (1957).
Osborne, Harold, *Bolivia: A Land Divided* (3d ed., 1964).
Ostria Gutiérrez, Alberto, *The Tragedy of Bolivia: A People Crucified* (1958).
Silvert, K. H., *Chile Yesterday and Today* (1965).
Subercaseaux, Benjamín, *Chile, A Geographic Extravaganza* (tr. by A. Flores) (1943).
Wright, J. H., *Chile: Economic and Commercial Conditions* (1958).

CHAPTER XIX: THE PLATA STATES

Barrett, W. E., *Woman on Horseback: The Story of Francisco Lopez and Elisa Lynch* (1952).
Burgin, Miron, *The Economic Aspects of Argentine Federalism, 1820–1852* (1946).
Cunninghame Graham, R. B., *Portrait of a Dictator: Francisco Solano López* (1933).
Ferguson, J. H., *The River Plata Republics* (1965).
Fitzgibbon, R. H., *Uruguay: Portrait of a Democracy* (1966).
Hudson, W. H., *Tales of the Gauchos* (ed. by Elizabeth Coatsworth) (1946).
Kennedy, J. J., *Catholicism, Nationalism and Democracy in Argentina* (1958).
Kroeber, C. B., *The Growth of the Shipping Industry in the Río de la Plata, 1794–1860* (1957).
Levene, Ricardo, *A History of Argentina* (tr. and ed. by W. S. Robertson) (1937).
Luper, A. T., *The Music of Argentina* (1942).
Macdonald, A. F., *Government of the Argentine Republic* (1942).
Nichols, M. W., *The Gaucho* (1942).
Raine, Phillip, *Paraguay* (1956).
Scobie, J. R., *Revolution on the Pampas: a Social History of Argentina, 1860–1910* (1964).

Whitaker, A. P., *Argentina* (1964).
————, *The United States and Argentina* (1964 ed.).

CHAPTER XX: BRAZIL

Bandeira, Manuel, *Brief History of Brazilian Literature* (1958).
Cruz Costa, João, *A History of Ideas in Brazil* (1964).
Cunha, Euclides da, *Rebellion in the Backlands* (tr. by Samuel Putnam, 1944).
Faust, A. F., *Brazil: Education in an Expanding Economy* (1959).
Freyre, Gilberto, *The Masters and the Slaves* (tr. by Samuel Putnam) (2d ed., 1956).
Haring, C. H., *Empire in Brazil: A New World Experiment with Monarchy* (1958).
Harris, Marvin, *Town and Country in Brazil* (1956).
Havinghurst, R. J., *Society and Education in Brazil* (1965).
Hutchinson, H. W., *Village and Plantation Life in Northeastern Brazil* (1957).
James, P. E., *Brazil* (1946).
Loewenstein, Karl, *Brazil under Vargas* (1942).
Luper, A. T., *The Music of Brazil* (1943).
Manchester, A. K., *British Preeminence in Brazil* (1965).
Marshall, Andrew, *Brazil* (1966).
Mindlin, H. E., *Modern Architecture in Brazil* (tr. by John Knox) (1956).
Nist, John, *Modern Brazilian Poetry, An Anthology* (1962).
Pandiá Calógeras, João, *A History of Brazil* (tr. by P. A. Martin) (1939).
Ramos, Arthur, *The Negro in Brazil* (tr. by Richard Pattee) (1939).
Sayers, R. S., *The Negro in Brazilian Literature* (1956).
Schurz, W. L., *Brazil: The Infinite Country* (1961).
Smith, T. L., *Brazil: People and Institutions* (3d ed., 1963).
Veríssimo, Erico, *Brazilian Literature: An Outline* (1945).
Wagley, Charles, *Brazil: Crisis and Change* (1964).
Williams, M. W., *Dom Pedro, the Magnanimous* (1937).
Wythe, George, et al., *Brazil: An Expanding Economy* (1949).

CHAPTER XXI: THE CARIBBEAN INSULAR STATES

Arciniegas, Germán, *Caribbean, Sea of the New World* (tr. by Harriet de Onís) (1946).
Chester, E. A., *A Sergeant Named Batista* (1954).
Clark, E. P., *West Indian Cookery* (1945).
Deren, Maya, *Divine Horsemen: The Living Gods of Haiti* (1953).
Foner, P. S., *A History of Cuba and Its Relations with the United States* (Vol. I, 1962).
Goldenberg, Boris, *The Cuban Revolution and Latin America* (1965).
Holly, M. A., *Agriculture in Haiti* (1955).
Lizaso, Félix, *Martí, Martyr of Cuban Independence* (tr. by E. E. Shuler) (1953).
Ornes, G. E., *Trujillo, Little Caesar of the Caribbean* (1958).
Pattee, Richard, et al., *Catholic Life in the West Indies* (1946).
Phillips, R. H., *Cuba, Island of Paradox* (1959).
Rodman, Selden, *Haiti, the Black Republic* (1954).
Smith, R. F., *The United States and Cuba: Business and Diplomacy, 1917–1960* (1961).
Townsend, F. E., *Quisqueya: A Panoramic Anthology of Dominican Verse* (1954).
Underwood, Edna, *The Poets of Haiti, 1782–1934* (1934).
Wilgus, A. C. (ed.), *The Caribbean at Mid-Century* (1951); *The Caribbean: Peoples, Problems, and Prospects* (1952); *The Caribbean: Contemporary Trends* (1953); *The Caribbean: Its Economy* (1954); *The Caribbean: Its Culture* (1955); *The Caribbean: Its Political Problems* (1956); *The Caribbean: Contemporary International Relations* (1957); *The Caribbean: British, Dutch, French, United States* (1958); *The Caribbean: Natural Resources* (1959); *The Caribbean: Contemporary Education* (1960).
Williams, Eric, *The Negro in the Caribbean* (1945).

PART FOUR (CHAPTERS XXII–XXV): INTERNATIONAL RELATIONS SINCE INDEPENDENCE

Abel, Elie, *The Missile Crisis* (1966).

Allen, R. L., *Soviet Influence in Latin America: The Role of Economic Relations* (1959).

Bates, Margaret (ed.), *The Migration of Peoples to Latin America* (1957).

Bernstein, M. D., *Foreign Investment in Latin America* (1966).

Callcott, W. H., *The Caribbean Policy of the United States, 1890–1920* (1942).

Carey, J. C., *Peru and the United States, 1900–62* (1965).

Castañeda, J. E., *Mexico and the United Nations* (1958).

Crary, R. W., *Latin America and the World Struggle for Freedom* (1943).

Dale, W. B., *Brazil: Factors Affecting Foreign Investment* (1959).

Fernández Artucio, Hugo, *The Nazi Underground in South America* (1942).

Ferns, H. S., *Britain and Argentina in the Nineteenth Century* (1960).

Fitzgibbon, R. H., *Cuba and the United States, 1900–1935* (1964).

Glick, E. B., *Latin America and the Palestine Problem* (1958).

Hill, L. F., *Diplomatic Relations between the United States and Brazil* (1932).

Hill, R. R., *Fiscal Intervention in Nicaragua* (1933).

Holland, H. F., *Objectives of United States Foreign Policy in Latin America* (1955).

Houston, J. A., *Latin America in the United Nations* (1956).

Ireland, Gordon, *Boundaries, Possessions, and Conflicts in South America* (1938).

———, *Boundaries, Possessions, and Conflicts in Central and North America and the Caribbean* (1941).

Johnsen, J. E., *Canada and the Western Hemisphere* (1944).

———, *Latin American Relations with the League of Nations* (1930).

Kirkpatrick, F. A., *South America and the War* (1918).

Logan, R. W., *Diplomatic Relations of the United States with Haiti, 1776–1891* (1941).

McCain, W. D., *The United States and the Republic of Panama* (1937).

McGann, T. F., *Argentina, the United States, and the Inter-American System, 1880–1914* (1958).

Madariaga, Salvador de, *Latin America between the Eagle and the Bear* (1962).

Manger, William, *Pan America in Crisis: The Future of the O.A.S.* (1961).

———, *The Americas and the War: Measures for the Defense of the Continent* (1944).

Matthews, H. L. (ed.), *The United States and Latin America* (1960).

Mecham, J. Lloyd, *A Survey of United States-Latin American Relations* (1965).

Montague, L. L., *Haiti and the United States, 1714–1938* (1940).

Mosher, A. T., *Technical Co-operation in Latin-American Agriculture* (1957).

Normano, J. F., and Gerbi, Antonello, *The Japanese in South America* (1943).

Palmer, T. W., *The Search for a Latin American Policy* (1957).

Parks, E. T., *Colombia and the United States, 1765–1934* (1935).

Perkins, Dexter, *A History of the Monroe Doctrine* (rev. ed., 1955).

Peterson, H. F., *Argentina and the United States, 1810–1960* (1964).

Pizer, Samuel, *United States Investments in the Latin American Economy* (1958).

Quintanilla, Luis, *A Latin American Speaks* (1943).

Reidy, Joseph W., *Strategy for the Americas* (1966).

Rippy, J. F., *British Investments in Latin America, 1822–1949* (1959).

———, *South America and Hemisphere Defense* (1941).

Singletary, O. A., *The Mexican War* (1960).

Thomas, Ann and A. J., *Non-intervention: The Law and Its Import in the Americas* (1956).

Weinberg, A. K., *Manifest Destiny: A Study of Nationalist Expansion in American History* (1958).

Whitaker, A. P., *The Western Hemisphere Idea: Its Rise and Decline* (1965 ed.).

Wood, Bryce, *The Making of the Good Neighbor Policy* (1965).

Wythe, George, *The United States and Inter-American Relations* (1964).